ENGLISH SHORT STORIES

1900 to the present

selected and introduced by Giles Gordon

Modern Short Stories 1940–80

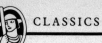

EVERYMAN ● CLASSICS

ENGLISH SHORT STORIES

1900 to the present

Selected and introduced by
Giles Gordon

Dent: London
EVERYMAN'S LIBRARY

First published as an Everyman Classic, 1988
© Selection, Introduction and Notes, Giles Gordon, 1988

Printed in Great Britain by
Cox and Wyman Reading
for
J.M. Dent & Sons Ltd,
91 Clapham High Street, London SW4 7TA

British Library Cataloguing in Publication Data
English short stories 1900-80.
1. Gordon, Giles, 1940-
823'.01'08[FS]
ISBN 0–460–01445–5

Contents

INTRODUCTION

After the First World War, not only life but literature would never be the same again.

Of the twenty-six contributors to this book of short stories, all but six were born prior to 1914, and only one later than 1945. Not one had died by the start of hostilities, yet all but four of the stories were written after what, at the time, was known inevitably as the Great War. Thus twenty-two of the stories were written with a knowledge of what mankind was capable of doing to itself in our century. Certainly a similar kind of selection of stories from an earlier period would not suggest to such an extent that the world is so relentlessly dark, gloomy and depressing. The most recent stories, too, it goes without saying, are written with the long shadow of the Holocaust as part of the writer's (and reader's) moral equipment and consciousness.

And yet every writer represented here is in the tradition of English letters; there is no escaping the writers who came before; nor should there be. No writer, no story exists in a vacuum. Indeed, it is interesting how many of the contributors both knew each other and even dedicated books to one another. Thus, as with Saint Peter and Popes and the laying on of hands, the handing down of tradition, continuity (however isolated the individual writer) is a fundamental part of the art of English fiction. But never more so than in our century in which the old has made way for the new.

At first glance it is strange that of our twenty-six authors no fewer than sixteen were born in the nineteenth century. Yet, plainly, no baby, however precocious and wise, starts urgently penning distinguished short stories: the cultivation of experience (if not necessarily of education and maturity) is required. As if to give the lie to that assertion Muriel Spark's deliciously severe 'The First Year of My Life' has a baby – more writer prodigy than writer manqué; a very recording angel with an inbuilt sense of destiny – declare: 'I was born on the first day of the second month of the last year of the First World War, a Friday.' Mrs Spark was born in 1918.

No story published in the nineteenth century has been included here. Of my chosen writers, only H.G.Wells, it seems to me, wrote most of his most typical stories in the final years of the previous century. But 'The Truth about Pyecraft', published in 1903, is a satisfyingly *modern* story – in the telling as much as the tale; and it is 'modern' if not modernist to make *that* distinction – and that to me, so far as this book is concerned, is the point.

Our response as readers to individual stories is influenced by our awareness of our era, of particular events and decades. Arguably the greatest (but how meaningless in the context that adjective is) short story writer of the twentieth century is Rudyard Kipling. A few years ago we would have hailed him for his jungle or historical tales, more so now for the complexity and weight of his prose and mind. As Craig Raine, in the introduction to his recent formidable work of reclamation and celebration (*A Choice of Kipling's Prose*), writes: 'Kipling, more than any other writer, except perhaps Chekhov, mastered the stipulated economy. His openings are packed.' And, of the late stories, of which 'Dayspring Mishandled' (1932) is a stunning example, Raine adds: 'Links are suppressed to involve the reader in the tale: close reading implicates the reader as he deciphers the encoded text.' Anyone approaching the densely written prose of 'Dayspring Mishandled' expecting something of the straightforward, patriotic resonances of Empire will be in for a surprise. The story is diffuse, complex, as hermetic as a series of Chinese boxes. The experience of reading it is not altogether dissimilar to trying to solve the *Times* crossword.

Kipling a modernist? What a shock, the shock of the new. Joyce's *Dubliners* was published in 1914, *Ulysses* in 1922, and Kipling was not unaware of them. The best writers, axiomatically, are not those who need labels attached to them but those who interpret their times in an individual, idiosyncratic way that resonates with the reader. The work of most interesting writers changes, too, as they grow older, live longer. (It doesn't necessarily 'develop', usually doesn't. Thus early Kipling and early Joyce are *different* from late Kipling and late Joyce. *Ulysses* isn't 'better' than the short story collection *Dubliners*; or vice versa.) There are exceptions. H.H.Munro's ('Saki') 135 stories are much of an elegant, polished, fastidious piece. In 'Sredni Vashtar' the comedy is counterpointed by the darkness in which neurotic urbanity engages with grimmest fantasy; yet, by the end, you believe that the Damoclean ferret has in reality purged the boy's detested guardian. Saki, the seventh writer represented in the book to be born, was the first to die, killed in France in 1916, a private in the Royal Fusiliers. His prose, though, is that of a commanding officer.

The nearest we get in these pages to a story *about* the First World War is Joseph Conrad's unhelpfully titled 'The Tale'. Although written in 1917, it was not published until 1925. The story is uncannily 'modern', so much so that neither the protagonist, a ship's commanding officer on patrol during the war, nor the reader, knows whether a rival vessel which he dispatches to destruction is or is not a collaborator with the enemy, or whether the rival ship goes to her fate knowingly, suicidally, or by mischance, in innocence.

D.H.Lawrence's 'The Prussian Officer' slyly introduces much realism into this look at an earlier, more 'romantic' war. This, surely, is an indisputably great story. There is a massiveness to the prose that suggests sculpture hewn from stone, a three-dimensional representation of two men locked together, the sadistic world-weary officer and his handsome young orderly and the inevitability of the younger man's attraction to the officer. That the orderly has a girl is equally inevitable but, in the male world of war depicted, the girl can be but an incidental, an irrelevance. The story is written in a robust, virile prose, though not without much lyricism. The fate of the two men, the one having killed the other having first been destroyed by him, is, again, inevitable, and tragic. The last sentence – 'The bodies of the two men lay together, side by side, in the mortuary, the one white and slender, but laid rigidly at rest, the other looking as if every moment it must rouse into life again, so young and unused, from a slumber' – recalls, surely, nothing so much as the last scene of *Romeo and Juliet*.

Only one story, Elizabeth Bowen's 'Mysterious Kôr', is set, almost sociologically, in the Second World War. It was originally published in *Penguin New Writing* in 1944, and I first encountered it in a yellowed, disintegrating copy of that influential periodical, a strangely moving experience that heightened the effect of the story. The Anglo-Irish Elizabeth Bowen is, perhaps, best-known for her cool appraisals of upper middle class Anglo-Irish mores. But she is also, as Angus Wilson (who edited her *Collected Stories*) has remarked, along with Henry Green one of the best two writers on what life was like in London during the Blitz. A young soldier, home for a night or two of snatched leave, says to his beloved's flatmate as his sweetheart sleeps: 'They forget war's not just only war; it's years out of people's lives that they've never had before and won't have again.'

Angus Wilson himself, in two collections published in the late '40s, early '50s, captured lethally the dandruff-like lives of the genteel, beleaguered middle classes in the frugal post-war years. 'Et Dona Ferentes' portrays an English family and the effect upon it of Sven, a Swedish student living with them, their son having previously stayed with Sven's family in Sweden. Monica, the boy's mother, says to Sven: '"I'm afraid we lost all our manners here while we were busy fighting the war." Two sharp points of red glowed suddenly on the Swedish boy's cheekbones and his already slanting eyes narrowed and blinked.' A world of Englishness versus 'foreigners' is encapsulated in those two sentences. It is rarely safe to trust the surface of Angus Wilson's sentences. Worlds teem below.

Sir Angus is a tireless exponent of and enthusiast for other writers, frequently younger than himself. He first encountered and encouraged the youngest author in this book, Ian McEwan, when the latter was a student studying writing at the University of East Anglia and Wilson a professor there. Of the work of our younger writers, Ian McEwan's first collections ('Solid Geometry' is taken from *First Love, Last Rites*, 1975) are likely in future years to be read as images of the macabre depravities, in actuality and in the mind, of the 1970s; as if, as Anthony Thwaite observed, '. . . some of the characters from early Angus Wilson had been painted by Francis Bacon'.

So this is not a collection of 'best' twentieth century stories. It is a compilation of outstanding stories which are finely crafted, enjoyable to read and, in every case, say quite a lot about the time in which they were written and what was going on in the English mind, the authors' minds. The only writer I struck out from my original list was Sir Arthur Conan Doyle, whose final Sherlock Holmes stories were published in the first decade of our century. But they are not, by any means, the best Holmes stories, and – crucially – their diction, pace and social attitudinising make them seem to belong to the certainties of an earlier age. G.K. Chesterton's ruminative Father Brown detective stories ('The Honour of Israel Gow' is a masterly, sophisticated performance, published in 1911) could almost have been written today.

The same, admittedly – except perhaps in 'genre' ghost stories, an intrinsically 'reactionary' form – could not be said of 'Oh, Whistle, and I'll Come to You, My Lad' by M.R. James, published in 1904. But as the master of the English ghost story, it is right that James should be represented. He might be regarded as, if you'll allow the epithet, a donnish Donne. 'Oh, Whistle...' works as seamlessly as it does because it is a ghost story and doesn't pretend to be a horror story, something else altogether. I still believe in the bed unslept in by man or woman with the linen, in the morning, crumpled up by human form.

Walter de la Mare didn't only write ghost stories, and 'Bad Company' is as much morality tale as depiction of a haunting. It troubles, disturbs, on both levels. It's a gloss on the tradition of the *doppelgänger*, of James Hogg's *Confessions of a Justified Sinner*, *Dr Jekyll and Mr Hyde*, *Dorian Gray* and in its turn to be followed by Muriel Spark's *The Ballad of Peckham Rye*. The difference, in de la Mare's pungent little piece, is that *both* faces of the man observed by the narrator are evil personified. How then could he survive? And where is God?

The best stories in a 'genre' clearly transcend that genre. We have here the detective tale and the ghost story. We also have science fiction. J.G. Ballard, like George Eliot, is a stern moralist who spins his fables into the future. He writes, in his own lucid phrase, about inner rather than outer space, though the former does not sometimes preclude the latter. His visions of the future, as in 'The Intensive Care Unit', the most recently written story in the book, published in 1982, are as horrifying as they are precisely evoked because Ballard doesn't write in a social or political vacuum. He is always conscious of our heritage and tradition of literature and the achievements of the other arts.

The English tradition in the short story is different from but, inevitably, parallel to the English tradition in the novel. (John Bayley wrote recently: 'The short story form seems peculiarly well suited to the exercise of personal fantasy, because its ready-made spareness and detachment can conceal the author as the full-length novel can scarcely do.') Thus a history of the modern English short story would, to some extent, name different names and draw different conclusions than would a history of the modern English novel. This, above all, for two reasons. First, because not all significant modern English novelists (by 'English' I am thinking, for the sake of this book, of writers in the language other than Americans) have practised, or exercised seriously and with artistic success, the form of the short story, preferring to expend all their energies and best ideas on the longer, baggier form. It seems to me that, for instance, Evelyn Waugh and Graham Greene, both of whom have published stories, fit into this category. Conversely, certain writers (they include, restricting the list to contributors to these pages, Kipling, Saki, Maugham, Pritchett and Bates) are at their best in the short story form although they also write novels.

Second, because some writers use the short story either for recreation – doodles of ideas that don't, in their view, merit being trucked out to the length of novels – or, paradoxically, to practise something different, big, brave and original. Readers will frequently tolerate, even be intrigued by 'experimental fiction' in the shorter form – let's agree that a short story tends not to be longer than 10,000 words; thereafter it's veering towards the novella – that they might not be inclined to stomach if stretched to novel length.

This is one of the reasons – the glancing blow; the emotional trauma; facets of lives, of society; the clash of cultures, of language and dialect; the prejudiced, angled view – why, to readers, the concentrated intensity of a short story is so satisfying. There can be no slackness in the prose, no false notes, no fudging of situations or characters although much may – will – be left to the enterprise of the co-author's imagination; the reader's, that is. A short story, or 'short fiction' as these days it is sometimes fashionably referred to (as if 'story' is a kindergarden word and 'fiction' more for grown-ups), can be perfect in ways a novel rarely is. It can meticulously get things right, as a poem can. When this happens, you cannot discover one wrong or false word, or imagine a sentence or paragraph expressed differently.

With a novel, the writer and subsequently the reader can take his or her time in getting to the gist, the heart of the matter. There is no pressure, provided the reader's interest is sustained. With a short story, the first sentence is the most important for, if the potentially fickle reader is not satisfied, he or she may turn the pages or change to another writer. The reader doesn't have to be shocked, only hooked. 'The Van Dorth Hotel at Singapore was far from grand', W.Somerset Maugham begins 'The Four Dutchmen'. A simple sentence indeed, but how much it tells. It delivers an exotic location followed immediately by the suggestion of seediness, an intriguing combination. The English short story, and in Maugham as much as anyone, has specialised in 'abroad', how lives are lived there, how they differ from at home. Maugham is a popular storyteller *par excellence*, whose every sentence leads the reader on.

The New Zealander Katherine Mansfield, in 'Je Ne Parle Pas Français', takes us to Paris, a city ever special to the young and romantic English, but (she writes in 1923, too) she propounds a less than perfect liaison. No story in this book is more heartless (the narrator's voice, that is), more despairing of relationships. I reread the story to see if I had missed something. I hadn't. It seems straightforward but the implications, the consequences to the characters, go on nagging at the mind – as the author surely intended. In 'The Evils of Spain' – written in 1935, published in 1938 – V.S.Pritchett takes us not, as might be assumed from the title and date of the story's composition – to fascistic horrors. Instead of being about solemn matters this light, impressionistic anecdote sparkles deliciously and reveals much about the differences between the English character and that of the Mediterranean. It is, technically, extremely adroit and advanced for its time, evoking French painters of the period rather than English.

In his introduction to *Seven by Five* by H.E.Bates, Henry Miller likens Bates's stories to paintings by Bonnard or Renoir. This is particularly apt for that beautiful story 'The Kimono', which tells the life (not just one or two incidents therein) of a young man coming to London from the provinces in 1911 in search of a job and enough money to keep his fiancée when he marries her. He lands a job and falls for a shopgirl in a kimono. In truth he falls, as the reader realises, more for the kimono and what it fails to hide than for the girl herself. Come the First World War and he is away and his girl seeks solace elsewhere. Years later, he hears on the wireless that his wife is dying. But he can't go to see her after all these absent years. It is a deceptively easy story. The whole of human life is here, happiness and unhappiness, hope and hopelessness. England is touched in sufficiently for us to believe wholeheartedly these flesh-and-blood lives.

Two of the (six) women writers represented also deal, in their stories reprinted here, with matters of the heart, and in utterly contrasting ways. 'Till September Petronella' was drafted by Jean Rhys years before the finished version was published (1968). It is a lovely, translucent piece evoking, also, the work of French Impressionists and Post-Impressionists, although assuredly set in London and the English countryside. Jean Rhys in her stories pins down as no one else does the languour and vacuousness of Bohemia and its mascots, chorus girls, models and artists. There is a terrible sadness, too, of people almost wanting to waste their lives. Virginia Woolf's 'Lappin and Lapinova', about the first years of a marriage, is in contrast brutally unromantic, tough, realistic. It begins: 'They were married.' And concludes: 'So that was the end of their marriage.' But the marriage referred to in the final sentence is not, at least overtly, that of the couple depicted in the story.

James Joyce is the pivotal literary figure of the century. Accurate, moving, mature and compassionate though 'A Painful Case' is, it has to be conceded that it is not the equal of his masterpiece in the form, 'The Dead'. However, that longest story from *Dubliners* appears in most of the anthologies and I preferred, with Joyce as with every other contributor, to opt for the less frequently reprinted story, if only to prove that the writers here are, none of them, producers of merely hackneyed anthology pieces. For this reason I have resisted Maugham's 'Rain', Mansfield's 'The Garden Party', Dylan Thomas's 'A Child's Christmas in Wales', and so on.

Thomas's dark early story, 'The Vest', is less flowery, less in thrall to the verbal palette than most of his later work, and for this reason has, for me, greater power. This Celtic world, of solitude and the void, is not that distant from the visions of an Irishman born eight years before the Welsh writer, Samuel Beckett. Sean O'Faolain's 'An Enduring Friendship' is a delicious piece of whimsy that, nonetheless, says more than many a more solemn diatribe about the vagaries of the Irish character. Likewise, William Trevor's humane, gentle eye has both celebrated and poked fun at the Irish, although 'Angels at the Ritz' is one of his 'English' stories. It explores constancies and inconstancies in marriage. (Marriage gets a *very* bad press in this book – but happy marriages lead to soporific reading.) Trevor's sense of humour and humanity makes the reader feel compassion for the story's fallen angels. 'There but for the grace of God,' you think; then realise that there's more than a little of yourself in the ridiculousness of the characters' pathetic lives.

There is a long tradition in English, not least by Irish writers, of the comic story. When written by the English, in its depiction of the mannered classes, of gentlemen's gentlemen being infinitely brighter than their lords and masters, it reached its zenith in the rotten snobbish England depicted by P. G. Wodehouse. 'Jeeves and the Hard-Boiled Egg' goes one better, and makes mockery of America and Americans, too.

From the world of Wodehouse to the worlds of the Rhodesian-born Doris Lessing is quite a jump. Her 'England versus England' is probably the most politically overt story in the book, and all the more instructive as a result. First published in 1963, it maps with devastating accuracy an England of social change; a country, that is, of two nations, of middle class and working class and of the agonies of the working class as it aspires to assimilate with the middle class. 'O! Let me not be mad, not mad, sweet heaven' cries King Lear. Charlie, a miner's son who makes it to Oxford, feels he is going that way. He even has two accents, one for back home and a posh one for university.

Schizophrenia rules in 'England versus England', and clearly the title is meant in itself to comment, if not make judgement, on an England as divided against itself as much as ever it was during the years recorded in Shakespeare's History plays. The divisions today may be less obvious, more subversive, but this results – as I hope readers will discover for themselves – in more complex and subtle stories than otherwise would be the case. There are few absolutes, few solutions.

Without wanting to sound either pompous or portentous, I'd submit that these twenty-six stories taken as a whole chart the shedding of the skins of Empire and show a country and a language – for English belongs more than ever to the world – trying, on the whole with not too much success, to find new clothes that fit.

Historically, the best literature of any country has usually been written out of adversity. What writing there is in these pages!

Giles Gordon
February 1988

JOSEPH CONRAD

The Tale

Outside the large single window the crepuscular light was dying out slowly in a great square gleam without colour, framed rigidly in the gathering shades of the room.

It was a long room. The irresistible tide of the night ran into the most distant part of it, where the whispering of a man's voice, passionately interrupted and passionately renewed, seemed to plead against the answering murmurs of infinite sadness.

At last no answering murmur came. His movement when he rose slowly from his knees by the side of the deep, shadowy couch holding the shadowy suggestion of a reclining woman revealed him tall under the low ceiling, and sombre all over except for the crude discord of the white collar under the shape of his head and the faint, minute spark of a brass button here and there on his uniform.

He stood over her a moment, masculine and mysterious in his immobility, before he sat down on a chair near by. He could see only the faint oval of her upturned face and, extended on her black dress, her pale hands, a moment before abandoned to his kisses and now as if too weary to move.

He dared not make a sound, shrinking as a man would do from the prosaic necessities of existence. As usual, it was the woman who had the courage. Her voice was heard first – almost conventional while her being vibrated yet with conflicting emotions.

'Tell me something,' she said.

The darkness hid his surprise and then his smile. Had he not just said to her everything worth saying in the world – and that not for the first time !

'What am I to tell you ?' he asked, in a voice creditably steady.

He was beginning to feel grateful to her for that something final in her tone which had eased the strain.

'Why not tell me a tale?'

'A tale!' He was really amazed.

'Yes. Why not?'

These words came with a slight petulance, the hint of a loved woman's capricious will, which is capricious only because it feels itself to be a law, embarrassing sometimes and always difficult to elude.

'Why not?' he repeated, with a slightly mocking accent, as though he had been asked to give her the moon. But now he was feeling a little angry with her for that feminine mobility that slips out of an emotion as easily as out of a splendid gown.

He heard her say, a little unsteadily with a sort of fluttering intonation which made him think suddenly of a butterfly's flight:

'You used to tell – your – your simple and – and professional – tales very well at one time. Or well enough to interest me. You had a – a sort of art – in the days – the days before the war.'

'Really?' he said, with involuntary gloom. 'But now, you see, the war is going on,' he continued in such a dead, equable tone that she felt a slight chill fall over her shoulders. And yet she persisted. For there's nothing more unswerving in the world than a woman's caprice.

'It could be a tale not of this world,' she explained.

'You want a tale of the other, the better world?' he asked, with a matter-of-fact surprise. 'You must evoke for that task those who have already gone there.'

'No. I don't mean that. I mean another – some other – world. In the universe – not in heaven.'

'I am relieved. But you forget that I have only five days' leave.'

'Yes. And I've also taken a five days' leave from – from my duties.'

'I like that word.'

'What word?'

'Duty.'

'It is horrible – sometimes.'

'Oh, that's because you think it's narrow. But it isn't. It contains infinities, and – and so –'

'What is this jargon?'

He disregarded the interjected scorn. 'An infinity of absolution, for instance,' he continued. 'But as to this "another world" – who's going to look for it and for the tale that is in it ?'

'You,' she said, with a strange, almost rough, sweetness of assertion.

He made a shadowy movement of assent in his chair, the irony of which not even the gathered darkness could render mysterious.

'As you will. In that world, then, there was once upon a time a Commanding Officer and a Northman. Put in the capitals, please, because they had no other names. It was a world of seas and continents and islands –'

'Like the earth,' she murmured, bitterly.

'Yes. What else could you expect from sending a man made of our common, tormented clay on a voyage of discovery ? What else could he find ? What else could you understand or care for, or feel the existence of even ? There was comedy in it, and slaughter.'

'Always like the earth,' she murmured.

'Always. And since I could find in the universe only what was deeply rooted in the fibres of my being there was love in it, too. But we won't talk of that.'

'No. We won't,' she said, in a neutral tone which concealed perfectly her relief – or her disappointment. Then after a pause she added : 'It's going to be a comic story.'

'Well – ' he paused, too. 'Yes, In a way. In a very grim way. It will be human, and, as you know, comedy is but a matter of the visual angle. And it won't be a noisy story. All the long guns in it will be dumb – as dumb as so many telescopes.'

'Ah, there are guns in it, then ! And may I ask – where ?'

'Afloat. You remember that the world of which we speak had its seas. A war was going on in it. It was a funny world and terribly in earnest. Its war was being carried on over the land, over the water, under the water, up in the air, and even under the ground. And many young men in it, mostly in wardrooms and messrooms, used to say to each other – pardon the unparliamentary word – they used to say, "It's a damned bad war, but it's better than no war at all." Sounds flippant, doesn't it ?'

He heard a nervous, impatient sigh in the depths of the couch while he went on without a pause.

'And yet there is more in it than meets the eye. I mean more wisdom. Flippancy, like comedy, is but a matter of visual first-impression. That world was not very wise. But there was in it a certain amount of common working sagacity. That, however, was mostly worked by the neutrals in diverse ways, public and private, which had to be watched; watched by acute minds and also by actual sharp eyes. They had to be very sharp indeed, too, I assure you.'

'I can imagine,' she murmured, appreciatively.

'What is there that you can't improve?' he pronounced, soberly. 'You have the world in you. But let us go back to our commanding officer, who, of course, commanded a ship of a sort. My tales if often professional (as you remarked just now) have never been technical. So I'll tell you that the ship was of a very ornamental sort once, with lots of grace and elegance and luxury about her. Yes, once! She was like a pretty woman who had suddenly put on a suit of sackcloth and stuck revolvers in her belt. But she floated lightly, she moved nimbly, she was quite good enough.'

'That was the opinion of the commanding officer?' said the voice from the couch.

'It was. He used to be sent out with her along certain coasts to see – what he could see. Just that. And sometimes he had some preliminary information to help him, and sometimes he had not. And it was all one, really. It was about as useful as information trying to convey the locality and intentions of a cloud, of a phantom taking shape here and there and impossible to seize, would have been.

'It was in the early days of the war. What at first used to amaze the commanding officer was the unchanged face of the waters, with its familiar expression, neither more friendly nor more hostile. On fine days the sun strikes sparks upon the blue; here and there a peaceful smudge of smoke hangs in the distance, and it is impossible to believe that the familiar clear horizon traces the limit of one great circular ambush.

'Yes, it is impossible to believe, till some day you see a ship not your own ship (that isn't so impressive), but some ship in company, blow up all of a sudden and plop under almost before you know what has happened to her. Then you begin to believe. Henceforth you go out for the work to see – what you can see, and you keep on at it with the conviction that some day you will die from something you have not seen. One envies the soldiers at the end of the day, wiping the sweat and blood from their faces, counting the dead fallen to their hands, looking at the devastated fields, the torn earth that seems to suffer and bleed with them. One does, really. The final brutality of it – the taste of primitive passion – the ferocious frankness of the blow struck with one's hand – the direct call and the straight response. Well, the sea gave you nothing of that, and seemed to pretend that there was nothing the matter with the world.'

She interrupted, stirring a little.

'Oh, yes. Sincerity – frankness – passion – three words of your gospel. Don't I know them !'

'Think ! Isn't it ours – believed in common ?' he asked, anxiously, yet without expecting an answer, and went on at once : 'Such were the feelings of the commanding officer. When the night came trailing over the sea, hiding what looked like the hypocrisy of an old friend, it was a relief. The night blinds you frankly – and there are circumstances when the sunlight may grow as odious to one as falsehood itself. Night is all right.

'At night the commanding officer could let his thoughts get away – I won't tell you where. Somewhere where there was no choice but between truth and death. But thick weather, though it blinded one, brought no such relief. Mist is deceitful, the dead luminosity of the fog is irritating. It seems that you *ought* to see.

'One gloomy, nasty day the ship was steaming along her beat in sight of a rocky, dangerous coast that stood out intensely black like an Indian-ink drawing on gray paper. Presently the second in command spoke to his chief. He thought he saw something on the water, to seaward. Small wreckage, perhaps.

'"But there shouldn't be any wreckage here, sir," he remarked.

'"No," said the commanding officer. "The last reported submarined ships were sunk a long way to the westward. But one never knows. There may have been others since then not reported nor seen. Gone with all hands."

'That was how it began. The ship's course was altered to pass the object close ; for it was necessary to have a good look at what one could see. Close, but without touching ; for it was not advisable to come in contact with objects of any form whatever floating casually about. Close, but without stopping or even diminishing speed; for in those times it was not prudent to linger on any particular spot, even for a moment. I may tell you at once that the object was not dangerous in itself. No use in describing it. It may have been nothing more remarkable than, say, a barrel of a certain shape and colour. But it was significant.

'The smooth bow-wave hove it up as if for a closer inspection, and then the ship, brought again to her course, turned her back on it with indifference, while twenty pairs of eyes on her deck stared in all directions trying to see – what they could see.

'The comanding officer and his second in command discussed the object with understanding. It appeared to them to be not so much a proof of the sagacity as of the activity of certain neutrals. This activity had in many cases taken the form of replenishing the stories of certain submarines at sea. This was generally believed, if not absolutely known. But the very nature of things in those early days pointed that way. The object, looked at closely and turned away from with apparent indifference, put it beyond doubt that something of the sort had been done somewhere in the neighbourhood.

'The object in itself was more than suspect. But the fact of its being left in evidence roused other suspicions. Was it the result of some deep and devilish purpose? As to that all speculation soon appeared to be a vain thing. Finally the two officers came to the conclusion that it was left there most likely by accident, complicated possibly by some unforeseen necessity; such, perhaps, as the sudden need to get away quickly from the spot, or something of that kind.

'Their discussion had been carried on in curt, weighty phrases, separated by long, thoughtful silences. And all the time their eyes roamed about the horizon in an everlasting, almost mechanical effort of vigilance. The younger man summed up grimly:

'"Well, it's evidence. That's what it is. Evidence of what we were pretty certain of before. And plain, too."

'"And much good it will do to us;" retorted the commanding officer. "The parties are miles away; the submarine, devil only knows where, ready to kill; and the noble neutral slipping away to the eastward, ready to lie!"

'The second in command laughed a little at the tone. But he guessed that the neutral wouldn't even have to lie very much. Fellows like that, unless caught in the very act, felt themselves pretty safe. They could afford to chuckle. That fellow was probably chuckling to himself. It's very possible he had been before at the game and didn't care a rap for the bit of evidence left behind. It was a game in which practice made one bold and successful, too.

'And again he laughed faintly. But his commanding officer was in revolt against the murderous stealthiness of method and the atrocious callousness of complicities that seemed to taint the very source of men's deep emotions and noblest activities; to corrupt their imagination which builds up the final conceptions of life and death. He suffered – '

The voice from the sofa interrupted the narrator.

'How well I can understand that in him!'

He bent forward slightly.

'Yes. I, too. Everything should be open in love and war. Open as the day, since both are the call of an ideal which is so easy, so terribly easy, to degrade in the name of Victory.'

He paused; then went on:

'I don't know that the commanding officer delved so deep as that into his feelings. But he did suffer from them – a sort of disenchanted sadness. It is possible, even, that he suspected himself of folly. Man is various. But he had no time for much introspection, because from the southwest a wall of fog had advanced upon his ship. Great convolutions of vapours flew over, swirling about masts and funnel, which looked as if they were beginning to melt. Then they vanished.

'The ship was stopped, all sounds ceased, and the very fog became motionless, growing denser and as if solid in its amazing dumb immobility. The men at their stations lost sight of each other. Footsteps sounded stealthy; rare voices, impersonal and remote, died out without resonance. A blind white stillness took possession of the world.

'It looked, too, as if it would last for days. I don't mean to say that the fog did not vary a little in its density. Now and then it would thin out mysteriously, revealing to the men a more or less ghostly presentment of their ship. Several times the shadow of the coast itself swam darkly before their eyes through the fluctuating opaque brightness of the great white cloud clinging to the water.

'Taking advantage of these moments, the ship had been

moved cautiously nearer the shore. It was useless to remain out in such thick weather. Her officers knew every nook and cranny of the coast along their beat. They thought that she would be much better in a certain cove. It wasn't a large place, just ample room for a ship to swing at her anchor. She would have an easier time of it till the fog lifted up.

'Slowly, with infinite caution and patience, they crept closer and closer, seeing no more of the cliffs than an evanescent dark loom with a narrow border of angry foam at its foot. At the moment of anchoring the fog was so thick that for all they could see they might have been a thousand miles out in the open sea. Yet the shelter of the land could be felt. There was a peculiar quality in the stillness of the air. Very faint, very elusive, the wash of the ripple against the encircling land reached their ears, with mysterious sudden pauses.

'The anchor dropped, the leads were laid in. The commanding officer went below into his cabin. But he had not been there very long when a voice outside his door requested his presence on deck. He thought to himself: "What is it now?" He felt some impatience at being called out again to face the wearisome fog.

'He found that it had thinned again a little and had taken on a gloomy hue from the dark cliffs which had no form, no outline, but asserted themselves as a curtain of shadows all round the ship, except in one bright spot, which was the entrance from the open sea. Several officers were looking that way from the bridge. The second in command met him with the breathlessly whispered information that there was another ship in the cove.

'She had been made out by several pairs of eyes only a couple of minutes before. She was lying at anchor very near the entrance — a mere vague blot on the fog's brightness. And the commanding officer by staring in the direction pointed out to him by eager hands ended by distinguishing it at last himself. Indubitably a vessel of some sort.

'"It's a wonder we didn't run slap into her when coming in," observed the second in command.

'"Send a boat on board before she vanishes," said the commanding officer. He surmised that this was a coaster. It could hardly be anything else. But another thought came into his head suddenly. "It is a wonder," he said to his second in command, who had rejoined him after sending the boat away.

'By that time both of them had been struck by the fact that the ship so suddenly discovered had not manifested her presence by ringing her bell.

'"We came in very quietly, that's true," concluded the younger officer. "But they must have heard our leadsmen at least. We couldn't have passed her more than fifty yards off. The closest shave ! They may even have made us out, since they were aware of something coming in. And the strange thing is that we never heard a sound from her. The fellows on board must have been holding their breath."

'"Aye," said the commanding officer, thoughtfully.

'In due course the boarding-boat returned, appearing suddenly alongside, as though she had burrowed her way under the fog. The officer in charge came up to make his report, but the commanding officer didn't give him time to begin. He cried from a distance :

'"Coaster, isn't she ?"

'"No, sir. A stranger – a neutral," was the answer.

'"No. Really ! Well, tell us all about it. What is she doing here ?"

'The young man stated then that he had been told a long and complicated story of engine troubles. But it was plausible enough from a strictly professional point of view and it had the usual features : disablement, dangerous drifting along the shore, weather more or less thick for days, fear of a gale, ultimately a resolve to go on and anchor anywhere on the coast, and so on. Fairly plausible.

'"Engines still disabled ?" inquired the commanding officer.

'"No, sir. She has steam on them."

'The commanding officer took his second aside. "By Jove !" he said, "you were right ! They were holding their breaths as we passed them. They were."

'But the second in command had his doubts now.

'"A fog like this does muffle small sounds, sir," he remarked. "And what could his object be, after all ?"

'"To sneak out unnoticed," answered the commanding officer.

'"Then why didn't he ? He might have done it, you know. Not exactly unnoticed, perhaps. I don't suppose he could have slipped his cable without making some noise. Still, in a minute or so he would have been lost to view – clean gone before we had made him out fairly. Yet he didn't."

'They looked at each other. The commanding officer shook his head. Such suspicions as the one which had entered his head are not defended easily. He did not even state it openly. The boarding officer finished his report. The cargo of the ship was of a harmless and useful character. She was bound to an English port. Papers and everything in perfect order. Nothing suspicious to be detected anywhere.

'Then passing to the men, he reported the crew on deck as the usual lot. Engineers of the well-known type, and very full of their achievement in repairing the engines. The mate surly. The master rather a fine specimen of a Northman, civil enough, but appeared to have been drinking. Seemed to be recovering from a regular bout of it.

'"I told him I couldn't give him permission to proceed. He said he wouldn't dare to move his ship her own length out in such weather as this, permission or no permission. I left a man on board, though."

'"Quite right."

'The commanding officer, after communing with his suspicions for a time, called his second aside.

'"What if she were the very ship which had been feeding some infernal submarine or other?" he said in an undertone.

'The other started. Then, with conviction:

'"She would get off scot-free. You couldn't prove it, sir."

'"I want to look into it myself."

'"From the report we've heard I am afraid you couldn't even make a case for reasonable suspicion, sir."

'"I'll go on board all the same."

'He had made up his mind. Curiosity is the great motive power of hatred and love. What did he expect to find? He could not have told anybody – not even himself.

'What he really expected to find there was the atmosphere, the atmosphere of gratuitous treachery, which in his view nothing could excuse; for he thought that even a passion of unrighteousness for its own sake could not excuse that. But could he detect it? Sniff it? Taste it? Receive some mysterious communication which would turn his invincible suspicions into a certitude strong enough to provoke action with all its risks?

'The master met him on the after-deck, looming up in the fog amongst the blurred shapes of the usual ship's fittings. He was a robust Northman, bearded, and in the force of his age. A round leather cap fitted his head closely. His hands were rammed deep into the pockets of his short leather jacket. He kept them there while he explained that at sea he lived in the chartroom, and led the way there, striding carelessly. Just before reaching the door under the bridge he staggered a little, recovered himself, flung it open, and stood aside, leaning his shoulder as if involuntarily against the side of the house, and staring vaguely into the fog-filled space. But he followed the commanding officer at once, flung the door to, snapped on the electric light, and hastened to thrust his hands back into his pockets, as though afraid of being seized by them either in friendship or in hostility.

'The place was stuffy and hot. The usual chart-rack overhead was full, and the chart on the table was kept unrolled by an empty cup standing on a saucer half-full of some spilt dark liquid. A slightly nibbled biscuit reposed on the chronometer-case. There were two settees, and one of them had been made up into a bed with a pillow and some blankets, which were now very much tumbled. The Northman let himself fall on it, his hands still in his pockets.

'"Well, here I am," he said, with a curious air of being surprised at the sound of his own voice.

'The commanding officer from the other settee observed the handsome, flushed face. Drops of fog hung on the yellow beard and moustaches of the Northman. The much darker eyebrows ran together in a puzzled frown, and suddenly he jumped up.

'"What I mean is that I don't know where I am. I really don't," he burst out, with extreme earnestness. "Hang it all ! I got turned around somehow. The fog has been after me for a week. More than a week. And then my engines broke down. I will tell you how it was."

'He burst out into loquacity. It was not hurried, but it was insistent. It was not continuous for all that. It was broken by the most queer, thoughtful pauses. Each of these pauses lasted no more than a couple of seconds, and each had the profundity of an endless meditation. When he began again nothing betrayed in him the slightest consciousness of these intervals. There was the same fixed glance, the same unchanged earnestness of tone. He didn't know. Indeed, more than one of these pauses occurred in the middle of a sentence.

'The commanding officer listened to the tale. It struck him as more plausible than simple truth is in the habit of being. But that, perhaps, was prejudice. All the time the Northman was speaking the commanding officer has been aware of an inward voice, a grave murmur in the depth of his very own self, telling another tale, as if on purpose to keep alive in him his indignation and his anger with that baseness of greed or of mere outlook which lies often at the root of simple ideas.

'It was the story that had been already told to the boarding officer an hour or so before. The commanding officer nodded slightly at the Northman from time to time. The latter came to an end and turned his eyes away. He added, as an afterthought:

'"Wasn't it enough to drive a man out of his mind with worry? And the ship's my own. Your officer has seen the papers. She isn't much, as you can see for yourself. Just an old cargo-boat. Bare living for my family."

'He raised a big arm to point at a row of photographs plastering the bulkhead. The movement was ponderous, as if the arm had been made of lead. The commanding officer said, carelessly:

'"You will be making a fortune yet for your family with this old ship."

'"Yes, if I don't lose her," said the Northman, gloomily.

'"I mean – out of this war," added the commanding officer.

'The Northman stared at him in a curiously unseeing and at the same time interested manner, as only eyes of a particular blue shade can stare.

'"And you wouldn't be angry at it," he said, "would you? You are too much of a gentleman. We didn't bring this on you. And suppose we sat down and cried. What good would that be? Let those cry who made the trouble," he concluded, with energy. "Time's money, you say. Well – *this* time *is* money. Oh! isn't it!"

'The commanding officer tried to keep under the feeling of immense disgust. He said to himself that it was unreasonable. Men are like that – moral cannibals feeding on each other's misfortunes. He said aloud:

'"You have made it perfectly plain how it is that you are here.

Your log-book confirms you very minutely. Of course, a log-book may be cooked. Nothing easier."

'The Northman never moved a muscle. He was gazing at the floor; he seemed not to have heard. He raised his head after a while.

'"But you can't suspect me of anything," he muttered, negligently.

'The commanding officer thought: "Why should he say this?"

'Immediately afterwards the man before him added: "My cargo is for an English port."

'His voice had turned husky for the moment. The commanding officer reflected: "That's true. There can be nothing. I can't suspect him. Yet why was he lying with steam up in this fog – and then, hearing us come in, why didn't he give some sign of life? Why? Could it be anything else but a guilty conscience? He could tell by the leadsmen that this was a man-of-war.'

'Yes – why? The commanding officer went on thinking: "Suppose I ask him and then watch his face. He will betray himself in some way. It's perfectly plain that the fellow *has* been drinking. Yes, he has been drinking; but he will have a lie ready all the same." The commanding officer was one of those men who are made morally and almost physically uncomfortable by the mere thought of having to beat down a lie. He shrank from the act in scorn and disgust, which were invincible because more temperamental than moral.

'So he went out on deck instead and had the crew mustered formally for his inspection. He found them very much what the report of the boarding officer had led him to expect. And from their answers to his questions he could discover no flaw in the log-book story.

'He dismissed them. His impression of them was – a picked lot; have been promised a fistful of money each if this came off; all slightly anxious, but not frightened. Not a single one of them likely to give the show away. They don't feel in danger of their life. They know England and English ways too well!

'He felt alarmed at catching himself thinking as if his vaguest suspicions were turning into a certitude. For, indeed, there was no shadow of reason for his inferences. There was nothing to give away.

'He returned to the chart-room. The Northman had lingered behind there; and something subtly different in his bearing, more bold in his blue, glassy stare, induced the commanding officer to conclude that the fellow had snatched at the opportunity to take another swig at the bottle he must have had concealed somewhere.

'He noticed, too, that the Northman on meeting his eyes put on an elaborately surprised expression. At least, it seemed elaborated. Nothing could be trusted. And the Englishman felt himself with astonishing conviction faced by an enormous lie, solid like a wall, with no way round to get at the truth, whose ugly murderous face he seemed to see peeping over at him with a cynical grin.

'"I dare say," he began, suddenly, "you are wondering at my proceedings, though I am not detaining you, am I? You wouldn't dare to move in this fog?"

'"I don't know where I am," the Northman ejaculated, earnestly. "I really don't."

'He looked around as if the very chart-room fittings were strange to him. The commanding officer asked him whether he had not seen an unusual objects floating about while he was at sea.

'"Objects! What objects? We were groping blind in the fog for days."

'"We had a few clear intervals," said the commanding officer. "And I'll tell you what we have seen and the conclusion I've come to about it."

'He told him a few words. He heard the sound of a sharp breath indrawn through closed teeth. The Northman with his hand on the table stood absolutely motionless and dumb. He stood as if thunderstruck. Then he produced a fatuous smile.

'Or at least so it appeared to the comanding officer. Was this significant, or of no meaning whatever? He didn't know, he couldn't tell. All the truth had departed out of the world as if drawn in, absorbed in this monstrous villainy this man was – or was not – guilty of.

'"Shooting's too good for people that conceive neutrality in this pretty way," remarked the commanding officer, after a silence.

'"Yes, yes, yes," the Northman assented, hurriedly – then

added an unexpected and dreamy-voiced "Perhaps."

'Was he pretending to be drunk, or only trying to appear sober? His glance was straight, but it was somewhat glazed. His lips outlined themselves firmly under his yellow moustache. But they twitched. Did they twitch? And why was he drooping like this in his attitude?

'"There's no perhaps about it," pronounced the commanding officer sternly.

'The Northman had straightened himself. And unexpectedly he looked stern, too.

'"No, But what about the tempters? Better kill that lot off. There's about four, five, six million of them," he said, grimly; but in a moment changed into a whining key. "But I had better hold my tongue. You have some suspicions."

'"No, I've no suspicions," declared the commanding officer.

'He never faltered. At that moment he had the certitude. The air of the chart-room was thick with guilt and falsehood braving the discovery, defying simple right, common decency, all humanity of feeling, every scruple of conduct.

'The Northman drew a long breath. "Well, we know that you English are gentlemen. But let us speak the truth. Why should we love you so very much? You haven't done anything to be loved. We don't love the other people, of course. They haven't done anything for that either. A fellow comes along with a bag of gold ... I haven't been in Rotterdam my last voyage for nothing."

'"You may be able to tell something interesting, then, to our people when you come into port," interjected the officer.

'"I might. But you keep some people in your pay at Rotterdam. Let them report. I am a neutral – am I not? ... Have you ever seen a poor man on one side and a bag of gold on the other? Of course, I couldn't be tempted. I haven't the nerve for it. Really I haven't. It's nothing to me. I am just talking openly for once."

'"Yes. And I am listening to you," said the commanding officer, quietly.

'The Northman leaned forward over the table. "Now that I know you have no suspicions, I talk. You don't know what a poor man is. I do. I am poor myself. This old ship, she isn't much, and she is mortgaged too. Bare living, no more. Of course, I wouldn't have the nerve. But a man who has nerve! See. The stuff he takes aboard looks like any other cargo – packages, barrels, tins, copper tubes – what not. He doesn't see it work. It isn't real to him. But he sees the gold. That's real. Of course, nothing could induce me. I suffer from an internal disease. I would either go crazy from anxiety – or – or – take to drink or something. The risk is too great. Why – ruin !"

'"It should be death." The commanding officer got up, after this curt declaration, which the other received with a hard stare oddly combined with an uncertain smile. The officer's gorge rose at the atmosphere of murderous complicity which surrounded him, denser, more impenetrable, more acrid than the fog outside.

'"It's nothing to me," murmured the Northman, swaying visibly.

'"Of course not," assented the commanding officer, with a great effort to keep his voice calm and low. The certitude was strong within him. "But I am going to clear all you fellows off this coast at once. And I will begin with you. You must leave in half an hour."

'By that time the officer was walking along the deck with the Northman at his elbow.

'"What ! In this fog ?" the latter cried out, huskily.

'"Yes, you will have to go in this fog."

'"But I don't know where I am. I really don't."

'The commanding officer turned round. A sort of fury possessed him. The eyes of the two men met. Those of the Northman expressed a profound amazement.

'"Oh, you don't know how to get out." The commanding officer spoke with composure, but his heart was beating with anger and dread. "I will give you your course. Steer south-by-east-half-east for about four miles and then you will be clear to haul to the eastward for your port. The weather will clear up before very long."

'"Must I ? What could induce me ? I haven't the nerve."

'"And yet you must go. Unless you want to – "

'"I don't want to," panted the Northman. "I've enough of it."

'The commanding officer got over the side. The Northman remained still as if rooted to the deck. Before his boat reached the ship the commanding officer heard the steamer beginning to pick up her anchor. Then, shadowy in the fog, she steamed out on the given course.

'"Yes," he said to his officers, "I let him go."'

The narrator bent forwards towards the couch, where no movement betrayed the presence of a living person.

'Listen,' he said, forcibly. 'That course would lead the Northman straight on a deadly ledge of rock. And the commanding officer gave it to him. He steamed out — ran on it — and went down. So he had spoken the truth. He did not know where he was. But it proves nothing. Nothing either way. It may have been the only truth in all his story. And yet ... He seems to have been driven out by a menacing stare — nothing more.'

'Yes, I gave that course to him. It seemed to me a supreme test. I believe — no, I don't believe. I don't know. At the time I was certain. They all went down; and I don't know whether I have done stern retribution — or murder; whether I have added to the corpses that litter the bed of the unreadable sea the bodies of men completely innocent or basely guilty. I don't know. I shall never know.'

He rose. The woman on the couch got up and threw her arms round his neck. Her eyes put two gleams in the deep shadow of the room. She knew his passion for truth, his horror of deceit, his humanity.

'Oh, my poor, poor — '

'I shall never know,' he repeated, sternly, disengaged himself, pressed her hands to his lips, and went out.

M. R. JAMES

'Oh, Whistle, and I'll come to You, My Lad'

'I suppose you will be getting away pretty soon, now Full Term is over, Professor,' said a person not in the story to the Professor of Ontography, soon after they had sat down next to each other at a feast in the hospitable hall of St James's College.

The Professor was young, neat, and precise in speech.

'Yes,' he said; 'my friends have been making me take up golf this term, and I mean to go to the East Coast – in point of fact to Burnstow – (I dare say you know it) for a week or ten days, to improve my game. I hope to get off tomorrow.'

'Oh, Parkins,' said his neighbour on the other side, 'if you are going to Burnstow, I wish you would look at the site of the Templars' preceptory, and let me know if you think it would be any good to have a dig there in the summer.'

It was, as you might suppose, a person of antiquarian pursuits who said this, but, since he merely appears in this prologue, there is no need to give his entitlements.

'Certainly,' said Parkins, the Professor: 'If you will describe to me whereabouts the site is, I will do my best to give you an idea of the lie of the land when I get back; or I could write to you about it, if you would tell me where you are likely to be.'

'Don't trouble to do that, thanks. It's only that I'm thinking of taking my family in that direction in the Long, and it occurred to me that, as very few of the English preceptories have ever been properly planned, I might have an opportunity of doing something useful on off-days.'

The Professor rather sniffed at the idea that planning out a preceptory could be described as useful. His neighbour continued:

'The site – I doubt if there is anything showing above ground – must be down quite close to the beach now. The sea has encroached tremendously, as you know, all along that bit of coast. I should think, from the map, that it must be about three-quarters of a mile from the Globe Inn, at the north end of the town. Where are you going to stay?'

'Well, *at* the Globe Inn, as a matter of fact,' said Parkins: 'I have engaged a room there. I couldn't get in anywhere else; most of the lodging-houses are shut up in winter, it seems; and, as it is, they tell me that the only room of any size I can have is really a double-bedded one, and that they haven't a corner in which to store the other bed, and so on. But I must have a fairly large room, for I am taking some books down, and mean to do a bit of work; and though I don't quite fancy having an empty bed – not to speak of two – in what I may call for the time being my study, I suppose I can manage to rough it for the short time I shall be there.'

'Do you call having an extra bed in your room roughing it, Parkins?' said a bluff person opposite. 'Look here, I shall come down and occupy it for a bit; it'll be company for you.'

The Professor quivered, but managed to laugh in a courteous manner.

'By all means, Rogers; there's nothing I should like better. But I'm afraid you would find it rather dull; you don't play golf, do you?'

'No, thank Heaven!' said rude Mr Rogers.

'Well, you see, when I'm not writing I shall most likely be out on the links, and that, as I say, would be rather dull for you, I'm afraid.'

'Oh, I don't know! There's certain to be somebody I know in the place; but, of course, if you don't want me, speak the word, Parkins; I shan't be offended. Truth, as you always tell us, is never offensive.'

Parkins was, indeed, scrupulously polite and strictly truthful. It is to be feared that Mr Rogers sometimes practised upon his knowledge of these characteristics. In Parkin's breast there was a conflict now raging, which for a moment or two did not allow him to answer. That interval being over, he said:

'Well, if you want the extact truth, Rogers, I was considering whether the room I speak of would really be large enough to accommodate us both comfortably; and also whether (mind, I shouldn't have said this if you hadn't pressed me) you would not constitute something in the nature of a hindrance to my work.'

Rogers laughed loudly.

'Well done, Parkins!' he said. 'It's all right. I promise not to interrupt your work; don't you disturb yourself about that. No, I won't come if you don't want me; but I thought I should do so nicely to keep the ghosts off.' Here he might have been seen to wink and to nudge his next neighbour. Parkins might also have been seen to become pink. 'I beg pardon, Parkins,' Rogers continued; 'I oughtn't to have said that. I forgot you didn't like levity on these topics.'

'Well,' Parkins said, 'as you have mentioned the matter, I freely own that I do *not* like careless talk about what you call ghosts. A man in my positon,' he went on, raising his voice a little, 'cannot, I find, be too careful about appearing to sanction the current beliefs on such subjects. As you know, Rogers, or as you ought to know; for I think I have never concealed my views – '

'No, you certainly have not, old man,' put in Rogers *sotto voce*.

' – I hold that any semblance, any appearance of concession to the view that such things might exist is equivalent to a renunciation of all that I hold most sacred. But I'm afraid I have not succeeded in securing your attention.'

'Your *undivided* attention, was what Dr Blimber actually *said*,'* Rogers interrupted, with every appearance of an earnest desire for accuracy. 'But I beg your pardon, Parkins: I'm stopping you.'

'No, not at all,' said Parkins. 'I don't remember Blimber; perhaps he was before my time. But I needn't go on. I'm sure you know what I mean.'

'Yes, yes,' said Rogers, rather hastily – 'just so. We'll go into it fully at Burnstow, or somewhere.'

In repeating the above dialogue I have tried to give the impression which it made on me, that Parkins was something of an old woman – rather henlike, perhaps, in his little ways; totally destitute, alas! of the sense of humour, but at the same time dauntless and sincere in his convictions, and a man deserving of the greatest respect. Whether or not the reader has

---

* Mr Rogers was wrong, *vide Dombey and Son*, chapter xii.

gathered so much, that was the character which Parkins had.

On the following day Parkins did, as he had hoped, succeed in getting away from his college, and in arriving at Burnstow. He was made welcome at the Globe Inn, was safely installed in the large double-bedded room of which we have heard, and was able before retiring to rest to arrange his materials for work in apple-pie order upon a commodious table which occupied the outer end of the room, and was surrounded on three sides by windows looking out seaward; that is to say, the central window looked straight out to sea, and those on the left and right commanded prospects along the shore to the north and south respectively. On the south you saw the village of Burnstow. On the north no houses were to be seen, but only the beach and the low cliff backing it. Immediately in front was a strip – not considerable – of rough grass, dotted with old anchors, capstans, and so forth; then a broad path; then the beach. Whatever may have been the original distance between the Globe Inn and the sea, not more than sixty yards now separated them.

The rest of the population of the inn was, of course, a golfing one, and included few elements that call for a special description. The most conspicuous figure was, perhaps, that of an *ancien militaire*, secretary of a London club, and possessed of a voice of incredible strength, and of views of a pronouncedly Protestant type. These were apt to find utterance after his attendance upon the ministrations of the Vicar, an estimable man with inclinations towards a picturesque ritual, which he gallantly kept down as far as he could out of deference to East Anglian tradition.

Professor Parkins, one of whose principal characteristics was pluck, spent the greater part of the day following his arrival at Burnstow in what he had called improving his game, in company with this Colonel Wilson: and during the afternoon – whether the process of improvement were to blame or not, I am not sure – the Colonel's demeanour assumed a colouring so lurid that even Parkins jibbed at the thought of walking home with him from the links. He determined, after a short and furtive look at that bristling moustache and those incarnadined features, that it would be wiser to allow the influences of tea and tobacco to do what they could with the Colonel before the dinner-hour should render a meeting inevitable.

'I might walk home tonight along the beach,' he reflected – 'yes, and take a look – there will be light enough for that – at the ruins of which Disney was talking. I don't exactly know where they are, by the way; but I expect I can hardly help stumbling on them.'

This he accomplished, I may say, in the most literal sense, for in picking his way from the links to the shingle beach his foot caught, partly in a gorse-root and partly in a biggish stone, and over he went. When he got up and surveyed his surroundings, he found himself in a patch of somewhat broken ground covered with small depressions and mounds. These latter, when he came to examine them, proved to be simply masses of flints embedded in mortar and grown over with turf. He must, he quite rightly concluded, be on the site of the preceptory he had promised to look at. It seemed not unlikely to reward the spade of the explorer; enough of the foundations was probably left at no great depth to throw a good deal of light on the general plan. He remembered vaguely that the Templars, to whom this site had belonged, were in the habit of building round churches, and he thought a particular series of the humps or mounds near him did appear to be arranged in something of a circular form. Few people can resist the temptation to try a little amateur research in a department quite outside their own, if only for the satisfaction of showing how successful they would have been had they only taken it up seriously. Our Professor, however, if he felt something of this mean desire, was also truly anxious to oblige Mr Disney. So he paced with care the circular area he had noticed, and wrote down its rough dimensions in his pocket-book. Then he proceeded to examine an oblong eminence which lay east of the centre of the circle, and seemed to his thinking likely to be the base of a platform or altar. At one end of it, the northern, a patch of the turf was gone – removed by some boy or other creature *ferae naturae*. It might, he thought, be as well to probe the soil here for evidences of masonry, and he took out his knife and began scraping away the earth. And now followed another little discovery: a portion of soil fell inward as he scraped, and disclosed a small cavity. He lighted one match after another to help him to see of what nature the hole was, but the wind was too strong for them all. By tapping and scratching the sides with his knife, however, he was able to make out that it must be an artificial hole in masonry. It was rectangular, and the sides, top, and bottom, if not actually plastered, were smooth and regular. Of course it was empty. No ! As he withdrew the knife he heard a metallic clink, and when he introduced his hand it met with a cylindrical object lying on the floor of the hole. Naturally enough, he picked it up, and when he brought it into the light, now fast fading, he could see that it, too, was of man's making – a metal tube about four inches long, and evidently of some considerable age.

By the time Parkins had made sure that there was nothing else in this odd receptacle, it was too late and too dark for him to think of undertaking any further search. What he had done had proved so unexpectedly interesting that he determined to sacrifice a little more of the daylight on the morrow to archaeology. The object which he now had safe in his pocket was bound to be of some slight value at least, he felt sure.

Bleak and solemn was the view on which he took a last look before starting homeward. A faint yellow light in the west showed the links, on which a few figures moving towards the club-house were still visible, the squat martello tower, the lights of Aldsey village, the pale ribbon of sand intersected at intervals by black wooden groynings, the dim and murmuring sea. The wind was bitter from the north, but was at his back when he set out for the Globe. He quickly rattled and clashed through the shingle and gained the sand, upon which, but for the groynings which had to be got over every few yards, the going was both good and quiet. One last look behind, to measure the distance he had made since leaving the ruined Templars' church, showed him a prospect of company on his walk, in the shape of a rather indistinct personage, who seemed to be making great efforts to catch up with him, but made little, if any, progress. I mean that there was an appearance of running about his movements, but that the distance between him and Parkins did not seem materially to lessen. So, at least, Parkins thought, and decided that he almost certainly did not know him, and that it would be absurd to wait until he came up. For all that, company, he began to think, would really be very welcome on that lonely shore, if only you could choose your companion. In his unenlightened days he had read of meetings in such places which even now would hardly bear thinking of. He went on thinking of them, however, until he reached home, and particularly of one which catches most people's fancy at some time of their childhood. 'Now I saw in my dream that Christian had gone but a very little way when he saw a foul fiend coming over the field to meet him.' 'What should I do now,' he thought, 'if I looked back and caught sight of a black figure sharply defined against the yellow sky, and saw that it had horns and wings ? I wonder whether I should stand or run for it. Luckily, the gentleman behind is not of that kind, and he seems to be about as far off now as when I saw him first. Well, at this rate, he won't get his dinner as soon as I shall ; and, dear me ! it's within a quarter of an hour of the time now. I must run !'

Parkins had, in fact, very little time for dressing. When he met the Colonel at dinner, Peace – or as much of her as the gentleman could manage – reigned once more in the military bosom ; nor was she put to flight in the hours of bridge that followed dinner, for Parkins was a more than respectable player. When, therefore, he retired towards twelve o'clock, he felt that he had spent his evening in quite a satisfactory way, and that, even for so long as a fortnight or three weeks, life at the Globe would be supportable under similar conditions – 'especially,' thought he, 'if I go on improving my game.'

As he went along the passages he met the boots of the Globe, who stopped and said :

'Beg your pardon, sir, but as I was abrushing your coat just now there was something fell out of the pocket. I put it on your chest of drawers, sir, in your room, sir – a piece of a pipe of somethink of that, sir. Thank you, sir. You'll find it on your chest of drawers, sir – yes, sir. Good night, sir.'

The speech served to remind Parkins of his little discovery of that afternoon. It was with some considerable curiosity that he turned it over by the light of his candles. It was of bronze, he now saw, and was shaped very much after the manner of the modern dog-whistle ; in fact it was – yes, certainly it was – actually no more nor less than a whistle. He put it to his lips, but it was quite full of a fine, caked-up sand or earth, which would not yield to knocking, but must be loosened with a knife. Tidy as ever in his habits, Parkins cleared out the earth on to a piece of paper, and took the latter to the window to empty it out. The night was clear and bright, as he saw when he had opened the casement, and he stopped for an instant to look at the sea and note a belated wanderer stationed on the shore in front of the inn. Then he shut the window, a little surprised at the late hours people kept at Burnstow, and took his whistle to the light again. Why, surely there were marks on it, and not merely marks, but letters! A very little rubbing rendered the deeply-cut inscription quite legible, but the Professor had to confess, after some earnest thought, that the meaning of it was as obscure to him as the writing on the wall to Belshazzar. There were legends both on the front and on the back of the whistle. The one read thus:

𝕱𝕷𝕬

𝕱𝖀𝕽   𝕭𝕴𝕾

𝕱𝕷𝕰

𝕼𝖀𝕴𝕾 𝕰𝕾𝕿 𝕴𝕾𝕿𝕰 𝕼𝖀𝕴 𝖁𝕰𝕹𝕴𝕿

'I ought to be able to make it out,' he thought; 'but I suppose I am a little rusty in my Latin. When I come to think of it, I don't believe I even know the word for a whistle. The long one does seem simple enough. It ought to mean: "Who is this who is coming?" Well, the best way to find out is evidently to whistle for him.'

He blew tentatively and stopped suddenly, startled and yet pleased at the note he had elicited. It had a quality of infinite distance in it, and, soft as it was, he somehow felt it must be audible for miles round. It was a sound, too, that seemed to have the power (which many scents possess) of forming pictures in the brain. He saw quite clearly for a moment a vision of a wide, dark expanse at night, with a fresh wind blowing, and in the midst a lonely figure – how employed, he could not tell. Perhaps he would have seen more had not the picture been broken by the sudden surge of a gust of wind against his casement, so sudden that it made him look up, just in time to see the white glint of a seabird's wing somewhere outside the dark panes.

The sound of the whistle had so fascinated him that he could not help trying it once more, this time more boldly. The note was little, if at all, louder than before, and repetition broke the illusion – no picture followed, as he had half hoped it might. 'But what is this ? Goodness ! what force the wind can get up in a few minutes ! What a tremendous gust ! There ! I knew that window-fastening was no use ! Ah ! I thought so – both candles out. It is enough to tear the room to pieces.'

The first thing was to get the window shut. While you might count twenty Parkins was struggling with the small casement, and felt almost as if he were pushing back a sturdy burglar, so strong was the pressure. It slackened all at once, and the window banged to and latched itself. Now to relight the candles and see what damage, if any, had been done. No, nothing seemed amiss ; no glass even was broken in the casement. But the noise had evidently roused at least one member of the household : the Colonel was to be heard stumping in his stockinged feet on the floor above, and growling.

Quickly as it had risen, the wind did not fall at once. On it went, moaning and rushing past the house, at times rising to a cry so desolate that, as Parkins disinterestedly said, it might have made fanciful people feel quite uncomfortable ; even the unimaginative, he thought after a quarter of an hour, might be happier without it.

Whether it was the wind, or the excitement of golf, or of the researches in the preceptory that kept Parkins awake, he was not sure. Awake he remained, in any case, long enough to fancy (as I am afraid I often do myself under such conditions) that he was the victim of all manner of fatal disorders : he would lie counting the beats of his heart, convinced that it was going to stop work every moment, and would entertain grave suspicions of his lungs, brain, liver, etc. – suspicions which he was sure would be dispelled by the return of daylight, but which until then refused to be put aside. He found a little vicarious comfort in the idea that someone else was in the same boat. A near neighbour (in the darkness it was not easy to tell his direction) was tossing and rustling in his bed, too.

The next stage was that Parkins shut his eyes and determined to give sleep every chance. Here again over-excitement asserted itself in another form – that of making pictures. *Experto crede*, pictures do come to the closed eyes of one trying to sleep, and are often so little to his taste that he must open his eyes and disperse them.

Parkins's experience on this occasion was a very distressing one. He found that the picture which presented itself to him was continuous. When he opened his eyes, of course, it went; but when he shut them once more it framed itself afresh, and acted itself out again, neither quicker nor slower than before. What he saw was this:

A long stretch of shore – shingle edged by sand, and intersected at short intervals with black groynes running down to the water – a scene, in fact, so like that of his afternoon's walk that, in the absence of any land-mark, it could not be distinguished therefrom. The light was obscure, conveying an impression of gathering storm, late winter evening, and slight cold rain. On this bleak stage at first no actor was visible. Then, in the distance, a bobbing black object appeared; a moment more, and it was a man running, jumping, clambering over the groynes, and every few seconds looking eagerly back. The nearer he came the more obvious it was that he was not only anxious, but even terribly frightened, though his face was not to be distinguished. He was, moreover, almost at the end of his strength. On he came; each successive obstacle seemed to cause him more difficulty than the last. 'Will he get over this next one?' thought Parkins; 'it seems a little higher than the others.' Yes; half climbing, half throwing himself, he did get over, and fell all in a heap on the other side (the side nearest to the spectator). There, as if really unable to get up again, he remained crouching under the groyne, looking up in an attitude of painful anxiety.

So far no cause whatever for the fear of the runner had been shown; but now there began to be seen, far up the shore, a little flicker of something light-coloured moving to and fro with great swiftness and irrgularity. Rapidly growing larger, it, too, declared itself as a figure in pale, fluttering draperies, ill-defined. There was something about its motion which made Parkins very unwilling to see it at close quarters. It would stop, raise arms, bow itself towards the sand, then run stooping across the beach to the water-edge and back again; and then, rising upright, once more continue its course forward at a speed that was startling and terrifying. The moment came when the pursuer was hovering about from left to right only a few yards beyond the groyne where the runner lay in hiding. After two or three ineffectual castings hither and thither it came to a stop, stood upright, with arms raised high, and then darted straight forward towards the groyne.

It was at this point that Parkins always failed in his resolution to keep his eyes shut. With many misgivings as to incipient failure of eyesight, overworked brain, excessive smoking, and so on, he finally resigned himself to light his candle, get out a book, and pass the night walking, rather than be tormented by this persistent panorama, which he saw clearly enough could only be a morbid reflection of his walk and his thoughts on that very day.

The scraping of match on box and the glare of light must have startled some creatures of the night – rats or what not – which he heard scurry across the floor from the side of his bed with much rustling. Dear, dear! the match is out! Fool that it is! But the second one burnt better, and a candle and book were duly procured, over which Parkins pored till sleep of a wholesome kind came upon him, and that in no long space. For about the first time in his orderly and prudent life he forget to blow out the candle, and when he was called next morning at eight there was still a flicker in the socket and a sad mess of guttered grease on the top of the little table.

After breakfast he was in his room, putting the finishing touches to his golfing costume – fortune had again allotted the Colonel to him for a partner – when one of the maids came in.

'Oh, if you please,' she said, 'would you like any extra blankets on your bed, sir!'

'Ah! thank you,' said Parkins. 'Yes, I think I should like one. It seems likely to turn rather colder.'

In a very short time the maid was back with the blanket.

'Which bed should I put it on, sir?' she asked.

'What? Why, that one – the one I slept in last night,' he said, pointing to it.

'Oh yes! I beg your pardon, sir, but you seemed to have tried both of 'em; leastways, we had to make 'em both up this morning.'

'Really! How very absurd!' said Parkins. 'I certainly never touched the other, except to lay some things on it. Did it actually seem to have been slept in ?'

'Oh yes, sir !' said the maid. 'Why, all the things was crumpled and throwed about all ways, if you'll excuse me, sir – quite as if anyone 'adn't passed but a very poor night, sir.'

'Dear me,' said Parkins. 'Well, I may have disordered it more than I thought when I unpacked my things. I'm very sorry to have given you the extra trouble, I'm sure. I expect a friend of mine soon, by the way – a gentleman from Cambridge – to come and occupy it for a night or two. That will be all right, I suppose, won't it ?'

'Oh yes, to be sure, sir. Thank you, sir. It's no trouble, I'm sure,' said the maid, and departed to giggle with her colleagues.

Parkins set forth, with a stern determination to improve his game.

I am glad to be able to report that he succeeded so far in this enterprise that the Colonel, who had been rather repining at the prospect of a second day's play in his company, became quite chatty as the morning advanced ; and his voice boomed out over the flats, as certain also of our own minor poets have said, 'like some great bourdon in a minster tower'.

'Extraordinary wind, that, we had last night,' he said. 'In my old home we should have said someone had been whistling for it.'

'Should you, indeed !' said Parkins. 'Is there a superstition of that kind still current in your part of the country ?'

'I don't know about superstition,' said the Colonel. 'They believe in it all over Denmark and Norway, as well as on the Yorkshire coast ; and my experience is, mind you, that there's generally something at the bottom of what these country-folk hold to, and have held to for generations. But it's your drive' (or whatever it might have been : the golfing reader will have to imagine appropriate digressions at the proper intervals).

When conversation was resumed, Parkins said, with a slight hesitancy :

'A propos of what you were saying just now, Colonel, I think I ought to tell you that my own views on such subjects are very strong. I am, in fact, a convinced disbeliever in what is called the "supernatural".'

'What !' said the Colonel, 'do you mean to tell me you don't believe in second-sight, or ghosts, or anything of that kind ?'

'In nothing whatever of that kind,' returned Parkins firmly.

'Well', said the Colonel, 'but it appears to me at that rate, sir, that you must be little better than a Sadducee.'

Parkins was on the point of answering that, in his opinion, the Sadducees were the most sensible persons he had ever read of in the Old Testament; but feeling some doubt as to whether much mention of them was to be found in that work, he preferred to laugh the accusation off.

'Perhaps I am,' he said; 'but – Here, give me my cleek, boy! – Excuse me one moment, Colonel.' A short interval. 'Now, as to whistling for the wind, let me give you my theory about it. The laws which govern winds are really not at all perfectly known – to fisherfolk and such, of course, not known at all. A man or woman of eccentric habits, perhaps, or a stranger, is seen repeatedly on the beach at some unusual hour, and is heard whistling. Soon afterwards a violent wind rises; a man who could read the sky perfectly or who possessed a barometer could have foretold that it would. The simple people of a fishing-village have no barometers, and only a few rough rules for prophesying weather. What more natural than that the eccentric personage I postulated should be regarded as having raised the wind, or that he or she should clutch eagerly at the reputation of being able to do so? Now, take last night's wind: as it happens, I myself was whistling. I blew a whistle twice, and the wind seemed to come absolutely in answer to my call. If anyone had seen me—'

The audience had been a little restive under this harangue, and Parkins had, I fear, fallen somewhat into the tone of a lecturer; but at the last sentence the Colonel stopped.

'Whistling, were you?' he said. 'And what sort of whistle did you use? Play this stroke first.' Interval.

'About that whistle you were asking. Colonel. It's rather a curious one. I have it in my – No; I see I've left it in my room. As a matter of fact, I found it yesterday.'

And then Parkins narrated the manner of his discovery of the whistle, upon hearing which the Colonel grunted, and opined that, in Parkins's place, he should himself be careful about using a thing that had belonged to a set of Papists, of whom, speaking generally, it might be affirmed that you never knew what they might not have been up to. From this topic he diverged to the enormities of the Vicar, who had given notice on the previous Sunday that Friday would be the Feast of St Thomas the Apostle, and that there would be service at eleven o'clock in the church. This and other similar proceedings constituted in the Colonel's view a strong presumption that the Vicar was a concealed Papist, if not a Jesuit; and Parkins, who could not very readily follow the Colonel in this region, did not disagree with him. In fact, they got on so well together in the morning that there was not talk on either side of their separating after lunch.

Both continued to play well during the afternoon, or at least, well enough to make them forget everything else until the light began to fail them. Not until then did Parkins remember that he had meant to do some more investigating at the preceptory; but it was of no great importance, he reflected. One day was as good as another; he might as well go home with the Colonel.

As they turned the corner of the house, the Colonel was almost knocked down by a boy who rushed into him at the very top of his speed, and then, instead of running away, remained hanging on to him and panting. The first words of the warrior were naturally those of reproof and objurgation, but he very quickly discerned that the boy was almost speechless with fright. Inquiries were useless at first. When the boy got his breath he began to howl, and still clung to the Colonel's legs. He was at last detached, but continued to howl.

'What in the world *is* the matter with you? What have you been up to? What have you seen?' said the two men.

'Ow, I seen it wive at me out of the winder,' wailed the boy, 'and I don't like it.'

'What window?' said the irritated Colonel. 'Come pull yourself together, my boy.'

'The front winder it was, at the 'otel,' said the boy.

At this point Parkins was in favour of sending the boy home, but the Colonel refused; he wanted to get to the bottom of it, he said; it was most dangerous to give a boy such a fright as this one had had, and if it turned out that people had been playing jokes, they should suffer for it in some way. And by a series of questions he made out this story: The boy had been playing about on the grass in front of the Globe with some others; then they had gone home to their teas, and he was just going, when he happened to look up at the front winder and see it a-wiving at him. *It* seemed to be a figure of some sort, in white as far as he knew – couldn't see its face; but it wived at him, and it warn't a right thing – not to say not a right person. Was there a light in the room? No, he didn't think to look if there was a light. Which was the window? Was it the top one or the second one? The seckind one it was – the big winder what got two little uns at the sides.

'Very well, my boy,' said the Colonel, after a few more questions. 'You run away home now. I expect it was some person trying to give you a start. Another time, like a brave English boy, you just throw a stone – well, no, not that exactly, but you go and speak to the waiter, or to Mr Simpson, the landlord, and – yes – and say that I advised you to do so.'

The boy's face expressed some of the doubt he felt as to the likelihood of Mr Simpson's lending a favourable ear to his complaint, but the Colonel did not appear to perceive this, and went on:

'And here's a sixpence – no, I see it's a shilling – and you be off home, and don't think any more about it.'

The youth hurried off with agitated thanks, and the Colonel and Parkins went round to the front of the Globe and reconnoitred. There was only one window answering to the description they had been hearing.

'Well, that's curious,' said Parkins; 'it's evidently my window the lad was talking about. Will you come up for a moment, Colonel Wilson? We ought to be able to see if anyone has been taking liberties in my room.'

They were soon in the passage, and Parkins made as if to open the door. Then he stopped and felt in his pockets.

'This is more serious than I thought,' was his next remark. 'I remember now that before I started this morning I locked the door. It is locked now, and, what is more, here is the key.' And he held it up. 'Now,' he went on, 'if the servants are in the habit of going into one's room during the day when one is away, I can only say that – well, that I don't approve of it at all.' Conscious of a somewhat weak climax, he busied himself in opening the door (which was indeed locked) and in lighting candles. 'No,' he said, 'nothing seems disturbed.'

'Except your bed,' put in the Colonel.

'Excuse me, that isn't my bed,' said Parkins. 'I don't use that one. But it does look as if someone had been playing tricks with it.'

It certainly did: the clothes were bundled up and twisted together in a most tortuous confusion. Parkins pondered.

'That must be it,' he said at last. 'I disordered the clothes last night in unpacking, and they haven't made it since. Perhaps they came in to make it, and that boy saw them through the window; and then they were called away and locked the door after them. Yes, I think that must be it.'

'Well, ring and ask,' said the Colonel, and this appealed to Parkins as practical.

The maid appeared, and, to make a long story short, deposed that she had made the bed in the morning when the gentleman was in the room, and hadn't been there since. No, she hadn't no other key. Mr Simpson, he kep' the keys; he'd be able to tell the gentleman if anyone had been up.

This was a puzzle. Investigation showed that nothing of value had been taken, and Parkins remembered the disposition of the small objects on tables and so forth well enough to be pretty sure that no pranks had been played with them. Mr and Mrs Simpson furthermore agreed that neither of them had given the duplicate key of the room to any person whatever during the day. Nor could Parkins, fair-minded man as he was, detect anything in the demeanour of master, mistress, or maid that indicated guilt. He was much more inclined to think that the boy had been imposing on the Colonel.

The latter was unwontedly silent and pensive at dinner and throughout the evening. When he bade goodnight to Parkins, he murmured in a gruff undertone:

'You know where I am if you want me during the night.'

'Why, yes, thank you, Colonel Wilson. I think I do; but there isn't much prospect of my disturbing you, I hope. By the way,' he added, 'did I show you that old whistle I spoke of? I think not. Well, here it is.'

The Colonel turned it over gingerly in the light of the candle.

'Can you make anything of the inscription?' asked Parkins, as he took it back.

'No, not in this light. What do you mean to do with it?'

'Oh, well, when I get back to Cambridge I shall submit it to some of the archaeologists there, and see what they think of it;

and very likely, if they consider it worth having, I may present it to one of the museums.'

''M!' said the Colonel. 'Well, you may be right. All I know is that, if it were mine, I should chuck it straight into the sea. It's no use talking, I'm well aware, but I expect that with you it's a case of live and learn. I hope so, I'm sure, and I wish you a good night.'

He turned away, leaving Parkins in act to speak at the bottom of the stair, and soon each was in his own bedroom.

By some unfortunate accident, there was neither blinds nor curtains to the windows of the Professor's room. The previous night he had thought little of this, but tonight there seemed every prospect of a bright moon rising to shine directly on his bed, and probably wake him later on. When he noticed this he was a good deal annoyed, but, with an ingenuity which I can only envy, he succeeded in rigging up, with the help of a railway-rug, some safety-pins, and a stick and umbrella, a screen which, if it only held together, would completely keep the moonlight off his bed. And shortly afterwards he was comfortably in that bed. When he had read a somewhat solid work long enough to produce a decided wish to sleep, he cast a drowsy glance round the room, blew out the candle, and fell back upon the pillow.

He must have slept soundly for an hour or more, when a sudden clatter shook him up in a most unwelcome manner. In a moment he realized what had happened: his carefully-constructed screen had given way, and a very bright frosty moon was shining directly on his face. This was highly annoying. Could he possibly get up and reconstruct the screen? or could he manage to sleep if he did not?

For some minutes he lay and pondered over all the possibilities; then he turned over sharply, and with his eyes open lay breathlessly listening. There had been a movement, he was sure, in the empty bed on the opposite side of the room. Tomorrow he would have it moved, for there must be rats or something playing about in it. It was quiet now. No! the commotion began again. There was a rustling and shaking: surely more than any rat could cause.

I can figure to myself something of the Professor's bewilderment and horror, for I have in a dream thirty years back seen the same thing happen; but the reader will hardly, perhaps, imagine how dreadful it was to him to see a figure suddenly sit up in what he had known was an empty bed. He was out of his own bed in one bound, and made a dash towards the window, where he lay his only weapon, the stick with which he had propped his screen. This was, as it turned out, the worst thing he could have done, because the personage in the empty bed, with a sudden smooth motion, slipped from the bed and took up a position, with outspread arms, between the two beds, and in front of the door. Parkins watched it in a horrid perplexity. Somehow, the idea of getting past it and escaping through the door was intolerable to him; he could not have borne – he didn't know why – to touch it; and as for its touching him, he would sooner dash himself through the window than have that happen. It stood for the moment in a band of dark shadow, and he had not seen what its face was like. Now it began to move, in a stooping posture, and all at once the spectator realized, with some horror and some relief, that it must be blind, for it seemed to feel about it with its muffled arms in a groping and random fashion. Turning half way from him, it became suddenly conscious of the bed he had just left, and darted towards it, and bent and felt over the pillows in a way which made Parkins shudder as he had never in his life thought it possible. In a very few moments it seemed to know that the bed was empty, and then, moving forward into the area of light and facing the window, it showed for the first time what manner of thing it was.

Parkins, who very much dislikes being questioned about it, did once describe something of it in my hearing, and I gathered that what he chiefly remembers about it is a horrible, an intensely horrible, face *of crumpled linen*. What expression he read upon it he could not or would not tell, but that the fear of it went nigh to maddening him is certain.

But he was not at leisure to watch it for long. With formidable quickness it moved into the middle of the room, and, as it groped and waved, one corner of its draperies swept across Parkins's face. He could not, though he knew how perilous a sound was – he could not keep back a cry of disgust, and this gave the searcher an instant clue. It leapt towards him upon the instant, and the next moment he was half-way through the window backwards, uttering cry upon cry at the utmost pitch of his voice, and the linen face was thrust close into his own. At this, almost the last possible second, deliverance came, as you will have guessed: the Colonel burst the door open, and was just in time to see the dreadful group at the window. When he reached the figures only one was left. Parkins sank forward into the room in a faint, and before him on the floor lay a tumbled heap of bed-clothes.

Colonel Wilson asked no questions, but busied himself in keeping everyone else out of the room and in getting Parkins back to his bed; and himself, wrapped in a rug, occupied the other bed, for the rest of the night. Early on the next day Rogers arrived, more welcome than he would have been a day before, and the three of them held a very long consultation in the Professor's room. At the end of it the Colonel left the hotel door carrying a small object between his finger and thumb, which he cast as far into the sea as a very brawny arm could send it. Later on the smoke of a burning ascended from the back premises of the Globe.

Exactly what explanation was patched up for the staff and visitors at the hotel I must confess I do not recollect. The Professor was somehow cleared of the ready suspicion of delirium tremens, and the hotel of the reputation of a troubled house.

There is not much question as to what would have happened to Parkins if the Colonel had not intervened when he did. He would either have fallen out of the window or else lost his wits. But it is not so evident what more the creature that came in answer to the whistle could have done than frighten. There seemed to be absolutely nothing material about it save the bed-clothes of which it had made itself a body. The Colonel, who remembered a not very dissimilar occurrence in India, was of the opinion that if Parkins had closed with it it could really have done very little, and that its one power was that of frightening. The whole thing, he said, served to confirm his opinion of the Church of Rome.

There is really nothing more to tell, but, as you may imagine, the Professor's views on certain points are less clear cut than they used to be. His nerves, too, have suffered: he cannot even now see a surplice hanging on a door quite unmoved, and the spectacle of a scarecrow in a field late on a winter afternoon has cost him more than one sleepless night.

RUDYARD KIPLING

Dayspring Mishandled

C'est moi, c'est moi, c'est moi !
Je suis la Mandragore !
La fille des beaux qui s'éveille à l'aurore –
Et qui chan'e pour toi !

C.Nodier

In the days beyond compare and before the Judgments, a genius called Graydon foresaw that the advance of education and the standard of living would submerge all mind-marks in one mudrush of standardized reading-matter, and so created the Fictional Supply Syndicate to meet the demand.

Since a few days' work for him brought them more money than a week's elsewhere, he drew many young men – some now eminent – into his employ. He bade them keep their eyes on the *Sixpenny Dream Book*, the Army and Navy Stores Catalogue (this for backgrounds and furniture as they changed), and *The Hearthstone Friend*, a weekly publication which specialized unrivalledly in the domestic emotions. Yet, even so, youth would not be denied, and some of the collaborated love-talk in 'Passion Hath Peril', and 'Ena's Lost Lovers', and the account of the murder of the earl in 'The Wickwire Tragedies' – to name but a few masterpieces now never mentioned for fear of blackmail – was as good as anything to which their authors signed their real names in more distinguished years.

Among the young ravens driven to roost awhile on Graydon's ark was James Andrew Manallace – a darkish, slow northerner of the type that does not ignite, but must be detonated. Given written or verbal outlines of a plot, he was useless; but, with a half-dozen pictures round which to write his tale, he could astonish.

And he adored that woman who afterwards became the mother of Vidal Benzaquen,* and who suffered and died because she loved one unworthy. There was, also, among the company a mannered, bellied person called Alured Castorley, who talked

*'The Village that voted the Earth was Flat.' *A Diversity of Creatures.*

and wrote about 'Bohemia', but was always afraid of being 'compromised' by the weekly suppers at Neminaka's Café in Hestern Square, where the Syndicate work was apportioned, and where everyone looked out for himself. He, too, for a time, had loved Vidal's mother, in his own way.

Now, one Saturday at Neminaka's, Graydon, who had given Manallace a sheaf of prints — torn from an extinct children's book called *Philippa's Queen* — on which to improvise, asked for results. Manallace went down into his ulster-pocket, hesitated a moment, and said the stuff had turned into poetry on his hands.

'Bosh !'

'That's what it isn't', the boy retorted. 'It's rather good.'

'Then it's no use to us.' Graydon laughed. 'Have you brought back the cuts ?'

Manallace handed them over. There was a castle in the series ; a knight or so in armour ; an old lady in a horned head-dress ; a young ditto ; a very obvious Hebrew ; a clerk, with pen and inkhorn, checking wine-barrels on a wharf ; and a Crusader. On the back of one of the prints was a note, 'If he doesn't want to go, why can't he be captured and held to ransom ?' Graydon asked what it all meant.

'I don't know yet. A comic opera, perhaps,' said Manallace.

Graydon, who seldom wasted time, passed the cuts on to someone else, and advanced Manallace a couple of sovereigns to carry on with, as usual ; at which Castorley was angry and would have said something unpleasant but was suppressed. Half-way through supper, Castorley told the company that a relative had died and left him an independence ; and that he now withdrew from 'hackwork' to follow 'Literature'. Generally, the Syndicate rejoiced in a comrade's good fortune, but Castorley had gifts of waking dislike. So the news was received with a vote of thanks, and he went out before the end, and, it was said, proposed to 'Dal Benzaquen's mother, who refused him. He did not come back. Manallace, who had arrived a little exalted, got so drunk before midnight that a man had to stay and see him home. But liquor never touched him above the belt, and when he had slept awhile, he recited to the gas-chandelier the poetry he had made out of the pictures ; said that, on second thoughts, he would convert it into comic opera ; deplored the Upas-tree influence of Gilbert and Sullivan : sang somewhat to illustrate his point; and – after words, by the way, with a negress in yellow satin – was steered to his rooms.

In the course of a few years, Graydon's foresight and genius were rewarded. The public began to read and reason upon higher planes, and the Syndicate grew rich. Later still, people demanded of their printed matter what they expected in their clothing and furniture. So, precisely as the three-guinea handbag is followed in three weeks by its thirteen and sevenpence ha'penny, indistinguishable sister, they enjoyed perfect synthetic substitutes for Plot, Sentiment, and Emotion. Graydon died before the cinema-caption school came in, but he left his widow twenty-seven thousand pounds.

Manallace made a reputation, and, more important, money for Vidal's mother when her husband ran away and the first symptoms of her paralysis showed. His line was the jocundly-sentimental Wardour Street brand of adventure, told in a style that exactly met, but never exceeded, every expectation.

As he once said when urged to 'write a real book': 'I've got my label, and I'm not going to chew it off. If you save people thinking, you can do anything with 'em.' His output apart, he was genuinely a man of letters. He rented a small cottage in the country and economized on everything, except the care and charges of Vidal's mother.

Castorley flew higher. When his legacy freed him from 'hackwork', he became first a critic – in which calling he loyally scalped all his old associates as they came up – and then looked for some speciality. Having found it (Chaucer was the prey), he consolidated his position before he occupied it, by his careful speech, his cultivated bearing, and the whispered words of his friends whom he, too, had saved the trouble of thinking. It followed that, when he published his first serious articles on Chaucer, all the world which is interested in Chaucer said: 'This is an authority.' But he was no impostor. He learned and knew his poet and his age; and in a month-long dogfight in an austere literary weekly, met and mangled a recognized Chaucer expert of the day. He also, 'for old sake's sake', as he wrote to a friend, went out of his way to review one of Manallace's books with an intimacy of unclean deduction (this was before the days of Freud) which long stood as a record. Some member of the extinct Syndicate took occasion to ask him if he would – for old sake's sake – help Vidal's mother to a new treatment. He answered that he had 'known the lady very slightly and the calls on his purse were so heavy that', etc. The writer showed the letter to Manallace, who said he was glad Castorley hadn't interfered. Vidal's mother was then wholly paralysed. Only her eyes could move, and those always looked for the husband who had left her. She died thus in Manallace's arms in April of the first year of the war.

During the war he and Castorley worked as some sort of departmental dishwashers in the Office of Co-ordinated Supervisals. Here Manallace came to know Castorley again. Castorley, having a sweet tooth, cadged lumps of sugar for his tea from a typist, and when she took to giving them to a younger man, arranged that she should be reported for smoking in unauthorized apartments. Manallace possessed himself of every detail of the affair, as compensation for the review of his book. Then there came a night when, waiting for a big air-raid, the two men had talked humanly, and Manallace spoke of Vidal's mother. Castorley said something in reply, and from that hour – as was learned several years later – Manallace's real life-work and interests began.

The war over, Castorley set about to make himself Supreme Pontiff on Chaucer by methods not far removed from the employment of poison gas. The English Pope was silent, through private griefs, and influenza had carried off the learned Hun who claimed continental allegiance. Thus Castorley crowed unchallenged from Upsala to Seville, while Manallace went back to his cottage with the photo of Vidal's mother over the mantelpiece. She seemed to have emptied out his life, and left him only fleeting interests in trifles. His private diversions were experiments of uncertain outcome, which, he said, rested him after a day's gadzooking and vitalstapping. I found him, for instance, one weekend, in his toolshed-scullery, boiling a brew of slimy barks which were, if mixed with oak-galls, vitriol and wine, to become an ink-powder. We boiled it till the Monday, and it turned into an adhesive stronger than birdlime, and entangled us both.

At other times, he would carry me off, once in a few weeks, to sit at Castorley's feet, and hear him talk about Chaucer. Castorley's voice, bad enough in youth, when it could be shouted down, had, with culture and tact, grown almost insupportable. His mannerisms, too, had multiplied and set. He minced and mouthed, postured and chewed his words throughout those terrible evenings; and poisoned not only Chaucer, but every shred of English literature which he used to embellish him. He was shameless, too, as regarded self-advertisement and 'recognition' – weaving elaborate intrigues; forming petty friendships and confederacies, to be dissolved next week in favour of more promising alliances; fawning, snubbing, lecturing, organizing and lying as unrestingly as a politician, in chase of the knighthood due not to him (he always called on his Maker to forbid such a thought) but as tribute to Chaucer. Yet, sometimes, he could break from his obsession and prove how a man's work will try to save the soul of him. He would tell us charmingly of copyists of the fifteenth century in England and the Low Countries, who had multiplied the Chaucer MSS., of which there remained – he gave us the exact number – and how each scribe could by him (and, he implied, by him alone) be distinguished from every other by some peculiarity of letter-formation, spacing or like trick of pen-work; and how he could fix the dates of their work within five years. Sometimes he would give us an hour of really interesting stuff and then return to his overdue 'recognition'. The changes sickened me, but Manallace defended him, as a master in his own line who had revealed Chaucer to at least one grateful soul.

This, as far as I remembered, was the autumn when Manallace holidayed in the Shetlands or the Faroes, and came back with a stone 'quern' – a hand corn-grinder. He said it interested him from the ethnological standpoint. His whim lasted till next harvest, and was followed by a religious spasm which, naturally, translated itself into literature. He showed me a battered and mutilated Vulgate of 1485, patched up the back with bits of legal parchment, which he had bought for thirty-five shillings. Some monk's attempt to rubricate chapter-initials had caught, it seemed, his forlorn fancy, and he dabbled in shells of gold and silver paint for weeks.

That also faded out, and he went to the Continent to get local colour for a love-story, about Alva and the Dutch, and the next year I saw practically nothing of him. This released me from seeing much of Castorley, but, at intervals, I would go there to dine with him, when his wife — an unappetizing, ash-coloured woman — made no secret that his friends wearied her almost as much as he did. But at a later meeting, not long after Manallace had finished his Low Countries' novel, I found Castorley charged to bursting-point with triumph and high information hardly withheld. He confided to me that a time was at hand when great matters would be made plain, and 'recognition' would be inevitable. I assumed, naturally, that there was fresh scandal or heresy afoot in Chaucer circles, and kept my curiosity within bounds.

In time, New York cabled that a fragment of a hitherto unknown Canterbury Tale lay safe in the steel-walled vaults of the seven-million-dollar Sunnapia Collection. It was news on an international scale — the New World exultant — the Old deploring the 'burden of British taxation which drove such treasures, etc.', and the lighter-minded journals disporting themselves according to their publics; for 'our Dan', as one earnest Sunday editor observed, 'lies closer to the national heart than we wot of'. Common decency made me call on Castorley, who, to my surprise, had not yet descended into the arena. I found him, made young again by joy, deep in just-passed proofs.

Yes, he said, it was all true. He had, of course, been in it from the first. There had been found one hundred and seven new lines of Chaucer tacked on to an abridged end of *The Persone's Tale*, the whole the work of Abraham Mentzius, better known as Mentzel of Antwerp (1388–1438/9) — I might remember he had talked about him — whose distinguishing peculiarities were a certain Byzantine formation of his 'g's, the use of a 'sickle-slanted' reed-pen, which cut into the vellum at certain letters; and, above all, a tendency to spell English words on Dutch lines, whereof the manuscript carried one convincing proof. For instance (he wrote it out for me), a girl praying against an undesired marriage, says:

'Ah Jesu-Moder, pitie my oe peyne.
Daiespringe mishandeelt cometh nat agayne.'

Would I, please note the spelling of 'mishandeelt'? Stark Dutch and Mentzel's besetting sin ! But in *his* position one took nothing for granted. The page had been part of the stiffening of the side of an old Bible, bought in a parcel by Dredd, the big dealer, because it had some rubricated chapter-initials, and by Dredd shipped, with a consignment of similar odds and ends, to the Sunnapia Collection, where they were making a glass-cased exhibit of the whole history of illumination and did not care how many books they gutted for that purpose. There, someone who noticed a crack in the back of the volume had unearthed it. He went on: 'They didn't know what to make of the thing at first. But they knew about *me*! They kept quiet till I'd been consulted. You might have noticed I was out of England for three months.

'I was over there, of course. It was what is called a "spoil" – a page Mentzel had spoiled with his Dutch spelling – I expect he had had the English dictated to him – then had evidently used the vellum for trying out his reeds; and then, I suppose, had put it away. The "spoil" had been doubled, pasted together, and slipped in as stiffening to the old book-cover. I had it steamed open, and analysed the wash. It gave the flour-grains in the paste-coarse, because of the old millstone – and there were traces of the grit itself. What? Oh, possibly a handmill of Mentzel's own time. He may have doubled the spoilt page and used it for part of a pad to steady woodcuts on. It may have knocked about his workshop for years. That, indeed, is practically certain because a beginner from the Low Countries has tried his reed on a few lines of some monkish hymn – not a bad lilt tho' – which must have been common form. Oh yes, the page may have been used in other books before it was used for the Vulgate. That doesn't matter, but *this* does. Listen! I took a wash, for analysis, from a blot in one corner – that would be after Mentzel had given up trying to make a possible page of it, and had grown careless – and I got the actual *ink* of the period! It's a practically eternal stuff compounded on – I've forgotten his name for the minute – the scribe at Bury St Edmunds, of course – hawthorn bark and wine. Anyhow, on *his* formula. *That* wouldn't interest you either, but, taken with all the other testimony, it clinches the thing. (You'll see it all in my statement to the press on Monday.) Overwhelming, isn't it?'

'Overwhelming,' I said, with sincerity. 'Tell me what the tale was about, though. That's more in my line.'

'I know it; but *I* have to be equipped on all sides. The verses are relatively easy for one to pronounce on. The freshness, the fun, the humanity, the fragrance of it all, cries – no, shouts –

itself as Dan's work. Why "Daiespringe mishandled" alone stamps it from Dan's mint. Plangent as doom, my dear boy – plangent as doom! It's all in my statement. Well, substantially, the fragment deals with a girl whose parents wish her to marry an elderly suitor. The mother isn't so keen on it, but the father, an old knight, is. The girl, of course, is in love with a younger and a poorer man. Common form? Granted. Then the father, who doesn't in the least want to, is ordered off to a Crusade and, by way of passing on the kick, as we used to say during the war, orders the girl to be kept in duresse till his return or her consent to the old suitor. Common form, again? Quite so. That's too much for her mother. She reminds the old knight of his age and infirmities, and the discomforts of crusading. Are you sure I'm not boring you?'

'Not at all,' I said, though time had begun to whirl backward through my brain to a red-velvet, pomatum-scented side-room at Neminaka's and Manallace's set face intoning to the gas.

'You'll read it all in my statement next week. The sum is that the old lady tells him of a certain knight-adventurer on the French coast, who, for a consideration, waylays knights who don't relish crusading and holds them to impossible ransoms till the trooping-season is over, or they are returned sick. He keeps a ship in the Channel to pick 'em up and transfers his birds to his castle ashore, where he as a reputation for doing 'em well. As the old lady points out:

'And if perchance thou fall into his honde
By God how canstow ride to Holilonde?'

'You see? Modern in essence as Gilbert and Sullivan, but handled as only Dan could! And she reminds him that "Honour and olde bones" parted company long ago. He makes one splendid appeal for the spirit of chivalry:

Lat all men change as Fortune may send,
But Knighthood beareth service to the end,

and *then*, of course, he gives in:

For what his woman willeth to be don
Her manne must or wauken Hell anon.

'Then she hints that the daughter's young lover, who is in the

Bordeaux wine trade, could open negotiations for a kidnapping without compromising him. And *then* that careless brute Mentzel spoils his page and chucks it! But there's enough to show what's going to happen. You'll see it all in my statement. Was there ever anything in literary finds to hold a candle to it? ... And they give grocers knighthoods for selling cheese!'

I went away before he could get into his stride on that course. I wanted to think, and to see Manallace. But I waited till Castorley's statement came out. He had left himself no loophole. And when, a little later, his (nominally the Sunnapia people's) 'scientific' account of their analyses and tests appeared, criticism ceased, and some journals began to demand 'public recognition'. Manallace wrote me on this subject, and I went down to his cottage, where he at once asked me to sign a memorial on Castorley's behalf. With luck, he said, we might get him a KBE in the next Honours List. Had I read the statement?

'I have,' I replied. 'But I want to ask you something first. Do you remember the night you got drunk at Neminaka's, and I stayed behind to look after you?'

'Oh, *that* time,' said he, pondering. 'Wait a minute! I remember Graydon advancing me two quid. He was a generous paymaster. And I remember – now, who the devil rolled me under the sofa – and what for?'

'We all did,' I replied. 'You wanted to read us what you'd written to those Chaucer cuts.'

'I don't remember that. No! I don't remember anything after the sofa-episode ... *You* always said that you took me home – didn't you?'

'I did, and you told Kentucky Kate outside the old Empire that you had been faithful, Cynara, in your fashion.'

'Did I?' said he. 'My God! Well, I suppose I have.' He stared into the fire. 'What else?'

'Before we left Neminaka's you recited me what you had made out of the cuts – the whole tale! So – you see?'

'Ye-es.' He nodded. 'What are you going to do about it?'

'What are *you*?'

'I'm going to help him get his knighthood – first.'

'Why?'

'I'll tell you what he said about 'Dal's mother – the night there was that air-raid on the offices.'

He told it.

'That's why,' he said. 'Am I justified?'

He seemed to me entirely so.

'But after he gets his knighthood?' I went on.

'That depends. There are several things I can think of. It interests me.'

'Good Heavens! I've always imagined you a man without interests.'

'So I was. I owe my interests to Castorley. He gave me every one of 'em except the tale itself.'

'How did *that* come?'

'Something in those ghastly cuts touched off something in me – a sort of possession, I suppose. I was in love too. No wonder I got drunk that night. I'd *been* Chaucer for a week.! Then I thought the notion might make a comic opera. But Gilbert and Sullivan were too strong.'

'So I remember you told me at the time.'

'I kept it by me, and it made me interested in Chaucer – philologically and so on. I worked on it on those lines for years. There wasn't a flaw in the wording even in 'Fourteen. I hardly had to touch it after that.'

'Did you ever tell it to anyone except me?'

'No, only 'Dal's mother – when she could listen to anything – to put her to sleep. But when Castorley said – what he did about her, I thought I might use it. 'Twasn't difficult. *He* taught me. D'you remember my birdlime experiments, and the stuff on our hands? I'd been trying to get that ink for more than a year. Castorley told me where I'd find the formula. And your falling over the quern, too?'

'That accounted for the stone-dust under the microscope?'

'Yes. I grew the wheat in the garden here, and ground it myself. Castorley gave me Mentzel complete. He put me on to an MS. in the British Museum which he said was the finest sample of his work. I copied his "Byzantine 'g's" for months.'

'You nick one edge of your reed till it drags and scratches on the curves of the letters. Castorley told me about Mentzel's spacing and margining. I only had to get the hang of his script.'

'How long did that take you?'

'On and off – some years. I was too ambitious at first – I wanted to give the whole poem. That would have been risky.

Then Castorley told me about spoiled pages and I took the hint. I spelt "Dayspring mishandeelt" Mentzel's way – to make sure of him. It's not a bad couplet in itself. Did you see how he admires the "plangency" of it?'

'Never mind him. Go on!' I said.

He did. Castorley had been his unfailing guide throughout, specifying in minutest detail every trap to be set later for his own feet. The actual vellum was an Antwerp find, and its introduction into the cover of the Vulgate was begun after a long course of amateur bookbinding. At last, he bedded it under pieces of an old deed, and a printed page (1686) of Horace's *Odes*, legitimately used for repairs by different owners in the seventeenth and eighteenth centuries; and at the last moment, to meet Castorley's theory that spoiled pages were used in workshops by beginners, he had written a few Latin words in fifteenth century script – the statement gave the exact date – across an open part of the fragment. The thing ran: *'Illa alma Mater ecca, secum afferens me acceptum. Nicolaus Atrib.'* The disposal of the thing was easiest of all. He had merely hung about Dredd's dark bookshop of fifteen rooms, where he was well known, occasionally buying but generally browsing, till, one day, Dredd Senior showed him a case of cheap black-letter stuff, English and Continental – being packed for the Sunnapia people – into which Manallace tucked his contribution, taking care to wrench the back enough to give a lead to an earnest seeker.

'And then?' I demanded.

'After six months or so Castorley sent for me. Sunnapia had found it, and as Dredd had missed it, and there was no money-motive sticking out, they were half-convinced it was genuine from the start. But they invited him over. He conferred with their experts, and suggested the scientific tests. *I* put that into his head, before he sailed. That's all. And now, will you sign our memorial?'

I signed. Before we had finished hawking it round there was a host of influential names to help us, as well as the impetus of all the literary discussion which arose over every detail of the glorious trove. The upshot was a KBE* for Castorley in the next

---

*Officially it was on account of his good work in the Departmental of Coordinated Supervisals, but all true lovers of literature knew the real reason, and told the papers so.

Honours List ; and Lady Castorley, her cards duly printed, called on friends that same afternoon.

Manallace invited me to come with him, a day or so later, to convey our pleasure and satisfaction to them both. We were rewarded by the sight of a man relaxed and ungirt – not to say wallowing naked – on the crest of success. He assured us that 'The Title' should not make any difference to our future relations, seeing it was in no sense personal, but, as he had often said, a tribute to Chaucer ; 'and, after all,' he pointed out, with a glance at the mirror over the mantelpiece, 'Chaucer was the prototype of the "veray parfit gentil Knight" of the British Empire so far as that then existed.'

On the way back, Manallace told me he was considering either an unheralded revelation in the baser press which should bring Castorley's reputation about his own ears some breakfast-time, or a private conversation, when he would make clear to Castorley that he must now back the forgery as long as he lived, under threat of Manallace's betraying it if he flinched.

He favoured the second plan. 'If I pull the string of the shower-bath in the papers,' he said, 'Castorley might go off his veray parfit gentil nut. I want to keep his intellect.'

'What about your own position ? The forgery doesn't matter so much. But if you tell this you'll kill him,' I said.

'I intend that. Oh – my position ? I've been dead since – April Fourteen, it was. But there's no hurry. What was it *she* was saying to you just as we left ?'

'She told me how much your sympathy and understanding had meant to him. She said she thought that even Sir Alured did not realize the full extent of his obligations to you.'

'She's right, but I don't like putting it that way.'

'It's only common form – as Castorley's always saying.'

'Not with *her*. She can hear a man think.'

'She never struck me in that light.'

'*You* aren't playing against her.'

'Guilty conscience, Manallace ?'

'H'm ! I wonder. Mine or hers ? I *wish* she hadn't said that. "More even than *he* realizes it." I won't call again for awhile.'

He kept away till we read that Sir Alured, owing to slight indisposition, had been unable to attend a dinner given in his honour.

Inquiries brought word that it was but natural reaction, after strain, which, for the moment, took the form of nervous dyspepsia, and he would be glad to see Manallace at any time. Manallace reported him as rather pulled and drawn, but full of his new life and position, and proud that his efforts should have martyred him so much. He was going to collect, collate and expand all his pronouncements and inferences into one authoritative volume.

'I must make an effort of my own,' said Manallace. 'I've collected nearly all his stuff about the find that has appeared in the papers, and he's promised me everything that's missing. I'm going to help him. It will be a new interest.'

'How will you treat it ?' I asked.

'I expect I shall quote his deductions on the evidence, and parallel 'em with my experiments – the ink and the paste and the rest of it. It ought to be rather interesting.'

'But even then there will only be your word. It's hard to catch up with an established lie,' I said. 'Especially when you've started it yourself.'

He laughed. 'I've arranged for *that* – in case anything happens to me. Do you remember the "Monkish Hymn" ?'

'Oh yes ! There's quite a literature about it already.'

'Well, you write those ten words above each other, and read down the first and second letters of 'em ; and see what you get.* My bank has the formula.'

He wrapped himself lovingly and leisurely round his new task, and Castorley was as good as his word in giving him help. The two practically collaborated, for Manallace suggested that all Castorley's strictly scientific evidence should be in one place, with his deductions and dithyrambs as appendices. He assured him that the public would prefer this arrangement, and, after grave consideration, Castorley agreed.

*Illa
alma
Mater
ecca
secum
afferens
me
acceptum
Nicolaus
Atrib.

'That's better,' said Manallace to me. 'Now I shan't have so many hiatuses in my extracts. Dots always give the reader the idea you aren't dealing fairly with your man. I shall merely quote him solid, and rip him up, proof for proof, and date for date, in parallel columns. His book's taking more out of him than I like, though. He's been doubled up twice with tummy attacks since I've worked with him. And he's just the sort of flatulent beast who may go down with appendicitis.'

We learned before long that the attacks were due to gall-stones, which would necessitate an operation. Castorley bore the blow very well. He had full confidence in his surgeon, an old friend of theirs; great faith in his own constitution; a strong conviction that nothing would happen to him till the book was finished, and, above all, the Will to Live.

He dwelt on these assets with a voice at times a little out of pitch and eyes brighter than usual beside a slightly-sharpening nose.

I had only met Gleeag, the surgeon, once or twice at Castorley's house, but had always heard him spoken of as a most capable man. He told Castorley that his trouble was the price exacted, in some shape or other, from all who had served their country; and that, measured in units of strain, Castorley had practically been at the front through those three years he had served in the Office of Co-ordinated Supervisals. However, the thing had been taken betimes, and in a few weeks he would worry no more about it.

'But suppose he dies?' I suggested to Manallace.

'He won't. I've been talking to Gleeag. He says he's all right.'

'Wouldn't Gleeag's talk be common form?'

'I *wish* you hadn't said that. But, surely, Gleeag wouldn't have the face to play with me – or her.'

'Why not? I expect it's been done before.'

But Manallace insisted that, in this case, it would be impossible.

The operation was a success and, some weeks later, Castorley began to recast the arrangement and most of the material of his book. 'Let me have my way,' he said, when Manallace protested. 'They are making too much of a baby of me. I really don't need Gleeag looking in every day now.' But Lady Castorley told us that he required careful watching. His heart had felt the strain, and fret or disappointment of any kind must be avoided. 'Even,' she turned to Manallace, 'though you know ever so much better how his book should be arranged than he does himself.'

'But really,' Manallace began. 'I'm very careful not to fuss –'

She shook her finger at him playfully. 'You don't think you do; but, remember, he tells me everything that you tell him, just the same as he told me everything that he used to tell *you*. Oh, I don't mean the things that men talk about. I mean about his Chaucer.'

'I didn't realize that,' said Manallace, weakly.

'I thought you didn't. He never spares me anything; but *I* don't mind,' she replied with a laugh, and went off to Gleeag, who was paying his daily visit. Gleeag said he had no objection to Manallace working with Castorley on the book for a given time – say, twice a week – but supported Lady Castorley's demand that he should not be over-taxed in what she called 'the sacred hours'. The man grew more and more difficult to work with, and the little check he had heretofore set on his self-praise went altogether.

'He says there has never been anything in the History of Letters to compare with it.' Manallace groaned. 'He wants now to inscribe – he never dedicates, you know – inscribe it to me, as his "most valued assistant". The devil of it is that *she* backs him up in getting it out soon. Why? How much do you think she knows?'

'Why should she know anything at all?'

'You heard her say he had told her everything that he had told me about Chaucer? (I *wish* she hadn't said that!) If she puts two and two together, she can't help seeing that every one of his notions and theories had been played up to. But then – but then ... Why is she trying to hurry publication? She talks about me fretting him. *She's* at him, all the time, to be quick.'

Castorley must have over-worked, for, after a couple of months, he complained of a stitch in his right side, which Gleeag said was a slight sequel, a little incident of the operation. It threw him back awhile, but he returned to his work undefeated.

The book was due in the autumn. Summer was passing, and his publisher urgent, and – he said to me, when after a longish interval I called – Manallace had chosen this time, of all, to take holiday. He was not pleased with Manallace, once his indefatigable aide, but now dilatory, and full of time-wasting objections. Lady Castorley had noticed it, too.

Meantime, with Lady Castorley's help, he himself was doing the best he could to expedite the book: but Manallace had mislaid (did I think through jealousy?) some essential stuff which had been dictated to him. And Lady Castorley wrote Manallace, who had been delayed by a slight motor accident abroad, that the fret of waiting was prejudicial to her husband's health. Manallace, on his return from the Continent, showed me the letter.

'He has fretted a little, I believe,' I said.

Manallace shuddered. 'If I stay abroad, I'm helping to kill him. If I help him to hurry up the book, I'm expected to kill him. *She* knows,' he said.

'You're mad. You've got this thing on the brain.'

'I have not! Look here! You remember that Gleeag gave me from four to six, twice a week, to work with him. She called them the "sacred hours". You heard her? Well, they *are*! They are Gleeag's and hers. But she's so infernally plain, and I'm such a fool, it took me weeks to find it out.'

'That's their affair,' I answered. 'It doesn't prove she knows anything about the Chaucer.'

'She *does*! He told her everything that he had told me when I was pumping him, all those years. She put two and two together when the thing came out. She saw exactly how I had set my traps. I know it! She's been trying to make me admit it.'

'What did you do?'

'Didn't understand what she was driving at, of course. And then she asked Gleeag, before me, if he didn't think the delay over the book was fretting Sir Alured. He didn't think so. He said getting it out might deprive him of an interest. He had that much decency. *She's* the devil!'

'What do you suppose is her game, then?'

'If Castorley knows he's been had, it'll kill him. She's at me all the time, indirectly, to let it out. I've told you she wants to make it a sort of joke between us. Gleeag's willing to wait. He knows Castorley's a dead man. It slips out when they talk. They say "He was", not "He is". Both of 'em know it. But *she* wants him finished sooner.'

'I don't believe it. What are you going to do?'

'What can I? I'm not going to have him killed, though.'

Manlike, he invented compromises whereby Castorley might be lured up by-paths of interest, to delay publication. This was not a success. As autumn advanced Castorley fretted more, and suffered from returns of his distressing colics. At last, Gleeag told him that he thought they might be due to an overlooked gallstone working down. A second comparatively trivial operation would eliminate the bother once and for all. If Castorley cared for another opinion, Gleeag named a surgeon of eminence. 'And then,' he said, cheerily, 'the two of us can talk you over.' Castorley did not want to be talked over. He was oppressed by pains in his side, which, at first, had yielded to the liver-tonics Gleeag prescribed; but now they stayed – like a toothache – behind everything. He felt most at ease in his bedroom-study, with his proofs round him. If he had more pain than he could stand, he would consider the second operation. Meantime Manallace – 'the meticulous Manallace', he called him – agreed with him in thinking that the Mentzel page-facsimile, done by the Sunnapia Library, was not quite good enough for the great book, and the Sunnapia people were, very decently, having it reprocessed. This would hold things back till early spring, which had its advantages, for he could run a fresh eye over all in the interval.

One gathered these news in the course of stray visits as the days shortened. He insisted on Manallace keeping to the 'sacred hours', and Manallace insisted on my accompanying him when possible. On these occasions he and Castorley would confer apart for half an hour or so, while I listened to an unendurable clock in the drawing-room. Then I would join them and help wear out the rest of the time, while Castorley rambled. His speech, now, was often clouded and uncertain – the result of the 'liver-tonics'; and his face came to look like old vellum.

It was a few days after Christmas – the operation had been postponed till the following Friday – that we called together. She met us with word that Sir Alured had picked up an irritating little winter cough, due to a cold wave, but we were not, therefore, to abridge our visit. We found him in steam perfumed with Friar's Balsam. He waved the old Sunnapia facsimile at us. We agreed that it ought to have been more worthy. He took a dose of his mixture, lay back and asked us to lock the door.

There was, he whispered, something wrong somewhere. He could not lay his finger on it, but it was in the air. He felt he was being played with. He did not like it. There was something wrong all round him. Had we noticed it? Manallace and I severally and slowly denied that we had noticed anything of the sort.

With no longer break than a light fit of coughing, he fell into the hideous helpless panic of the sick – those worse than captives who lie at the judgment and mercy of the hale for every office and hope. He wanted to go away. Would we help him to pack his Gladstone? Or, if that would attract too much attention in certain quarters, help him to dress and go out? There was an urgent matter to be set right, and now that he had The Title and knew his own mind it would all end happily and he would be well again. *Please* would we let him go out, just to speak to – he named her; he named her by her 'little' name out of the old Neminaka days? Manallace quite agreed, and recommended a pull at the 'liver-tonic' to brace him after so long in the house. He took it, and Manallace suggested that it would be better if, after his walk, he came down to the cottage for a weekend and brought the revise with him. They could then re-touch the last chapter. He answered to that drug and to some praise of his work, and presently simpered drowsily. Yes, it *was* good – though he said it who should not. He praised himself awhile till, with a puzzled forehead and shut eyes, he told us that *she* had been saying lately that it was too good – the whole thing, if we understood, was *too* good. He wished us to get the exact shade of her meaning. She had suggested, or rather implied, this doubt. She had said – he would let us draw our own inferences – that the Chaucer find had 'anticipated the wants of humanity'. Johnson, of course. No need to tell *him* that. But what the hell was her implication? Oh God! Life had always been one long innuendo! *And* she had said that a man could do anything with anyone if he saved him the trouble of thinking. What did she mean by that? *He* had never shirked thought. He had thought sustainedly all his life. It *wasn't* too good, was it? Manallace didn't think it was too good – did he? But this pick-pick-picking at a man's brain and work was too bad, wasn't it? *What* did she mean? Why did she always bring in Manallace, who was only a friend – no scholar, but a lover of the game – Eh? – Manallace could confirm this if he were here, instead of loafing on the Continent just when he was most needed.

'I've come back,' Manallace interrupted, unsteadily. 'I can confirm every word you've said. You've nothing to worry about. It's *your* find – *your* credit – *your* glory and – all the rest of it.'

'Swear you'll tell her so then,' said Castorley. She doesn't believe a word I say. She told me she never has since before we were married. Promise !'

Manallace promised, and Castorley added that he had named him his literary executor, the proceeds of the book to go to his wife. 'All profits without deduction,' he gasped. 'Big sales if it's properly handled. *You* don't need money ... Graydon'll trust *you* to any extent. It 'ud be a long ...'

He coughed, and, as he caught breath, his pain broke through all the drugs, and the outcry filled the room. Manallace rose to fetch Gleeag, when a full, high, affected voice, unheard for a generation, accompanied, as it seemed, the clamour of a beast in agony, saying : 'I wish to God someone would stop that old swine howling there ! I can't ... I was going to tell you fellows that it would be a dam' long time before Graydon advanced *me* two quid.'

We escaped together, and found Gleeag waiting, with Lady Castorley, on the landing. He telephoned me, next morning, that Castorley had died of bronchitis, which his weak state made it impossible for him to throw off. 'Perhaps it's just as well,' he added, in reply to the condolences I asked him to convey to the widow. 'We might have come across something we couldn't have coped with.'

Distance from that house made me bold.

'You knew all along, I suppose ? What was it, really ?

'Malignant kidney-trouble – generalized at the end. No use worrying him about it. We let him through as easily as possible. Yes ! A happy release ... What ? ... Oh ! Cremation. Friday, at eleven.'

There, then Manallace and I met. He told me that she had asked him whether the book need now be published ; and he had told her this was more than ever necessary, in her interests as well as Castorley's.

'She is going to be known as his widow – for a while, at any rate. Did I perjure myself much with him ?'

'Not explicitly,' I answered.

'Well, I have now – with *her* – explicitly,' said he, and took out his black gloves ...

As, on the appointed words, the coffin crawled sideways through the noiselessly-closing door-flaps, I saw Lady Castorley's eyes turn towards Gleeag.

GERTRUDE'S PRAYER

(*Modernized from the 'Chaucer' of Manallace.*)

That which is married at birth Time shall not mend,
   Nor water out of bitter well make clean;
All evil thing returneth at the end,
   Or elseway walketh in our blood unseen.
Whereby the more is sorrow in certaine –
Dayspring mishandled cometh not againe.

To-bruized be that slender, sterting spray
   Out of the oake's rind that should betide
A branch of girt and goodliness, straightway
   Her spring is turned on herself, and wried
And knotted like some gall or veiney wen. –
Dayspring mishandled cometh not agen.

Noontide repayeth never morning-bliss –
   Sith noon to morn is incomparable;
And, so it be our dawning goth amiss,
   None other after-hour serveth well.
Ah! Jesu-Moder, pitie my oe paine –
Dayspring mishandled cometh not againe!

H. G. WELLS

The Truth about Pyecraft

He sits not a dozen yards away. If I glance over my shoulder I can see him. And if I catch his eye – and usually I catch his eye – it meets me with an expression –

It is mainly an imploring look – and yet with suspicion in it.

Confound his suspicion! If I wanted to tell on him I should have told long ago. I don't tell and I don't tell, and he ought to feel at his ease. As if anything so gross and fat as he could feel at ease! Who would believe me if I did tell!

Poor old Pyecraft! Great, uneasy jelly of substance! The fattest clubman in London.

He sits at one of the little club tables in the huge bay by the fire, stuffing. What is he stuffing? I glance judiciously and catch him biting at the round of hot buttered teacake, with his eyes on me. Confound him! – with his eyes on me!

That settles it, Pyecraft! Since you *will* be abject, since you *will* behave as though I was not a man of honour, here, right under your embedded eyes, I write the thing down – the plain truth about Pyecraft. The man I helped, the man I shielded, and who has requited me by making my club unendurable, absolutely unendurable, with his liquid appeal, with the perpetual 'don't tell' of his looks.

And, besides, why does he keep on eternally eating?

Well, here goes for the truth, the whole truth, and nothing but the truth!

Pyecraft – I made the acquaintance of Pyecraft in this very smoking-room. I was a young, nervous new member, and he saw it. I was sitting all alone, wishing I new more of the members, and suddenly he came, a great rolling front of chins and abdomina, towards me, and grunted and sat down in a chair close by me, and wheezed for a space, and scraped for a space with a match and lit a cigar, and then addressed me. I forget what he said — something about the matches not lighting properly, and afterwards as he talked he kept stopping the waiters one by one as they went by, and telling them about the matches in that thin, fluty voice he has. But, anyhow, it was in some such way we began our talking.

He talked about various things and came round to games. And thence to my figure and complexion. 'You ought to be a good cricketer,' he said. I suppose I am slender, slender to what some people would call lean, and I suppose I am rather dark, still — I am not ashamed of having a Hindu great-grandmother, but, for all that, I don't want casual strangers to see through me at a glance to *her*. So that I was set against Pyecraft from the beginning.

But he only talked about me in order to get to himself.

'I expect,' he said, 'you take no more exercise than I do, and probably you eat no less' (Like all excessively obese people he fancied he ate nothing.) 'Yet' — and he smiled an oblique smile — 'we differ.'

And then he began to talk about his fatness and his fatness; all he did for his fatness and all he was going to do for his fatness; what people had advised him to do for his fatness and what he had heard of people doing for fatness similar to his. '*A priori*,' he said, 'one would think a question of nutrition could be answered by dietary and a question of assimilation by drugs.' It was stifling. It was dumpling talk. It made me feel swelled to hear him.

One stands that sort of thing once in a way at a club, but a time came when I fancied I was standing too much. He took to me altogether too conspicuously. I could never go into the smoking-room but he would come wallowing towards me and sometimes he came and gormandised round and about me while I had my lunch. He seemed at times almost to be clinging to me. He was a bore, but not so fearful a bore as to be limited to me; and from the first there was something in his manner — almost as though he knew, almost as though he penetrated to the fact that I *might* — that there was a remote, exceptional chance in me that no one else presented.

'I'd give anything to get it down,' he would say — 'anything,' and peer at me over his vast cheeks and pant.

Poor old Pyecraft! He has just gonged, no doubt to order another buttered teacake!

He came to the actual thing one day. 'Our Pharmacopoeia,' he said, 'our Western Pharmacopoeia, is anything but the last word of medical science. In the East, I've been told – '

He stopped and stared at me. It was like being at an aquarium.

I was quite suddenly angry with him. 'Look here,' I said, 'who told you about my great-grandmother's recipes?'

'Well,' he fenced.

'Every time we've met for a week,' I said – 'and we've met pretty often – you've given me a broad hint or so about that little secret of mine.'

'Well,' he said, 'now the cat's out of the bag, I'll admit, yes, it is so. I had it –'

'From Pattison?'

'Indirectly,' he said, which I believe was lying, 'yes.'

'Pattison,' I said, 'took that stuff at his own risk.'

He pursed his mouth and bowed.

'My great-grandmother's recipes,' I said, 'are queer things to handle. My father was near making me promise – '

'He didn't?'

'No. But he warned me. He himself used one – once.'

'Ah!... But do you think – ? Suppose – suppose there did happen to be one – '

'The things are curious documents,' I said. 'Even the smell of 'em ... No!'

But after going so far Pyecraft was resolved I should go farther. I was always a little afraid if I tried his patience too much he would fall on me suddenly and smother me. I own I was weak. But I was also annoyed with Pyecraft. I had got to that state of feeling for him that disposed me to say, 'Well, *take* the risk!' The little affair of Pattison to which I have alluded was a different matter altogether. What it was doesn't concern us now, but I knew, anyhow, that the particular recipe I used then was safe. The rest I didn't know so much about, and, on the whole, I was inclined to doubt their safety pretty completely.

Yet even if Pyecraft got poisoned –

I must confess the poisoning of Pyecraft stuck me as an immense undertaking.

That evening I took that queer, old-scented sandalwood box

out of my safe and turned the rustling skins over. The gentleman who wrote the recipes for my great-grandmother evidently had a weakness for skins of a miscellaneous origin, and his handwriting was cramped to the last degree. Some of the things are quite unreadable to me – though my family, with its Indian Civil Service associations, has kept up a knowledge of Hindustani from generation to generation – and none are absolutely plain sailing. But I found the one that I knew was there soon enough, and sat on the floor by my safe for some time looking at it.

'Look here,' said I to Pyecraft next day, and snatched the slip away from his eager grasp.

'So far as I can make it out, this is a recipe for Loss of Weight. ('Ah!' said Pyecraft.) I'm not absolutely sure, but I think it's that. And if you take my advice you'll leave it alone. Because, you know – I blacken my blood in your interest, Pyecraft – my ancestors on that side were, so far as I can gather, a jolly queer lot. See?'

'Let me try it,' said Pyecraft.

I leant back in my chair. My imagination made one mighty effort and fell flat within me. 'What in Heaven's name, Pyecraft,' I asked, 'do you think you'll look like when you get thin?'

He was impervious to reason. I made him promise never to say a word to me about his disgusting fatness again whatever happened – never, and then I handed him that little piece of skin.

'It's nasty stuff,' I said.

'No matter,' he said, and took it.

He goggled at it. 'But – but —' he said.

He had just discovered that it wasn't English.

'To the best of my ability,' I said, 'I will do you a translation.'

I did my best. After that we didn't speak for a fortnight. Whenever he approached me. I frowned and motioned him away, and he respected our compact, but at the end of the fortnight he was as fat as ever. And then he got a word in.

'I must speak,' he said. 'It isn't fair. There's something wrong. It's done me no good. You're not doing your great-grandmother justice.'

'Where's the recipe?'

He produced it gingerly from his pocket-book.

I ran my eye over the items. 'Was the egg addled?' I asked.

'No. Ought it to have been?'

'That,' I said, 'goes without saying in all my poor dear great-grandmother's recipes. When condition or quality is not specified you must get the worst. She was drastic or nothing ... And there's one or two possible alternatives to some of these other things. You got *fresh* rattlesnake venom?'

'I got rattlesnake from Jamrach's. It cost – it cost –'

'That's your affair, anyhow. This last item – '

'I know a man who – '

'Yes, H'm. Well, I'll write the alternatives down. So far as I know the language, the spelling of this recipe is particularly atrocious. By-the-bye, dog here probably means pariah dog.'

For a month after that I saw Pyecraft constantly at the club and as fat and anxious as ever. He kept our treaty, but at times he broke the spirit of it by shaking his head despondently. Then one day in the cloak-room he said, 'Your great-grandmother – '

'Not a word against her,' I said : and he held his peace.

I could have fancied he had desisted, and I saw him one day talking to three new members about his fatness as though he was in search of other recipes. And then, quite unexpectedly his telegram came.

'Mr Formalyn !' bawled a page-boy under my nose and I took the telegram and opened it at once.

'For Heaven's sake come. – Pyecraft.'

'H'm,' said I, and to tell the truth I was so pleased at the rehabilitation of my great-grandmother's reputation this evidently promised that I made a most excellent lunch.

I got Pyecraft's address from the hall porter. Pyecraft inhabited the upper half of a house in Bloomsbury, and I went there as soon as I had done my coffee and Trappistine. I did not wait to finish my cigar.

'Mr Pyecraft ?' said I, at the front door.

They believed he was ill ; he hadn't been out for two days.

'He expects me,' said I, and they sent me up.

I rang the bell at the lattice-door upon the landing.

'He shouldn't have tried it, anyhow,' I said to myself. 'A man who eats like a pig ought to look like a pig.'

An obviously worthy woman, with an anxious face and a carelessly placed cap, came and surveyed me through the lattice.

I gave my name and she opened his door for me in a dubious fashion.

'Well?' said I, as we stood together inside Pyecraft's piece of the landing.

''E said you was to come in if you came,' she said, and regarded me, making no motion to show me anywhere. And then, confidentially, ''E's locked in, sir.'

'Locked in?'

'Locked himself in yesterday morning and 'asn't let anyone in since, sir. And ever and again *swearing*. Oh, my!'

I stared at the door she indicated by her glances. 'In there?' I said.

'Yes, sir.'

'What's up?'

She shook her head sadly. ''E keeps on calling for vittles, sir. *'Eavy* vittles 'e wants. I get 'im what I can. Pork 'e's 'ad, sooit puddin', sossiges, noo bread. Everythink like that. Left outside, if you please, and me go away. 'Es' eatin' sir, something *awful*.'

There came a piping bawl from inside the door: 'That Formalyn?'

'That you, Pyecraft?' I shouted, and went and banged the door.

'Tell her to go away.'

I did.

Then I could hear a curious pattering upon the door, almost like someone feeling for the handle in the dark, and Pyecraft's familiar grunts.

'It's all right,' I said, 'she's gone.'

But for a long time the door didn't open.

I heard the key turn. Then Pyecraft's voice said, 'Come in.'

I turned the handle and opened the door. Naturally I expected to see Pyecraft.

Well, you know, he wasn't there!

I never had such a shock in my life. There was his sitting-room in a state of untidy disorder, plates and dishes among the books and writing things, and several chairs overturned, but Pyecraft –

'It's all right, o' man; shut the door,' he said, and then I discovered him.

There he was right up close to the cornice in the corner by the door, as though someone had glued him to the ceiling. His face was anxious and angry. He panted and gesticulated. 'Shut the door,' he said. 'If that woman gets hold of it –'

'If anything gives way and you tumble down,' I said, 'you'll break your neck, Pyecraft.'

'I wish I could,' he wheezed.

'A man of your age and weight getting up to kiddish gynmastics – '

'Don't' he said, and looked agonized. 'Your damned great-grandmother – '

'Be careful,' I warned him.

'I'll tell you,' he said, and gesticulated.

'How the deuce,' said I, 'are you holding on up there ?'

And then abruptly I realized that he was not holding on at all, that he was floating up there – just as a gas-filled bladder might have floating in the same position. He began a struggle to thrust himself away from the ceiling and to clamber down the wall to me. 'It's that prescription,' he panted, as he did so. 'Your great-gran –'

'*No !*' I cried.

He took hold of a framed engraving rather carelessly as he spoke and it gave way, and he flew back to the ceiling again, while the picture smashed on to the sofa. Bump he went against the ceiling, and I knew then why he was all over white on the more salient curves and angles of his person. He tried again more carefully, coming down by way of the mantel.

It was really a most extraordinary spectacle, that great, fat, apoplectic-looking man upside down and trying to get from the ceiling to the floor. 'That prescription,' he said. 'Too successful.'

'How ?'

'Loss of weight – almost complete.'

And then, of course, I understood.

'By Jove, Pyecraft,' said I, 'what you wanted was a cure for fatness ! But you always called it weight. You would call it weight.'

Somehow I was extremely delighted. I quite liked Pyecraft for the time. 'Let me help you !' I said, and took his hand and pulled him down. He kicked about, trying to get foothold somewhere. It was very like holding a flag on a windy day.

'That table,' he said, pointing, 'is solid mahogany and very heavy. If you can put me under that –'

I did, and there he wallowed about like a captive balloon, while I stood on his hearthrug and talked to him.

I lit a cigar. 'Tell me,' I said, 'what happened?'

'I took it,' he said.

'How did it taste?'

'Oh, *beastly!*'

I should fancy they all did. Whether one regards the ingredients or the probable compound or the possible results, almost all my great-grandmother's remedies appear to me at least to be extraordinarily uninviting. For my own part —

'I took a little sip first.'

'Yes?'

'And as I felt lighter and better after an hour, I decided to take the draught.'

'My dear Pyecraft!'

'I held my nose,' he explained. 'And then I kept on getting lighter and lighter — and helpless, you know.'

He gave way suddenly to a burst of passion. 'What the goodness am I to *do?*' he said.

'There's one thing pretty evident,' I said, 'that you mustn't do. If you go out of doors you'll go up and up.' I waved an arm upward. 'They'd have to send Santos-Dumont* after you to bring you down again.'

'I suppose it will wear off?'

I shook my head. 'I don't think you can count on that,' I said.

And then there was another burst of passion, and he kicked out at adjacent chairs and banged the floor. He behaved just as I should have expected a great, fat, self-indulgent man to behave under trying circumstances — that is to say, very badly. He spoke of me and of my great-grandmother with an utter want of discretion.

'I never asked you to take the stuff,' I said.

And generously disregarding the insults he was putting upon me, I sat down in his armchair and began to talk to him in a sober, friendly fashion.

I pointed out to him that this was a trouble he had brought upon himself, and that it had almost an air of poetical justice. He

* Albert Santos-Dumont (1873–1932) was a successful experimenter in aerial navigation, his most notable flights being made in Paris and at Monte Carlo. He visited London in 1903, the year Wells wrote this story; thus the allusion was highly topical (*ed.*).

had eaten too much. This he disputed, and for a time we argued the point.

He became noisy and violent, so I desisted from this aspect of his lesson. 'And then,' said I, 'you committed the sin of euphuism. You called it, not Fat, which is just and inglorious, but Weight. You —'

He interrupted to say that he recognised all that. What was he to *do*?

I suggested he should adapt himself to his new conditions. So we came to the really sensible part of the business. I suggested that it would not be difficult for him to learn to walk about on the ceiling with his hands —

'I can't sleep,' he said.

But that was no great difficulty. It was quite possible, I pointed out, to make a shake-up under a wire mattress, fasten the under things on with tapes, and have a blanket, sheet, and coverlid to button at the side. He would have to confide in his housekeeper, I said; and after some squabbling he agreed to that. (Afterwards it was quite delightful to see the beautifully matter-of-fact way with which the good lady took all these amazing inversions.) He could have a library ladder in his room, and all his meals could be laid on the top of his bookcase. We also hit on an ingenious device by which he could get to the floor whenever he wanted, which was simply to put the *British Encyclopaedia* (tenth edition) on the top of his open shelves. He just pulled out a couple of volumes and held on, and down he came. And we agreed there must be iron staples along the skirting, so that he could cling to those whenever he wanted to get about the room on the lower level.

As we got on with the thing I found myself almost keenly interested. It was I who called in the housekeeper and broke matters to her, and it was I chiefly who fixed up the inverted bed. In fact, I spent two whole days at his flat. I am a handy, interfering sort of man with a screwdriver, and I made all sorts of ingenious adaptations for him — ran a wire to bring his bell within reach, turned all his electric lights up instead and down, and so on. The whole affair was extremely curious and interesting to me, and it was delightful to think of Pyecraft like some great, fat blow-fly, crawling about on his ceiling and clambering round the lintel of his doors from one room to another, and never, never, never coming to the club any more. . . .

Then, you know, my fatal ingenuity got the better of me. I was sitting by his fire drinking his whisky, and he was up in his favourite corner by the cornice, tacking a Turkey carpet to the ceiling, when the idea struck me. 'By Jove, Pyecraft!' I said, 'all this is totally unnecessary.'

And before I could calculate the complete consequences of my notion I blurted it out. 'Lead underclothing,' said I, and the mischief was done.

Pyecraft received the thing almost in tears. 'To be right ways up again – ' he said.

I gave him the whole secret before I was where it would take me. 'Buy sheet lead,' I said, 'stamp it into discs. Sew 'em all over your underclothes until you have enough. Have lead-soled boots, carry a bag of solid lead, and the thing is done! Instead of being a prisoner here you may go abroad again, Pyecraft! you may travel – '

A still happier idea came to me. 'You need never fear a shipwreck. All you need do is just slip off some or all of your clothes, take the necessary amount of luggage in your hand, and float up in the air – '

In his emotion he dropped the tack-hammer within a ace of my head. 'By Jove!' he said, 'I shall be able to come back to the club again.'

The thing pulled me up short. 'By Jove!' I said, faintly. 'Yes. Of course – you will.'

He did. He does. There he sits behind me now stuffing – as I live! – a third go of buttered cake. And no one in the whole world knows – except his housekeeper and me – that he weighs practically nothing; that he is a mere boring mass of assimilatory matters, mere clouds in clothings, *niente, nefas,* and most inconsiderable of men. There he sits watching until I have done his writing. Then, if he can, he will waylay me. He will come billowing up to me . . .

He will tell me over again all about it, how it feels, how it doesn't feel, how he sometimes hopes it is passing off a little. And always somewhere in that fat, abundant discourse he will say, 'The secret's keeping, eh? If anyone knew of it – I should be so ashamed. . . . Makes a fellow look such a fool, you know.

Crawling about on a ceiling and all that. ...'

And now to elude Pyecraft, occupying, as he does, an admirable strategic position between me and the door.

ARNOLD BENNETT

The Idiot

William Froyle, ostler at the Queen's Arms at Moorthorne, took the letter, and, with a curt nod which stifled the loquacity of the village postman, went at once from the yard into the coach-house. He had recognized the hand-writing on the envelope, and the recognition of it gave form and quick life to all the vague suspicions that had troubled him some months before, and again during the last few days. He felt suddenly the near approach of a frightful calamity which had long been stealing towards him.

A wire-sheathed lantern, set on a rough oaken table, cast a wavering light round the coach-house, and dimly showed the inner stable. Within the latter could just be distinguished the mottle-gray flanks of a fat cob which dragged its chain occasionally, making the large slow movements of a horse comfortably lodged in its stall. The pleasant odour of animals and hay filled the wide spaces of the shed, and through the half-open door came a fresh thin mist rising from the rain-soaked yard in the November evening.

Froyle sat down on the oaken table, his legs dangling, and looked again at the envelope before opening it. He was a man about thirty years of age, with a serious and thoughtful, rather heavy countenance. He had a long light moustache, and his skin was a fresh, rosy salmon colour ; his straw-tinted hair was cut very short, except over the forehead, where it grew full and bushy. Dressed in his rough stable corduroys, his forearms bare and white, he had all the appearance of the sturdy Englishman, the sort of Englishman that crosses the world in order to find vent for his taciturn energy on virgin soils. From the whole village he commanded and received respect. He was known for a scholar, and it was his scholarship which had obtained for him the proud position of secretary to the provident society styled the Queen's Arms Slate Club. His respectability and his learning combined had enabled him to win with dignity the hand of Susie Trimmer, the grocer's daughter, to whom he had been engaged about a year. The village could not make up its mind concerning that match; without doubt it was a social victory for Froyle, but everyone wondered that so sedate and sagacious a man should have seen in Susie a suitable mate.

He tore open the envelope with his huge forefinger, and, bending down towards the lantern, began to read the letter. It ran:

'OLDCASTLE STREET,
'BURSLEY.

'DEAR WILL,
'I asked father to tell you, but he would not. He said I must write. Dear Will, I hope you will never see me again. As you will see by the above address, I am now at Aunt Penrose's at Burnsley. She is awful angry, but I was obliged to leave the village because of my shame. I have been a wicked girl. It was in July. You know the man, because you asked me about him one Sunday night. He is no good. He is a villain. Please forget all about me. I want to go to London. So many people know me here, and what with people coming in from the village, too. Please forgive me.

'S. TRIMMER.'

After reading the letter a second time, Froyle folded it up and put it in his pocket. Beyond a slight unaccustomed pallor of the red cheeks, he showed no sign of emotion. Before the arrival of the postman he had been cleaning his master's bicycle, which stood against the table. To this he returned. Kneeling down in some fresh straw, he used his dusters slowly and patiently — rubbing, then stopping to examine the result, and then rubbing again. When the machine was polished to his satisfaction, he wheeled it carefully into the stable, where it occupied a stall next to that of the cob. As he passed back agan, the animal leisurely turned its head and gazed at Froyle with its large liquid eyes. He slapped the immense flank. Content, the animal returned to its feed, and the weighted chain ran down with a rattle.

The fortnightly meeting of the Slate Club was to take place at eight o'clock that evening. Froyle had employed part of the afternoon in making ready his books for the event, to him always so solemn and ceremonious; and the affairs of the club were now prominent in his mind. He was sorry that it would be impossible for him to attend the meeting; fortunately, all the usual preliminaries were complete.

He took a piece of notepaper from a little hanging cupboard, and, sprawling across the table, began to write under the lantern. The pencil seemed a tiny toy in his thick roughened fingers:

> 'To Mr Andrew McCall, Chairman
> Queen's Arms Slate Club

'DEAR SIR,
  'I regret to inform you that I shall not be at the meeting tonight. You will find the books in order ...'

Here he stopped, biting the end of the pencil in thought. He put down the pencil and stepped hastily out of the stable, across the yard, and into the hotel. In the large room, the room where cyclists sometimes took tea and cold meat during the summer season, the long deal table and the double line of oaken chairs stood ready for the meeting. A fire burnt warmly in the big grate, and the hanging lamp had been lighted. On the wall was a large card containing the rules of the club, which had been written out in a fair hand by the schoolmaster. It was to this card that Froyle went. Passing his thumb down the card, he paused at Rule VII:

> 'Each member shall, on the death of another member, pay 1s. for benefit of widow or nominee of deceased, same to be paid within one month after notice given.'

'Or nominee – nominee,' he murmured reflectively, staring at the card. He mechanically noticed, what he had noticed often before with disdain, that the chairman had signed the rules without the use of capitals.

He went back to the dusk of the coach-house to finish his letter, still murmuring the word 'nominee,' of whose meaning he was not quite sure:

'I request that the money due to me from the Slate Club on my death shall be paid to my nominee, Miss Susan Trimmer, now staying with her aunt, Mrs Penrose, at Bursley.

'Yours respectfully,
'WILLIAM FROYLE.'

After further consideration he added:

'P.S. – My annual salary of sixpence per member would be due at the end of December. If so be the members would pay that, or part of it, should they consider the same due, to Susan Trimmer as well, I should be thankful. Yours resp, W.F.'

He put the letter in an envelope, and, taking it to the large room, laid it carefully at the end of the table opposite the chairman's seat. Once more he returned to the coach-house. From the hanging cupboard he now produced a piece of rope. Standing on the table he could just reach, by leaning forward, a hook in the ceiling, that was sometimes used for the slinging of bicycles. With difficulty he made the rope fast to the hook. Putting a noose on the other end, he tightened it round his neck. He looked up at the ceiling and down at the floor in order to judge whether the rope was short enough.

'Good-bye, Susan, and everyone,' he whispered, and then stepped off the table.

The tense rope swung him by his neck halfway across the coach-house. He swung twice to and fro, but as he passed under the hook for the fifth time his toes touched the floor. The rope had stretched. In another second he was standing firm on the floor, purple and panting, but ignominiously alive.

'Good-even to you, Mr Froyle. Be you committing suicide?' The tones were drawling, uncertain, mildly astonished.

He turned round hastily, his hands busy with the rope, and saw in the doorway the figure of Daft Jimmy, the Moorthorne idiot.

He hesitated before speaking, but he was not confused. No one could have been confused before Daft Jimmy. Neither man nor woman in the village considered his presence more than that of a cat.

'Yes, I am,' he said.

The middle-aged idiot regarded him with a vague, interested smile, and came into the coach-house.

'You'n gotten the rope too long, Mr Froyle. Let me help you.'

Froyle calmly assented. He stood on the table, and the two rearranged the noose and made it secure. As they did so the idiot gossiped:

'I was going to Bursley tonight to buy me a pair o'boots, and when I was at top o' th' hill I remembered as I'd forgotten the measure o' my feet. So I ran back again for it. Then I saw the light in here, and I stepped up to bid ye good-evening.'

Someone had told him the ancient story of the fool and his boots, and, with the pride of an idiot in his idiocy, he had determined that it should be related of himself.

Froyle was silent.

The idiot laughed with a dry cackle.

'Now you go,' said Froyle, when the rope was fixed.

'Let me see ye do it,' the idiot pleaded with pathetic eyes.

'No; out you get!'

Protesting, the idiot went forth, and his irregular clumsy footsteps sounded on the pebble-paved yard. When the noise of them ceased in the soft roadway. Froyle jumped off the table again. Gradually his body, like a stopping pendumum, came to rest under the hook, and hung twitching, with strange disconnected movements. The horse in the stable, hearing unaccustomed noises, rattled his chain and stamped about in the straw of his box.

Furtive steps came down the yard again, and Daft Jimmy peeped into the coach-house.

'He done it! He done it!' the idiot cried gleefully. 'Damned if he hasna'.' He slapped his leg and almost danced. The body still twitched occasionally. 'He done it!'

'Done what, Daft Jimmy? You're making a fine noise there! Done what?'

The idiot ran out of the stable. At the side-entrance to the hotel stood the barmaid, the outline of her fine figure distinct against the light from within.

The idiot continued to laugh.

'Done what?' the girl repeated, calling out across the dark yard in clear, pleasant tones of amused inquiry. 'Done what?'

'What's that to you, Miss Tucker?'

'Now none of your sauce, Daft Jimmy! Is Willie Froyle in there?'

The idiot roared with laughter.

'Yes, he is, miss.'

'Well, tell him his master wants him. I don't want to cross this mucky, messy yard.'

'Yes, miss,'

The girl closed the door.

The idiot went into the coach-house, and, slapping William's body in a friendly way so that it trembled on the rope, he spluttered out between his laughs:

'Master wants ye, Mr Froyle.'

Then he walked out into the village street, and stood looking up the muddy road, still laughing quietly. It was quite dark, but the moon aloft in the clear sky showed the highway with its shining ruts leading in a straight line over the hill to Bursley.

'Them shoes!' the idiot ejaculated suddenly. 'Well, I be an idiot, and that's true! They can take the measure from my feet, and I never thought on it till this minute!'

Laughing again, he set off at a run up the hill.

SAKI

Sredni Vashtar

Conradin was ten years old, and the doctor had pronounced his professional opinion that the boy would not live another five years. The doctor was silky and effete, and counted for little, but his opinion was endorsed by Mrs De Ropp, who counted for nearly everything. Mrs De Ropp was Conradin's cousin and guardian, and in his eyes she represented those three-fifths of the world that are necessary and disagreeable and real; the other two-fifths, in perpetual antagonism to the foregoing, were summed up in himself and his imagination. One of these days Conradin supposed he would succumb to the mastering pressure of wearisome necessary things – such as illness and coddling restrictions and drawn-out dullness. Without his imagination, which was rampant under the spur of loneliness, he would have succumbed long ago.

Mrs De Ropp would never, in her honestest moments, have confessed to herself that she disliked Conradin, though she might have been dimly aware that thwarting him 'for his good' was a duty which she did not find particularly irksome. Conradin hated her with a desperate sincerity which he was perfectly able to mask. Such few pleasures as he could contrive for himself gained an added relish from the likelihood that they would be displeasing to his guardian, and from the realm of his imagination she was locked out – an unclean thing, which should find no entrance.

In the dull, cheerless garden, overlooked by so many windows that were ready to open with a message not to do this or that, or a reminder that medicines were due, he found little attraction. The few fruit-trees that it contained were set jealously apart from his plucking, as though they were rare specimens of their kind blooming in an arid waste; it would probably have been

74

difficult to find a market-gardener who would have offered ten shillings for the entire yearly produce. In a forgotten corner, however, almost hidden behind a dismal shrubbery, was a disused tool-shed of respectable proportions, and within its walls Conradin found a haven, something that took on the varying aspects of a playroom and a cathedral. He had peopled it with a legion of familiar phantoms, evoked partly from fragments of history and partly from his own brain, but it also boasted two inmates of flesh and blood. In one corner lived a ragged-plumaged Houdan hen, on which the boy lavished an affection that had scarcely another outlet. Further back in the gloom stood a large hutch, divided into two compartments, one of which was fronted with close iron bars. This was the abode of a large polecat-ferret, which a friendly butcher-boy had once smuggled, cage and all, into its present quarters, in exchange for a long-secreted hoard of small silver. Conradin was dreadfully afraid of the lithe, sharp-fanged beast, but it was his most treasured possession. Its very presence in the tool-shed was a secret and fearful joy, to be kept scrupulously from the knowledge of the Woman, as he privately dubbed his cousin. And one day, out of Heaven knows what material, he spun the beast a wonderful name, and from that moment it grew into a god and a religion. The Woman indulged in religion once a week at a church near by, and took Conradin with her, but to him the church service was an alien rite in the House of Rimmon. Every Thursday, in the dim and musty silence of the tool-shed, he worshipped with mystic and elaborate ceremonial before the wooden hutch where dwelt Sredni Vashtar, the great ferret. Red flowers in their season and scarlet berries in the winter-time were offered at his shrine, for he was a god who laid some special stress on the fierce impatient side of things, as opposed to the Woman's religion, which, as far as Conradin could observe, went to great lengths in the contrary direction. And on great festivals powdered nutmeg was strewn in front of his hutch, an important feature of the offering being that the nutmeg had to be stolen. These festivals were of irregular occurrence, and were chiefly appointed to celebrate some passing event. On one occasion, when Mrs De Ropp suffered from acute toothache for three days, Conradin kept up the festival during the entire three days, and almost succeeded in persuading himself that Sredni

Vashtar was personally responsible for the toothache. If the malady had lasted for another day the supply of nutmeg would have given out.

The Houdan hen was never drawn into the cult of Sredni Vashtar. Conradin had long ago settled that she was an Anabaptist. He did not pretend to have the remotest knowledge as to what an Anabaptist was, but he privately hoped that it was dashing and not very respectable. Mrs De Ropp was the ground plan on which he based and detested all respectability.

After a while Conradin's absorption in the tool-shed began to attract the notice of his guardian. 'It is not good for him to be pottering down there in all weathers,' she promptly decided, and at breakfast one morning she announced that the Houdan hen had been sold and taken away overnight. With her short-sighted eyes she peered at Conradin, waiting for an outbreak of rage and sorrow, which she was ready to rebuke with a flow of excellent precepts and reasoning. But Conradin said nothing: there was nothing to be said. Something perhaps in his white set face gave her a momentary qualm, for at tea that afternoon there was toast on the table, a delicacy which she usually banned on the ground that it was bad for him; also because the making of it 'gave trouble,' a deadly offence in the middle-class feminine eye.

'I thought you liked toast,' she exclaimed, with an injured air, observing that he did not touch it.

'Sometimes,' said Conradin.

In the shed that evening there was an innovation in the worship of the hutch-god. Conradin had been wont to chant his praises, tonight he asked a boon.

'Do one thing for me, Sredni Vashtar.'

The thing was not specified. As Sredni Vashtar was a god he must be supposed to know. And choking back a sob as he looked at the other empty corner, Conradin went back to the world he so hated.

And every night, in the welcome darkness of his bedroom, and every evening in the dusk of the tool-shed, Conradin's bitter litany went up: 'Do one thing for me, Sredni Vashtar.'

Mrs De Ropp noticed that the visits to the shed did not cease, and one day she made a further journey of inspection.

'What are you keeping in that locked hutch?' she asked. 'I believe it's guinea-pigs. I'll have them all cleared away.'

Conradin shut his lips tight, but the Woman ransacked his bedroom till she found the carefully hidden key, and forthwith marched down to the shed to complete her discovery. It was a cold afternoon, and Conradin had been bidden to keep to the house. From the furthest window of the dining-room the door of the shed could just be seen beyond the corner of the shrubbery, and there Conradin stationed himself. He saw the Woman enter, and then he imagined her opening the door of the sacred hutch and peering down with her short-sighted eyes into the thick straw bed where his god lay hidden. And Conradin fervently breathed his prayer for the last time. But he knew as he prayed that he did not believe. He knew that the Woman would come out presently with that pursed smile he loathed so well on her face, and that in an hour or two the gardener would carry away his wonderful god, a god no longer, but a simple brown ferret in a hutch. And he knew that the Woman would triumph always as she triumphed now, and that he would grow ever more sickly under her pestering and domineering, and superior wisdom, till one day nothing would matter much more with him, and the doctor would be proved right. And in the sting and misery of his defeat, he began to chant loudly and defiantly the hymn of his threatened idol:

Sredni Vashtar went forth,
His thoughts were red thoughts and his teeth were white.
His enemies called for peace, but he brought them death.
Sredni Vashtar the Beautiful.

And then of a sudden he stopped his chanting and drew closer to the window-pane. The door of the shed still stood ajar as it had been left, and the minutes were slipping by. They were long minutes, but they slipped by nevertheless. He watched the starlings running and flying in little parties across the lawn; he counted them over and over again, with one eye always on that swinging door. A sour-faced maid came in to lay the table for tea, and still Conradin stood and waited and watched. Hope had crept by inches into his heart, and now a look of triumph began to blaze in his eyes that had only known the wistful patience of defeat. Under his breath, with a furtive exultation, he began once again the paean of victory and devastation. And presently his eyes were rewarded: out through that doorway came a long, low, yellow-and-brown beast, with eyes a-blink at the waning daylight, and dark wet stains around the fur of jaw and throat. Conradin dropped on his knees. The great polecat ferret made its way down to a small brook at the foot of the garden, drank for a moment, then crossed a little plank bridge and was lost to sight in the bushes. Such was the passing of Sredni Vashtar.

'Tea is ready,' said the sour-faced maid; 'where is the mistress?'

'She went down to the shed some time ago,' said Conradin.

And while the maid went to summon her mistress to tea, Conradin fished a toasting-fork out of the sideboard drawer and proceeded to toast himself a piece of bread. And during the toasting of it and the buttering of it with much butter and the slow enjoyment of eating it, Conradin listened to the noises and silences which fell in quick spasms beyond the dining-room door. The loud foolish screaming of the maid, the answering chorus of wondering ejaculations from the kitchen region, the scuttering footsteps and hurried embassies for outside help, and then, after a lull, the scared sobbings and the shuffling tread of those who bore a heavy burden into the house.

'Whoever will break it to the poor child? I couldn't for the life of me!' exclaimed a shrill voice. And while they debated the matter among themselves, Conradin made himself another piece of toast.

WALTER DE LA MARE

Bad Company

It is very seldom that one encounters what would appear to be sheer unadulterated evil in a human face ; an evil, I mean, active, deliberate, deadly, dangerous. Folly, heedlessness, vanity, pride, craft, meanness, stupidity – yes. But even Iagos in this world are few, and devilry is as rare as witchcraft.

One winter's evening some little time ago, bound on a visit to a friend in London, I found myself on the platform of one of its many subterranean railway stations. It is an ordeal that one may undergo as seldom as one can. The glare and glitter, the noise, the very air one breathes affect nerves and spirits. One expects vaguely strange meetings in such surroundings. On this occasion, the expectation was justified. The mind is at times more attentive than the eye. Already tired, and troubled with personal cares and problems, which a little wisdom and enterprise should have refused to entertain, I had seated myself on one of the low, wooden benches to the left of the entrance to the platform, when, for no conscious reason, I was prompted to turn my head in the direction of a fellow traveller, seated across the gangway on the fellow to my bench some few yards away.

What was wrong with him ? He was enveloped in a loose cape or cloak, sombre and motionless. He appeared to be wholly unaware of my abrupt scrutiny. And yet I doubt it ; for the next moment, although the door of the nearest coach gaped immediately opposite him, he had shuffled into the compartment I had entered myself, and now in its corner, confronted me, all but knee to knee. I could have touched him with my hand. We had, too, come at once into an even more intimate contact than that of touch. Our eyes – his own fixed in a dwelling and lethargic stare – had instantly met, and no less rapidly mine had uncharitably recoiled, not only in misgiving, but in something

79

little short of disgust. The effect resembled that of an acid on milk, and for the time being cast my thoughts into confusion. Yet that one glance had taken him in.

He was old – over seventy. A wide-brimmed rusty and dusty black hat concealed his head – a head fringed with wisps of hair, lank and paper-grey. His loose, jaded cheeks were of the colour of putty; the thin lips above the wide unshaven and dimpled chin showing scarcely a trace of red. The cloak suspended from his shoulders mantled him to his shins. One knuckled, cadaverous, mittened hand clasped a thick ash stick, its handle black and polished with long usage. The only sign of life in his countenance was secreted in his eyes – fixed on mine – hazed and dully glistening, as a snail in winter is fixed to a wall. There was a dull deliberate challenge in them, and, as I fancied, something more than that. They suggested that he had been in wait for me; that for him, it was almost 'well met!'

For minutes together I endeavoured to accept their challenge, to make sure. Yet I realized, fascinated the while, that he was well aware of the futility of this attempt, as a snake is of the restless, fated bird in the branches above its head.

Such a statement, I am aware, must appear wildly exaggerated, but I can only record my impression. It was already lateish – much later than I had intended. The passengers came and went, and, whether intentionally or not, none consented to occupy the seat vacant beside him. I fixed my eyes on an advertisement – that of a Friendly Society I remember! – immediately above his head, with the intention of watching him in the field of an eye that I could not persuade to meet his own in full focus again.

He had instantly detected this ingenuous device. By a fraction of an inch he had shifted his grasp upon his stick. So intolerable, at length, became the physical – and psychical – effect of his presence on me that I determined to leave the train at the next station, and there to await the next. And at this precise moment, I was conscious that he had not only withdrawn his eyes but closed them.

I was not so easily to free myself of his company. A glance over my shoulder as, after leaving the train, I turned towards the lift, showed him hastily groping his way out of the carriage. The metal gate clanged. The lift slid upwards and, such is the contrariness of human nature, a faint disappointment followed. One may, for example, be appalled and yet engrossed in reading an account of some act of infamous cruelty.

Concealing myself as best I could at the bookstall, I awaited the next lift-load. Its few passengers having dispersed, he himself followed. In spite of age and infirmity, he *had*, then, ascended alone the spiral staircase. Glancing, it appeared, neither to right nor left, he passed rapidly through the barrier. And yet – *had* he not seen me?

The Collector raised his head, opened his mouth, watched his retreating figure, but made no attempt to retrieve his ticket. It was dark now – the dark of London. In my absence underground, minute frozen pellets of snow had fallen, whitening the streets and lulling the sound of the traffic. On emerging into the street, he turned in the direction of the next station – my own. Yet again – had he, or had he not, been aware that he was being watched? However that might be, my journey lay his way, and that way my feet directed me; although I was already later than I intended. I followed him, led on no doubt in part merely by the effect he had had on me. Some twenty or thirty yards ahead, his dark shapelessness showed – distinct against the whitening pavement.

The waters of the Thames, I was aware, lay on my left. A muffled blast from the siren of a tug announced its presence. Keeping my distance, I followed him on. One lamp-post – two – three. At that, he seemed to pause for a moment, as if to listen, momentarily glanced back (as I fancied) and vanished.

When I came up with it, I found that this third lamp-post vaguely illuminated the mouth of a narrow, lightless alley between highish walls. It led me, after a while, into another alley, yet dingier. The wall on the left of this was evidently that of a large garden; on the right came a row of nondescript houses, looming up in their neglect against a starless sky.

The first of these houses *appeared* to be occupied. The next two were vacant. Dingy curtains, soot-grey against their snowy window-sills, hung over the next. A litter of paper and refuse – abandoned by the last long gust of wind that must have come whistling round the nearer angle of the house – lay under the broken flight of steps up to a mid-Victorian porch. The small snow clinging to the bricks and to the worn and weathered cement of the wall only added to its gaunt lifelessness.

In the faint hope of other company coming my way, and vowing that I would follow no farther than to the outlet of yet another pitch-black and uninviting alley or court – which might indeed prove a dead end – I turned into it. It was then that I observed, in the rays of the lamp over my head, that in spite of the fineness of the snow and the brief time that had elapsed, there seemed to be no trace on its surface of recent footsteps.

A faintly thudding echo accompanied me on my way. I have found it very useful – in the country – always to carry a small electric torch in my greatcoat pocket; but for the time being I refrained from using it. This alley proved not to be blind. Beyond a patch of waste ground, a nebulous, leaden-grey vacancy marked a loop here of the Thames – I decided to go no farther; and then perceived a garden gate in the wall to my right. It was ajar, but could not long have been so because no more than an instant's flash of my torch showed marks in the snow of its recent shifting. And yet there was little wind. On the other hand, here was the open river; just a breath of a breeze across its surface might account for this. The cracked and blistered paint was shimmering with a thin coat of rime – of hoarfrost, and as if a finger had but just now scrawled it there, a clumsy arrow showed, its 'V' pointing inward. A tramp, an errand-boy, mere accident might have accounted for this. It may indeed have been a mark made some time before the paint.

I paused in an absurd debate with myself, chiefly I think because I felt some little alarm at the thought of what might follow; yet led on also by the conviction that I had been intended, decoyed to follow. I pushed the gate a little wider open, peered in, and made my way up a woody path beneath ragged unpruned and leafless fruit trees towards the house. The snow's own light revealed a ramshackle flight of steps up to a poor, frenchified sort of canopy above french windows, one-half of their glazed doors ajar. I ascended, and peered into the intense gloom beyond it. And thus and then prepared to retrace my steps as quickly as possible, I called (in tones as near those of a London policeman as I could manage):

'Hello there! Is anything wrong? Is anyone wanted?'

After all, I could at least explain to my fellow passenger if he appeared that I found both his gate and his window open; and the house was hardly pleasantly situated.

No answer was returned to me. In doubt and disquietude, but with a conviction that all was not well, I flashed my torch over the walls and furniture of the room and its heavily framed pictures. How could anything be well – with unseen company such as this besieging one's senses! Ease and pleasant companionship, the room may once have been capable of giving; in its dirt, cold, and neglect it showed nothing of that now. I crossed it, paused again in the passage beyond it, and listened. I then entered the room beyond. Venetian blinds, many of the slats of which had outworn their webbing, and heavy, crimson chenille side-curtains concealed its windows. The ashes of a fire showed beyond rusty bars of the grate under a black marble mantelpiece. An oil lamp on the table, with a green shade, exuded a stink of paraffin; beyond was a table littered with books and papers, and an overturned chair. There I could see the bent-up old legs, perceptibly lean beneath the trousers, of the occupant of the room. In no doubt of whose remains these were, I drew near, and with bared teeth and icy, trembling fingers, drew back the fold of the cloak that lay over the face. Death has a strange sorcery. A shuddering revulsion of feeling took possession of me. This cold, once genteel, hideous, malignant room – and this!

The skin of the blue loose cheek was drawn tight over the bone; the mouth lay a little open, showing the dislodged false teeth beneath; the dull unspeculative eyes stared out from beneath lowered lids towards the black mouth of the chimney above the fireplace. Vileness and iniquity had left their marks on the lifeless features, and yet it was rather with compassion than with horror and disgust that I stood regarding them. What desolate solitude, what misery must this old man, abandoned to himself, have experienced during the last years of his life; encountering nothing but enmity and the apprehension of his fellow creatures. I am not intending to excuse or even commiserate what I cannot understand, but the almost complete absence of any goodness in the human spirit cannot but condemn the heart to an appalling isolation. Had he been murdered, or had he come to a violent but natural end? In either case, horror and terror must have supervened. That I had been enticed, deliberately led on, to this discovery I hadn't the least doubt, extravagant though this, too, may seem. Why? What for?

I could not bring myself to attempt to light the lamp. Besides, in that last vigil, it must have burnt itself out. My torch revealed a stub of candle on the mantelpiece. I lit that. He seemed to have been engaged in writing when the enemy of us all had approached him in silence and had struck him down. A long and unsealed envelope lay on the table. I drew out the contents – a letter and a Will, which had been witnessed some few weeks before, apparently by a tradesman's boy and, possibly, by some derelict charwoman, Eliza Hinks. I knew enough about such things to be sure that the Will was valid and complete. This old man had been evidently more than fairly rich in this world's goods, and reluctant to surrender them. The letter was addressed to his two sisters: 'To my two Sisters, Amelia and Maude.' Standing there in the cold and the silence, and utterly alone – for, if any occupant of the other world had decoyed me there, there was not the faintest hint in consciousness that he or his influence was any longer present with me – I read the vilest letter that has ever come my way. Even in print. It stated that he knew the circumstances of these two remaining relatives – that he was well aware of their poverty and physical conditions. One of them, it seemed, was afflicted with Cancer. He then proceeded to explain that, although they should by the intention of their mother have had a due share in her property and in the money she had left, it rejoiced him to think that his withholding of this knowledge must continually have added to their wretchedness. Why he so hated them was only vaguely suggested.

The Will he had enclosed with the letter left all that he died possessed of to – of all human establishments that need it least – the authorities of Scotland Yard. It was to be devoted, it ran, to the detection of such evil-doers as are ignorant or imbecile enough to leave their misdemeanours and crimes detectable.

It is said that confession is good for the soul. Well then, as publicly as possible, I take this opportunity of announcing that, there and then, I made a little heap of envelope, letter and Will on the hearth and put a match to them. When every vestige of the paper had been consumed, I stamped the ashes down. I had touched nothing else. I would leave the vile, jaded, forsaken house to reveal its own secret; and I might ensure that that would not be long delayed.

What continues to perplex me is that so far as I can see no

other agency but that of this evil old recluse himself had led me to my discovery. Why? Can it have been with this very intention? I stooped down and peeped and peered narrowly in under the lowered lids in the light of my torch, but not the feeblest flicker, remotest signal – or faintest syllabling echo of any message rewarded me. Dead fish are less unseemly.

And yet. Well – we are all of us, I suppose, at any extreme *capable* of remorse and not utterly shut against repentance. Is it possible that this priceless blessing is not denied us even when all that's earthly else appears to have come to an end?

G. K. CHESTERTON

The Honour of Israel Gow

A stormy evening of olive and silver was closing in, as Father
Brown, wrapped in a grey Scotch plaid, came to the end of a grey
Scotch valley and beheld the strange castle of Glengyle. It
stopped one end of the glen or hollow like a blind alley ; and it
looked like the end of the world. Rising in steep roofs and spires
of seagreen slate in the manner of the Old French-Scottish
châteaux, it reminded an Englishman of the sinister steeple-hats
of witches in fairy tales ; and the pine woods that rocked round
the green turrets looked, by comparison, as black as numberless
flocks of ravens. This note of a dreamy, almost a sleepy devilry,
was no mere fancy from the landscape. For there did rest on the
place one of those clouds of pride and madness and mysterious
sorrow which lie more heavily on the noble houses of Scotland
than on any other of the children of men. For Scotland has a
double dose of the poison called heredity ; the sense of blood in
the aristrocrat, and the sense of doom in the Calvinist.

The priest had snatched a day from his business at Glasgow to
meet his friend Flambeau, the amateur detective, who was at
Glengyle Castle with another more formal officer investigating
the life and death of the late Earl of Glengyle. That mysterious
person was the last representative of a race whose valour,
insanity, and violent cunning had made them terrible even
among the sinister nobility of their nation in the sixteenth
century. None were deeper in that labyrinthine ambition, in
chamber within chamber of that palace of lies that was built up
around Mary Queen of Scots.

The rhyme in the country-side attested the motive and the
result of their machinations candidly :

'As green sap to the simmer trees
Is red gold to the Ogilvies.'

For many centuries there had never been a decent lord in Glengyle Castle; and with the Victorian era one would have thought that all eccentricities were exhausted. The last Glengyle, however, satisfied his tribal tradition by doing the only thing that was left for him to do; he disappeared. I do not mean that he went abroad; by all accounts he was still in the castle, if he was anywhere. But though his name was in the church register and the big red Peerage, nobody ever saw him under the sun.

If anyone saw him it was a solitary man-servant, something between a groom and a gardener. He was so deaf that the more business-like assumed him to be dumb; while the more penetrating declared him to be half-witted. A gaunt, red-haired labourer, with a dogged jaw and chin, but quiet black-blue eyes, he went by the name of Israel Gow, and was the only silent servant on that deserted estate. But the energy with which he dug potatoes, and the regularity with which he disappeared into the kitchen gave people an impression that he was providing for the meals of a superior, and that the strange earl was still concealed in the castle. If society needed any further proof that he was there, the servant persistently asserted that he was not at home. One morning the provost and the minister (for the Glengyles were Presbyterian) were summoned to the castle. There they found that the gardener, groom and cook had added to his many professions that of an undertaker, and had nailed up his noble master in a coffin. With how much or how little further inquiry this odd fact was passed, did not as yet very plainly appear; for the thing that never been legally investigated till Flambeau had gone north two or three days before. By then the body of Lord Glengyle (if it was the body) had lain for some time in the little churchyard on the hill.

As Father Brown passed through the dim garden and came under the shadow of the château, the clouds were thick and the whole air damp and thundery. Against the last stripe of the green-gold sunset he saw a black human silhouette; a man in a chimney-pot hat, with a big spade over his shoulder. The combination was queerly suggestive of a sexton; but when Brown remembered the deaf servant who dug potatoes, he thought it natural enough. He knew something of the Scotch peasant; he knew the respectability which might well feel it necessary to wear 'blacks' for an official inquiry; he knew also the economy that would not lose an hour's digging for that. Even the man's start and suspicious stare as the priest went by were consonant enough with the vigilance and jealousy of such a type.

The great door was opened by Flambeau himself, who had with him a lean man with iron-grey hair and papers in his hand : Inspector Craven from Scotland Yard. The entrance hall was mostly stripped and empty ; but the pale, sneering faces of one or two of the wicked Ogilvies looked down out of the black periwigs and blackening canvas.

Following them into an inner room, Father Brown found that the allies had been seated at a long oak table, of which their end was covered with scribbled papers, flanked with whisky and cigars. Through the whole of its remaining length it was occupied by detached objects arranged at intervals ; objects about as inexplicable as any objects could be. One looked like a small heap of glittering broken glass. Another looked like a high heap of brown dust. A third appeared to be a plain stick of wood.

'You seem to have a sort of geological museum here,' he said, as he sat down, jerking his head briefly in the direction of the brown dust and the crystalline fragments.

'Not a geological museum,' replied Flambeau ; 'say a psychological museum.'

'Oh, for the Lord's sake,' cried the police detective, laughing, 'don't let's begin with such long words.'

'Don't you know what psychology means ?' asked Flambeau with friendly surprise. 'Psychology means being off your chump.'

'Still I hardly follow,' replied the official.

'Well,' said Flambeau, with decision ; 'I mean that we've only found out one thing about Lord Glengyle. He was a maniac.'

The black silhouette of Gow with his top hat and spade passed the window, dimly outlined against the darkening sky. Father Brown stared passively at it and answered :

'I can understand there must have been something odd about the man, or he wouldn't have buried himself alive – nor been in such a hurry to bury himself dead. But what makes you think it was lunacy ?'

'Well,' said Flambeau ; 'you just listen to the list of things Mr

Craven has found in the house.'

'We must get a candle,' said Craven, suddenly. 'A storm is getting up, and it's too dark to read.'

'Have you found any candles,' asked Brown smiling, 'among your oddities?'

Flambeau raised a grave face, and fixed his dark eyes on his friend.

'That is curious, too,' he said. 'Twenty-five candles, and not a trace of a candlestick.'

In the rapidly darkening room and rapidly rising wind, Brown went along the table to where a bundle of wax candles lay among the other scrappy exhibits. As he did so he bent accidentally over the heap of red-brown dust; and a sharp sneeze cracked the silence.

'Hullo!' he said; 'snuff!'

He took one of the candles, lit it carefully, came back and stuck it in the neck of the whisky bottle. The unrestful night air, blowing through the crazy window, waved the long flame like a banner. And on every side of the castle they could hear the miles and miles of black pine wood seething like a black sea around a rock.

'I will read the inventory,' began Craven gravely, picking up one of the papers, 'the inventory of what we found loose and unexplained in the castle. You are to understand that the place generally was dismantled and neglected; but one or two rooms had plainly been inhabited in a simple but not squalid style by somebody; somebody who was not the servant Gow. The list is as follows:

'First item. A very considerable hoard of precious stones, nearly all diamonds, and all of them loose, without any setting whatever. Of course, it is natural that the Ogilvies should have family jewels; but those are exactly the jewels that are almost always set in particular articles of ornament. The Ogilvies would seem to have kept theirs loose in their pockets, like coppers.

'Second item. Heaps and heaps of loose snuff, not kept in a horn, or even a pouch, but lying in heaps on the mantelpieces, on the sideboard, on the piano, anywhere. It looks as if the old gentleman would not take the trouble to look in a pocket or lift a lid.

'Third item. Here and there about the house curious little

heaps of minute pieces of metal, some like steel springs and some in the form of microscopic wheels. As if they had gutted some mechanical toy.

'Fourth item. The wax candles, which have to be stuck in bottle necks because there is nothing else to stick them in. Now I wish you to note how very much queerer all this is than anything we anticipated. For the central riddle we are prepared; we have all seen at a glance there was something wrong about the last earl. We have come here to find out whether he really lived here, whether he really died here, whether that red-haired scarecrow who did his burying had anything to do with his dying. But suppose the worst in all this, the most lurid or melodramatic solution you like. Suppose, the servant really killed the master, or suppose the master isn't really dead, or suppose the master is dressed up as the servant, or suppose the servant is buried for the master; invent what Wilkie Collins's tragedy you like, and you still have not examined a candle without a candlestick, or why an elderly gentleman of good family should habitually spill snuff on the piano. The core of the tale we could imagine; it is the fringes that are mysterious. By no stretch of fancy can the human mind connect together snuff and diamonds and wax and loose clockwork.'

'I think I see the connection' said the priest. 'This Glengyle was mad against the French Revolution. He was an enthusiast for the *ancien régime,* and was trying to re-enact literally the family life of the last Bourbons. He had snuff because it was the eighteenth-century luxury; wax candles, because they were the eighteenth-century lighting; the mechanical bits of iron represented the locksmith hobby of Louis XVI; the diamonds are for the Diamond Necklace of Marie Antoinette.'

Both the other men were staring at him with round eyes. 'What a perfectly extraordinary notion!' cried Flambeau. 'Do you really think that is the truth?'

'I am perfectly sure it isn't,' answered Father Brown, 'only you said that nobody could connect snuff and diamonds and clockwork and candles. I give you that connection off-hand. The real truth, I am very sure, lies deeper.'

He paused a moment and listened to the wailing of the wind in the turrets. Then he said: 'The late Earl of Glengyle was a thief. He lived a second and darker life as a desperate housebreaker.

He did not have any candlesticks because he only used these candles cut short in the lantern he carried. The snuff he employed as the fiercest French criminals have used pepper : to fling it suddenly in dense masses in the face of a captor or pursuer. But the final proof is in the curious coincidence of the diamonds and the small steel wheels. Surely that makes everything plain to you ? Diamonds and small steel wheels are the only two instruments with which you can cut out a pane of glass.'

The bough of a broken pine tree lashed heavily in the blast against the window-pane behind them, as if in parody of a burglar, but they did not turn round. Their eyes were fastened on Father Brown.

'Diamonds and small wheels,' repeated Craven ruminating. 'Is that all that makes you think it the true explanation ?'

'I don't think it the true explanation,' replied the priest placidly; 'but you said that nobody could connect the four things. The true tale, of course, is something much more humdrum. Glengyle had found, or thought he had found, precious stones on his estate. Somebody had bamboozled him with those loose brilliants, saying they were found in the castle caverns. The little wheels are some diamond-cutting affair. He had to do the thing very roughly and in a small way, with the help of a few shepherds or rude fellows on these hills. Snuff is the one great luxury of such Scotch shepherds; 'it's the one thing with which you can bribe them. They didn't have candlesticks because they didn't want them; they held the candles in their hands when they explored the caves.'

'Is that all ?' asked Flambeau after a long pause. 'Have we got to the dull truth at last ?'

'Oh, no,' said Father Brown.

As the wind died in the most distant pine woods with a long hoot as of mockery, Father Brown, with an utterly impassive face, went on :

'I only suggested that because you said one could not plausibly connect snuff with clockwork or candles with bright stones. Ten false philosophies will fit the universe ; ten false theories will fit Glengyle Castle. But we want the real explanation of the castle and the universe. But are there no other exhibits ?'

Craven laughed, and Flambeau rose smiling to his feet and

strolled down the long table.

'Items five, six, seven, etc.,' he said, 'are certainly more varied than instructive. A curious collection, not of lead pencils, but of lead out of lead pencils. A senseless stick of bamboo, with the top rather splintered. It might be the instrument of the crime. Only, there isn't any crime. The only other things are a few old missals and little Catholic pictures, which the Ogilvies kept, I suppose, from the Middle Ages – their family pride being stronger than their Puritanism. We only put them in the museum because they seem curiously cut about and defaced.'

The heady tempest without drove a dreadful wrack of clouds across Glengyle and threw the long room into darkness as Father Brown picked up the little illuminated pages to examine them. He spoke before the drift of darkness had passed; but it was the voice of an utterly new man.

'Mr Craven,' said he, talking like a man ten years younger: 'You have got a legal warrant, haven't you to go up and examine that grave? The sooner we do it the better, and get to the bottom of this horrible affair. If I were you I should start now.'

'Now,' repeated the astonished detective, 'and why now?'

'Because this is serious,' answered Brown; 'this is not spilt snuff or loose pebbles, that might be there for a hundred reasons. There is only one reason I know of for *this* being done; and the reason goes down to the roots of the world. These religious pictures are not just dirtied or torn or scrawled over, which might be done in idleness or bigotry, by children or by Protestants. These have been treated very carefully – and very queerly. In every place where the great ornamented name of God comes in the old illuminations it has been elaborately taken out. The only other thing that has been removed is the halo round the head of the Child Jesus. Therefore, I say, let us get our warrant and our spade and our hatchet, and go and break open that coffin.'

'What *do* you mean?' demanded the London officer.

'I mean,' answered the little priest, and his voice seemed to rise slightly in the roar of the gale, 'I mean that the great devil of the universe may be sitting on the top tower of this castle at this moment, as big as a hundred elephants, and roaring like the Apocalypse. There is black magic somewhere at the bottom of this.'

'Black magic,' repeated Flambeau in a low voice, for he was too enlightened a man not to know of such things ; 'but what can these other things mean ?'

'Oh, something damnable, I suppose,' replied Brown impatiently. 'How should I know ? How can I guess all their mazes down below ? Perhaps you can make a torture out of snuff and bamboo. Perhaps lunatics lust after wax and steel filings. Perhaps there is a maddening drug made of lead pencils ! Our shortest cut to the mystery is up the hill to the grave.'

His comrades hardly knew that they had obeyed and followed him till a blast of the night wind nearly flung them on their faces in the garden. Nevertheless they had obeyed him like automata ; for Craven found a hatchet in his hand and the warrant in his pocket ; Flambeau was carrying the heavy spade of the strange gardener ; Father Brown was carrying the little gilt book from which had been torn the name of God.

The path up the hill to the churchyard was crooked but short ; only under the stress of wind it seemed laborious and long. Far as the eye could see, farther and farther as they mounted the slope, were seas beyond seas of pines, now all aslope one way under the wind. And that universal gesture seemed as vain as it was vast, as vain as if that wind were whistling about some unpeopled and purposeless planet. Through all that infinite growth of grey-blue forest sang, shrill and high, that ancient sorrow that is in the heart of all heathen things. One could fancy that the voices from the underworld of unfathomable foliage were cries of the lost and wandering pagan gods ; gods who had gone roaming in that irrational forest, and who will never find their way back to heaven.

'You see,' said Father Brown in low but easy tone, 'Scotch people before Scotland existed were a curious lot. In fact, they're a curious lot still. But in the prehistoric times I fancy they really worshipped demons. That,' he added genially, 'is why they jumped at the Puritan theology.'

'My friend,' said Flambeau, turning in a kind of fury, 'what does all that snuff mean ?'

'My friend,' replied Brown, with equal seriousness, 'there is one mark of all genuine religions : materialism. Now, devil-worship is a perfectly genuine religion.'

They had come up on the grassy scalp of the hill, one of the few bald spots that stood clear of the crashing and roaring pine forest. A mean enclosure, partly timber and partly wire, rattled in the tempest to tell them the border of the graveyard. But by the time Inspector Craven had come to the corner of the grave, and Flambeau had planted his spade point downwards and leaned on it, they were both almost as shaken as the shaky wood and wire. At the foot of the grave grew great tall thistles, grey and silver in their decay. Once or twice, when a ball of thistle-down broke under the breeze and flew past them, Craven jumped slightly as if it had been an arrow.

Flambeau drove the blade of his spade through the whistling grass into the wet clay below. Then he seemed to stop and lean on it as on a staff.

'Go on,' said the priest very gently. 'We are only trying to find the truth. What are you afraid of?'

'I am afraid of finding it,' said Flambeau.

The London detective spoke suddenly in a high crowing voice that was meant to be conversational and cheery. 'I wonder why he really did hide himself like that. Something nasty, I suppose; was he a leper?'

'Something worse than that,' said Flambeau.

'And what do you imagine,' asked the other, 'would be worse than a leper?'

'I don't imagine it,' said Flambeau.

He dug for some dreadful minutes in silence, and then said in a choked voice: 'I am afraid of his not being the right shape.'

'Nor was that piece of paper, you know,' said Father Brown quietly, 'and we survived even that piece of paper.'

Flambeau dug on with a blind energy. But the tempest had shouldered away the choking grey clouds that clung to the hills like smoke and revealed grey fields of faint starlight before he cleared the shape of a rude timber coffin, and somehow tipped it upon the turf. Craven stepped forward with his axe; a thistle-top touched, and he flinched. Then he took a firmer stride, and hacked and wrenched with an energy like Flambeau's till the lid was torn off, and all that was there lay glimmering in the grey starlight.

'Bones,' said Craven; and then he added, 'but it is a man,' as if that were something unexpected.

'Is he,' asked Flambeau in a voice that went oddly up and

down, 'is he all right?'

'Seems so,' said the officer huskily, bending over the obscure and decaying skeleton in the box. 'Wait a minute.'

A vast heave went over Flambeau's huge figure. 'And now I come to think of it,' he cried, 'why in the name of madness shouldn't he be all right? What is it gets hold of a man on these cursed cold mountains? I think it's the black, brainless repetition; all these forests, and over all an ancient horror of unconsciousness. It's like the dream of an atheist. Pine-trees and more pine-trees and millions more pine-trees – '

'God!' cried the man by the coffin; 'but he hasn't got a head.'

While the others stood rigid the priest, for the first time, showed a leap of startled concern.

'No head!' he repeated. *'No head?'* as if he had almost expected some other deficiency.

Half-witted visions of a headless baby born to Glengyle, of a headless youth hiding himself in the castle, of a headless man pacing those ancient halls or that gorgeous garden, passed in panorama through their minds. But even in that stiffened instant the tale took no root in them and seemed to have no reason in it. They stood listening to the loud woods and the shrieking sky quite foolishly, like exhausted animals. Thought seemed to be something enormous that had suddenly slipped out of their grasp.

'There are three headless men,' said Father Brown: 'standing round this open grave.'

The pale detective from London opened his mouth the speak, and left it open like a yokel, while a long scream of wind tore the sky then he looked at the axe in his hands as if it did not belong to him, and dropped it.

'Father,' said Flambeau in that infantile and heavy voice he used very seldom, 'what are we to do?'

His friend's reply came with the pent promptitude of a gun going off.

'Sleep!' cried Father Brown. 'Sleep. We have come to the end of the ways. Do you know what sleep is? Do you know that every man who sleeps believes in God? It is a sacrament; for it is an act of faith and it is a food. And we need a sacrament, if only a natural one. Something has fallen on us that falls very seldom on men; perhaps the worst thing that can fall on them.'

Craven's parted lips came together to say: 'What do you mean?'

The priest turned his face to the castle as he answered:

'We have found the truth; and the truth makes no sense.'

He went down the path in front of them with a plunging and reckless step very rare with him, and when they reached the castle again he threw himself upon sleep with the simiplicity of a dog.

Despite his mystic praise of slumber, Father Brown was up earlier than anyone else except the silent gardener; and was found smoking a big pipe and watching that expert at his speechless labours in the kitchen garden. Towards daybreak the rocking storm had ended in roaring rains, and the day came with a curious freshness. The gardener seemed even to have been conversing, but at sight of the detective he planted his spade sullenly in a bed and, saying something about his breakfast, shifted along the lines of cabbages and shut himself in the kitchen. 'He's a valuable man, that,' said Father Brown. 'He does the potatoes amazingly. Still,' he added with a dispassionate charity, 'he has his faults; which of us hasn't? He doesn't dig this bank quite regularly. There, for instance,' and he stamped suddenly on one spot. 'I'm really very doubtful about that potato.'

'And why?' asked Craven, amused with the little man's new hobby.

'I'm doubtful about it,' said the other, 'because old Gow was doubtful about it himself. He put his spade in methodically in every place but just this. There must be a mighty fine potato just there.'

Flambeau pulled up the spade and impetuously drove it into the place. He turned up, under a load of soil, something that did not look like a potato, but rather like a monstrous, overdomed mushroom. But it stuck the spade with a cold click; it rolled over like a ball, and grinned up at them.

'The Earl of Glengyle,' said Brown sadly, and looked down heavily at the skull.

Then, after a momentary meditation, he plucked the spade from Flambeau, and, saying: 'We must hide it again,' clamped the skull down in the earth. Then he leaned his little body and huge head on the great handle of the spade, that stood up stiffly in the earth, and his eyes were empty and his forehead full of wrinkles. 'If one could only conceive,' he muttered, 'the meaning of this last monstrosity.' And leaning on the large spade handle, he buried his brows in his hands, as men do in church.

All the corners of the sky were brightening into blue and silver; the birds were chattering in the tiny garden trees; so loud it seemed as if the trees themselves were talking. But the three men were silent enough.

'Well, I give it all up,' said Flambeau at last boisterously. 'My brain and this world don't fit each other; and there's an end of it. Snuff, spoilt Prayer Books, and the insides of muscial boxes – what – '

Brown threw up his bothered brow and rapped on the spade handle with an intolerance quite unusual with him. 'Oh, tut, tut, tut, tut !' he cried. 'All that is as plain as a pikestaff. I understood the snuff and clockwork, and so on, when I first opened my eyes this morning. And since then I've had it out with old Gow, the gardener, who is neither so deaf nor so stupid as he pretends. There's something amiss about the loose items. I was wrong about the torn mass-book, too; there's no harm in that. But it's this last business. Desecrating graves and stealing dead men's heads – surely there's harm in that ? Surely there's black magic still in that ? That doesn't fit in to the quite simple story of the snuff and the candles.' And, striding about again, he smoked moodily.

'My friend,' said Flambeau, with a grim humour, 'you must be careful with me and remember I was once a criminal. The great advantage of that estate was that I always made up the story myself, and acted it as quick as I chose. This detective business of waiting about is too much for my French impatience. All my life, for good or evil, I have done things at the instant; I always fought duels the next morning; I always paid bills on the nail; I never even put off a visit to the dentist – '

Father Brown's pipe fell out of his mouth and broke into three pieces on the gravel path. He stood rolling his eyes, the exact picture of an idiot. 'Lord, what a turnip I am !' he kept saying. 'Lord, what a turnip !' Then, in a somewhat groggy kind of way, he began to laugh.

'The dentist !' he repeated. 'Six hours in the spiritual abyss, and all because I never thought of the dentist ! Such a simple, such a beautiful and peaceful thought ! Friends, we have passed a night in hell ; but now the sun is risen, the birds are singing, and the radiant form of the dentist consoles the world.'

'I will get some sense out of this,' cried Flambeau, striding forward, 'if I use the tortures of the Inquisition.'

Father Brown repressed what appeared to be a momentary disposition to dance on the now sunlit lawn and cried quite piteously, like a child : 'Oh, let me be silly a little. You don't know how unhappy I have been. And now I know that there has been no deep sin in this business at all. Only a little lunacy, perhaps — and who minds that ?'

He spun round once, then faced them with gravity.

'This is not a story of crime,' he said, 'rather it is the story of a strange and crooked honesty. We are dealing with the one man on earth, perhaps, who has taken no more than his due. It is a study in the savage living logic that has been the religion of this race.

'That old local rhyme about the house of Glengyle —

'"As green sap to the simmer trees
Is red gold to the Ogilvies"

was literal as well as metaphorical. It did not merely mean that the Glengyles sought for wealth ; it was also true that they literally gathered gold ; they had a huge collection of ornaments and utensils in that metal. They were, in fact, misers whose mania took that turn. In the light of that fact, run through all the things we found in the castle. Diamonds without their gold rings ; candles without their gold candlesticks ; snuff without the gold snuff-boxes ; pencil-leads without the gold pencil-cases ; a walking-stick without its gold top ; clockwork without the gold clocks — or rather watches. And, mad as it sound, because the haloes and the name of God in the old missals were of real gold, these also were taken away.'

The garden seemed to brighten, the grass to grow gayer in the strengthening sun, as the crazy truth was told. Flambeau lit a cigarette as his friend went on.

'Were taken away,' continued Father Brown ; 'were taken away — but not stolen. Thieves would never have left this mystery. Thieves would have taken the gold snuff-boxes, snuff and all ; the gold pencil-cases, lead and all. We have to deal with a man with a peculiar conscience, but certainly a conscience. I found that mad moralist this morning in a kitchen garden yonder, and I heard the whole story.

'The late Archbishop Ogilvie was the nearest approach to a good man ever born at Glengyle. But his bitter virtue took the turn of the misanthrope; he moped over the dishonesty of his ancestors, from which, somehow, he generalized a dishonesty of all men. More especially he distrusted philantrophy or free-giving; and he swore if he could find one man who took his exact rights he should have all the gold of Glengyle. Having delivered this defiance to humanity he shut himself up, without the smallest expectation of its being answered. One day, however, a deaf and seemingly senseless lad from a distant village brought him a belated telegram; and Glengyle, in his acrid pleasantry, gave him a new farthing. At least he thought he had done so, but when he turned over his change he found the new farthing still there and a sovereign gone. The accident offered him vistas of sneering speculation. Either way, the boy would show the greasy greed of the species. Either he would vanish, a thief stealing a coin; or he would sneak back with it virtuously, a snob seeking a reward. In the middle of the night Lord Glengyle was knocked up out of his bed – for he lived alone – and forced to open the door to the deaf idiot. The idiot brought with him, not the sovereign, but exactly nineteen shillings and eleven pence three-farthings in change.

'Then the wild exactitude of this action took hold of the mad lord's brain like fire. He swore he was Diogenes, that had long sought an honest man, and at last had found one. He made a new will, which I have seen. He took the literal youth into his huge, neglected house, and trained him up as his solitary servant and – after an odd manner – his heir. And whatever that queer creature understands, he understood absolutely his lord's two fixed ideas: first, that the letter of right is everything; and second, that he himself was to have the gold of Glengyle. So far, that is all; and that is simple. He has stripped the house of gold, and taken not a grain that was not gold; not so much as a grain of snuff. He lifted the gold leaf off an old illumination, fully satisfied that he left the rest unspoilt. All that I understand; but I could not understand this skull business. I was really uneasy about the human buried among the potatoes. It distressed me –

till Flambeau said the word.

'It will be all right. He will put the skull back in the grave, when he has taken the gold out of the tooth.'

And indeed, when Flambeau crossed the hill that morning, he saw the strange being, the just miser, digging at the desecrated grave, the plaid round his throat thrashing out in the mountain wind; the sober top hat on his head.

W. Somerset Maugham

The Four Dutchmen

The Van Dorth Hotel at Singapore was far from grand. The bedrooms were dingy and the mosquito nets patched and darned; the bath-houses, all in a row and detached from the bed-rooms, were dank and smelly. But it had character. The people who stayed there, masters of tramps whose round ended at Singapore, mining engineers out of a job and planters taking a holiday, to my mind bore a more romantic air than the smart folk, globe-trotters, government officials and their wives, wealthy merchants, who gave luncheon-parties at the Europe and played golf and danced and were fashionable. The Van Dorth had a billiard-room, with a table with a threadbare cloth, where ships' engineers and clerks in insurance offices played snooker. The dining-room was large and bare and silent. Dutch families on the way to Sumatra ate solidly through their dinner without exchanging a word with one another, and single gentlemen on a business trip from Batavia devoured a copious meal while they intently read their paper. On two days a week there was rijstafel and then a few residents of Singapore who had a fancy for this dish came for tiffin. The Van Dorth Hotel should have been a depressing place, but somehow it wasn't; its quaintness saved it. It had a faint aroma of something strange and half-forgotten. There was a scrap of garden facing the street where you could sit in the shade of trees and drink cold beer. In that crowded and busy city, though motors whizzed past and rickshaws passed continuously, the coolies' feet pattering on the road and their bells ringing, it had the remote peacefulness of a corner of Holland. It was the third time I had stayed at the Van Dorth. I had been told about it first by the skipper of a Dutch tramp, the S.S. *Utrecht*, on which I had travelled from Merauke in New Guinea to Macassar. The journey took the best part of a

101

month, since the ship stopped at a number of islands in the Malay Archipelago, the Aru and the Kei Islands, Banda-Neira, Amboina and others of which I have even forgotten the names, sometimes for an hour or two, sometimes for a day, to take on or discharge cargo. It was a charming, monotonous and diverting trip. When we dropped anchor the agent came out in his launch, and generally the Dutch Resident, and we gathered on deck under the awning and the captain ordered beer. The news of the island was exchanged for the news of the world. We brought papers and mail. If we were staying long enough the Resident asked us to dinner and, leaving the ship in charge of the second officer, we all (the captain, the chief officer, the engineer, the supercargo and I) piled into the launch and went ashore. We spent a merry evening. These little islands, one so like another, allured my fancy just because I knew that I should never see them again. It made them strangely unreal, and as we sailed away and they vanished into the sea and sky it was only by an effort of the imagination that I could persuade myself that they did not with my last glimpse of them cease to exist.

But there was nothing illusive, mysterious or fantastic about the captain, the chief officer, the chief engineer and the supercargo. Their solidity was amazing. They were the four fattest men I ever saw. At first I had great difficulty in telling them apart, for though one, the supercargo, was dark and the others were fair, they looked astonishingly alike. They were all big, with large round bare red faces, with large fat arms and large fat legs and large fat bellies. When they went ashore they buttoned up their stengah-shifters and then their great double chins bulged over the collars and they looked as though they would choke. But generally they wore them unbuttoned. They sweated freely and wiped their shiny faces with bandanas and vigorously fanned themselves with palm-leaf fans.

It was a treat to see them at tiffin. Their appetites were enormous. They had rijstafel every day, and each seemed to vie with the other how high he could pile his plate. They loved it hot and strong.

'In dis country you can't eat a ting onless it's tasty,' said the skipper.

'De only way to keep yourself up in dis country is to eat

hearty,' said the chief.

They were the greatest friends, all four of them ; they were like schoolboys together, playing absurd little pranks with one another. They knew each other's jokes by heart and no sooner did one of them start the familiar lines than he would splutter with laughter so violently, the heavy shaking laughter of the fat man, that the could not go on, and then the others began to laugh too. They rolled about in their chairs, and grew redder and redder, hotter and hotter, till the skipper shouted for beer, and each, gasping but happy, drank his bottle in one enchanted draught. They had been on this run together for five years and when, a little time before, the chief officer had been offered a ship of his own he refused it. He would not leave his companions. They had made up their minds that when the first of them retired they would all retire.

'All friends and a good ship. Good grub and good beer. Vot can a sensible man vant more ?'

At first they were a little stand-offish with me. Although the ship had accommodation for half a dozen passengers, they did not often get any, and never one whom they did not know. I was a stranger and a foreigner. They liked their bit of fun and did not want anyone to interfere with it. But they were all of them very fond of bridge, and on occasion the chief and the engineer had duties that prevented one or the other from playing. They were willing to put up with me when they discovered that I was ready to make a fourth whenever I was wanted. Their bridge was as incredibly fantastic as they were. They played for infinitesimal stakes, five cents a hundred : they did not want to win one another's money, they said, it was the game they liked. But what a game ! Each was wildly determined to play the hand and hardly one was dealt without at least a small slam being declared. The rule was that if you could get a peep at somebody's else's cards you did and if you could get away with a revoke you told your partner when there was no danger it could be claimed and you both roared with laughter till the tears rolled down your fat cheeks. But if your partner had insisted on taking the bid away from you and had called a grand slam on five spades to the queen, whereas you were positive on your seven little diamonds you could have made it easily, you could always score him off by redoubling without a trick in your hand. He went down two or three thousand and the glasses on the table danced with the laughter that shook your opponents.

I could never remember their difficult Dutch names, but knowing them anonymously as it were, only by the duties they performed, as one knows the characters Pantaloon, Harlequin and Punchinello, of the old Italian comedy, added grotesquely to their drollery. The mere sight of them, all four together, set you laughing, and I think they got a good deal of amusement from the astonishment they caused in strangers. They boasted that they were the four most famous Dutchmen in the East Indies. To me not the least comic part of them was their serious side. Sometimes late at night, when they had given up all pretence of still wearing their uniforms, and one or the other of them lay by my side on a long chair in a pyjama jacket and a sarong, he would grow sentimental. The chief engineer, due to retire soon, was meditating marriage with a widow whom he had met when last he was home and spending the rest of his life in a little town with old red-brick houses on the shores of the Zuyder Zee. But the captain was very susceptible to the charms of the native girls and his thick English became almost unintelligible from emotion when he described to me the effect they had on him. One of these days he would buy himself a house on the hills in Java and marry a pretty little Javanese. They were so small and so gentle and they made no noise, and he would dress her in silk sarongs and give her gold chains to wear round her neck and gold bangles to put on her arms. But the chief mocked him.

'Silly all dat is. Silly. She goes mit all your friends and de house boys and everybody. By de time you retire, my dear, vot you'll vant vill be a nurse, not a vife.'

'Me' cried the skipper. 'I shall want a vife ven I'm eighty!'

He had picked up a little thing last time the ship was at Macassar and as we approached that port he began to be all of a flutter. The chief officer shrugged fat and indulgent shoulders. The captain was always losing his head over one brazen hussy after another, but his passion never survived the interval between one stop at a port and the next, and then the chief was called in to smooth out the difficulties that ensued. And so it would be this time.

'De old man suffers from fatty degeneration of de heart. But so long as I'm dere to look after him not much harm comes of it. He vastes his money and dat's a pity, but as long as he's got it to vaste, why shouldn't he?'

The chief officer had a philosophic soul.

At Macassar then I disembarked, and bade farewell to my four fat friends.

'Make another journey with us,' they said. 'Come back next year or the year after. You'll find us all here just the same as ever.'

A good many months had passed since then and I had wandered through more than one strange land. I had been to Bali and Java and Sumatra; I had been to Cambodia and Annam; and now, feeling as though I were home again, I sat in the garden of the Van Dorth Hotel. It was cool in the very early morning and having had breakfast I was looking at back numbers of the *Straits Times* to find out what had been happening in the world since last I had been within reach of papers. Nothing very much. Suddenly my eyes caught a headline: *The* Utrecht *Tragedy. Supercargo and Chief Engineer. Not Guilty.* I read the paragraph carelessly and then I sat up. The *Utrecht* was the ship of my four fat Dutchmen and apparently the supercargo and the chief engineer had been on trial for murder. It couldn't be my two fat friends. The names were given, but the names meant nothing to me. The trial had taken place in Batavia. No details were given in this paragraph; it was only a brief announcement that after the judges had considered the speeches of the prosecution and of the defence their verdict was as stated. I was astounded. It was incredible that the men I knew could have committed a murder. I could not find out who had been murdered. I looked through back numbers of the paper. Nothing.

I got up and went to the manager of the hotel, a genial Dutchman, who spoke admirable English, and showed him the paragraph.

'That's the ship I sailed on. I was in her for nearly a month. Surely these fellows aren't the men I knew. The men I knew were enormously fat.'

'Yes, that's right,' he answered. 'They were celebrated all through the Dutch East Indies, the four fattest men in the service. It's been a terrible thing. It made a great sensation. And they were friends. I knew them all. The best fellows in the world.'

'But what happened?'

He told me the story and answered my horrified questions. But there were things I wanted to know that he couldn't tell me. It was all confused. It was unbelievable. What actually had happened was only conjecture. Then someone claimed the manager's attention and I went back to the garden. It was getting hot now and I went up to my room. I was strangely shattered.

It appeared that on one of the trips the captain took with him a Malay girl that he had been carrying on with and I wondered if it was the one he had been so eager to see when I was on board. The other three had been against her coming – what did they want with a woman in the ship? It would spoil everything – but the captain insisted and she came. I think they were all jealous of her. On that journey they didn't have the fun they generally had. When they wanted to play bridge the skipper was dallying with the girl in his cabin; when they touched at a port and went ashore the time seemed long to him till he could get back to her. He was crazy about her. It was the end of all their larks. The chief officer was more bitter against her than anybody: he was the captain's particular chum, they had been shipmates ever since they first came out from Holland; more than once high words passed between them on the subject of the captain's infatuation. Presently those old friends spoke to one another only when their duties demanded it. It was the end of the good fellowship that had so long obtained between the four fat men. Things went from bad to worse. There was a feeling among the junior officers that something untoward was pending. Uneasiness. Tension. Then one night the ship was aroused by the sound of a shot and the screams of the Malay girl. The supercargo and the chief engineer tumbled out of their bunks and they found the captain, a revolver in his hand, at the door of the chief officer's cabin. He pushed past them and went on deck. They entered and found the chief officer dead and the girl cowering behind the door. The captain had found them in bed together and had killed the chief. How he had discovered what was going on didn't seem to be known, nor what was the meaning of the intrigue. Had the chief induced the girl to come to his cabin in order to get back on the captain, or had she, knowing his ill-will and anxious to placate him, lured him to become her lover? It was a mystery that would never be solved. A dozen possible explanations flashed across my mind. While the engineer and the supercargo were in the cabin, horror-struck at the sight before them, another shot was heard. They knew at once what had happened. They rushed up the companion. The captain had gone to his cabin and blown his brains out. Then the story grew dark and enigmatic. Next morning the Malay girl was nowhere to be found and when the second officer, who had taken command of the ship, reported this to the supercargo, the supercargo said: 'She's probably jumped overboard. It's the best thing she could have done. Good riddance to bad rubbish.' But one of the sailors on the watch, just before dawn, had seen the supercargo and the chief engineer carry something up on deck, a bulky package, about the size of a native woman, look about them to see that they were unobserved, and drop it overboard; and it was said all over the ship that these two to avenge their friends had sought the girl out in her cabin and strangled her and flung her body into the sea. When the ship arrived at Macassar they were arrested and taken to Batavia to be tried for murder. The evidence was flimsy and they were acquitted. But all through the East Indies they knew that the supercargo and the chief engineer had executed justice on the trollop who had caused the death of the two men they loved.

And thus ended the comic and celebrated friendship of the four fat Dutchmen.

Jeeves and the Hard-boiled Egg

Sometimes of a morning, as I've sat in bed sucking down the early cup of tea and watched Jeeves flitting about the room and putting out the raiment for the day, I've wondered what the deuce I should do if the fellow ever took it into his head to leave me. It's not so bad when I'm in New York, but in London the anxiety is frightful. There used to be all sorts of attempts on the part of low blighters to sneak him away from me. Young Reggie Foljambe to my certain knowledge offered him double what I was giving him, and Alistair Bingham-Reeves, who's got a valet who had been known to press his trousers sideways, used to look at him, when he came to see me, with a kind of glittering, hungry eye which disturbed me deucedly. Bally pirates!

The thing, you see, is that Jeeves is so dashed competent. You can spot it even in the way he shoves studs into a shirt.

I rely on him absolutely in every crisis, and he never lets me down. And, what's more, he can always be counted on to extend himself on behalf of any pal of mine who happens to be to all appearances knee-deep in the bouillon. Take the rather rummy case, for instance, of dear old Bicky and his uncle, the hard-boiled egg.

It happened after I had been in America for a few months. I got back to the flat latish one night, and when Jeeves brought me the final drink he said:

'Mr Bickersteth called to see you this evening, sir, while you were out.'

'Oh?' I said.

'Twice, sir. He appeared a trifle agitated.'

'What, pipped?'

'He gave that impression, sir.'

I sipped the whisky. I was sorry if Bicky was in trouble, but, as a matter of fact, I was rather glad to have something I could discuss freely with Jeeves just then, because things had been a bit strained between us for some time, and it had been rather difficult to hit on anything to talk about that wasn't apt to take a personal turn. You see, I had decided – rightly or wrongly – to grow a moustache, and this had cut Jeeves to the quick. He couldn't stick the thing at any price, and I had been living ever since in an atmosphere of bally disapproval till I was getting jolly well fed up with it. What I mean is, while there's no doubt that in certain matters of dress Jeeves's judgment is absolutely sound and should be followed, it seemed to me that it was getting a bit too thick if he was going to edit my face as well as my costume. No one can call me an unreasonable chappie, and many's the time I've given in like a lamb when Jeeves has voted against one of my pet suits or ties; but when it comes to a valet's staking out a claim on your upper lip you've simply got to have a bit of the good old bulldog pluck and defy the blighter.

'He said that he would call again later, sir.'

'Something must be up, Jeeves.'

'Yes, sir.'

I gave the moustache a thoughtful twirl. It seemed to hurt Jeeves a good deal, so I chucked it.

'I see by the paper, sir, that Mr Bickersteth's uncle is arriving on the *Carmantic*.'

'Yes?'

'His Grace the Duke of Chiswick, sir.'

This was news to me, that Bicky's uncle was a duke. Rum, how little one knows about one's pals. I had met Bicky for the first time at a species of beano or jamboree down in Washington Square, not long after my arrival in New York. I suppose I was a bit homesick at the time, and I rather took to Bicky when I found that he was an Englishman and had, in fact, been up at Oxford with me. Besides, he was a frightful chump, so we naturally drifted together; and while we were taking a quiet snort in a corner that wasn't all cluttered up with artists and sculptors, he furthermore endeared himself to me by a most extraordinarily gifted imitation of a bull-terrier chasing a cat up a tree. But, though we had subsequently become extremely pally, all I really knew about him was that he was generally hard up, and had an uncle who relieved the strain a bit from time to time by sending him monthly remittances.

'If the Duke of Chiswick is his uncle,' I said, 'why hasn't he a title ? Why isn't he Lord What-Not ?'

'Mr Bickersteth is the son of His Grace's late sister, sir, who married Captain Rollo Bickersteth of the Coldstream Guards.'

Jeeves knows everything.

'Is Mr Bickersteth's father dead too ?'

'Yes, sir.'

'Leave any money ?'

'No, sir.'

I began to understand why poor old Bicky was always more or less on the rocks. To the casual and irreflective observer it may sound a pretty good wheeze having a duke for an uncle, but the trouble about old Chiswick was that, though an extremely wealthy old buster, owning half London and about five counties up north, he was notoriously the most prudent spender in England. He was what Americans call a hard-boiled egg. If Bicky's people hadn't left him anything and he depended on what he could prise out of the old duke, he was in a pretty bad way. Not that that explained why he was hunting me like this, because he was a chap who never borrowed money. He said he wanted to keep his pals, so never bit anyone's ear on principle.

At this juncture the door-bell rang. Jeeves floated out to answer it.

'Yes, sir. Mr Wooster has just returned,' I heard him say. And Bicky came beetling in, looking pretty sorry for himself.

'Hallo, Bicky,' I said. 'Jeeves told me you had been trying to get me. What's the trouble, Bicky ?'

'I'm in a hole, Bertie. I want your advice.'

'Say on, old lad.'

'My uncle's turning up to-morrow, Bertie.'

'So Jeeves told me.'

'The Duke of Chiswick, you know.'

'So Jeeves told me.'

Bicky seemed a bit surprised.

'Jeeves seems to know everything.'

'Rather rummily, that's exactly what I was thinking just now myself.'

'Well, I wish,' said Bicky, gloomily, 'that he knew a way to get me out of the hole I'm in.'

'Mr Bickersteth is in a hole, Jeeves,' I said, 'and wants you to rally round.'

'Very good, sir.'

Bicky looked a bit doubtful.

'Well, of course, you know, Bertie, this thing is by way of being a bit private and all that.'

'I shouldn't worry about that, old top. I bet Jeeves knows all about it already. Don't you, Jeeves?'

'Yes, sir.'

'Eh?' said Bicky, rattled.

'I am open to correction, sir, but is not your dilemma due to the fact that you are at a loss to explain to His Grace why you are in New York instead of in Colorado?'

Bicky rocked like a jelly in a high wind.

'How the deuce do you know anything about it?'

'I chanced to meet His Grace's butler before we left England. He informed me that he happened to overhear His Grace speaking to you on the matter, sir, as he passed the library door.'

Bicky gave a hollow sort of laugh.

'Well, as everybody seems to know all about it, there's no need to try to keep it dark. The old boy turfed me out, Bertie, because he said I was a brainless nincompoop. The idea was that he would give me a remittance on condition that I dashed out to some blighted locality of the name of Colorado and learned farming or ranching, or whatever they call it, at some bally ranch or farm, or whatever it's called. I didn't fancy the idea a bit. I should have had to ride horses and pursue cows, and so forth. At the same time, don't you know, I had to have that remittance.'

'I get you absolutely, old thing.'

'Well, when I got to New York it looked a decent sort of place to me, so I thought it would be a pretty sound notion to stop here. So I cabled to my uncle telling him that I had dropped into a good business wheeze in the city and wanted to chuck the ranch idea. He wrote back that it was all right, and here I've been ever since. He thinks I'm doing well at something or other over here. I never dreamed, don't you know, that he would ever come out here. What on earth am I to do?'

'Jeeves,' I said, 'what on earth is Mr Bickersteth to do?'

'You see,' said Bicky, 'I had a wireless from him to say that he was coming to stay with me – to save hotel bills, I suppose. I've always given him the impression that I was living in pretty good style. I can't have him to stay at my boarding-house.'

'Thought of anything, Jeeves?' I said.

'To what extent, sir, if the question is not a delicate one, are you prepared to assist Mr Bickersteth?'

'I'll do anything I can for you, of course, Bicky, old man.'

'Then, if I might make the suggestion, sir, you might lend Mr Bickersteth – '

'No, by Jove!' said Bicky firmly. 'I never have touched you, Bertie, and I'm not going to start now. I may be a chump, but it's my boast that I don't owe a penny to a single soul – not counting tradesmen, of course.'

'I was about to suggest, sir, that you might lend Mr Bickersteth this flat. Mr Bickersteth could give His Grace the impression that he was the owner of it. With your permission I could convey the notion that I was in Mr Bickersteth's employment and not in yours. You would be residing here temporarily as Mr Bickersteth's guest. His Grace would occupy the second spare bedroom. I fancy that you would find this answer satisfactorily, sir.'

Bicky had stopped rocking himself and was staring at Jeeves in an awed sort of way.

'I would advocate the dispatching of a wireless message to His Grace on board the vessel, notifying him of the change of address. Mr Bickersteth could meet His Grace at the dock and proceed directly here. Will that meet the situation, sir?'

'Absolutely.'

'Thank you, sir.'

Bicky followed him with his eye till the door closed.

'How does he do it, Bertie?' he said. 'I'll tell you what I think it is. I believe it's something to do with the shape of his head. Have you ever noticed his head, Bertie, old man? It sort of sticks out at the back!'

I hopped out of bed pretty early next morning, so as to be among those present when the old boy should arrive. I knew from experience that these ocean liners fetch up at the dock at a deucedly ungodly hour. It wasn't much after nine by the time I'd dressed and had my morning tea and was leaning out of the

window, watching the street for Bicky and his uncle. It was one
of those jolly, peaceful mornings that made a chappie wish he'd
got a soul or something, and I was just brooding on life in
general when I became aware of the dickens of a spat in progress
down below. A taxi had driven up, and an old boy in a top hat
had got out and was kicking up a frightful row about the fare. As
far as I could make out, he was trying to get the cabby to switch
from New York to London prices, and the cabby had apparently
never heard of London before, and didn't seem to think a lot of it
now. The old boy said that in London the trip would have set
him back a shilling ; and the cabby said he should worry. I called
to Jeeves.

'The duke has arrived, Jeeves.'

'Yes, sir ?'

'That'll be him at the door now.'

Jeeves made a long arm and opened the front door, and the
old boy crawled in.

'How do you do sir ?' I said, bustling up and being the ray of
sunshine. 'Your nephew went down to the dock to meet you, but
you must have missed him. My name's Wooster, don't you
know. Great pal of Bicky's, and all that sort of thing. I'm staying
with him, you know. Would you like a cup of tea ? Jeeves, bring
a cup of tea.'

Old Chiswick had sunk into an arm-chair and was looking
about the room.

'Does this luxurious flat belong to my nephew Francis ?'

'Absolutely.'

'It must be terribly expensive.'

'Pretty well, of course. Everything costs a lot over here, you
know.'

He moaned. Jeeves filtered in with the tea. Old Chiswick took
a stab at it to restore his tissues, and nodded.

'A terrible country, Mr Wooster ! A terrible country. Nearly
eight shillings for a short cab-drive. Iniquitious !' He took
another look round the room. It seemed to fascinate him. 'Have
you any idea how much my nephew pays for this flat, Mr
Wooster ?'

'About two hundred dollars a month, I believe.'

'What ! Forty pounds a month !'

I began to see that, unless I made the thing a bit more

plausible, the scheme might turn out a frost. I could guess what the old boy was thinking. He was trying to square all this prosperity with what he knew of poor old Bicky. And one had to admit that it took a lot of squaring, for dear old Bicky, though a stout fellow and absolutely unrivalled as an imitator of bull-terriers and cats, was in many ways one of the most pronounced fatheads that ever pulled on a suit of gents' underwear.

'I suppose it seems rummy to you,' I said, 'but the fact is New York often bucks fellows up and makes them show a flash of speed that you wouldn't have imagined them capable of. It sort of develops them. Something in the air, don't you know. I imagine that Bicky in the past, when you knew him, may have been something of a chump, but it's quite different now. Devilish efficient sort of bird, and looked on in commercial circles as quite the nib!'

'I am amazed! What is the nature of my nephew's business, Mr Wooster?'

'Oh, just business, don't you know. The same sort of thing Rockefeller and all these coves do, you know.' I slid for the door. 'Awfully sorry to leave you, but I've got to meet some of the lads elsewhere.'

Coming out of the lift I met Bicky bustling in from the street.

'Hallo, Bertie. I missed him. Has he turned up?'

'He's upstairs now, having some tea.'

'What does he think of it all?'

'He's absolutely rattled.'

'Ripping! I'll be toddling up, then. Toodle-oo, Bertie, old man. See you later.'

'Pip-pip, Bicky, dear boy.'

He trotted off, full of merriment and good cheer, and I went off to the club to sit in the window and watch the traffic coming up one way and going down the other.

It was latish in the evening when I looked in at the flat to dress for dinner.

'Where's everybody, Jeeves?' I said, finding no little feet pattering about the place. 'Gone out?'

'His Grace desired to see some of the sights of the city, sir. Mr Bickersteth is acting as his escort. I fancy their immediate objective was Grant's Tomb.'

'I suppose Mr Bickersteth is a bit bucked at the way things are going – what ?'

'Sir ?'

'I say, I take it that Mr Bickersteth is tolerably full of beans.'

'Not altogether, sir.'

'What's his trouble now ?'

'The scheme which I took the liberty of suggesting to Mr Bickersteth and yourself has, unfortunately, not answered entirely satisfactorily, sir.'

'Surely the duke believes that Mr Bickersteth is doing well in business, and all that sort of thing ?'

'Exactly, sir. With the result that he has decided to cancel Mr Bickersteth's monthly allowance, on the ground that, as Mr Bickersteth is doing so well on his own account, he no longer requires pecuniary assistance.'

'Great Scott, Jeeves ! This is awful !'

'Somewhat disturbing, sir.'

'I never expected anything like this !'

'I confess I scarcely anticipated the contingency myself, sir.'

'I suppose it bowled the poor blighter over absolutely ?'

'Mr Bickersteth appeared somewhat taken aback, sir.'

My heart bled for Bicky.

'We must do something, Jeeves.'

'Yes, sir.'

'Can you think of anything ?'

'Not at the moment, sir.'

'There must be something we can do.'

'It was the maxim of one of my former employers, sir – as I believe I mentioned to you once before – the present Lord Bridgworth, that there is always a way. No doubt we shall be able to discover some solution of Mr Bickersteth's difficulty, sir.'

'Well, have a stab at it, Jeeves.'

'I will spare no pains, sir.'

I went and dressed sadly. It will show you pretty well how pipped I was when I tell you that I as near as a toucher put on a white tie with a dinner-jacket. I sallied out for a bit of food more to pass the time than because I wanted it. It seemed brutal to be wading into the bill of fare with poor old Bicky headed for the breadline.

When I got back old Chiswick had gone to bed, but Bicky was there, hunched up in an arm-chair, brooding pretty tensely, with a cigarette hanging out of the corner of his mouth and a more or less glassy stare in his eyes.

'This is a bit thick, old thing – what!' I said.

He picked up his glass and drained it feverishly, overlooking the fact that it hadn't anything in it.

'I'm done, Bertie!' he said.

He had another go at the glass. It didn't seem to do him any good.

'If only this had happened a week later, Bertie! My next month's money was due to roll in on Saturday. I could have worked a wheeze I've been reading about in the magazine advertisements. It seems that you can made a dashed amount of money if you can only collect a few dollars and start a chicken-farm. Jolly life, too, keeping hens!' He had begun to get quite worked up at the thought of it, but he slopped back in his chair at this juncture with a good deal of gloom. 'But, of course, it's no good,' he said, 'because I haven't the cash.'

'You've only to say the word, you know, Bicky, old top.'

'Thanks awfully, Bertie, but I'm not going to sponge on you.'

That's always the way in this world. The chappies you'd like to lend money to won't let you, whereas the chappies you don't want to lend it to will do everything except actually stand you on your head and lift the specie out of your pockets. As a lad who has always rolled tolerably freely in the right stuff, I've had lots of experience of the second class. Many's the time, back in London, I've hurried along Piccadilly and felt the hot breath of the toucher on the back of my neck and heard his sharp, excited yapping as he closed in on me. I've simply spent my life scattering largesse to blighters I didn't care a hang for; yet here was I now, dripping doubloons and pieces of eight and longing to hand them over, and Bicky, poor fish, absolutely on his uppers, not taking any at any price.

'Well, there's only one hope then.'

'What's that?'

'Jeeves.'

'Sir?'

There was Jeeves, standing behind me, full of zeal. In this matter of shimmering into rooms the man is rummy to a degree. You're sitting in the old arm-chair, thinking of this and that, and then suddenly you look up, and there he is. He moves from point to point with as little uproar as a jelly-fish. The thing startled poor old Bicky considerably. He rose from his seat like a rocketing pheasant. I'm used to Jeeves now, but often in the days when he first came to me I've bitten my tongue freely on finding him unexpectedly in my midst.

'Did you call, sir?'

'Oh, there you are, Jeeves!'

'Precisely, sir.'

'Any ideas, Jeeves?'

'Why, yes, sir. Since we had our recent conversation I fancy I have found what may prove a solution. I do not wish to appear to be taking a liberty, sir, but I think that we have overlooked His Grace's potentialities as a source of revenue.'

Bicky laughed what I have sometimes seen described as a hollow, mocking laugh, a sort of bitter cackle from the back of the throat, rather like a gargle.

'I do not allude, sir,' explained, Jeeves, 'to the possibility of inducing His Grace to part with money. I am taking the liberty of regarding His Grace in the light of an at present – if I may say so – useless property, which is capable of being developed.'

Bicky looked at me in a helpless kind of way. I'm bound to say I didn't get it myself.

'Couldn't you make it a bit easier, Jeeves?'

'In a nutshell, sir, what I mean is this : His Grace is, in a sense, a prominent personage. The inhabitants of this country, as no doubt you are aware, sir, are peculiarly addicted to shaking hands with prominent personages. It occurred to me that Mr Bickersteth or yourself might know of persons who would be willing to pay a small fee – let us say two dollars or three – for the privilege of an introduction, including handshake, to His Grace.'

Bicky didn't seem to think much of it.

'Do you mean to say that anyone would be mug enough to part with solid cash just to shake hands with my uncle?'

'I have an aunt, sir, who paid five shillings to a young fellow for bringing a moving-picture actor to tea at her house one Sunday. It gave her social standing among the neighbours.'

Bicky wavered.

'If you think it could be done – '

'I feel convinced of it, sir.'

'What do you think, Bertie ?'

'I'm for it, old boy, absolutely. A very brainy wheeze.'

'Thank you, sir. Will there be anything further ? Good night, sir.'

And he flitted out, leaving us to discuss details.

Until we started this business of floating old Chiswick as a money-making proposition I had never realised what a perfectly foul time those Stock Exchange fellows must have when the public isn't biting freely. Nowadays I read that bit they put in the financial reports about 'The market opened quietly' with a sympathetic eye, for, by Jove, it certainly opened quietly for us. You'd hardly believe how difficult it was to interest the public and make them take a flutter on the old boy. By the end of a week the only name we had on our list was a delicatessen-store keeper down in Bicky's part of the town, and as he wanted us to take it out in sliced ham instead of cash that didn't help much. There was a gleam of light when the brother of Bicky's pawnbroker offered ten dollars, money down, for an introduction to old Chiswick, but the deal fell through, owing to its turning out that the chap was an anarchist and intended to kick the old boy instead of shaking hands with him. At that, it took me the deuce of a time to persuade Bicky not to grab the cash and let things take their course. He seemed to regard the pawnbroker's brother rather as a sportsman and benefactor of his species than otherwise.

The whole thing, I'm inclined to think, would have been off if it hadn't been for Jeeves. There is no doubt that Jeeves is in a class of his own. In the matter of brain and resource I don't think I have ever met a chappie so supremely like mother made. He trickled into my room one morning with the good old cup of tea, and intimated that there was something doing.

'Might I speak to you with regard to that matter of His Grace, sir ?'

'It's all off. We've decided to chuck it.'

'Sir ?'

'It won't work. We can't get anybody to come.'

'I fancy I can arrange that aspect of the matter, sir.'

'Do you mean to say you've managed to get anybody ?'

'Yes, sir. Eighty-seven gentlemen from Birdsburg, sir.'

I sat up in bed and spilt the tea.

'Birdsburg?'

'Birdsburg, Missouri, sir.'

'How did you get them?'

'I happened last night, sir, as you had intimated that you would be absent from home, to attend a theatrical performance, and entered into conversation between the acts with the occupant of the adjoining seat. I had observed that he was wearing a somewhat ornate decoration in his buttonhole, sir – a large blue button with the words 'Boost for Birdsburg' upon it in red letters, scarcely a judicious addition to a gentleman's evening costume. To my surprise I noticed that the auditorium was full of persons similarly decorated. I ventured to inquire the explanation, and was informed that these gentlemen, forming a party of eighty-seven, are a convention from a town of the name of Birdsburg in the State of Missouri. Their visit, I gathered, was purely of a social and pleasurable nature, and my informant spoke at some length of the entertainments arranged for their stay in the city. It was when he related with a considerable amount of satisfaction and pride that a deputation of their number had been introduced to and had shaken hands with a well-known prize-fighter that it occurred to me to broach the subject of His Grace. To make a long story short, sir, I have arranged, subject to your approval, that the entire convention shall be presented to His Grace to-morrow afternoon.'

I was amazed.

'Eighty-seven, Jeeves!' At how much a head?'

'I was obliged to agree to a reduction for quantity, sir. The terms finally arrived at were one hundred and fifty dollars for the party.'

I thought a bit.

'Payable in advance?'

'No, sir. I endeavoured to obtain payment in advance, but was not successful.'

'Well, anyway, when we get it I'll make it up to five hundred. Bicky'll never know. Do you suppose Mr Bickersteth would suspect anything, Jeeves, if I made it up to five hundred?'

'I fancy not, sir. Mr Bickersteth is an agreeable gentleman, but not bright.'

'All right, then. After breakfast run down to the bank and get me some money.'

'Yes, sir.'

'You know, you're a bit of a marvel, Jeeves.'

'Thank you, sir.'

'Right ho !'

'Very good, sir.'

When I took dear old Bicky aside in the course of the morning and told him what had happened he nearly broke down. He tottered into the sitting-room and buttonholed old Chiswick, who was reading the comic section of the morning paper with a kind of grim resolution.

'Uncle,' he said, 'are you doing anything special to-morrow afternoon ? I mean to say, I've asked a few of my pals in to meet you, don't you know.'

The old boy cocked a speculative eye at him.

'There will be no reporters among them ?'

'Reporters ? Rather not. Why ?'

'I refuse to be badgered by reporters. There were a number of adhesive young men who endeavoured to elicit from me my views on America while the boat was approaching the dock. I will not be subjected to this persecution again.'

'That'll be absolutely all right, uncle. There won't be a newspaper man in the place.'

'In that case I shall be glad to make the acquaintance of your friends.'

'You'll shake hands with them, and so forth ?'

'I shall naturally order my behaviour according to the accepted rules of civilised intercourse.'

Bicky thanked him heartily and came off to lunch with me at the club, where he babbled freely of hens, incubators, and other rotten things.

After mature consideration we had decided to unleash the Birdsburg contingent on the old boy ten at a time. Jeeves brought his theatre pal round to see us, and we arranged the whole thing with him. A very decent chappie, but rather inclined to collar the conversation and turn it in the direction of his home-town's new water-supply system. We settled that, as an hour was about all he would be likely to stand, each gang should consider itself entitled to seven minutes of the duke's society by Jeeves's stop-watch, and that when their time was up Jeeves should slide into the room and cough meaningly. Then we parted with what I believe are called mutual expressions of good-will, the Birdsburg chappie extending a cordial invitation to us all to pop out some day and take a look at the new water-supply system, for which we thanked him.

Next day the deputation rolled in. The first shift consisted of the cove we had met and nine others almost exactly like him in every respect. They all looked deuced keen and businesslike, as if from youth up they had been working in the office and catching the boss's eye and what not. They shook hands with the old boy with a good deal of apparent satisfaction – all except one chappie, who seemed to be brooding about something – and then they stood off and became chatty.

'What message have you for Birdsburg, duke?' asked our pal.

The old boy seemed a bit rattled.

'I have never been to Birdsburg.'

The chappie seemed pained.

'You should pay it a visit,' he said. 'The most rapidly-growing city in the country. Boost for Birdsburg!'

'"Boost for Birdsburg!" said the other chappie reverently.

The chappie who had been brooding suddenly gave tongue.

'Say!'

He was a stout sort of well-fed cove with one of those determined chins and a cold eye.

The assemblage looked at him.

'As a matter of business,' said the chappie – 'mind you, I'm not questioning anybody's good faith, but, as a matter of strict business – I think this gentleman here ought to put himself on record before witnesses as stating that he really is a duke.'

'What do you mean, sir?' cried the old boy, getting purple.

'No offence, simply business. I'm not saying anything, mind you, but there's one thing that seems kind of funny to me. This gentleman here says his name's Mr Bickersteth, as I understand it. Well, if you're the Duke of Chiswick, why isn't he Lord Percy Something? I've read English novels, and I know all about it.'

'This is monstrous!'

'Now don't get hot under the collar. I'm only asking. I've a right to know. You're going to take our money, so it's only fair that we should see that we get our money's worth.'

The water-supply cove chipped in:

'You're quite right, Simms. I overlooked that when making the agreement. You see, gentlemen, as business men we've a right to reasonable guarantees of good faith. We are paying Mr Bickersteth here a hundred and fifty dollars for this reception, and we naturally want to know – '

Old Chiswick gave Bicky a searching look; then he turned to the water-supply chappie. He was frightfully calm.

'I can assure you that I know nothing of this,' he said quite politely. 'I should be grateful if you would explain.'

'Well, we arranged with Mr Bickersteth that eighty-seven citizens of Birdsburg should have the privilege of meeting and shaking hands with you for a financial consideration mutually arranged, and what my friend Simms here means – and I'm with him – is that we have only Mr Bickersteth's word for it – and he is a stranger to us – that you are the Duke of Chiswick at all.'

Old Chiswick gulped.

'Allow me to assure you, sir,' he said in a rummy kind of voice, 'that I am the Duke of Chiswick.'

'Then that's all right,' said the chappie heartily. 'That was all we wanted to know. Let the thing go on.'

'I am sorry to say,' said old Chiswick, 'that it cannot go on. I am feeling a little tired. I fear I must ask to be excused.'

'But there are seventy-seven of the boys waiting round the corner at this moment, duke, to be introduced to you.'

'I fear I must disappoint them.'

'But in that case the deal would have to be off.'

'That is a matter for you and my nephew to discuss.'

The chappie seemed troubled.

'You really won't meet the rest of them?'

'No!'

'Well, then, I guess we'll be going.'

They went out, and there was a pretty solid silence. Then old Chiswick turned to Bicky:

'Well?'

Bicky didn't seem to have anything to say.

'Was it true what that man said?'

'Yes, uncle.'

'What do you mean by playing this trick?'

Bicky seemed pretty well knocked out, so I put in a word:

'I think you'd better explain the whole thing, Bicky, old top.'

Bicky's adam's-apple jumped about a bit; then he started.

'You see, you had cut off my allowance, uncle, and I wanted a bit of money to start a chicken farm. I mean to say it's an absolute cert if you once get a bit of capital. You buy a hen, and it lays an egg every day of the week, and you sell the eggs, say, seven for twenty-five cents. Keep of hen costs nothing. Profit practically – '

'What is all this nonsense about hens? You led me to suppose you were a substantial business man.'

'Old Bicky rather exaggerated, sir,' I said, helping the chappie out. 'The fact is, the poor old lad is absolutely dependent on that remittance of yours, and when you cut it off, don't you know, he was pretty solidly in the soup, and had to think of some way of closing in on a bit of the ready pretty quick. That's why we thought of this hand-shaking scheme.'

Old Chiswick foamed at the mouth.

'So you have lied to me! You have deliberately deceived me as to your financial status!'

'Poor old Bicky didn't want to go to that ranch,' I explained. 'He doesn't like cows and horses, but he rather thinks he would be hot stuff among the hens. All he wants is a bit of capital. Don't you think it would be rather a wheeze if you were to – '

'After what has happened? After this – this deceit and foolery? Not a penny!'

'But – '

'Not a penny!'

There was a respectful cough in the background.

'If I might make a suggestion, sir?'

Jeeves was standing on the horizon, looking devilish brainy.

'Go ahead, Jeeves!' I said.

'I would merely suggest, sir, that if Mr Bickersteth is in need of a little ready money, and is at a loss to obtain it elsewhere, he might secure the sum he requires by describing the occurrences of this afternoon for the Sunday issue of one of the more spirited and enterprising newspapers.'

'By Jove!' I said.

'By George!' said Bicky.

'Great heavens !' said old Chiswick.

'Very good, sir,' said Jeeves.

Bicky turned to old Chiswick with a gleaming eye.

'Jeeves is right ! I'll do it ! The *Chronicle* would jump at it. They eat that sort of stuff.'

Old Chiswick gave a kind of moaning howl.

'I absolutely forbid you, Francis, to do this thing !'

'That's all very well,' said Bicky, wonderfully braced, 'but if I can't get the money any other way – '

'Wait ! Er – wait, my boy ! You are so impetuous ! We might arrange something.'

'I won't go to that bally ranch.'

'No, no ! No, no, my boy ! I would not suggest it. I would not for a moment suggest it. I – I think – ' He seemed to have a bit of a struggle with himself. 'I – I think that, on the whole, it would be best if you returned with me to England. I – I might – in fact, I think I see my way to doing – to – I might be able to utilise your services in some secretarial position.'

'I shouldn't mind that.'

'I should not be able to offer you a salary, but, as you know, in English political life the unpaid secretary is a recognised figure –'

'The only figure I'll recognise,' said Bicky firmly, 'is five hundred quid a year, paid quarterly.'

'My dear boy !'

'Absolutely !'

'But your recompense, my dear Francis, would consist in the unrivalled opportunities you would have, as my secretary, to gain experience, to accustom yourself to the intricacies of political life, to – in fact, you would be in an exceedingly advantageous position.'

'Five hundred a year !' said Bicky, rolling it round his tongue. 'Why, that would be nothing to what I could make if I started a chicken farm. It stands to reason. Suppose you have a dozen hens. Each of the hens has a dozen chickens. After a bit the chickens grow up and have a dozen chickens each themselves, and then they all start laying eggs ! There's a fortune in it. You can get anything you like for eggs in America. Fellows keep them on ice for years and years, and don't sell them till they fetch about a dollar a whirl. You don't think I'm going to chuck a

future like this for anything under five hundred o' goblins a year
– what?'

A look of anguish passed over old Chiswick's face, then he
seemed to be resigned to it. 'Very well, my boy,' he said.

'What ho!' said Bicky. 'All right, then.'

'Jeeves,' I said. Bicky had taken the old boy off to dinner to
celebrate, and we were alone. 'Jeeves, this has been one of your
best efforts.'

'Thank you, sir.'

'It beats me how you do it.'

'Yes, sir?'

'The only trouble is you haven't got much out of it yourself.'

'I fancy Mr Bickersteth intends – I judge from his remarks – to
signify his appreciation of anything I have been fortunate
enough to do to assist him, at some later date when he is in a
more favourable position to do so.'

'It isn't enough, Jeeves!'

'Sir?'

It was a wrench, but I felt it was the only possible thing to be
done.

'Bring my shaving things.'

A gleam of hope shone in the man's eye, mixed with doubt.

'You mean, sir?'

'And shave off my moustache.'

There was a moment's silence. I could see the fellow was
deeply moved.

'Thank you very much indeed, sir,' he said, in a low voice.

JAMES JOYCE

A Painful Case

Mr James Duffy lived in Chapelizod because he wished to live as far as possibe from the city of which he was a citizen and because he found all the other suburbs of Dublin mean, modern, and pretentious. He lived in an old sombre house, and from his windows he could look into the disused distillery or upwards along the shallow river on which Dublin is built. The lofty walls of his uncarpeted room were free from pictures. He had himself bought every article of furniture in the room: a black iron bedstead, an iron washstand, four cane chairs, a clothes-rack, a coal-scuttle, a fender and irons, and a square table on which lay a double desk. A bookcase had been made in an alcove by means of shelves of white wood. The bed was clothed with white bed-clothes and a black and scarlet rug covered the foot. A little hand-mirror hung above the wash-stand and during the day a white-shaded lamp stood as the sole ornament of the mantel-piece. The books on the white wooden shelves were arranged from below upwards according to bulk. A complete Words-worth stood at one end of the lowest shelf and a copy of the *Maynooth Catechism*, sewn into the cloth cover of a notebook, stood at one end of the top shelf. Writing materials were always on the desk. In the desk lay a manuscript translation of Hauptmann's *Michael Kramer*, the stage directions of which were written in purple ink, and a little sheaf of papers held together by a brass pin. In these sheets a sentence was inscribed from time to time and, in an ironical moment, the headline of an advertisement for *Bile Beans* had been pasted on to the first sheet. On lifting the lid of the desk a faint fragrance escaped – the fragrance of new cedar-wood pencils or of a bottle of gum or of an over-ripe apple which might have been left there and forgotten.

Mr Duffy abhorred anything which betokened physical or mental disorder. A medieval doctor would have called him saturnine. His face, which carried the entire tale of his years, was of the brown tint of Dublin streets. On his long and rather large head grew dry black hair and a tawny moustache did not quite cover an unamiable mouth. His cheekbones also gave his face a harsh character; but there was no harshness in the eyes which, looking at the world from under their tawny eyebrows, gave the impression of a man ever alert to greet a redeeming instinct in others but often disappointed. He lived at a little distance from his body, regarding his own acts with doubtful side-glances. He had an odd autobiographical habit which led him to compose in his mind from time to time a short sentence about himself containing a subject in the third person and a predicate in the past tense. He never gave alms to beggars, and walked firmly, carrying a stout hazel.

He had been for many years cashier of a private bank in Baggot Street. Every morning he came in from Chapelizod by tram. At midday he went to Dan Burke's and took his lunch – a bottle of lager beer and a small trayful of arrow-root biscuits. At four o'clock he was set free. He dined in an eating-house in George's Street where he felt himself safe from the society of Dublin's gilded youth and where there was a certain plain honesty in the bill of fare. His evenings were spent either before his landlady's piano or roaming about the outskirts of the city. His liking for Mozart's music brought him sometimes to an opera or a concert: these were the only dissipations of his life.

He had neither companions nor friends, church nor creed. He lived his spiritual life without any communion with others, visiting his relatives at Christmas and escorting them to the cemetery when they died. He performed these two social duties for old dignity's sake, but conceded nothing further to the conventions which regulate the civic life. He allowed himself to think that in certain circumstances he would rob his bank but, as these circumstances never arose, his life rolled out evenly – an adventureless tale.

One evening he found himself sitting beside two ladies in the Rotunda. The house, thinly peopled and silent, gave distressing prophecy of failure. The lady who sat next him looked round at the deserted house once or twice and then said:

'What a pity there is such a poor house to-night! It's so hard on people to have to sing to empty benches.'

He took the remark as an invitation to talk. He was surprised that she seemed so little awkward. While they talked he tried to fix her permanently in his memory. When he learned that the young girl beside her was her daughter he judged her to be a year or so younger than himself. Her face, which must have been handsome, had remained intelligent. It was an oval face with strongly marked features. The eyes were very dark blue and steady. Their gaze began with a defiant note, but was confused by what seemed a deliberate swoon of the pupil into the iris, revealing for an instant a temperament of great sensibility. The pupil reasserted itself quickly, this half-disclosed nature fell again under the reign of prudence, and her astrakhan jacket, moulding a bosom of a certain fullness, struck the note of defiance more definitely.

He met her again a few weeks afterwards at a concert in Earlsfort Terrace and seized the moments when her daughter's attention was diverted to become intimate. She alluded once or twice to her husband, but her tone was not such as to make the allusion a warning. Her name was Mrs Sinico. Her husband's great, great-grandfather had come from Leghorn. Her husband was captain of a mercantile boat plying between Dublin and Holland; and they had one child.

Meeting her a third time by accident, he found courage to make an appointment. She came. This was the first of many meetings; they met always in the evening and chose the most quiet quarters for their walks together. Mr Duffy, however, had a distaste for underhand ways and, finding that they were compelled to meet stealthily, he forced her to ask him to her house. Captain Sinico encouraged his visits, thinking that his daughter's hand was in question. He had dismissed his wife so sincerely from his gallery of pleasures that he did not suspect that anyone else would take an interest in her. As the husband was often away and the daughter out giving music lessons, Mr Duffy had many opportunities of enjoying the lady's society. Neither he nor she had had any such adventure before and neither was conscious of any incongruity. Little by little he entangled his thoughts with hers. He lent her books, provided her with ideas, shared his intellectual life with her. She listened to all.

Sometimes in return for his theories she gave out some fact of her own life. With almost maternal solicitude she urged him to let his nature open to the full : she became his confessor. He told her that for some time he had assisted at the meetings of an Irish Socialist Party, where he had felt himself a unique figure amidst a score of sober workmen in a garret lit by an ineffecient oil-lamp. When the party had divided into three sections, each under its own leader and in its own garret, he had discontinued his attendances. The workmen's discussions, he said, were too timorous ; the interest they took in the question of wages was inordinate. He felt that they were hard-featured realists and that they resented an exactitude which was the produce of a leisure not within their reach. No social revolution, he told her, would be likely to strike Dublin for some centuries.

She asked him why did he not write out his thoughts. For what ? he asked her, with careful scorn. To compete with phrasemongers, incapable of thinking consecutively for sixty seconds ? To submit himself to the criticisms of an obtuse middle class which entrusted its morality to policemen and its fine arts to impresarios ?

He went often to her little cottage outside Dublin ; often they spent their evenings alone. Little by little, as their thoughts entangled, they spoke of subjects less remote. Her companion-ship was like a warm soil about an exotic. Many times she allowed the dark to fall upon them, refraining from lighting the lamp. The dark discreet room, their isolation, the music that still vibrated in their ears united them. This union exalted him, wore away the rough edges of his character, emotionalized his mental life. Sometimes he caught himself listening to the sound of his own voice. He thought that in her eyes he would ascend to an angelical stature ; and, as he attached the fervent nature of his companion more and more closely to him, he heard the strange impersonal voice which he recognized as his own, insisting on the soul's incurable loneliness. We cannot give ourselves, it said : we are our own. The end of these discourses was that one night, during which she had shown every sign of unusual excitement, Mrs Sinico caught up his hand passionately and pressed it to her cheek.

Mr Duffy was very much surprised. Her interpretation of his words disillusioned him. He did not visit her for a week ; then he wrote to her asking her to meet him. As he did not wish their last interview to be troubled by the influence of their ruined confessional they met in a little cakeshop near the Parkgate. It was cold autumn weather, but in spite of the cold they wandered up and down the roads of the Park for nearly three hours. They agreed to break off their intercourse: every bond, he said, is a bond to sorrow. When they came out of the Park they walked in silence towards the tram; but here she began to tremble so violently that, fearing another collapse on her part, he bade her good-bye quickly and left her. A few days later he received a parcel containing his books and music.

Four years passed. Mr Duffy returned to his even way of life. His room still bore witness of the order-liness of his mind. Some new pieces of music encumbered the music-stand in the lower room and on his shelves stood two volumes by Nietzsche: *Thus Spake Zarathustra* and *The Gay Science*. He wrote seldom in the sheaf of papers which lay in his desk. One of his sentences, written two months after his last interview with Mrs Sinico, read: Love between man and man is impossible because there must not be sexual intercourse, and friendship between man and woman is impossible because there must be sexual intercourse. He kept away from concerts lest he should meet her. His father died; the junior partner of the bank retired. And still every morning he went into the city by tram and every evening walked home from the city after having dined moderately in George's Street and read the evening paper for dessert.

One evening as he was about to put a morsel of corned beef and cabbage into his mouth his hand stopped. His eyes fixed themselves on a paragraph in the evening paper which he had propped against the water-carafe. He replaced the morsel of food on his plate and read the paragraph attentively. Then he drank a glass of water, pushed his plate to one side, doubled the paper down before him between his elbows and read the paragraph over and over again. The cabbage began to deposit a cold white grease on his plate. The girl came over to him to ask was his dinner not properly cooked. He said it was very good and ate a few mouthfuls of it with difficulty. Then he paid his bill and went out.

He walked along quickly through the November twilight, his stout hazel stick striking the ground regularly, the fringe of the buff *Mail* peeping out of a side-pocket of his tight reefer overcoat. On the lonely road which leads from the Parkgate to Chapelizod he slackened his pace. His stick struck the ground less emphatically, and his breath, issuing irregularly, almost with a sighing sound, condensed in the wintry air. When he reached his house he went up at once to his bedroom and, taking the paper from his pocket, read the paragraph again by the failing light of the window. He read it not aloud, but moving his lips as a priest does when he reads the prayers *Secreto*. This was the paragraph:

DEATH OF A LADY AT SYDNEY PARADE
A PAINFUL CASE

To-day at the City of Dublin Hospital the Deputy Coroner (in the absence of Mr Leverett) held an inquest on the body of Mrs Emily Sinico, aged forty-three years, who was killed at Sydney Parade Station yesterday evening. The evidence showed that the deceased lady while attempting to cross the line, was knocked down by the engine of the ten o'clock slow train from Kingstown, thereby sustaining injuries of the head and right side which led to her death.

James Lennon, driver of the engine, stated that he had been in the employment of the railway company for fifteen years. On hearing the guard's whistle he set the train in motion and a second or two afterwards brought it to rest in response to loud cries. The train was going slowly.

P. Dunne, railway porter, stated that as the train was about to start he observed a woman attempting to cross the lines. He ran towards her and shouted, but, before he could reach her, she was caught by the buffer of the engine and fell to the ground.

A juror. 'You saw the lady fall?'

Witness. 'Yes.'

Police-sergeant Croly deposed that when he arrived he found the deceased lying on the platform apparently dead. He had the body taken to the waiting-room pending the arrival of the ambulance.

Constable 57 corroborated.

Dr Halpin, assistant house-surgeon of the City of Dublin Hospital, stated that the deceased had two lower ribs fractured and had sustained severe contusions of the right shoulder. The right side of the head had been injured in the fall. The injuries were not sufficient to have caused death in a normal person. Death, in his opinion, had been probably due to shock and sudden failure of the heart's action.

Mr H.B.Patterson Finlay, on behalf of the railway company, expressed his deep regret at the accident. The company had always taken every precaution to prevent people crossing the lines except by the bridges, both by placing notices in every station and by the use of patent spring gates at level crossings. The deceased had been in the habit of crossing the lines late at night from platform to platform and, in view of certain other circumstances of the case, he did not think the railway officials were to blame.

Captain Sinico, of Leoville, Sydney Parade, husband of the deceased, also gave evidence. He stated that the deceased was his wife. He was not in Dublin at the time of the accident as he had arrived only that morning from Rotterdam. They had been married for twenty-two years and had lived happily until about two years ago, when his wife began to be rather intemperate in her habits.

Miss Mary Sinico said that of late her mother had been in the habit of going out at night to buy spirits. She, witness, had often tried to reason with her mother and had induced her to join a League. She was not at home until an hour after the accident.

The jury returned a verdict in accordance with the medical evidence and exonerated Lennon from all blame.

The Deputy-Coroner said it was a most painful case, and expressed great sympathy with Captain Sìnico and his daughter. He urged on the railway company to take strong measures to prevent the possibility of similar accidents in the future. No blame attached to anyone.

Mr Duffy raised his eyes from the paper and gazed out of his window on the cheerless evening landscape. The river lay quiet beside the empty distillery and from time to time a light appeared in some house on the Lucan road. What an end! The whole narrative of her death revolted him and it revolted him to think that he had ever spoken to her of what he held sacred. The threadbare phrases, the inane expressions of sympathy, the cautious words of a reporter won over to conceal the details of commonplace vulgar death attacked his stomach. Not merely had she degraded herself; she had degraded him. He saw the squalid tract of her vice, miserable and malodorous. His soul's companion! He thought of the hobbling wretches whom he had seen carrying cans and bottles to be filled by the barman. Just God, what an end! Evidently she had been unfit to live, without any strength of purpose, an easy prey to habits, one of the wrecks on which civilization has been reared. But that she could have sunk so low! Was it possible he had deceived himself so utterly about her? He remembered her outburst of that night and interpreted it in a harsher sense than he had ever done. He had no difficulty now in approving of the course he had taken.

As the light failed and his memory began to wander he thought her hand touched his. The shock which had first attacked his stomach was now attacking his nerves. He put on his overcoat and hat quickly and went out. The cold air met him on the threshold; it crept into the sleeves of his coat. When he came to the public-house at Chapelizod Bridge he went in and ordered a hot punch.

The proprietor served him obsequiously but did not venture to talk. There were five or six working-men in the shop discussing the value of a gentleman's estate in County Kildare. They drank at intervals from their huge pint tumblers and smoked, spitting often on the floor and sometimes dragging the sawdust over their spits with their heavy boots. Mr Duffy sat on his stool and gazed at them without seeing or hearing them. After a while they went out and he called for another punch. He sat a long time over it. The shop was very quiet. The proprietor sprawled on the counter reading the *Herald* and yawning. Now and again a tram was heard swishing along the lonely road outside.

As he sat there, living over his life with her and evoking alternately the two images in which he now conceived her, he realized that she was dead, that she had ceased to exist, that she had become a memory. He began to feel ill at ease. He asked himself what else could he have done. He could not have carried on a comedy of deception with her; he could not have lived with her openly. He had done what seemed to him best. How was he to blame? Now that she was gone he understood how lonely her life must have been, sitting night after night, alone in that room. His life would be lonely too until he, too, died, ceased to exist, became a memory — if anyone remembered him.

It was after nine o'clock when he left the shop. The night was cold and gloomy. He entered the Park by the first gate and walked along under the gaunt trees. He walked through the bleak alleys and where they had walked four years before. She seemed to be near him in the darkness. At moments he seemed to feel her voice touch his ear, her hand touch his. He stood still to listen. Why had he withheld life from her? Why had he sentenced her to death? He felt his moral nature falling to pieces.

When he gained the crest of the Magazine Hill he halted and looked along the river towards Dublin, the lights of which burned redly and hospitably in the cold night. He looked down the slope and, at the base, in the shadow of the wall of the Park, he saw some human figures lying. Those venal and furtive loves filled him with despair. He gnawed the rectitude of his life; he felt that he had been outcast from life's feast. One human being had seemed to love him and he had denied her life and happiness: he had sentenced her to ignominy, a death of shame. He knew that the prostrate creatures down by the wall were watching him and wished him gone. No one wanted him; he was outcast from life's feast. He turned his eyes to the grey gleaming river, winding along towards Dublin. Beyond the river he saw a goods train winding out of Kingsbridge Station, like a worm with a fiery head winding through the darkness, obstinately and laboriously. It passed slowly out of sight; but still he heard in his ears the laborious drone of the engine reiterating the syllables of her name.

He turned back the way he had come, the rhythm of the engine pounding in his ears. He began to doubt the reality of what memory told him. He halted under a tree and allowed the rhythm to die away. He could not feel her near him in the darkness nor her voice touch his ear. He waited for some minutes listening. He could hear nothing: the night was perfectly silent. He listened again: perfectly silent. He felt that he was alone.

VIRGINIA WOOLF

Lappin and Lapinova

They were married. The wedding march pealed out. The pigeons fluttered. Small boys in Eton jackets threw rice; a fox terrier sauntered across the path; and Ernest Thorburn led his bride to the car through that small inquisitive crowd of complete strangers which always collects in London to enjoy other people's happiness or unhappiness. Certainly he looked handsome and she looked shy. More rice was thrown, and the car moved off.

That was on Tuesday. Now it was Saturday. Rosalind had still to get used to the fact that she was Mrs. Ernest Thorburn. Perhaps she never would get used to the fact that she was Mrs. Ernest Anybody, she thought, as she sat in the bow window of the hotel looking over the lake to the mountains, and waited for her husband to come down to breakfast. Ernest was a difficult name to get used to. It was not the name she would have chosen. She would have preferred Timothy, Antony, or Peter. He did not look like Ernest either. The name suggested the Albert Memorial, mahogany sideboards, steel engravings of the Prince Consort with his family – her mother-in-law's dining-room in Porchester Terrace in short.

But here he was. Thank goodness he did not look like Ernest – no. But what did he look like? She glanced at him sideways. Well, when he was eating toast he looked like a rabbit. Not that anyone else would have seen a likeness to a creature so diminutive and timid in this spruce, muscular young man with the straight nose, the blue eyes, and the very firm mouth. But that made it all the more amusing. His nose twitched very slightly when he ate. So did her pet rabbit's. She kept watching his nose twitch; and then she had to explain, when he caught her looking at him, why she laughed.

'It's because you're like a rabbit, Ernest,' she said. 'Like a wild rabbit; a King Rabbit; a rabbit that makes laws for all the other rabbits.'

Ernest had no objection to being that kind of rabbit, and since it amused her to see him twitch his nose – he had never known that his nose twitched – he twitched it on purpose. And she laughed and laughed; and he laughed too, so that the maiden ladies and the fishing man and the Swiss waiter in his greasy black jacket all guessed right; they were very happy. But how long does such happiness last? they asked themselves; and each answered according to his own circumstances.

At lunch time, seated on a clump of heather beside the lake, 'Lettuce, rabbit?' said Rosalind, holding out the lettuce that had been provided to eat with the hard-boiled eggs. 'Come and take it out of my hand,' she added, and he stretched out and nibbled the lettuce and twitched his nose.

'Good rabbit, nice rabbit,' she said, patting him, as she used to pat her tame rabbit at home. But that was absurd. He was not a tame rabbit, whatever he was. She turned it into French. 'Lapin,' she called him. But whatever he was, he was not a French rabbit. He was simply and solely English – born at Porchester Terrace, educated at Rugby; now a clerk in His Majesty's Civil Service. So she tried 'Bunny' next; but that was worse. 'Bunny' was someone plump and soft and comic; he was thin and hard and serious. Still, his nose twitched. 'Lappin,' she exclaimed suddenly; and gave a little cry as if she had found the very word she looked for.

'Lappin, Lappin, King Lappin,' she repeated. It seemed to suit him exactly; he was not Ernest, he was King Lappin. Why? She did not know.

When there was nothing new to talk about on their long solitary walks – and it rained, as everyone had warned them that it would rain; or when they were sitting over the fire in the evening, for it was cold, and the maiden ladies had gone and the fishing man, and the waiter only came if you rang the bell for him, she let her fancy play with the story of the Lappin tribe. Under her hands – she was sewing; he was reading – they became very real, very vivid, very amusing. Ernest put down the paper and helped her. There were the black rabbits and the red; there were the enemy rabbits and the friendly. There were the wood in which they lived and the outlying prairies and the swamp. Above all there was King Lappin, who, far from having only the one trick – that he twitched his nose – became as the days passed an animal of the greatest character; Rosalind was always finding new qualities in him. But above all he was a great hunter.

'And what,' said Rosalind, on the last day of the honeymoon, 'did the King do to-day?'

In fact they had been climbing all day; and she had worn a blister on her heel; but she did not mean that.

'To-day,' said Ernest, twitching his nose as he bit the end off his cigar, 'he chased a hare.' He paused; struck a match, and twitched again.

'A woman hare,' he added.

'A white hare!' Rosalind exclaimed, as if she had been expecting this. 'Rather a small hare; silver grey; with big bright eyes?'

'Yes,' said Ernest, looking at her as she had looked at him, 'a smallish animal; with eyes popping out of her head, and two little front paws dangling.' It was exactly how she sat, with her sewing dangling in her hands; and her eyes, that were so big and bright, were certainly a little prominent.

'Ah, Lapinova,' Rosalind murmured.

'Is that what she's called?' said Ernest – 'the real Rosalind?' He looked at her. He felt very much in love with her.

'Yes; that's what she's called,' said Rosalind. 'Lapinova.' And before they went to bed that night it was all settled. He was King Lappin; she was Queen Lapinova. They were the opposite of each other; he was bold and determined; she wary and undependable. He ruled over the busy world of rabbits; her world was a desolate, mysterious place, which she ranged mostly by moonlight. All the same, their territories touched; they were King and Queen.

Thus when they came back from their honeymoon they possessed a private world, inhabited, save for the one white hare, entirely by rabbits. No one guessed that there was such a place, and that of course made it all the more amusing. It made them feel, more even than most young married couples, in league together against the rest of the world. Often they looked slyly at each other when people talked about rabbits and woods and traps and shooting. Or they winked furtively across the table when Aunt Mary said that she could never bear to see a hare in a dish – it looked so like a baby : or when John, Ernest's sporting brother, told them what price rabbits were fetching that autumn in Wiltshire, skins and all. Sometimes when they wanted a game-keeper, or a poacher or a Lord of the Manor, they amused themselves by distributing the parts among their friends. Ernest's mother, Mrs. Reginald Thorburn, for example, fitted the part of the Squire to perfection. But it was all secret – that was the point of it ; nobody save themselvs knew that such a world existed.

Without that world, how, Rosalind wondered, that winter could she have lived at all ? For instance, there was the golden-wedding party, when all the Thorburns assembled at Porchester Terrace to celebrate the fiftieth anniversary of that union which had been so blessed – had it not produced Ernest Thorburn ? and so fruitful – had it not produced nine other sons and daughters into the bargain, many themselves married and also fruitful ? She dreaded that party. But it was inevitable. As she walked upstairs she felt bitterly that she was an only child and an orphan at that ; a mere drop among all those Thorburns assembled in the great drawing-room with the shiny satin wallpaper and the lustrous family portraits. The living Thorburns much resembled the painted ; save that instead of painted lips they had real lips ; out of which came jokes ; jokes about school-rooms, and how they had pulled the chair from under the governess ; jokes about frogs and how they had put them between the virgin sheets of maiden ladies. As for herself, she had never even made an apple-pie bed. Holding her present in her hand she advanced toward her mother-in-law sumptuous in yellow satin ; and toward her father-in-law decorated with a rich yellow carnation. All round them on tables and chairs there were golden tributes, some nestling in cotton wool ; others branching resplendent – candle-sticks ; cigar boxes ; chains ; each stamped with a goldsmith's proof that it was solid gold, hall-marked, authentic. But her present was only a little pinchbeck box pierced with holes ; an old sand caster, an eighteenth-century relic, once used to sprinkle sand over wet ink. Rather a senseless present she felt – in an age of blotting paper ; and as she proffered it, she saw in front of her the stubby black handwriting in which her mother-in-law when they were engaged had expressed the hope that 'My son will make you happy.' No, she was not happy. Not at all happy. She looked at Ernest, straight as a ramrod with a nose like all the noses in the family portraits; a nose that never twitched at all.

Then they went down to dinner. She was half hidden by the great chrysanthemums that curled their red and gold petals into large tight balls. Everything was gold. A gold-edged card with gold initials intertwined recited the list of all the dishes that would be set one after another before them. She dipped her spoon in a plate of clear golden fluid. The raw white fog outside had been turned by the lamps into a golden mesh that blurred the edges of the plates and gave the pineapples a rough golden skin. Only she herself in her white wedding dress peering ahead of her with her prominent eyes seemed insoluble as an icicle.

As the dinner wore on, however, the room grew steamy with heat. Beads of perspiration stood out on the men's foreheads. She felt that her icicle was being turned to water. She was being melted; dispersed; dissolved into nothingness; and would soon faint. Then through the surge in her head and the din in her ears she heard a woman's voice exclaim, 'But they breed so !'

The Thorburns – yes; they breed so, she echoed; looking at all the round red faces that seemed doubled in the giddiness that overcame her; and magnified in the gold mist that enhaloed them. 'They breed so.' Then John bawled :

'Little devils ! ... Shoot 'em ! Jump on 'em with big boots ! That's the only way to deal with 'em ... rabbits !'

At that word, the magic word, she revived. Peeping between the chrysanthemums she saw Ernest's nose twitch. It rippled, it ran with successive twitches. And at that a mysterious catastrophe befell the Thorburns. The golden table became a moor with the gorse in full bloom; the din of voices turned to one peal of lark's laughter ringing down from the sky. It was a blue sky – clouds passed slowly. And they had all been changed – the Thorburns. She looked at her father-in-law, a furtive little man with dyed moustaches. His foible was collecting things – seals, enamel boxes, trifles from eighteenth-century dressing tables which he hid in the drawers of his study from his wife. Now she saw him as he was – a poacher, stealing off with his coat bulging with pheasants and partridges to drop them stealthily into a three-legged pot in his smoky little cottage. That was her real father-in-law – a poacher. And Celia, the unmarried daughter, who always nosed out other people's secrets, the little things they wished to hide – she was a white ferret with pink eyes, and a nose clotted with earth from her horrid underground nosings and pokings. Slung round men's shoulders, in a net, and thrust down a hole – it was a pitiable life – Celia's; it was none of her fault. So she saw Celia. And then she looked at her mother-in-law – whom they dubbed The Squire. Flushed, coarse, a bully – she was all that, as she stood returning thanks, but now that Rosalind – that is Lapinova – saw her, she saw behind her the decayed family mansion, the plaster peeling off the walls, and heard her, with a sob in her voice, giving thanks to her children (who hated her) for a world that had ceased to exist. There was a sudden silence. They all stood with their glasses raised; then it was over.

'Oh, King Lappin!' she cried as they went home together in the fog, 'if your nose hadn't twitched just at that moment, I should have been trapped!'

'But you're safe,' said King Lappin, pressing her paw.

'Quite safe,' she answered.

And they drove back through the Park, King and Queen of the marsh, of the mist, and of the gorse-scented moor.

Thus time passed; one year; two years of time. And on a winter's night, which happened by a coincidence to be the anniversary of the golden-wedding party – but Mrs. Reginald Thorburn was dead; the house was to let; and there was only a caretaker in residence – Ernest came home from the office. They had a nice little home; half a house above a saddler's shop in South Kensington, not far from the tube station. It was cold, with fog in the air, and Rosalind was sitting over the fire, sewing.

'What d'you think happened to me to-day?' she began as soon as he had settled himself down with his legs stretched to the blaze. 'I was crossing the stream when –'

'What stream?' Ernest interrupted her.

'The stream at the bottom, where our wood meets the black wood,' she explained.

Ernest looked completely blank for a moment.

'What the deuce are you talking about?' he asked.

'My dear Ernest!' she cried in dismay. 'King Lappin,' she added, dangling her little front paws in the firelight. But his nose did not twitch. Her hands – they turned to hands – clutched the stuff she was holding; her eyes popped half out of her head. It took him five minutes at least to change from Ernest Thorburn to King Lappin; and while she waited she felt a load on the back of her neck, as if somebody were about to wring it. At last he changed to King Lappin; his nose twitched; and they spent the evening roaming the woods much as usual.

But she slept badly. In the middle of the night she woke, feeling as if something strange had happened to her. She was stiff and cold. At last she turned on the light and looked at Ernest lying beside her. He was sound asleep. He snored. But even though he snored, his nose remained perfectly still. It looked as if it had never twitched at all. Was it possible that he was really Ernest; and that she was really married to Ernest? A vision of her mother-in-law's dining-room came before her; and there they sat, she and Ernest, grown old, under the engravings, in front of the sideboard ... It was their golden-wedding day. She could not bear it.

'Lappin, King Lappin!' she whispered, and for a moment his nose seemed to twitch of its own accord. But he still slept. 'Wake up, Lappin, wake up!' she cried.

Ernest woke; and seeing her sitting bolt upright beside him he asked: 'What's the matter?'

'I thought my rabbit was dead!' she whimpered. Ernest was angry.

'Don't talk such rubbish, Rosalind,' he said. 'Lie down and go to sleep.'

He turned over. In another moment he was sound asleep and snoring.

But she could not sleep. She lay curled up on her side of the bed, like a hare in its form. She had turned out the light, but the street lamp lit the ceiling faintly, and the trees outside made a lacy network over it as if there were a shadowy grove on the ceiling in which she wandered, turning, twisting, in and out, round and round, hunting, being hunted, hearing the bay of hounds and horns; flying, escaping ... until the maid drew the blinds and brought their early tea.

Next day she could settle to nothing. She seemed to have lost something. She felt as if her body had shrunk; it had grown small, and black and hard. Her joints seemed stiff too, and when she looked in the glass, which she did several times as she wandered about the flat, her eyes seemed to burst out of her head, like currants in a bun. The rooms also seemed to have shrunk. Large pieces of furniture jutted out at odd angles and she found herself knocking against them. At last she put on her hat and went out. She walked along the Cromwell Road; and every room she passed and peered into seemed to be a dining-room where people sat eating under steel engravings, with thick yellow lace curtains, and mahogany sideboards. At last she reached the Natural History Museum; she used to like it when she was a child. But the first thing she saw when she went in was a stuffed hare standing on sham snow with pink glass eyes. Somehow it made her shiver all over. Perhaps it would be better when dusk fell. She went home and sat over the fire, without a light, and tried to imagine that she was out alone on a moor; and there was a stream rushing; and beyond the stream a dark wood. But she could get no further than the stream. At last she squatted down on the bank on the wet grass, and sat crouched in her chair, with her hands dangling empty, and her eyes glazed, like glass eyes, in the firelight. Then there was the crack of a gun. . . . She started as if she had been shot. It was only Ernest, turning his key in the door. She waited, trembling. He came in and switched on the light. There he stood, tall, handsome, rubbing his hands that were red with cold.

'Sitting in the dark?' he said.

'Oh, Ernest, Ernest!' she cried, starting up in her chair.

'Well, what's up now?' he asked briskly, warming his hands at the fire.

'It's Lapinova . . .' she faltered, glancing wildly at him out of her great startled eyes. 'She's gone, Ernest. I've lost her!'

Ernest frowned. He pressed his lips tight together. 'Oh, that's what's up, is it?' he said, smiling rather grimly at his wife. For ten seconds he stood there, silent; and she waited, feeling hands tightening at the back of her neck.

'Yes,' he said at length. 'Poor Lapinova . . .' He straightened his tie at the looking-glass over the mantelpiece.

'Caught in a trap,' he said, 'killed,' and sat down and read the newspaper.

So that was the end of that marriage.

D. H. LAWRENCE

The Prussian Officer

They had marched more than thirty kilometres since dawn, along the white, hot road where occasional thickets of trees threw a moment of shade, then out into the glare again. On either hand, the valley, wide and shallow, glittered with heat; dark-green patches of rye, pale young corn, fallow and meadow and black pine woods spread in a dull, hot diagram under a glistening sky. But right in front the mountains ranged across, pale blue and very still, snow gleaming gently out of the deep atmosphere. And towards the mountains, on and on, the regiment marched between the rye-fields and the meadows, between the scraggy fruit trees set regularly on either side the high road. The burnished, dark-green rye threw off a suffocating heat, the mountains drew gradually nearer and more distinct. While the feet of the soldiers grew hotter, sweat ran through their hair under their helmets, and their knapsacks could burn no more in contact with their shoulders, but seemed instead to give off a cold, prickly sensation.

He walked on and on in silence, staring at the mountains ahead, that rose sheer out of the land, and stood fold behind fold, half earth, half heaven, the heaven, the barrier with slits of soft snow, in the pale, bluish peaks.

He could now walk almost without pain. At the start, he had determined not to limp. It had made him sick to take the first steps, and during the first mile or so, he had compressed his breath, and the cold drops of sweat had stood on his forehead. But he had walked it off. What were they after all but bruises! He had looked at them, as he was getting up: deep bruises on the backs of his thighs. And since he had made his first step in the morning, he had been conscious of them, till now he had a tight, hot place in his chest, with suppressing the pain, and holding

143

himself in. There seemed no air when he breathed. But he walked almost lightly.

The Captain's hand had trembled at taking his coffee at dawn : his orderly saw it again. And he saw the fine figure of the Captain wheeling on horseback at the farmhouse ahead, a handsome figure in pale-blue uniform with facings of scarlet, and the metal gleaming on the back helmet and the sword-scabbard, and dark streaks of sweat coming on the silky bay horse. The orderly felt he was connected with that figure moving so suddenly on horseback : he followed it like a shadow, mute and inevitable and damned by it. And the officer was always aware of the tramp of the company behind, the march of his orderly among the men.

The Captain was a tall man of about forty, grey at the temples. He had a handsome, finely-knit figure, and was one of the best horsemen in the West. His orderly, having to rub him down, admired the amazing riding-muscles of his loins.

For the rest, the orderly scarcely noticed the officer any more than he noticed himself. It was rarely he saw his master's face : he did not look at it. The Captain had reddish-brown, stiff hair, that he wore short upon his skull. His moustache was also cut short and bristly over a full, brutal mouth. His face was rather rugged, the cheeks thin. Perhaps the man was the more handsome for the deep lines in his face, the irritable tension of his brow, which gave him the look of a man who fights with life. His fair eyebrows stood bushy over light-blue eyes that were always flashing with cold fire.

He was a Prussian aristocrat, haughty and overbearing. But his mother had been a Polish countess. Having made too many gambling debts when he was young, he had ruined his prospects in the Army, and remained an infantry captain. He had never married : his position did not allow of it, and no woman had ever moved him to it. His time he spent riding – occasionally he rode one of his own horses at the races – and at the officers' club. Now and then he took himself a mistress. But after such an event, he returned to duty with his brow still more tense, his eyes still more hostile and irritable. With the men, however, he was merely impersonal, though a devil when roused ; so that, on the whole, they feared him, but had no great aversion from him. They accepted him as the inevitable.

To his orderly he was at first cold and just and indifferent: he did not fuss over trifles. So that his servant knew practically nothing about him, except just what orders he would give, and how he wanted them obeyed. That was quite simple. Then the change gradually came.

The orderly was a youth of about twenty-two, of medium height, and well built. He had strong, heavy limbs, was swarthy, with a soft, black, young moustache. There was something altogether warm and young about him. He had firmly marked eyebrows over dark, expressionless eyes, that seemed never to have thought, only to have received life direct through his senses, and acted straight from instinct.

Gradually the officer had become aware of his servant's young vigorous, unconscious presence about him. He could not get away from the sense of the youth's person, while he was in attendance. It was like a warm flame upon the older man's tense, rigid body, that had become almost unliving, fixed. There was something so free and self-contained about him, and something in the young fellow's movement, that made the officer aware of him. And this irritated the Prussian. He did not choose to be touched into life by his servant. He might easily have changed his man, but he did not. He now very rarely looked direct at his orderly, but kept his face averted, as if to avoid seeing him. And yet as the young soldier moved unthinking about the apartment, the elder watched him, and would notice the movement of his strong young shoulders under the blue cloth, the bend of his neck. And it irritated him. To see the soldier's young, brown, shapely peasant's hand grasp the loaf or the wine-bottle sent a flash of hate or of anger through the elder man's blood. It was not that the youth was clumsy: it was rather the blind, instinctive sureness of movement of an unhampered young animal that irritated the officer to such a degree.

Once, when a bottle of wine had gone over, and the red gushed out on to the tablecloth, the officer had started up with an oath, and his eyes, bluey like fire, had held those of the confused youth for a moment. It was a shock for the young soldier. He felt something sink deeper, deeper into his soul, where nothing had ever gone before. It left him rather blank and wondering. Some of his natural completeness in himself was gone, a little uneasiness took its place. And from that time an undiscovered feeling had held between the two men.

Henceforward the orderly was afraid of really meeting his master. His subconsciousness remembered those steely blue eyes and the harsh brows, and did not intend to meet them again. So he always stared past his master, and avoided him. Also, in a little anxiety, he waited for the three months to have gone, when his time would be up. He began to feel a constraint in the Captain's presence, and the soldier even more than the officer wanted to be left alone, in his neutrality as servant.

He had served the Captain for more than a year, and knew his duty. This he performed easily, as if it were natural to him. The officer and his commands he took for granted, as he took the sun and the rain, and he served as a matter of course. It did not implicate him personally.

But now if he were going to be forced into a personal interchange with his master he would be like a wild thing caught, he felt he must get away.

But the influence of the young soldier's being had penetrated through the officer's stiffened discipline, and perturbed the man in him. He, however, was a gentleman, with long, fine hands and cultivated movements, and was not going to allow such a thing as the stirring of his innate self. He was a man of passionate temper, who had always kept himself suppressed. Occasionally there had been a duel, an outburst before the soldiers. He knew himself to be always on the point of breaking out. But he kept himself hard to the idea of the Service. Whereas the young soldier seemed to live out his warm, full nature, to give it off in his very movements, which had a certain zest, such as wild animals have in free movement. And this irritated the officer more and more.

In spite of himself, the Captain could not regain his neutrality of feeling towards his orderly. Nor could he leave the man alone. In spite of himself, he watched him, gave him sharp orders, tried to take up as much of his time as possible. Sometimes he flew into a rage with the young soldier, and bullied him. Then the orderly shut himself off, as it were out of earshot, and waited, with sullen, flushed face, for the end of the noise. The words never pierced to his intelligence, he made himself, protectively, impervious to the feelings of his master.

He had a scar on his left thumb, a deep seam going across the knuckle. The officer had long suffered from it, and wanted to do something to it. Still it was there, ugly and brutal on the young, brown hand. At last the Captain's reserve gave way. One day, as the orderly was smoothing out the tablecloth, the officer pinned down his thumb with a pencil, asking:

'How did you come by that?'

The young man winced and drew back at attention.

'A wood axe, Herr Hauptmann,' he answered.

The officer waited for further explanation. None came. The orderly went about his duties. The elder man was sullenly angry. His servant avoided him. And the next day he had to use all his will-power to avoid seeing the scarred thumb. He wanted to get hold of it and — A hot flame ran in his blood.

He knew his servant would soon be free, and would be glad. As yet, the soldier had held himself off from the elder man. The Captain grew madly irritable. He could not rest when the soldier was away, and when he was present, he glared at him with tormented eyes. He hated those fine, black brows over the unmeaning, dark eyes, he was infuriated by the free movement of the handsome limbs, which no military discipline could make stiff. And he became harsh and cruelly bullying, using contempt and satire. The young soldier only grew more mute and expressionless.

'What cattle were you bred by, that you can't keep straight eyes? Look me in the eyes when I speak to you.'

And the soldier turned his dark eyes to the other's face, but there was no sight in them; he stared with the slightest possible cast, holding back his sight, perceiving the blue of his master's eyes, but receiving no look from them. And the elder man went pale, and his reddish eyebrows twitched. He gave his order, barrenly.

Once he flung a heavy military glove into the young soldier's face. Then he had the satisfaction of seeing the black eyes flare up into his own, like a blaze when straw is thrown on a fire. And he had laughed with a little tremor and a sneer.

But there were only two months more. The youth instinctively tried to keep himself intact: he tried to serve the officer as if the latter were an abstract authority and not a man. All his instinct was to avoid personal contact, even definite hate. But in spite of himself the hate grew, responsive to the officer's passion.

However, he put it in the background. When he had left the Army he could dare acknowledge it. By nature he was active, and had many friends. He thought what amazing good fellows they were. But, without knowing it, he was alone. Now this solitariness was intensified. It would carry him through his term. But the officer seemed to be going irritably insane, and the youth was deeply frightened.

The soldier had a sweetheart, a girl from the mountains, independent and primitive. The two walked together, rather silently. He went with her, not to talk, but to have his arm round her, and for the physical contact. This eased him, made it easier for him to ignore the Captain; for he could rest with her held fast against his chest. And she, in some unspoken fashion, was there for him. They loved each other.

The Captain perceived it, and was mad with irritation. He kept the young man engaged all the evenings long, and took pleasure in the dark look that came on his face. Occasionally, the eyes of the two men met, those of the younger sullen and dark, doggedly unalterable, those of the elder sneering with restless contempt.

The officer tried hard not to admit the passion that had got hold of him. He would not know that his feeling for his orderly was anything but that of a man incensed by his stupid, perverse servant. So, keeping quite justified and conventional in his consciousness, he let the other thing run on. His nerves, however, were suffering. At last he slung the end of a belt in his servant's face. When he saw the youth start back, the pain-tears in his eyes and the blood on his mouth, he had felt at once a thrill of deep pleasure and of shame.

But this, he acknowledged to himself, was a thing he had never done before. The fellow was too exasperating. His own nerves must be going to pieces. He went away for some days with a woman.

It was a mockery of pleasure. He simply did not want the woman. But he stayed on for his time. At the end of it, he came back in an agony of irritation, torment, and misery. He rode all the evening, then came straight in to supper. His orderly was out. The officer sat with his long, fine hands lying on the table, perfectly still, and all his blood seemed to be corroding.

At last his servent entered. He watched the strong, easy young figure, the fine eyebrows, the thick black hair. In a week's time the youth had got back his old well-being. The hands of the officer twitched and seemed to be full of mad flame. The young man stood at attention, unmoving, shut off.

The meal went in silence. But the orderly seemed eager. He made a clatter with the dishes.

'Are you in a hurry?' asked the officer, watching the intent, warm face of his servant. The other did not reply.

'Will you answer my question?' said the Captain.

'Yes sir,' replied the orderly, standing with his pile of deep Army plates. The Captain waited, looked at him, then asked again:

'Are you in a hurry?'

'Yes, sir,' came the answer, that sent a flash through the listener.

'For what?'

'I was going out, sir.'

'I want you this evening.'

There was a moment's hesitation. The officer had a curious stiffness of countenance.

'Yes sir,' replied the servant, in his throat.

'I want you to-morrow evening also – in fact you may consider your evenings occupied, unless I give you leave.'

The mouth with the young moustache set close.

'Yes sir,' answered the orderly, loosening his lips for a moment.

He again turned to the door.

'And why have you a piece of pencil in your ear?'

The orderly hestitated, then continued on his way without answering. He set the plates in a pile outside the door, took the stump of the pencil from his ear, and put it in his pocket. He had been copying a verse for his sweetheart's birthday card. He returned to finish clearing the table. The officer's eyes were dancing, he had a little, eager smile.

'Why have you a piece of pencil in your ear?' he asked.

The orderly took his hands full of dishes. His master was standing near the great green stove, a little smile on his face, his chin thrust forward. When the young soldier saw him his heart suddenly ran hot. He felt blind. Instead of answering, he turned dazedly to the door. As he was crouching to set down the dishes, he was pitched forward by a kick from behind. The pots went in a stream down the stairs, he clung to the pillar of the banisters. And as he was rising he was kicked heavily again and again, so that he clung sickly to the post for some moments. His master had gone swiftly into the room and closed the door. The maid-servant downstairs looked up the staircase and made a mocking face at the crockery disaster.

The officer's heart was plunging. He poured himself a glass of wine, part of which he spilled on the floor, and gulped the remainder, leaning against the cool, green stove. He heard his man collecting the dishes from the stairs. Pale, as if intoxicated, he waited. The servant entered again. The Captain's heart gave a pang, as of pleasure, seeing the young fellow bewildered and uncertain on his feet with pain.

'Schöner !' he said.

The soldier was a little slower in coming to attention.

'Yes, sir !'

The youth stood before him, with pathetic young moustache, and fine eyebrows very distinct on his forehead of dark marble.

'I asked you a question.'

'Yes, sir.'

The officer's tone bit like acid.

'Why had you a pencil in your ear ?'

Again the servant's heart ran hot, and he could not breathe. With dark, strained eyes, he looked at the officer, as if fascinated. And he stood there sturdily planted, unconscious. The withering smile came into the Captain's eyes, and he lifted his foot.

'I forgot it – sir,' panted the soldier, his dark eyes fixed on the other man's dancing blue ones.

'What was it doing there ?'

He saw the young man's breast heaving as he made an effort for words.

'I had been writing.'

'Writing what ?'

Again the soldier looked him up and down. The officer could hear him panting. The smile came into the blue eyes. The soldier worked his dry throat, but could not speak. Suddenly the smile lit like a flame on the officer's face, and a kick came heavily against the orderly's thigh. The youth moved sideways. His face went dead, with two black, staring eyes.

'Well?' said the officer.

The orderly's mouth had gone dry, and his tongue rubbed in it as on dry brown-paper. He worked his throat. The officer raised his foot. The servant went stiff.

'Some poetry, sir,' came the crackling, unrecognisable sound of his voice.

'Poetry, what poetry?' asked the Captain, with a sickly smile.

Again there was the working in the throat. The Captain's heart had suddenly gone down heavily, and he stood sick and tired.

'For my girl, sir,' he heard the dry, inhuman sound.

'Oh!' he said, turning away. 'Clear the table.'

'Click!' went the soldier's throat; then again, 'click!' and then the half-articulate:

'Yes, sir.'

The young soldier was gone, looking old, and walking heavily.

The officer, left alone, held himself rigid, to prevent himself from thinking. His instinct warned him that he must not think. Deep inside him was the intense gratification of his passion, still working powerfully. Then there was a counteraction, a horrible breaking down of something inside hm, a whole agony of reaction. He stood there for an hour motionless, a chaos of sensations, but rigid with a will to keep blank his consciousness, to prevent his mind grasping. And he held himself so until the worst of the stress had passed, when he began to drink, drank himself to an intoxication, till he slept obliterated. When he woke in the morning he was shaken to the base of his nature. But he had fought off the reliasation of what he had done. He had prevented his mind from taking it in, had suppressed it along with his instincts, and the conscious man had nothing to do with it. He felt only as after a bout of intoxication, weak, but the affair itself all dim and not to be recovered. Of the drunkenness of his passion he successfully refused remembrance. And when his orderly appeared with coffee, the officer assumed the same self he had had the morning before. He refused the event of the past night – denied it had ever been – and was successful in his denial. He had not done any such thing – not he himself. Whatever there might be lay at the door of a stupid insubordinate servant.

The orderly had gone about in a stupor all the evening. He

drank some beer because he was parched, but not much, the alcohol made his feeling come back, and he could not bear it. He was dulled, as if nine-tenths of the ordinary man in him were inert. He crawled about disfigured. Still, when he thought of the kicks, he went sick, and when he thought of the threat of more kicking, in the room afterwards, his heart went hot and faint, and he panted, remembering the one that had come. He had been forced to say : 'For my girl.' He was much too done even to want to cry. His mouth hung slightly open, like an idiot's. He felt vacant, and wasted. So, he wandered at his work, painfully, and very slowly and clumsily, fumbling blindly with the brushes, and finding it difficult, when he sat down, to summon the energy to move again. His limbs, his jaw, were slack and nerveless. But he was very tired. He got to bed at last, and slept inert, relaxed, in a sleep that was rather stupor than slumber, a dead night of stupefaction shot through with gleams of anguish.

In the morning were the manoeuvres. But he woke even before the bugle sounded. The painful ache in his chest, the dryness of his throat, the awful steady feeling of misery made his eyes come awake and dreary at once. He knew, without thinking, what had happened. And he knew that the day had come again, when he must go on with his round. The last bit of darkness was being pushed out of the room. He would have to move his inert body and go on. He was so young, and had known so little trouble, that he was bewildered. He only wished it would stay night, so that he could lie still, covered up by the darkness. And yet nothing would prevent the day from coming, nothing would save him from having to get up and saddle the Captain's horse, and make the Captain's coffee. It was there, inevitable. And then, he thought, it was impossible. Yet they would not leave him free. He must go and take the coffee to the Captain. He was too stunned to understand it. He only knew it was inevitable — inevitable, however long he lay inert.

At last, after heaving at himself, for he seemed to be a mass of inertia, he got up. But he had to force every one of his movements from behind, with his will. He felt lost, and dazed, and helpless. Then he clutched hold of the bed, the pain was so keen. And looking at the thighs he saw the darker bruises on his swarthy flesh, and he knew that if he pressed one of his fingers on one of the bruises, he should faint. But he did not want to faint – he did not want anybody to know. No one should ever know. It was between him and the Captain. There were only the two people in the world now – himself and the Captain.

Slowly, economically, he got dressed and forced himself to walk. Everything was obscure, except just what he had his hands on. But he managed to get through his work. The very pain revived his dull senses. The worst remained yet. He took the tray and went up to the Captain's room. The officer, pale and heavy, sat at the table. The orderly, as he saluted, felt himself put out of existence. He stood still for a moment submitting to his own nullification – then he gathered himself, seemed to regain himself, and then the Captain began to grow vague, unreal, and the younger soldier's heart beat up. He clung to this situation – that the Captain did not exist – so that he himself might live. But when he saw his officer's hand tremble as he took the coffee, he felt everything falling shattered. And he went away, feeling as if he himself were coming to pieces, disintegrated. And when the Captain was there on horseback, giving orders, while he himself stood, with rifle and knapsack, sick with pain, he felt as if he must shut his eyes – as if he must shut his eyes on everything. It was only the long agony of marching with a parched throat that filled him with one single, sleep-heavy intention : to save himself.

II

He was getting used even to his parched throat. That the snowy peaks were radiant among the sky, that the whity-green glacier-river twisted through its pale shoals, in the valley below, seemed almost supernatural. But he was going mad with fever and thirst. He plodded on uncomplaining. He did not want to speak, not to anybody. There were two gulls, like flakes of water and snow, over the river. The scent of green rye soaked in sunshine came like a sickness. And the march continued, monotonously, almost like a bad sleep.

At the next farmhouse, which stood low and broad near the high road, tubs of water had been put out. The soldiers clustered round to drink. They took off their helmets, and the steam mounted from their wet hair. The Captain sat on horseback, watching. He needed to see his orderly. His helmet threw a dark shadow over his light, fierce eyes, but his moustache and mouth and chin were distinct in the sunshine. The orderly must move under the presence of the figure of the horseman. It was not that he was afraid, or cowed. It was as if he was disembowelled, made empty, like an empty shell. He felt himself as nothing, a shadow creeping under the sunshine. And, thirsty as he was, he could scarcely drink, feeling the Captain near him. He would not take off his helmet to wipe his wet hair. He wanted to stay in shadow, not to be forced into consciousness. Starting, he saw the light heel of the officer prick the belly of the horse; the Captain cantered away, and he himself could relapse into vacancy.

Nothing, however, could give him back his living place in the hot, bright morning. He felt like a gap among it all. Whereas the Captain was prouder, overriding. A hot flash went through the young servant's body. The Captain was firmer and prouder with life, he himself was empty as a shadow. Again the flash went through him, dazing him out. But his heart ran a littler firmer.

The company turned up the hill, to make a loop for the return. Below, from among the trees, the farm-bell clanged. He saw the labourers, mowing bare-foot at the thick grass, leave off their work and go downhill, their scythes hanging over their shoulders, like long, bright claws curving down behind them. They seemed like dream-people, as if they had no relation to himself. He felt as in a blackish dream: as if all the other things were there and had form, but he himself was only a consciousness, a gap that could think and perceive.

The soldiers were tramping silently up the glaring hill-side. Gradually his head began to revolve, slowly, rhythmically. Sometimes it was dark before his eyes, as if he saw this world through a smoked glass, frail shadows and unreal. It gave him a pain in his head to walk.

The air was too scented, it gave no breath. All the lush green-stuff seemed to be issuing its sap, till the air was deathly, sickly with the smell of greenness. There was the perfume of clover, like pure honey and bees. Then there grew a faint acrid tang — they were near the beeches; and then a queer clattering noise, and a suffocating, hideous smell; they were passing a flock fo sheep, a shepherd in a black smock, holding his crook. Why shouldn't the sheep huddle together under this fierce sun ? He felt that the shepherd would not see him, though he could see the shepherd.

At last there was the halt. They stacked rifles in a conical stack, put down their kit in a scattered circle around it, and dispersed a little, sitting on a small knoll high on the hill-side. The chatter began. The soliders were steaming with heat, but were lively. He sat still, seeing the blue mountains rising upon the land, twenty kilometres away. There was a blue fold in the ranges, then out of that, at the foot, the broad, pale bed of the river, stretches of whity-green water between pinkish-grey shoals among the dark pine woods. There it was, spread out a long way off. And it seemed to come downhill, the river. There was a raft being steered, a mile away. It was a strange country. Nearer, a red-roofed, broad farm with white base and square dots of windows crouched beside the wall of beech foliage on the wood's edge. There were long strips of rye and clover and pale green corn. And just at his feet, below the knoll, was the darkish bog, where globe flowers stood breathless still on their slim stalks. And some of the pale gold bubbles were burst, and a broken fragment hung in the air. He thought he was going to sleep.

Suddenly something moved into this coloured mirage before his eyes. The Captain, a small, light-blue and scarlet figure, was trotting evenly between the strips of corn, along the level brow of the hill. And the man making flag-signals was coming on. Proud and sure moved the horseman's figure, the quick, bright thing, in which was concentrated all the light of this morning, which for the rest lay fragile, shining shadow. Submissive, apathetic, the young soldier sat and stared. But as the horse slowed to a walk, coming up the last steep path, the great flash flared over the body and soul of the orderly. He sat waiting. The back of his head felt as if it were weighted with a heavy piece of fire. He did not want to eat. His hands trembled slightly as he moved them. Meanwhile the officer on horseback was approaching slowly and proudly. The tension grew in the orderly's soul. Then again, seeing the Captain ease himself on the saddle, the flash blazed through him.

The Captain looked at the patch of light blue and scarlet, and dark heads, scattered closely on the hill-side. It pleased him. The command pleased him. And he was feeling proud. His orderly was among them in common subjection. The officer rose a little on his stirrups to look. The young soldier sat with averted, dumb face. The Captain relaxed on his seat. His slim-legged, beautiful horse, brown as a beech nut, walked proudly uphill. The Captain passed into the zone of the company's atmosphere : a hot smell of men, of sweat, of leather. He knew it very well. After a word with the lieutenant, he went a few paces higher, and sat there, a dominant figure, his sweat-marked horse swishing its tail, while he looked down on his men, on his orderly, a nonentity among the crowd.

The young soldier's heart was like fire in his chest, and he breathed with difficulty. The officer, looking downhill, saw three of the young soldiers, two pails of water between them, staggering across a sunny green field. A table had been set up under a tree, and there the slim lieutenant stood, importantly busy. Then the Captain summoned himself to an act of courage. He called his orderly.

The flame leapt into the young soldier's throat as he heard the command, and he rose blindly, stifled. He saluted, standing below the officer. He did not look up. But there was the flicker in the Captain's voice.

'Go to the inn and fetch me . . .' the officer gave his commands. 'Quick !' he added.

At the last word, the heart of the servant leapt with a flash, and he felt the strength come over his body. But he turned in mechanical obedience, and set off at a heavy run downhill, looking almost like a bear, his trousers bagging over his military boots. And the officer watched this blind, plunging run all the way.

But it was only the outside of the orderly's body that was obeying so humbly and mechanically. Inside had gradually accumulated a core into which all the energy of that young life was compact and concentrated. He executed his commission, and plodded quickly back uphill. There was a pain in his head as he walked that made him twist his features unknowingly. But hard there in the centre of his chest was himself, himself, firm, and not to be plucked to pieces.

The Captain had gone up into the wood. The orderly plodded through the hot, powerfully smelling zone of the company's atmosphere. He had a curious mass of energy inside him now. The Captain was less real than himself. He approached the green entrance to the wood. There, in the half-shade, he saw the horse standing, the sunshine and the flickering shadow of leaves dancing over his brown body. There was a clearing where timber had lately been felled. Here, in the gold-green shade beside the brilliant cup of sunshine, stood two figures, blue and pink, the bits of pink showing out plainly. The Captain was talking to his lieutenant.

The orderly stood on the edge of the bright clearing, where great trunks of trees, stripped and glistening, lay stretched like naked, brown-skinned bodies. Chips of wood littered the trampled floor, like splashed light, and the bases of the felled trees stood here and there, with their raw, level tops. Beyond was the brilliant, sunlit green of a beech.

'Then I will ride forward,' the orderly heard his Captain say. The lieutenant saluted and strode away. He himself went forward. A hot flash passed through his belly, as he tramped towards his officer.

The Captain watched the rather heavy figure of the young soldier stumble forward, and his veins, too, ran hot. This was to be man to man between them. He yielded before the solid, stumbling figure with bent head. The orderly stooped and put the food on a level-sawn tree-base. The Captain watched the glistening, sun-inflamed, naked hands. He wanted to speak to the young soldier, but could not. The servant propped a bottle against his thigh, pressed open the cork, and poured out the beer into the mug. He kept his head bent. The Captain accepted the mug.

'Hot !' he said, as if amiably.

The flame sprang out of the orderly's heart, nearly suffocating him.

'Yes, sir,' he replied, between shut teeth.

And he heard the sound of the Captain's drinking, and he clenched his fists, such a strong torment came into his wrists. Then came the faint clang of the closing of the pot-lid. He looked up. The Captain was watching him. He glanced swiftly away. Then he saw the officer stoop and take a piece of bread from the tree-base. Again the flash of flame went through the young soldier, seeing the stiff body stoop beneath him, and his hands jerked. He looked away. He could feel the officer was nervous. The bread fell as it was being broken. The officer ate the other piece. The two men stood tense and still, the master laboriously chewing his bread, the servant staring with averted face, his fist clenched.

Then the young soldier started. The officer has pressed open the lid of the mug again. The orderly watched the lip of the mug, and the white hand that clenched the handle, as if he were fascinated. It was raised. The youth followed it with his eyes. And then he saw the thin, strong throat of the elder man moving up and down as he drank, the strong jaw working. And the instinct which had been jerking at the young man's wrists suddenly jerked free. He jumped, feeling as if it were rent in two by a strong flame.

The spur of the officer caught a tree root, he went down backwards with a crash, the middle of his back thudding sickeningly against a sharp-edged tree-base, the pot flying away. And in a second the orderly, with serious, earnest young face, and underlip between his teeth, had got his knee in the officer's chest and was pressing the chin backward over the farther edge of the tree-stump, pressing, with all his heart behind in a passion of relief, the tension of his wrists exquisite with relief. And with the base of his palms he shoved at the chin, that hard jaw already slightly rough with beard, in his hands. He did not relax one hair's breadth, but, all the force of all his blood exulting in his thrust, he shoved back the head of the other man, till there was a little 'cluck' and a crunching sensation. Then he felt as if his head went to vapour. Heavy convulsions shook the body of the officer, frightening and horrifying the young soldier. Yet it pleased him, too, to repress them. It pleased him to keep his hands pressing back the chin, weight of his strong, young knees, to feel the hard twitchings of the prostrate body jerking his own whole frame, which was pressed down on it.

But it went still. He could look into the nostrils of the other man, the eyes he could scarcely see. How curiously the mouth was pushed out, exaggerating the full lips, and the moustache bristling up from them. Then, with a start, he noticed the nostrils gradually filled with blood. The red brimmed, hesitated, ran over, and went in a thin trickle down the face to the eyes.

It shocked and distressed him. Slowly, he got up. The body twitched and sprawled there, inert. He stood and looked at it in silence. It was a pity *it* was broken. It represented more than the thing which had kicked and bullied him. He was afraid to look at the eyes. They were hideous now, only the whites showing, and the blood running to them. The face of the orderly was drawn with horror at the sight. Well, it was so. In his heart he was satisfied. He had hated the face of the Captain. It was extinguished now. There was a heavy relief in the orderly's soul. That was as it should be. But he could not bear to see the long, military body lying broken over the tree-base, the fine fingers crisped. He wanted to hide it away.

Quickly, busily, he gathered it up and pushed it under the felled tree trunks, which rested their beautiful, smooth length either end of the logs. The face was horrible with blood. He covered it with the helmet. Then he pushed the limbs straight and decent, and brushed the dead leaves off the fine cloth of the uniform. So, it lay quite still in the shadow under there. A little strip of sunshine ran along the breast, from a chink between the logs. The orderly sat by it for a few minutes. Here his own life also ended.

Then, through his daze, he heard the lieutenant, in a loud voice, explaining to the men outside the wood, that they were to suppose the bridge on the river below was held by the enemy. Now they were to march to the attack in such and such a manner. The lieutenant had no gift of expression. The orderly, listening from habit, got muddled. And when the lieutenant began it all again he ceased to hear.

He knew he must go. He stood up. It surprised him that the leaves were glittering in the sun, and the chips of wood reflecting white from the ground. For him a change had come over the world. But for the rest it had not – all seemed the same. Only he had left it. And he could not go back. It was his duty to return with the beer-pot and the bottle. He could not. He had left all that. The lieutenant was still hoarsely explaining. He must go, or they would overtake him. And he could not bear contact with anyone now.

He drew his fingers over his eyes, trying to find out where he was. Then he turned away. He saw the horse standing in the path. He went up to it and mounted. It hurt him to sit in the saddle. The pain of keeping his seat occupied him as they cantered through the wood. He would not have minded anything, but he could not get away from the sense of being divided from the others. The path led out of the trees. On the edge of the wood he pulled up and stood watching. There in the spacious sunshine of the valley soldiers were moving in a little swarm. Every now and then, a man harrowing on a strip of fallow shouted to his oxen, at the turn. The village and the white-towered church was small in the sunshine. And he no longer belonged to it – he sat there, beyond, like a man outside in the dark. He had gone out from everyday life into the unknown and he could not, he even did not want to go back.

Turning from the sun-blazing valley, he rode deep into the wood. Tree trunks, like people standing grey and still, took no notice as he went. A doe, herself a moving bit of sunshine and shadow, went running through the flecked shade. There were bright green rents in the foliage. Then it was all pine wood, dark and cool. And he was sick with pain, and had an intolerable great pulse in his head, and he was sick. He had never been ill in his life. He felt lost, quite dazed with all this.

Trying to get down from the horse, he fell, astonished at the pain and his lack of balance. The horse shifted uneasily. He jerked its bridle and sent it cantering jerkily away. It was his last connection with the rest of things.

But he only wanted to lie down and not be disturbed. Stumbling through the trees, he came on a quiet place where beeches and pine trees grew on a slope. Immediately he had lain down and closed his eyes, his consciousness went racing on without him. A big pulse of sickness beat in him as if it throbbed through the whole earth. He was burning with dry heat. But he was too busy, too tearingly active in the incoherent race of delirium to observe.

III

He came to with a start. His mouth was dry and hard, his heart beat heavily, but he had not the energy to get up. His heart beat heavily. Where was he ? – the barracks – at home ? There was something knocking. And, making an effort, he looked round – trees, and litter of greenery, and reddish, bright, still pieces of sunshine on the floor. He did not believe he was himself, he did not believe what he saw. Something was knocking. He made a struggle towards consciousness, but relapsed. Then he struggled again. And gradually his surroundings fell into relationship with himself. He knew, and a great pang of fear went through his heart. Somebody was knocking. He could see the heavy, black rags of a fir tree overhead. Then everything went black. Yet he did not believe he had closed his eyes. He had not. Out of the blackness sight slowly emerged again. And someone was knocking. Quickly, he saw the blood-disfigured face of his Captain, which he hated. And he held himself still with horror. Yet, deep inside him, he knew that it was so, the Captain should be dead. But the physical delirium got hold of him. Someone was knocking. He lay perfectly still, as if dead, with fear. And he went unconscious.

When he opened his eyes again he started, seeing something creeping swiftly up a tree trunk. It was a little bird. And the bird was whistling overhead. Tap-tap-tap – it was the small, quick bird rapping the tree trunk with its beak, as if its head were a little round hammer. He watched it curiously. It shifted sharply, in its creeping fashion. Then, like a mouse, it slid down the bare trunk. Its swift creeping sent a flash of revulsion through him. He raised his head. It felt a great weight. Then, the little bird ran out of the shadow across a still patch of sunshine, its little head bobbing swiftly, its white legs twinkling brightly for a moment. How neat it was in its build, so compact, with piece of white on its wing. There were several of them. They were so pretty – but they crept like swift, erratic mice, running here and there among the beech-mast.

He lay down again exhausted, and his consciousness lapsed. He had a horror of the little creeping birds. All his blood seemed to be darting and creeping in his head. And yet he could not move.

He came to with a further ache of exhaustion. There was the pain in his head, and the horrible sickness, and his inability to move. He had never been ill in his life. He did not know where he was or what he was. Probably he had got sunstroke. Or what else ? – he had silenced the Captain for ever – some time ago – oh, a long time ago. There had been blood on his face, and his eyes had turned upwards. It was all right, somehow. It was peace. But now he had got beyond himself. He had never been here before. Was it life, or not life ? He was by himself. They were in a big, bright place, those others, and he was outside. The town, all the country, a big bright place of light : and he was outside, here, in the darkened open beyond, where each thing existed alone. But they would all have to come out there sometime, those others. Little, and left behind him, they all were. They had been father and mother and sweetheart. What did they all matter? This was the open land.

He sat up. Something scuffled. It was a little brown squirrel running in lovely undulating bounds over the floor, its red tail completing the undulation of its body – and then, as it sat up, furling and unfurling. He watched it, pleased. It ran on again, friskily, enjoying itself. It flew wildly at another squirrel, and they were chasing each other, and making little scolding, chattering noises. The soldier wanted to speak to them. But only a hoarse sound came out of his throat. The squirrels burst away – they flew up the trees. And then he saw the one peeping round at him, half-way up a tree trunk. A start of fear went through him, though in so far as he was conscious, he was amused. It still stayed, its little keen face staring at him half-way up the tree trunk, its little ears pricked up, its clawey little hands clinging to the bark, its white breast reared. He started from it in panic.

Struggling to his feet, he lurched away. He went on walking, walking, looking for something – for a drink. His brain felt hot and inflamed for want of water. He stumbled on. Then he did not know anything. He went unconscious as he walked. Yet he stumbled on, his mouth open.

When, to his dumb wonder, he opened his eyes on the world again, he no longer tried to remember what it was. There was thick, golden light behind golden-green glitterings, and tall, grey-purple shafts, and darknesses farther off, surrounding him, growing deeper. He was conscious of a sense of arrival. He was amid the reality, on the real, dark bottom. But there was the thirst burning in his brain. The air was muttering with thunder. He thought he was walking wonderfully swiftly and was coming straight to relief – or was it to water?

Suddenly he stood still with fear. There was a tremendous flare of gold, immense – just a few dark trunks like bars between him and it. All the young level wheat was burnished gold glaring on its silky green. A woman, full-skirted, a black cloth on her head for head-dress, was passing like a block of shadow through the glistening, green corn, into the full glare. There was a farm, too, pale blue in shadow, and the timber black. And there was a church spire, nearly fused away in the gold. The woman moved on, away from him. He had no language with which to speak to her. She was the bright, solid unreality. She would make a noise of words that would confuse him, and her eyes would look at him without seeing him. She was crossing there to the other side. He stood against a tree.

When at last he turned, looking down the long, bare grove whose flat bed was already filling dark, he saw the mountains in a wonder-light, not far away, and radiant. Behind the soft, grey ridge of the nearest range the farther mountains stood golden and pale grey, the snow all radiant like pure, soft gold. So still, gleaming in the sky, fashioned pure out of the ore of the sky, they shone in their silence. He stood and looked at them, his face illuminated. And like the golden, lustrous gleaming of the snow he felt his own thirst bright in him. He stood and gazed, leaning against a tree. And then everything slid away into space.

During the night the lightning fluttered perpetually, making the whole sky white. He must have walked again. The world hung livid round him for moments, fields a level sheen of grey-green light, trees in dark bulk, and the range of clouds black across a white sky. Then the darkness fell like a shutter, and the night was whole. A faint flutter of a half-revealed world, that could not quite leap out of the darkness! – Then there again stood a sweep of pallor for the land, dark shapes looming, a range of clouds hanging overhead. The world was a ghostly shadow, thrown for a moment upon the pure darkness, which returned ever whole and complete.

And the mere delirium of sickness and fever went on inside him – his brain opening and shutting like the night – then sometimes convulsions of terror from something with great eyes that stared round a tree – then the long agony of the march, and the sun decomposing his blood – then the pang of hate for the Captain, followed by a pang of tenderness and ease. But everything was distorted, born of an ache and resolving into an ache.

In the morning he came definitely awake. Then his brain flamed with the sole horror of thirstiness! The sun was on his face, the dew was steaming from his wet clothes. Like one possessed, he got up. There, straight in front of him, blue and cool and tender, the mountains ranged across the pale edge of the morning sky. He wanted them – he wanted them alone – he wanted to leave himself and be identified with them. They did not move, they were still and soft, with white, gentle markings of snow. He stood still, mad with suffering, his hands crisping and clutching. Then he was twisting in a paroxysm on the grass.

He lay still, in a kind of dream of anguish. His thirst seemed to have separated itself from him, and to stand apart, a single demand. Then the pain he felt was another single self. Then there was the clog of his body, another separate thing. He was divided among all kinds of separate things. There was some strange, agonised connection between them, but they were drawing farther apart. Then they would all split. The sun, drilling down on him, was drilling through the bond. Then they would all fall, fall through the everlasting lapse of space. Then again, his consciousness reasserted itself. He roused on to his elbow and stared at the gleaming mountains. There they ranked, all still and wonderful between earth and heaven. He stared till his eyes went black, and the mountains, as they stood in their beauty, so clean and cool, seemed to have it, that which was lost in him.

IV

When the soldiers found him, three hours later, he was lying with his face over his arm, his black hair giving off heat under the sun. But he was still alive. Seeing the open, black mouth the young soldiers dropped him in horror.

He died in the hospital at night, without having seen again.

The doctors saw the bruises on his legs, behind, and were silent.

The bodies of the two men lay together, side by side, in the mortuary, the one white and slender, but laid rigidly at rest, the other looking as if every moment it must rouse into life again, so young and unused, from a slumber.

KATHERINE MANSFIELD

Je Ne Parle Pas Français

I do not know why I have such a fancy for this little café. It's dirty and sad, sad. It's not as if it had anything to distinguish it from a hundred others – it hasn't ; or as if the same strange types came here every day, whom one could watch from one's corner and recognise and more or less (with a strong accent on the less) get the hang of.

But pray don't imagine that those brackets are a confession of my humility before the mystery of the human soul. Not at all ; I don't believe in the human soul. I never have. I believe that people are like portmanteaux – packed with certain things, started going, thrown about, tossed away, dumped down, lost and found, half emptied suddenly, or squeezed fatter than ever, until finally the Ultimate Porter swings them on to the Ultimate Train and away they rattle. ...

Not but what these portmanteaux can be very fascinating. Oh, but very ! I see myself standing in front of them, don't you know, like a Customs official.

'Have you anything to declare ? Any wines, spirits, cigars, perfumes, silks ?'

And the moment of hesitation as to whether I am going to be fooled just before I chalk that squiggle, and then the other moment of hesitation just after, as to whether I have been, are perhaps the two most thrilling instants in life. Yes, they are, to me.

But before I started that long and rather far-fetched and not frightfully original digression, what I meant to say quite simply was that there are no portmanteaux to be examined here because the clientele of this café, ladies and gentlemen, does not sit down. No, it stands at the counter, and it consists of a handful of workmen who come up from the river, all powdered over with

165

white flour, lime or something, and a few soldiers, bringing with them thin, dark girls with silver rings in their ears and market baskets on their arms.

Madame is thin and dark, too, with white cheeks and white hands. In certain lights she looks quite transparent, shining out of her black shawl with an extraordinary effect. When she is not serving she sits on a stool with her face turned, always, to the window. Her dark-ringed eyes search among and follow after the people passing, but not as if she was looking for somebody. Perhaps, fifteen years ago, she was; but now the pose has become a habit. You can tell from her air of fatigue and hopelessness that she must have given them up for the last ten years, at least. ...

And then there is the waiter. Not pathetic – decidedly not comic. Never making one of those perfectly insignificant remarks which amaze you so coming from a waiter (as though the poor wretch were a sort of cross between a coffee-pot and a wine bottle and not expected to hold so much as a drop of anything else). He is grey, flat-footed and withered, with long, brittle nails that set your nerves on edge while he scrapes up your two sous. When he is not smearing over the table or flicking at a dead fly or two, he stands with one hand on the back of a chair, in his far too long apron, and over his other arm the three-cornered dip of dirty napkin, waiting to be photographed in connection with some wretched murder. 'Interior of Café where Body was Found.' You've seen him hundreds of times.

Do you believe that every place has its hour of the day when it really does come alive? That's not exactly what I mean. It's more like this. There does seem to be a moment when you realize that, quite by accident, you happen to have come on to the stage at exactly the moment you were expected. Everything is arranged for you – waiting for you. Ah, master of the situation! You fill with important breath. And at the same time you smile, secretly, slyly, because Life seems to be opposed to granting you these entrances, seems indeed to be engaged in snatching them from you and making them impossible, keeping you in the wings until it is too late, in fact. ... Just for once you've beaten the old hag.

I enjoyed one of these moments the first time I ever came in here. That's why I keep coming back, I suppose. Revisiting the scene of my triumph, or the scene of the crime where I had the old bitch by the throat for once and did what I pleased with her.

Query : Why am I so bitter against Life ? And why do I see her as a rag-picker on the American cinema, shuffling along wrapped in a filthy shawl with her old claws crooked over a stick ?

Answer : The direct result of the American cinema acting upon a weak mind.

Anyhow, the 'short winter afternoon was drawing to a close', as they say, and I was drifting along, either going home or not going home, when I found myself in here, walking over to this seat in the corner.

I hung up my English overcoat and grey felt hat on the same peg behind me, and after I had allowed the waiter time for at least twenty photographs to snap their fill of him, I ordered a coffee.

He poured me out a glass of the familiar, purplish stuff with a green wandering light playing over it, and shuffled off, and I sat pressing my hands against the glass because it was bitterly cold outside.

Suddenly I realized that quite apart from myself, I was smiling. Slowly I raised my head and saw myself in the mirror opposite. Yes, there I sat, leaning on the table, smiling my deep, sly smile, the glass of coffee with its vague plume of steam before me and beside it the ring of white saucer with two pieces of sugar.

I opened my eyes very wide. There I had been for all eternity, as it were, and now at last I was coming to life. . . .

It was very quiet in the café. Outside, one could just see through the dusk that it had begun to snow. One could just see the shapes of horses and carts and people, soft and white, moving through the feathery air. The waiter disappeared and reappeared with a armful of straw. He strewed it over the floor from the door to the counter and round about the stove with humble, almost adoring gestures. One would not have been surprised if the door had opened and the Virgin Mary had come in, riding upon an ass, her meek hands folded over her big belly. . . .

That's rather nice, don't you think, that bit about the Virgin ? It comes from the pen so gently ; it has such a 'dying fall'. I thought so at the time and decided to make a note of it. One never knows when a little tag like that may come in useful to round off a paragraph. So, taking care to move as little as possible because the 'spell' was still unbroken (you know that ?), I reached over to the next table for a writing pad.

No paper or envelopes, of course. Only a morsel of pink blotting paper, incredibly soft and limp and almost moist, like the tongue of a little dead kitten, which I've never felt.

I sat – but always underneath, in this state of expectation, rolling the little dead kitten's tongue round my finger and rolling the soft phrase round my mind while my eyes took in the girls' names and dirty jokes and drawings of bottles and cups that would not sit in the saucers, scattered over the writing pad.

They are always the same, you know. The girls always have the same names, the cups never sit in the saucers ; all the hearts are stuck and tied up with ribbons.

But then, quite suddenly, at the bottom of the page, written in green ink, I fell on to that stupid, stale little phrase : *Je ne parle pas français*.

There ! it had come – the moment – the *geste* ! And although I was so ready, it caught me, it tumbled me over ; I was simply overwhelmed. And the physical feeling was so curious, so particular. It was as if all of me, except my head and arms, all of me that was under the table, had simply dissolved, melted, turned into water. Just my head remained and two sticks of arms pressing on to the table. But, ah ! the agony of that moment ! How can I describe it ? I didn't think of anything. I didn't even cry out to myself. Just for one moment I was not. I was Agony, Agony, Agony.

Then it passed, and the very second after I was thinking : 'Good God ! Am I capable of feeling as strongly as that ? But I was absolutely unconscious ! I hadn't a phrase to meet it with ! I was so overcome ! I was swept off my feet ! I didn't even try, in the dimmest way, to put it down. !'

And up I puffed and puffed, blowing off finally with : 'After all I must be first-rate. No second-rate mind could have experienced such an intensity of feeling so ... purely.'

The waiter has touched a spill at the red stove and lighted a bubble of gas under the spreading shade. It is no use looking out of the window, Madame ; it is quite dark now. Your white hands hover over your dark shawl. They are like two birds that have come home to roost. They are restless, restless. ... You tuck them, finally, under your warm little armpits.

Now the waiter has taken a long pole and clashed the curtains together. 'All gone,' as children say.

And besides, I've no patience with people who can't let go of things, who will follow after and cry out. When a thing's gone, it's gone. It's over and done with. Let it go then ! Ignore it, and comfort yourself, if you do want comforting, with the thought that you never do recover the same thing that you lose. It's always a new thing. The moment it leaves you it's changed. Why, that's even true of a hat you chase after ; and I don't mean superficially – I mean profoundly speaking – I have made it a rule of my life never to regret and never to look back. Regret is an appalling waste of energy, and no one who intends to be a writer can afford to indulge in it. You can't get it into shape ; you can't build on it ; it's only good for wallowing in. Looking back, of course, is equally fatal to Art. It's keeping yourself poor. Art can't and won't stand poverty.

Je ne parle pas français. Je ne parle pas français. All the while I wrote that last page my other self has been chasing up and down out in the dark there. It left me just when I began to analyse my grand moment, dashed off distracted, like a lost dog who thinks at last, at last, he hears the familiar step again.

'Mouse ! Mouse ! Where are you ? Are you near ? Is that you leaning from the high window and stretching out your arms for the wings of the shutters ? Are you this soft bundle moving towards me through the feathery snow ? Are you this little girl pressing through the swing-doors of the restaurant ? Is that your dark shadow bending forward in the cab ? Where are you ? Where are you ? Which way must I turn ? Which way shall I run ? And every moment I stand here hesitating you are farther away again. Mouse ! Mouse !'

Now the poor dog has come back into the café, his tail between his legs, quite exhausted.

'It was a ... false ... alarm. She's nowhere ... to ... be seen.'

'Lie down then ! Lie down ! Lie down !'

My name is Raoul Duquette. I am twenty-six years old and a

Parisian, a true Parisian. About my family – it really doesn't matter. I have no family ; I don't want any. I never think about my childhood. I've forgotten it.

In fact, there's only one memory that stands out at all. That is rather interesting because it seems to me now so very significant as regards myself from the literary point of view. It is this.

When I was about ten our laundress was an African woman, very big, very dark, with a check handkerchief over her frizzy hair. When she came to our house she always took particular notice of me, and after the clothes had been taken out of the basket she would lift me up into it and give me a rock while I held tight to the handles and screamed for joy and fright. I was tiny for my age, and pale, with a lovely little half-open mouth – I feel sure of that.

One day when I was standing at the door, watching her go, she turned round and beckoned to me, nodding and smiling in a strange secret way. I never thought of not following. She took me into a little outhouse at the end of the passage, caught me up in her arms and began kissing me. Ah, those kisses ! Especially those kisses inside my ears that nearly deafened me.

And then with a soft growl she tore open her bodice and put me to her. When she set me down she took from her pocket a little round fried cake covered with sugar and I reeled along the passage back to our door.

As this performance was repeated once a week it is no wonder that I remember it so vividly. Besides, from that very first afternoon, my childhood was, to put it prettily, 'kissed away'. I became very languid, very caressing, and greedy beyond measure. And so quickened, so sharpened, I seemed to understand everybody and be able to do what I liked with everybody.

I suppose I was in a state of more or less physical excitement, and that was what appealed to them. For all Parisians are more than half – oh, well, enough of that. And enough of my childhood, too. Bury it under a laundry basket instead of a shower of roses and *passons oultre*.

I date myself from the moment that I became the tenant of a small bachelor flat on the fifth floor of a tall, not too shabby house, in a street that might or might not be discreet. Very useful that. . . . There I emerged, came out into the light and put out my two horns with a study and a bedroom and a kitchen on my back. And real furniture planted in the rooms. In the bedroom a wardrobe with a long glass, a big bed covered with a yellow puffed-up quilt, a bed table with a marbled top and a toilet set sprinkled with tiny apples. In my study – English writing table with drawers, writing chair with leather cushions, books, armchair, side table with paper-knife and lamp on it and some nude studies on the walls. I didn't use the kitchen except to throw old papers into.

Ah, I can see myself that first evening, after the furniture men had gone and I'd managed to get rid of my atrocious old concierge – walking about on tip-toe, arranging and standing in front of the glass with my hands in my pockets and saying to that radiant vision : 'I am a young man who has his own flat. I write for two newspapers. I am going in for serious literature. I am starting a career. The book that I shall bring out will simply stagger the critics. I am going to write about things that have never been touched before. I am going to make a name for myself as a writer about the submerged world. But not as others have done before me. Oh, no ! Very naively, with a sort of tender humour and from the inside, as though it were all quite simple, quite natural. I see my way quite perfectly. Nobody has ever done it as I shall do it because none of the others have lived my experiences. I'm rich – I'm rich.'

All the same I had no more money than I have now. It's extraordinary how one can live without money. . . . I have quantities of good clothes, silk underwear, two evening suits, four pairs of patent leather boots with light uppers, all sorts of little things, like gloves and powder boxes and a manicure set, perfumes, very good soap, and nothing is paid for. If I find myself in need of right-down cash – well, there's always an African laundress and an outhouse, and I am very frank and *bon enfant* about plenty of sugar on the little fried cake afterwards. . . .

And here I should like to put something on record. Not from any strutting conceit, but rather with a mild sense of wonder. I've never yet made the first advances to any woman. It isn't as though I've known only one class of woman – not by any means. But from little prostitutes and kept women and elderly widows and shop girls and wives of respectable men, and even advanced modern literary ladies at the most select dinners and soirées (I've been there), I've met invariably with not only the same readiness, but with the same positive invitation. It surprised me at first. I used to look across the table and think 'Is that very distinguished young lady, discussing *le Kipling* with the gentleman with the brown beard, really pressing my foot?' And I was never really certain until I had pressed hers.

Curious, isn't it? Why should I be able to have any woman I want? I don't look at all like a maiden's dream. . . .

I am little and light with an olive skin, black eyes with long lashes, black silky hair cut short, tiny square teeth that show when I smile. My hands are supple and small. A woman in a bread shop once said to me: 'You have the hands for making fine little pastries.' I confess, without my clothes I am rather charming. Plump, almost like a girl, with smooth shoulders, and I wear a thin gold bracelet above my left elbow.

But, wait! Isn't it strange I should have writen all that about my body and so on? It's the result of my bad life, my submerged life. I am like a little woman in a café who has to introduce herself with a handful of photographs. 'Me in my chemise, coming out of an eggshell. . . . Me upside down in a swing, with a frilly behind like a cauliflower. . . .' You know the things.

If you think what I've written is merely superficial and impudent and cheap you're wrong. I'll admit it does sound so, but then it is not all. If it were, how could I have experienced what I did when I read that stale little phrase written in green ink, in the writing-pad? That proves there's more in me and that I really am important, doesn't it? Anything a fraction less than the moment of anguish I might have put on. But no! That was real.

'Waiter, a whisky.'

I hate whisky. Every time I take it into my mouth my stomach rises against it, and the stuff they keep here is sure to be particularly vile. I only ordered it because I am going to write about an Englishman. We French are incredibly old-fashioned and out of date still in some ways. I wonder I didn't ask him at the same time for a pair of tweed knickerbockers, a pipe, some long teeth and a set of ginger whiskers.

'Thanks, *mon vieux*. You haven't got perhaps a set of ginger whiskers?'

'No, monsieur,' he answers sadly. 'We don't sell American drinks.'

And having smeared a corner of the table he goes back to have another couple of dozen taken by artificial light.

Ugh! The smell of it! And the sickly sensation when one's throat contracts.

'It's bad stuff to get drunk on,' says Dick Harmon, turning his little glass in his fingers and smiling his slow, dreaming smile. So he gets drunk on it slowly and dreamily and at a certain moment begins to sing very low, very low, about a man who walks up and down trying to find a place where he can get some dinner.

Ah! how I loved that song, and how I loved the way he sang it, slowly, slowly, in a dark, soft voice.

> There was a man
> Walked up and down
> To get a dinner in the town ...

It seemed to hold, in its gravity and muffled measure, all those tall grey buildings, those fogs, those endless streets, those sharp shadows of policemen that mean England.

And then – the subject! The lean, starved creature walking up and down with every house barred against him because he had no 'home'. How extraordinarily English that is. ... I remember that it ended where he did at last 'find a place' and ordered a little cake of fish, but when he asked for bread the waiter cried contemptuously, in a loud voice: 'We don't serve bread with one fish ball.'

What more do you want? How profound those songs are! There is the whole psychology of a people; and how un-French – how un-French!

'Once more, Deeck, once more!' I would plead, clasping my hands and making a pretty mouth at him. He was perfectly content to sing it for ever.

There again. Even with Dick. It was he who made the first advances.

I met him at an evening party given by the editor of a new review. It was a very select, very fashionable affair. One or two of the older men were there and the ladies were extremely *comme il faut*. They sat on cubist sofas in full evening dress and allowed us to hand them thimbles of cherry brandy and to talk to them about their poetry. For, as far as I can remember, they were all poetesses.

It was impossible not to notice Dick. He was the only Englishman present, and instead of circulating gracefully round the room as we all did, he stayed in one place leaning against the wall, his hands in his pockets, that dreamy half smile on his lips, and replying in excellent French in his low, soft voice to anybody who spoke to him.

'Who is he?'

'An Englishman. From London. A writer. And he is making a special study of modern French literature.'

That was enough for me. My little book, *False Coins,* had just been published. I was a young, serious writer who was making a special study of modern English literature.

But I really had not time to fling my line before he said, giving himself a soft shake, coming right out of the water after the bait, as it were: 'Won't you come and see me at my hotel? Come about five o'clock and we can have a talk before going out to dinner.'

'Enchanted!'

I was so deeply, deeply flattered that I had to leave him then and there to preen and preen myself before the cubist sofas. What a catch! An Englishman, reserved, serious, making a special study of French literature. ...

The same night a copy of *False Coins* with a carefully cordial inscription was posted off, and a day or two later we did dine together and spent the evening talking.

Talking – but not only of literature. I discovered to my relief that it wasn't necessary to keep to the tendency of the modern novel, the need of a new form, or the reason why our young men appeared to be just missing it. Now and again, as if by accident, I threw in a card that seemed to have nothing to do with the game, just to see how he'd take it. But each time he gathered it into his hands with his dreamy look and smile unchanged. Perhaps he murmured: 'That's very curious.'

But not as if it were curious at all.

That calm acceptance went to my head at last. It fascinated me. It led me on and on till I threw every card that I possessed at him and sat back and watched him arrange them in his hand.

'Very curious and interesting. ...'

By that time we were both fairly drunk, and he began to sing his song very soft, very low, about the man who walked up and down seeking his dinner.

But I was quite breathless at the thought of what I had done. I had shown somebody both sides of my life. Told him everything as sincerely and truthfully as I could. Taken immense pains to explain things about my submerged life that really were disgusting and never could possibly see the light of literary day. On the whole I had made myself out far worse than I was – more boastful, more cynical, more calculating.

And there sat the man I had confided in, singing to himself and smiling. ... It moved me so that real tears came into my eyes. I saw them glittering on my long silky lashes – so charming.

After that I took Dick about with me everywhere, and he came to my flat, and sat in the arm-chair, very indolent, playing with the paper-knife. I cannot think why his indolence and dreaminess always gave me the impression he had been to sea. And all his leisurely slow ways seemed to be allowing for the movement of the ship. This impression was so strong that often when we were together and he got up and left a little woman just when she did not expect him to get up and leave her, but quite the contrary, I would explain : 'He can't help it, Baby. He has to go back to his ship.' And I believed it far more than she did.

All the while we were together Dick never went with a woman. I sometimes wondered whether he wasn't completely innocent. Why didn't I ask him ? Because I never did ask him anything about himself. But late one night he took out his pocket-book and a photograph dropped out of it. I picked it up and glanced at it before I gave it to him. It was of a woman. Not quite young. Dark, handsome, wild-looking, but so full in every line of a kind of haggard pride that even if Dick had not stretched out so quickly I wouldn't have looked longer.

'Out of my sight, you little perfumed fox-terrier of a

Frenchman,' said she. (In my very worst moments my nose reminds me of a fox-terrier's.)

'That is my Mother,' said Dick, putting up the pocket-book.

But if he had not been Dick I should have been tempted to cross myself, just for fun.

This is how we parted. As we stood outside his hotel one night waiting for the concierge to release the catch of the outer door, he said, looking up at the sky : 'I hope it will be fine to-morrow. I am leaving for England in the morning.'

'You're not serious.'

'Perfectly. I have to get back. I've some work to do that I can't manage here.'

'But – but have you made all your preparations ?'

'Preparations ?' He almost grinned. 'I've none to make.'

'But – *enfin*, Dick, England is not the other side of the boulevard.'

'It isn't much farther off,' said he. 'Only a few hours, you know.' The door cracked open.

'Ah, I wish I'd known at the beginning of the evening !'

I felt hurt. I felt as a woman must feel when a man takes out his watch and remembers an appointment that cannot possibly concern her, except that its claim is the stronger. 'Why didn't you tell me ?'

He put out his hand and stood, lightly swaying upon the step as though the whole hotel were his ship, and the anchor weighed.

'I forgot. Truly I did. But you'll write, won't you ? Good night, old chap. I'll be over again one of these days.'

And then I stood on the shore alone, more like a little fox-terrier than ever. ...

'But after all it was you who whistled to me, you who asked me to come ! What a spectacle I've cut wagging my tail and leaping round you, only to be left like this while the boat sails off in its slow, dreamy way. ... Curse these English ! No, this is too insolent altogether. Who do you imagine I am ? A little paid guide to the night pleasures of Paris ? ... No, monsieur. I am a young writer, very serious, and extremely interested in modern English literature. And I have been insulted – insulted.'

Two days after came a long, charming letter from him, written in French that was a shade too French, but saying how he missed me and counted on our friendship, on keeping in touch.

I read it standing in front of the (unpaid for) wardrobe mirror. It was early morning. I wore a blue kimono embroidered with white birds and my hair was still wet; it lay on my forehead, wet and gleaming.

'Portrait of Madame Butterly,' said I, 'on hearing of the arrival of *ce cher Pinkerton.*'

According to the books I should have felt immensely relieved and delighted. ' ... Going over to the window he drew apart the curtains and looked out at the Paris trees, just breaking into buds and green. ... Dick! Dick! My English friend!'

I didn't. I merely felt a little sick. Having been up for my first ride in an aeroplane I didn't want to go up again, just now.

That passed, and months after, in the winter, Dick wrote that he was coming back to Paris to stay indefinitely. Would I take rooms for him? He was bringing a woman friend with him.

Of course I would. Away the little fox-terrier flew. It happened most usefully, too; for I owed much money at the hotel where I took my meals, and two English people requiring rooms for an indefinite time was an excellent sum on account.

Perhaps I did rather wonder, as I stood in the larger of the two rooms with Madame, saying 'Admirable,' what the woman friend would be like, but only vaguely. Either she would be very severe, flat back and front, or she would be tall, fair, dressed in mignonette green, name – Daisy, and smelling of rather sweetish lavender water.

You see, by this time, according to my rule of not looking back, I had almost forgotten Dick, I even got the tune of his song about the unfortunate man a little bit wrong when I tried to hum it. ...

I very nearly did not turn up at the station after all. I had arranged to, and had, in fact, dressed with particular care for the occasion. For I intended to take a new line with Dick this time. No more confidences and tears on eyelashes.

No, thank you !

'Since you left Paris,' said I, knotting my black silver-spotted tie in the (also unpaid for) mirror over the mantelpiece, 'I have been very successful, you know. I have two more books in preparation, and then I have written a serial story, *Wrong Doors,* which is just on the point of publication and will bring me in a lot of money. And then my little book of poems,' I cried, seizing the clothes-brush and brushing the velvet collar of my new indigo-blue overcoat, 'my little book – *Left Umbrellas* – really did create,' and I laughed and waved the brush, 'an immense sensation !'

It was impossible not to believe this of the person who surveyed himself finally, from top to toe, drawing on his soft grey gloves. He was looking the part; he was the part.

That gave me an idea. I took out my notebook, and still in full view, jotted down a note or two. . . . How can one look the part and not be the part ? Or be the part and not look it ? Isn't looking – being ? Or being – looking ? At any rate who is to say that it is not ? . . .

This seemed to me extraordinarily profound at the time, and quite new. But I confess that something did whisper as, smiling, I put up the notebook : 'You – literary ? you look as though you've taken down a bet on a racecourse !' But I didn't listen. I went out, shutting the door of the flat with a soft, quick pull so as not to warn the concierge of my departure, and ran down the stairs quick as a rabbit for the same reason.

But ah ! the old spider. She was too quick for me. She let me run down the last little ladder of the web and the she pounced. 'One moment, One little moment, Monsieur,' she whispered, odiously confidential. 'Come in. Come in.' And she beckoned with a dripping soup ladle. I went to the door, but that was not good enough. Right inside and the door shut before she would speak.

There are two ways of managing your concierge if you haven't any money. One is – to take the high hand, make her your enemy, bluster, refuse to discuss anything; the other is – to keep in with her, butter her up to the two knots of the black rag tying up her jaws, pretend to confide in her, and rely on her to arrange with the gas man and to put off the landlord.

I had tried the second. But both are equally detestable and

unsuccessful. At any rate whichever you're trying is the worse, the impossible one.

It was the landlord this time. ... Imitation of the landlord by the concierge threatening to toss me out. ... Imitation of the concierge by the concierge taming the wild bull. ... Imitation of the landlord rampant again, breathing in the concierge's face. I was the concierge. No, it was too nauseous. And all the while the black pot on the gas ring bubbling away, stewing out the hearts and livers of every tenant in the place.

'Ah !' I cried, staring at the clock on the mantelpiece, and then, realizing that it didn't go, striking my forehead as though the idea had nothing to do with it. 'Madame, I have a very important appointment with the director of my newspaper at nine-thirty. Perhaps to-morrow I shall be able to give you. ...'

Out, out. And down the métro and squeezed into a full carriage. The more the better. Everybody was one bolster the more between me and the concierge. I was radiant.

'Ah ! pardon, Monsieur !' said the tall charming creature in black with a big full bosom and a great bunch of violets dropping from it. As the train swayed it thrust the bouquet right into my eyes. 'Ah ! pardon, Monsieur !'

But I looked up at her, smiling mischievously.

'There is nothing I love more, Madame, than flowers on a balcony.'

At the very moment of speaking I caught sight of the huge man in a fur coat against whom my charmer was leaning. He poked his head over her shoulder and he went white to the nose ; in fact his nose stood out a sort of cheese green.

'What was that you said to my wife ?'

Gare Saint Lazare saved me. But you'll own that even as the author of *False Coins, Wrong Doors, Left Umbrellas,* and two in preparation, it was not too easy to go on my triumphant way.

At length, after countless trains had steamed into my mind, and countless Dick Harmons had come rolling towards me, the real train came. The little knot of us waiting at the barrier moved up close, craned forward, and broke into cries as though we were some kind of many-headed monster, and Paris behind us nothing but a great trap we had set to catch these sleepy innocents.

Into the trap they walked and were snatched and taken off to be devoured. Where was my prey?

'Good God!' My smile and my lifted hand fell together. For one terrible moment I thought this was the woman of the photograph, Dick's mother, walking towards me in Dick's coat and hat. In the effort — and you saw what an effort it was — to smile, his lips curled in just the same way and he made for me, haggard and wild and proud.

What had happened? What could have changed him like this? Should I mention it?

I waited for him and was even conscious of venturing a fox-terrier wag or two to see if he could possibly respond, in the way I said: 'Good evening, Dick! How are you, old chap? All right?'

'All right. All right.' He almost gasped. 'You've got the rooms?'

Twenty times, good God! I saw it all. Light broke on the dark waters and my sailor hadn't been drowned. I almost turned a somersault with amusement.

It was nervousness, of course. It was embarrassment. It was the famous English seriousness. What fun I was going to have! I could have hugged him.

'Yes, I've got the rooms,' I nearly shouted. 'But where is Madame?'

'She's been looking after the luggage,' he panted. 'Here she comes, now.'

Not this baby walking beside the old porter as though he were her nurse and had just lifted her out of her ugly perambulator while he trundled the boxes on it.

'And she's not Madame,' said Dick, drawling suddenly.

At that moment she caught sight of him and hailed him with her minute muff. She broke away from her nurse and ran up and said something, very quick, in English; but he replied in French: 'Oh, very well. I'll manage.'

But before he turned to the porter he indicated me with a vague wave and muttered something. We were introduced. She held out her hand in that strange boyish way Englishwomen do, and standing very straight in front of me with her chin raised and making — she too — the effort of her life to control her preposterous excitement, she said, wringing my hand (I'm sure she didn't know it was mine), *Je ne parle pas français.*

'But I'm sure you do,' I answered, so tender, so reassuring, I might have been a dentist about to draw her first little milk tooth.

'Of course she does.' Dick swerved back to us. 'Here, can't we get a cab or taxi or something? We don't want to stay in this cursed station all night. Do we?'

This was so rude that it took me a moment to recover; and he must have noticed, for he flung his arm round my shoulder in the old way, saying: 'Ah, forgive me, old chap. But we've had a loathsome, hideous journey. We've taken years to come. Haven't we?' To her. But she did not answer. She bent her head and began stroking her grey muff; she walked beside us stroking her grey muff all the way.

'Have I been wrong?' thought I. 'Is this simply a case of frenzied impatience on their part? Are they merely "in need of a bed", as we say? Have they been suffering agonies on the journey?' Sitting, perhaps, very close and warm under the same travelling rug?' and so on and so on while the driver strapped on the boxes. That done –

'Look here, Dick. I go home by métro. Here is the address of your hotel. Everything is arranged. Come and see me as soon as you can.'

Upon my life I thought he was going to faint. He went white to the lips.

'But you're coming back with us,' he cried. 'I thought it was all settled. Of course you're coming back. You're not going to leave us.' No, I gave it up. It was too difficult, too English for me.

'Certainly, certainly. Delighted. I only thought, perhaps. ...'

'You must come!' said Dick to the little fox-terrier. And again he made that big awkward turn towards her.

'Get in, Mouse.'

And Mouse got in the black hole and sat stroking Mouse II and not saying a word.

Away we jolted and rattled like three little dice that life had decided to have a fling with.

I had insisted on taking the flap seat facing them because I would not have missed for anything those occasional flashing glimpses I had as we broke through the white circles of lamplight.

They revealed Dick, sitting far back in his corner, his coat collar turned up, his hands thrust in his pockets, and his broad dark hat shading him as if it were a part of him – a sort of wing he hid under. They showed her, sitting up very straight, her lovely little face more like a drawing than a real face – every line was so full of meaning and so sharp cut against the swimming dark.

For Mouse was beautiful. She was exquisite, but so fragile and fine that each time I looked at her it was as if for the first time. She came upon you with the same kind of shock that you feel when you have been drinking tea out of a thin innocent cup and suddenly, at the bottom, you see a tiny creature, half butterfly, half woman, bowing to you with her hands in her sleeves.

As far as I could make out she had dark hair and blue or black eyes. Her long lashes and the two little feathers traced above were most important.

She wore a long dark cloak such as one sees in old-fashioned pictures of Englishwomen abroad. Where her arms came out of it there was grey fur – fur round her neck, too, and her close-fitting cap was furry.

'Carrying out the mouse idea,' I decided.

Ah, not how intriguing it was – how intriguing! Their excitement came nearer and nearer to me, while I ran out to meet it, bathed in it, flung myself far out of my depth, until at last I was at hard put to it to keep control as they.

But what I wanted to do was to behave in the most extraordinary fashion – like a clown. To start singing, with large extravagant gestures, to point out of the window and cry: 'We are now passing, ladies and gentlemen, one of the sights for which *notre Paris* is justly famous'; to jump out of the taxi while it was going, climb over the roof and dive in by another door; to hang out of the window and look for the hotel through the wrong end of a broken telescope, which was also a peculiarly ear-splitting trumpet.

I watched myself do all this, you understand, and even managed to applaud in a private way by putting my gloved

hands gently together, while I said to Mouse: 'And is this your
first visit to Paris?'

'Yes, I've not been here before.'

'Ah, then you have a great deal to see.'

And I was just going to touch lightly upon the objects of
interest and the museums when we wrenched to a stop.

Do you know – it's very absurd – but as I pushed open the
door for them and followed up the stairs to the bureau on the
landing I felt somehow that this hotel was mine.

There was a vase of flowers on the window sill of the bureau
and I even went so far as to re-arrange a bud or two and to stand
off and note the effect while the manageress welcomed them.
And when she turned to me and handed me the keys (the *garçon*
was hauling up the boxes) and said: 'Monsieur Duquette will
show you your rooms' – I had a longing to tap Dick on the arm
with a key and say, very confidentially: 'Look here, old chap. As
a friend of mine I'll be only too willing to make a slight
reduction. . . .'

Up and up we climbed. Round and round. Past an occasional
pair of boots (why is it one never sees an attractive pair of boots
outside a door?). Higher and higher.

'I'm afraid they're rather high up,' I murmured idiotically.
'But I chose them because. . . .'

They so obviously did not care why I chose them that I went
no further. They accepted everything. They did not expect
anything to be different. This was just part of what they were
going through – that was how I analysed it.

'Arrived at last.' I ran from one side of the passage to the
other, turning on the lights, explaining.

'This one I thought for you, Dick. The other is larger and it
has a little dressing-room in the alcove.'

My 'proprietary' eye noted the clean towels and covers, and
the bed linen embroidered in red cotton. I thought them rather
charming rooms, sloping, full of angles, just the sort of rooms
one would expect to find if one had not been to Paris before.

Dick dashed his hat down on the bed.

'Oughtn't I to help that chap with the boxes?' he asked –
nobody.

'Yes, you ought,' replied Mouse, 'they're dreadfully heavy.'

And she turned to me with the first glimmer of a smile: 'Books, you know.' Oh, he darted such a strange look at her before he rushed out. And he not only helped, he must have torn the box off the *garçon's* back, for he staggered back, carrying one, dumped it down and then fetched in the other.

'That's yours, Dick,' said she.

'Well, you don't mind it standing here for the present, do you?' he asked, breathless, breathing hard (the box must have been tremendously heavy). He pulled out a handful of money. 'I suppose I ought to pay this chap.'

The *garçon,* standing by, seemed to think so too.

'And will you require anything further, Monsieur?'

'No! No!' said Dick impatiently.

But at that Mouse stepped forward. She said, too deliberately, not looking at Dick, with her quaint clipped English accent: 'Yes, I'd like some tea. Tea for three.'

And suddenly she raised her muff as though her hands were clasped inside it, and she was telling the pale, sweaty *garçon* by that action that she was at the end of her resources, that she cried out to him to save her with 'Tea. Immediately!'

This seemed to me so amazingly in the picture, so exactly the gesture and cry that one would expect (thought I couldn't have imagined it) to be wrung out of an Englishwoman faced with a great crisis, that I was almost tempted to hold up my hand and protest.

'No! No! Enough. Enough. Let us leave off there. At the word – tea. For really, really, you've filled your greediest subscriber so full that he will burst if he has to swallow another word.'

It even pulled Dick up. Like someone who has been unconsious for a long long time he turned slowly to Mouse and slowly looked at her with his tired, haggard eyes, and murmured with the echo of his dreamy voice: 'Yes. That's a good idea.' And then: 'You must be tired, Mouse. Sit down.'

She sat down in a chair with lace tabs on the arms; he leaned against the bed, and I estabished myself on a straight-backed chair, crossed my legs and brushed some imaginary dust off the knees of my trousers. (The Parisian at his ease.)

There came a tiny pause. Then he said: 'Won't you take off your coat, Mouse?'

'No, thanks. Not just now.'

Were they going to ask me? Or should I hold up my hand and call out in a baby voice: 'It's my turn to be asked.'

No, I shouldn't. They didn't ask me.

The pause became a silence. A real silence.

'... Come, my Parisian fox-terrier! Amuse these sad English! It's no wonder they are such a nation for dogs.'

But, after all – why should I? It was not my "job", as they would say. Nevertheless, I made a vivacious little bound at Mouse.

'What a pity it is that you did not arrive by daylight. There is such a charming view from these two windows. You know, the hotel is on a corner and each window looks down an immensely long, straight street.'

'Yes,' she said.

'Not that that sounds very charming,' I laughed. 'But there is so much animation – so many absurd little boys on bicycles and people hanging out of windows and – oh, well, you'll see for yourself in the morning. ... Very amusing. Very animated.'

'Oh, yes,' said she.

If the pale, sweaty *garçon* had not come in at that moment, carrying the tea-tray high on one hand as if the cups were cannon-balls and he a heavy weight lifter on the cinema. ...

He managed to lower it on to a round table.

'Bring the table over here,' said Mouse. The waiter seemed to be the only person she cared to speak to. She took her hands out of her muff, drew off her gloves and flung back the old-fashioned cape.

'Do you take milk and sugar?'

'No milk, thank you, and no sugar.'

I went over for mine like a little gentleman. She poured out another cup.

'That's for Dick.'

And the faithful fox-terrier carried it across to him and laid it at his feet, as it were.

'Oh, thanks,' said Dick.

And then I went back to my chair and she sank back in hers.

But Dick was off again. He stared wildly at the cup of tea for a moment, glanced round him, put it down on the bed-table, caught up his hat and stammered at a full gallop: 'Oh, by the way, do you mind posting a letter for me? I want to get it off by to-night's post. I must. It's very urgent. ....' Feeling her eyes on him, he flung: 'It's to my mother.' To me: 'I won't be long. I've got everything I want. But it must go off to-night. You don't mind? It ... it won't take any time.'

'Of course I'll post it. Delighted.'

'Won't you drink your tea first?' suggested Mouse softly.

... Tea? Tea? Yes, of course. Tea ... A cup of tea on the bed-table. ... In his racing dream he flashed the brightest, most charming smile at his little hostess.

'No, thanks. Not just now.'

And still hoping it would not be any trouble to me he went out of the room and closed the door, and we heard him cross the passage.

I scalded myself with mine in my hurry to take the cup back to the table and to say as I stood there: 'You must forgive me if I am impertinent. ... if I am too frank. But Dick hasn't tried to disguise it – has he? There is something the matter. Can I help?'

(Soft music. Mouse gets up, walks the stage for a moment or so before she returns to her chair and pours him out, oh, such a brimming, such a burning cup that the tears come into the friend's eyes while he sips – while he drains it to the bitter dregs ....)

I had time to do all this before she replied. First she looked in the teapot, filled it with hot water, and stirred it with a spoon.

'Yes, there is something the matter. No, I'm afraid you can't help, thank you.' Again I got that glimmer of a smile. 'I'm awfully sorry. It must be horrid for you.'

Horrid, indeed! Ah, why couldn't I tell her that it was months and months since I had been so entertained?

'But you are suffering,' I ventured softly, as though that was what I could not bear to see.

She didn't deny it. She nodded and bit her under-lip and I thought I saw her chin tremble.

'And there is really nothing I can do?' More softly still.

She shook her head, pushed back the table and jumped up.

'Oh, it will be all right soon,' she breathed, walking over to the dressing-table and standing with her back towards me. 'It will be all right. It can't go on like this.'

'But of course it can't.' I agreed, wondering whether it would look heartless if I lit a cigarette; I had a sudden longing to smoke.

In some way she saw my hand move to my breast pocket, half draw out my cigarette case and put it back again, for the next thing she said was: 'Matches ... in ... candlestick. I noticed them.'

And I heard from her voice that she was crying.

'Ah, thank you. Yes. Yes. I've found them.' I lighted my cigarette and walked up and down, smoking.

It was so quiet it might have been two o'clock in the morning. It was so quiet you heard the boards creak and pop as one does in a house in the country. I smoked the whole cigarette and stabbed the end into my saucer before Mouse turned round and came back to the table.

'Isn't Dick being rather a long time?'

'You are very tired. I expect you want to go to bed,' I said kindly. (And pray don't mind me if you do, said my mind.)

'But isn't he being a very long time?' she insisted.

I shrugged. 'He is, rather.'

Then I saw she looked at me strangely. She was listening.

'He's been gone ages,' she said, and she went with little light steps to the door, opened it, and crossed the passage into his room.

I waited. I listened too, now. I couldn't have borne to miss a word. She had left the door open. I stole across the room and looked after her. Dick's door was open, too. But – there wasn't a word to miss.

You know I had the mad idea that they were kissing in that quiet room – a long comfortable kiss. One of those kisses that not only puts one's grief to bed, but nurses it and warms it and tucks it up and keeps it fast enfolded until it is sleeping sound. Ah! how good that is.

It was over at last. I heard some one move and tip-toed away.

It was Mouse. She came back. She felt her way into the room carrying the letter for me. But it wasn't in an envelope; it was just a sheet of paper and she held it by the corner as though it was still wet.

Her head was bent so low — so tucked in her furry collar that I hadn't a notion — until she let the paper fall and almost fell herself on to the floor by the side of the bed, leaned her cheek against it, flung out her hands as though the last of her poor little weapons was gone and now she let herself be carried away, washed out into the deep water.

Flash! went my mind. Dick has shot himself, and then a succession of flashes while I rushed in, saw the body, head unharmed, small blue hole over temple, roused hotel, arranged funeral, attended funeral, closed cab, new morning coat. ...

I stooped down and picked up the paper and would you believe it — so ingrained is my Parisian sense of *comme il faut* — I murmured 'pardon' before I read it.

'Mouse, my little Mouse,

It's no good. It's impossible. I can't see it through. Oh, I do love you. I do love you, Mouse, but I can't hurt her. People have been hurting her all her life. I simply dare not give her this final blow. You see, though she's stronger than both of us, she's so frail and proud. I would kill her — kill her, Mouse. And, oh God, I can't kill my mother! Not even for you. Not even for us. You do see that — don't you.

It all seemed so possible when we talked and planned, but the very moment the train started it was all over. I felt her drag me back to her — calling. I can hear her now as I write. And she's alone and she doesn't know. A man would have to be a devil to tell her and I'm not a devil, Mouse. She mustn't know. Oh, Mouse, somewhere, somewhere in you don't you agree? It's all so unspeakably awful that I don't know if I want to go or not. Do I? Or is Mother just dragging me? I don't know. My head is too tired. Mouse, Mouse — what will you do? But I can't think of that, either. I dare not. I'd break down. And I must not break down. All I've got to do is — just to tell you this and go. I couldn't have gone off without telling you. You'd have been frightened. And you must not be frightened. You won't — will you? I can't bear — but no more of that. And don't write. I should not have the courage to answer your letters and the sight of your spidery handwriting —

Forgive me. Don't love me any more. Yes. Love me. Love me. Dick.'

What do you think of that? Wasn't it a rare find? My relief at his not having shot himself was mixed with a wonderful sense of elation. I was even – more than even with my 'that's very curious and interesting' Englishman. ...

She wept so strangely. With her eyes shut, with her face quite calm except for the quivering eyelids. The tears pearled down her cheeks and she let them fall.

'You've read it?'

Her voice was quite calm, but it was not her voice any more. It was like the voice you might imagine coming out of a tiny, cold sea-shell swept high and dry at last by the salt tide. ...

I nodded, quite overcome, you understand, and laid the letter down.

'It's incredible! incredible!' I whispered.

At that she got up from the floor, walked over the wash-stand dipped her handkerchief into the jug and sponged her eyes, saying: 'Oh, no. It's not incredible at all.' And still pressing the wet ball to her eyes she came back to me, to her chair with the lace tabs, and sank into it.

'I knew all along, of course,' said the cold, salty little voice. 'From the very moment that we started. I felt it all through me, but I still went on hoping –' and here she took the handkerchief down and gave me a final glimmer – 'as one so stupidly does, you know.'

'As one does.'

Silence.

'But what will you do? You'll go back? You'll see him?'

That made her sit right up and stare across at me.

'What an extraordinary idea!' she said, more coldly than ever. 'Of course I shall not dream of seeing him. As for going back – that is quite out of the question. I can't go back.'

'But. ...'

'It's impossible. For one thing all my friends think I am married.'

I put out my hand – 'Ah, my poor little friend.'

But she shrank away. (False move.)

Of course there was one question that has been at the back of my mind all this time. I hated it.

'Have you any money?'

'Yes, I have twenty pounds – here,' and she put her hand on

her breast. I bowed. It was a great deal more than I had expected.

'And what are your plans ?'

Yes, I know. My question was the most clumsy, the most idiotic one I could have put. She had been so tame, so confiding, letting me, at any rate spiritually speaking, hold her tiny quivering body in one hand and stroke her furry head – and now, I'd thrown her away. Oh, I could have kicked myself.

She stood up. 'I have no plans. But – it's very late. You must go now, please.'

How could I get her back ? I wanted her back, I swear I was not acting then.

'Do feel that I am your friend,' I cried. 'You will let me come to-morrow, early ? You will let me look after you a little – take care of you a little ? You'll use me just as you think fit ?'

I succeeded. She came out of her hole ... timid ... but she came out.

'Yes, you're very kind. Yes. Do come to-morrow. I shall be glad. It makes things rather difficult because –' and again I clasped her boyish hand – '*je ne parle pas français.*'

Not until I was half-way down the boulevard did it come over me – the full force of it.

Why, they were suffering ... those two ... really suffering. I have seen two people suffer as I don't suppose I ever shall again .... And. .... 'Good-night, my little cat,' said I, impudently, to the fattish old prostitute picking her way home through the slush ... I didn't give her time to reply.

Of course you know what to expect. You anticipate, fully, what I am going to write. It wouldn't be me, otherwise.

I never went near the place again.

Yes, I still owe that considerable amount for lunches and dinners, but that's beside the mark. It's vulgar to mention it in the same breath with the fact that I never saw Mouse again.

Naturally, I intended to. Started out – got to the door – wrote and tore up letters – did all those things. But I simply could not make the final effort.

Even now I don't fully understand why. Of course I knew that I couldn't have kept it up. That had a great deal to do with it. But you would have thought, putting it at its lowest, curiosity couldn't have kept my fox-terrier nose away. . . .

Je ne parle pas français. That was her swan song for me.

But how she makes me break my rules. Oh, you've seen for yourself, but I could give you countless examples.

. . . Evenings, when I sit in some gloomy café, and an automatic piano starts playing a 'mouse' tune (there are dozens of tunes that evoke just her) I begin to dream things like. . . .

A little house on the edge of the sea, somewhere far, far away. A girl outside in a frock rather like Red Indian women wear, hailing a light, bare-foot boy who runs up from the beach.

'What have you got ?'

'A fish.' I smile and give it to her.

. . . The same girl, the same boy, different costumes – sitting at an open window, eating fruit and leaning out and laughing.

'All the wild strawberries are for you, Mouse. I won't touch one.'

. . . A wet night. They are going home together under an umbrella. They stop on the door to press their wet cheeks together.

And so one and so on until some dirty old gallant comes up to my table and sits opposite and begins to grimace and yap. Until I hear myself saying : 'But I've got the little girl for you, *mon vieux*. So little . . . so tiny. And a virgin.' I kiss the tips of my fingers – 'A virgin' – and lay them upon my heart. 'I give you my word of honour as a gentleman, a writer, serious, young, and extremely interested in modern English literature.'

I must go. I must go. I reach down my coat and hat. Madame knows me. 'You haven't dined yet ?' she smiles.

'No, not yet, Madame.'

I'd rather like to dine with her. Even to sleep with her afterwards. Would she be pale like that all over ?

But no. She's have large moles. They go with that kind of skin. And I can't bear them. They remind me somehow, disgustingly, of mushrooms.

Jean Rhys

Till September Petronella

There was a barrel organ playing at the corner of Torrington Square. It played 'Destiny' and 'La Palome' and 'Le Rêve Passe', all tunes I liked, and the wind was warm and kind not spiteful, which doesn't often happen in London. I packed the striped dress that Estelle had helped me to choose, and the cheap white one that fitted well, and my best underclothes, feeling very happy while I was packing. A bit of a change, for that had not been one of my lucky summers.

I would tell myself it was the colour of the carpet or something about my room which was depressing me, but it wasn't that. And it wasn't anything to do with money either. I was making nearly five pounds a week – very good for me, and different from when I first started, when I was walking round trying to get work. *No* Hawkers, *No* Models, some of them put up, and you stand there, your hands cold and clammy, afraid to ring the bell. But I had got past that state ; this depression had nothing to do with money.

I often wished I was like Estelle, this French girl who lived in the big room on the ground floor. She had everything so cut-and-dried, she walked the tightrope so beautifully, not even knowing she was walking it. I'd think about the talks we had, and her clothes and her scent and the way she did her hair, and that when I went into her room it didn't seem like a Bloomsbury bed-sitting room – and when it comes to Bloomsbury bed-sitting rooms I know what I'm talking about. No, it was like a room out of one of those long, romantic novels, six hundred and fifty pages of small print, translated from French or German or Hungarian or something – because few of the English ones have the exact feeling I mean. And you read one page of it or even one phrase of it, and then you gobble up all the rest and go about in a dream for weeks afterwards, for months afterwards – perhaps all your life, who knows? – surrounded by those six hundred and fifty pages, the houses, the streets, the snow, the river, the roses, the girls, the sun, the ladies' dresses and the gentlemen's voices, the old, wicked, hard-hearted women and the old, sad women, the waltz music, everything. What is not there you put in afterwards, for it is alive, this book, and it grows in your head. 'The house I was living in when I read that book,' you think, or 'This colour reminds me of that book.'

It was after Estelle left, telling me she was going to Paris and wasn't sure whether she was coming back, that I struck a bad patch. Several of the people I was sitting to left London in June, but, instead of arranging for more work, I took long walks, zig-zag, always the same way – Euston Road, Hampstead Road, Camden Town – though I hated those streets, which were like a grey nightmare in the sun. You saw so many old women, or women who seemed old, peering at the vegetables in the Camden Town market, looking at you with hatred, or blankly, as though they had forgotten your language, and talked another one. 'My God,' I would think, 'I hope I never live to be old. Anyway, however old I get, I'll never let my hair go grey. I'll dye it black, red, any colour you like, but I'll never let it go grey. I hate grey too much.' Coming back from one of these walks the thought came to me suddenly, like a revelation, that I could kill myself any time I liked and so end it. After that I put a better face on things.

When Marston wrote and I told the landlord I was going away for a fortnight, he said 'So there's a good time coming for the ladies, is there? – a good time coming for the girls? About time too.'

Marston said, 'You seem very perky, my dear. I hardly recognized you.'

I looked along the platform, but Julian had not come to meet me. There was only Marston, his long, white face and his pale-blue eyes, smiling.

'What a gigantic suitcase,' he said. 'I have my motorbike here, but I suppose I'd better leave it. We'll take a cab.'

It was getting dark when we reached the cottage, which stood by itself on rising ground. There were two elm trees in a field near the veranda, but the country looked bare, with low, grassy hills.

As we walked up the path through the garden I could hear Julian laughing and a girl talking, her voice very high and excited, though she put on a calm, haughty expression as we came into the room. Her dress was red, and she wore several coloured glass bangles which tinkled when she moved.

Marston said, 'This is Frankie. You've met the great Julian, of course.'

Well, I knew Frankie Morell by sight, but as she didn't say anything about it I didn't either. We smiled at each other cautiously, falsely.

The table was laid for four people. The room looked comfortable but there were no flowers. I had expected that they would have it full of flowers. However, there were some sprays of honeysuckle in a green jug in my bedroom and Marston, standing in the doorway, said 'I walked miles to get you that honeysuckle this morning. I thought about you all the time I was picking it.'

'Don't be long,' he said. 'We're all very hungry.'

We ate ham and salad and drank perry. It went to my head a bit. Julian talked about his job which he seemed to dislike. He was the music critic of one of the daily papers. 'It's a scandal. One's forced to down the right people and praise the wrong people.'

'Forced?' said Marston.

'Well, they drop very strong hints.'

'I'll take the plates away,' Frankie told me. 'You can start tomorrow. Not one of the local women will do a thing for us. We've only been here a fortnight, but they've got up a hate you wouldn't believe. Julian says he almost faints when he thinks of it. I say, why think of it?'

When she came back she turned the lamp out. Down there it was very still. The two trees outside did not move, or the moon.

Julian lay on the sofa and I was looking at his face and his hair when Marston put his arms round me and kissed me. But I watched Julian and listened to him whistling – stopping, laughing, beginning again.

'What was that music?' I said, and Frankie answered in a patronizing voice, '*Tristan*, second act duet.'

'I've never been to that opera.'

I had never been to any opera. All the same, I could imagine it.

I could imagine myself in a box, wearing a moonlight-blue dress and silver shoes, and when the lights went up everybody asking, 'Who's that lovely girl in that box?' But it must happen quickly or it will be too late.

Marston squeezed my hand. 'Very fine performance, Julian,' he said, 'very fine. Now forgive me, my dears, I must leave you. All this emotion –'

Julian lighted the lamp, took a book from the shelf and began to read.

Frankie blew on the nails of one hand and polished them on the edge of the other. Her nails were nice – of course, you could get a manicure for a bob then – but her hands were large and too white for her face. 'I've seen you at the Apple Tree, surely.' The Apple Tree was a night club in Greek Street.

'Oh yes, often.'

'But you've cut your hair. I wanted to cut mine, but Julian asked me not to. He begged me not to. Didn't you Julian?'

Julian did not answer.

'He said he'd lose his strength if I cut my hair.'

Julian turned over a page and went on reading.

'This is not a bad spot, is it?' Frankie said. 'Not one of those places where the ceiling's on top of your head and you've got to walk four miles in the dark to the lavatory. There are two other bedrooms besides the one Marston gave you. Come and have a look at them. You can change over if you want to. We'll never tear Julian away from his book. It's about the biological inferiority of women. That's what you told me, Julian, isn't it?'

'Oh, *go* away,' Julian said.

We ended up in her room, where she produced some head and figure studies, photographs.

'Do you like these?' Do you know this man? He says I'm the best model he's ever had. He says I'm far and away the best model in London.'

'Beautiful. Lovely photographs.'

But Frankie, sitting on the big bed, said, 'Aren't people swine? Julian says I never think. He's wrong, sometimes I think quite a lot. The other day I spent a long time trying to decide which were worse – men or women.'

'I wonder.'

'Women are worse.'

She had long, calm black hair, drawn away from her face and hanging smoothly almost to her waist, and a calm, clear little voice and a calm, haughty expression.

'They'll kick your face to bits if you let them. And shriek with laughter at the damage. But I'm not going to let them — oh no. ... Marston's always talking about you,' she said. 'He's very fond of you, poor old Marston. Do you know that picture as you go into his studio — in the entrance place? What's he say it is?'

'The Apotheosis of Lust.'

'Yes, the Apotheosis of Lust. I have to laugh when I think of that, for some reason. Poor old Andy Marston ... But I don't know why I should say "Poor old Andy Marston". He'll always have one penny to tinkle against another. His family's very wealthy, you know.'

'He makes me go cold.'

I thought, 'Why did I say that?' Because I like Marston.

'So that's how you feel about him, is it?' She seemed pleased, as if she had heard something she wanted to hear, had been waiting to hear.

'Are you tired?' Marston said.

I was looking out of the bedroom window at some sheep feeding in the field where the elm trees grew.

'A bit,' I said. 'A bit very.'

His mouth drooped, disappointed.

'Oh Marston, thank you for asking me down here. It's lovely to get away from London; it's like a dream.'

'A dream, my God! However, when it comes to dreams, why shouldn't they be pleasant?'

He sat down on the windowsill.

'The great Julian's not so bad, is he?'

'Why do you call him the great Julian? As if you were gibing at him.'

'Gibing at him? Good Lord, far be it from me to gibe at him. He *is* the great Julian. He's going to be very important, so far as an English musician can be important. He's horribly conceited, though. Not about his music, of course — he's conceited about his personal charm. I can't think why. He's a very ordinary type really. You see that nose and mouth and hear that voice all over the place. You rather dislike him, don't you?'

'Do I?'

'Of course you do. Have you forgotten how annoyed you were when I told you that he'd have to *see* a female before he could consent to live at close quarters with her for two weeks? You were quite spirited about it, I thought. Don't say that was only a flash in the pan, you poor devil of a female, female, female, in a country where females are only tolerated at best! What's going to become of you, Miss Petronella Gray, living in a bed-sitting room in Torrington Square, with no money, no background and no nous? ... Is Petronella your real name?'

'Yes.'

'You worry me, whatever your name is. I bet it isn't Gray.'

I thought, 'What does it matter? If you knew how bloody my home was you wouldn't be surprised that I wanted to change my name and forget all about it.'

I said, not looking at him, 'I was called after my grandmother – Julia Petronella.'

'Oh, you've got a grandmother, have you? Fancy that! Now, for Heaven's sake don't put on that expression. Take my advice and grow another skin or two and sharpen your claws before it's too late. *Before it's too late*, mark those words. If you don't, you're going to have a hell of a time.'

'So that I long for death?'

He looked startled. 'Why do you say that?'

'It was only the first thing that came into my head from nowhere. I was joking.'

When he did not answer, 'Well, good night,' I said. 'Sleep tight.'

'I shan't sleep,' he said. 'I shall probably have to listen to those two for quite a time yet. When they're amorous they're noisy and when they fight it's worse. She goes for him with a pen-knife. Mind you, she only does that because she likes it, but her good nature is a pretence. She's a bitch really. Shut your door and you won't hear anything. Will you be sad tomorrow?'

'Of course not.'

'Don't look as if you'd lost a shilling and found a sixpence then,' he said, and went out.

That's the way they always talk. 'You look as if you'd lost a shilling and found sixpence,' they say; 'You look very perky, I hardly recognized you,' they say; '*Look gay*,' they say; 'My dear

Petronella, I have an entirely new idea of you. I'm going to paint you out in the opulent square. So can you wear something gay tomorrow afternoon? Not one of those drab affairs you usually clothe yourself in. Gay – do you know the meaning of the word? Think about it, it's very important.'

Once, left alone in a very ornate studio, I went up to a plaster cast – the head of a man, one of those Greek heads – and kissed it, because it was so beautiful. Its mouth felt warm, not cold. It was smiling. When I kissed it the room went dead silent and I was frightened. I told Estelle about this one day. 'Does that sound mad?' She didn't laugh. She said, 'Who hasn't kissed a picture or a photograph and suddenly been frightened?'

The music Julian had been whistling was tormenting me. That, and the blind eyes of the plaster cast, and the way the sun shone on the black iron bedstead in my room in Torrington Square on fine days. The bars of the bedstead grin at me. Sometimes I count the knobs on the chest of drawers three times over. 'One of those drab affairs! ...'

I began to talk to Julian in my head. Was it to Julian? 'I'm not like that. I'm not at all like that. They're trying to make me like that, but I'm not like that.'

After a while I took a pencil and paper and wrote, 'I love Julian. Julian, I kissed you once, but you didn't know.'

I folded the paper several times and hid it under some clothes in my suitcase. Then I went to bed and slept at once.

Where our path joined the main road there were some cottages. As Marston and I came back from our walk next morning we passed two women in their gardens, which were full of lupins and poppies. They looked at us sullenly, as though they disliked us. When Marston said 'Good morning,' they did not answer.

'Surly, priggish brutes,' he muttered, 'but that's how they are.'

The grass round our cottage was long and trampled in places. There were no flowers.

'They're back,' Marston said. 'There's the motorbike.'

They came out on to the veranda, very spruce; Frankie in her red frock with her hair tied up in a red and blue handkerchief, Julian wearing a brown coat over a blue shirt and shabby grey trousers like Marston's. Very gay, I thought. (*Gay – do you know the meaning of the word* ?)

'What's the matter with you, Marston ?' Julian said. 'You look frightful.'

'You do seem a bit upset,' Frankie said. 'What happened ? Do tell.'

'Don't tell her anything,' said Marston. 'I'm going to dress up too. Why should I be the only one in this resplendent assembly with a torn shirt and stained bags ? Wait till you see what I've got – and I don't mean what you mean.'

'Let's get the food ready,' Frankie said to me.

The kitchen table was covered with things they had brought from Cheltenham, and there were several bottles of white wine cooling in a bucket of water in the corner.

'What have you done to Marston ?'

'Nothing. What on earth do you mean ?'

Nothing had happened. We were sitting under a tree, looking at a field of corn, and Marston put his head in my lap and then a man came along and yelled at us. I said, 'What do you think we're doing to your corn ? Can't we even look at your corn ?' But Marston only mumbled, 'I'm fearfully sorry. I'm dreadfully sorry,' and so on. And then we went walking along the main road in the sun, not talking much because I was hating him.

'Nothing happened,' I said.

'Oh well, it's a pity, because Julian's in a bad mood today. However, don't take any notice of him. Don't start a row whatever you do, just smooth it over.'

'Look at the lovely bit of steak I got,' she said. 'Marston says he can't touch any meat except cold ham, I ask you, and he does the cooling. Cold ham and risotto, risotto and cold ham. And curried eggs. That's what we've been living on ever since we came down here.'

When we went in with the food they had finished a bottle of wine. Julian said, 'Here's luck to the ruddy citizens I saw this morning. May they be flourishing and producing offspring exactly like themselves, but far, far worse, long after we are all in our dishonoured graves.'

Marston was now wearing black silk pyjamas with a pattern of red and green dragons. His long, thin neck and sad face looked extraordinary above this get-up. Frankie and I glanced at each other and giggled. Julian scowled at me.

Marston went over to the mirror. 'Never mind,' he said softly to his reflection, 'never mind, never mind.'

'It's ham and salad again,' Frankie said. 'But I've got some prunes.'

The table was near the window. A hot, white glare shone in our eyes. We tried pulling the blinds down, but one got stuck and we went on eating in the glare.

Then Frankie talked about the steak again. 'You must have your first bite tonight, Marston.'

'It won't be my first bite,' Marston said. 'I've been persuaded to taste beef before.'

'Oh, you never told me that. No likee?'

'I thought it would taste like sweat,' Marston said, 'and it did.'

Frankie looked annoyed. 'The trouble with you people is that you try to put other people off just because you don't fancy a thing. If you'd just not like it and leave it at that, but you don't *rest* till you've put everybody else off.'

'Oh God, let's get tight,' Julian said. 'There are bottles and bottles of wine in the kitchen. Cooling, I hope.'

'We'll get them,' Frankie said, 'we'll get them.'

Frankie sat on the kitchen table. 'I think Julian's spoiling for a fight. Let him calm down a bit ... you're staving Marston off, aren't you? And he doesn't like it; he's very disconsolate. You've got to be careful of these people, they can be as hard as nails.'

Far away a dog barked, a cock crew, somebody was sawing wood. I hardly noticed what she had said because again it came, that feeling of happiness, the fish-in-water feeling, so that I couldn't even remember having been unhappy.

Frankie started on a long story about a man called Petersen who had written a play about Northern gods and goddesses and Yggdrasil.

'I thought Yggdrasil was a girl, but it seems it's a tree.'

Marston and Julian and all that lot had taken Petersen up, she said. They used to ask him out and make him drunk. Then he would take his clothes off and dance about and if he did not do it somebody would be sure to say, 'What's the matter? Why don't you perform?' But as soon as he got really sordid they had dropped him like a hot brick. He simply disappeared.

'I met an old boy who knew him and asked what had happened. The old boy said, "A gigantic man has swallowed Petersen. ..." Maw, what a word! It reminds me of Julian's mother – she's a maw if you like. Well, I'd better take these bottles along now.'

So we took the four bottles out of the bucket and went back into the sitting-room. It was still hot and glaring, but not quite so bad as it had been.

'Now it's my turn to make a speech,' said Marston. 'But you must drink, pretty creatures, drink.' He filled our glasses and I drank mine quickly. He filled it up again.

'My speech,' he said, 'my speech ... Let's drink to afternoon, the best of all times. Cruel morning is past, fearful, unpredictable, lonely night is yet to come. Here's to heartrending afternoon. ... I will now recite a poem. It's hackneyed and pawed about, like so many other things, but beautiful. "*C'est bien la pire peine de ne savoir pourquoi* –"'

He stopped and began to cry. We all looked at him. Nobody laughed; nobody knew what to say. I felt shut in by the glare.

Marston blew his nose, wiped his eyes and gabbled on: '"*Pourquoi, sans amour et sans haine, Mon coeur a tant de peine. ...*"'

'"*Sans amour*" is right,' Julian said, staring at me. I looked back into his eyes.

'"But for loving, why, you would not, Sweet,"' Marston went on, '"Though we prayed you, Paid you, brayed out. In a mortar – for you could not, Sweet."'

'The motorbike was altogether a bit of luck,' Frankie said. 'Julian had a fight with a man on the bus going in. I thought he'd have a fit.'

'Fight?' Julian said. 'I never fight. I'm frightened.'

He was still staring at me.

'Well then, you were very rude.'

'I'm never rude, either,' Julian said. 'I'm far too frightened ever to be rude! I suffer in silence.'

'I shouldn't do that if I were you,' I said. The wine was making me giddy. So was the glare, and the way he was looking at me.

'What's this young creature up to?' he said. 'I can't quite make her out.'

'Ruddy respectable citizens never can.'

'Ha-hah,' Frankie said. 'One in the eye for you, Julian. You're always going on about respectable people, but you know *you* are respectable, whatever you say and whatever you do, and you'll be respectable till you die, however you die, and that way you miss something, believe it or not.'

'You keep out of this, Phoenician,' Julian said. 'You've got nothing to say. Retire under the table, because that's where I like you best.'

Frankie crawled under the table. She darted her head out now and again, pretending to bite his legs, and every time she did that he would shiver and scream.

'Oh, come on out,' he said at last. 'It's too hot for these antics.'

Frankie crawled out again, very pleased with herself, went to the mirror and arranged the handkerchief round her hair. 'Am I really like a Phoenician?'

'Of course you are. A Phoenician from Cornwall, England. Direct descent, I should say.'

'And what's she?' Frankie said. Her eyes looked quite different, like snake's eyes. We all looked quite different — it's funny what drink does.

'That's very obvious too,' Julian said.

'All right, why don't you come straight out with it?' I said. 'Or are you frightened?'

'Sometimes words fail.'

Marston waved his arms about. 'Julian, you stop this. I won't have it.'

'You fool,' Julian said, 'you fool. Can't you see she's fifth rate. Can't you see?'

'You ghastly cross between a barmaid and a chorus-girl,' he said. 'You female spider,' he said; 'You've been laughing at him for weeks,' he said, 'jeering at him, sniggering at him. Stopping him from working — the best painter in this damnable island, the only one in my opinion. And when I try to get him away from you, of course you follow him down here.'

'That's not it at all,' Marston said. 'You're not being fair to the girl. You don't understand her a bit.'

'She doesn't care,' Julian said. 'Look at her — she's giggling her stupid head off.'

'Well, what are you to do when you come up against a mutual admiration society?' I said.

'You're letting your jealousy run away with you,' said Marston.

'Jealousy?' Julian said. 'Jealousy!' He was unrecognizable. His beautiful eyes were little, mean pits and you looked down them into nothingness.

'Jealous of what?' he shrieked. 'Why, do you know that she told Frankie last night that she can't bear you and that the only reason she has anything to do with you is because she wants money. What do you think of that? Does that open your eyes?'

'Now, *Julian*!' Frankie's voice was as loud and high as his. 'You'd no right to repeat that. You promised you wouldn't and anyway you've exaggerated it. It's all very well for you to talk about how inferior women are, but you get more like your horrible mother every moment.'

'You do,' Marston said, quite calmly now. 'Julian, you really do.'

'Do you know what all this is about?' Frankie said, nodding at Julian. 'It's because he doesn't want me to go back to London with him. He wants me to go and be patronized and educated by his detestable mother in her dreary house in the dreary country, who will then say that the case is hopeless. Wasn't she a good sort and a saint to try? But the girl is *quite impossible*. Do you think I don't know that trick? It's as old as the hills.

'You're mean,' she said to Julian, 'and you hate girls really. Don't imagine I don't see through you. You're trying to get me down. But you won't do it. If you think you're the only man in the world who's fond of me *or* that I'm a goddamned fool, you're making the hell of a big mistake, you and your mother.'

She plucked a hairpin from her hair, bent it into the shape of pince-nez and went on in a mincing voice. 'Do Ay understend you tew say thet *may* sonn –' she placed the pince-nez on her nose and looked over it sourly '– with *one* connection –'

'Damn you,' said Julian, 'damn you, damn you.'

'Now they're off,' Marston said placidly. 'Drinking on a hot afternoon is a mistake. The pen-knife will be out in a minute. . . . Don't go. Stay and watch the fun. My money on Frankie every time.'

But I went into the bedroom and shut the door. I could hear them wrangling and Marston, very calm and superior, putting in a word now and again. Then nothing. They had gone on to the veranda.

I got the letter I had written and tore it very carefully into four pieces. I spat on each piece. I opened the door – there was not sign of them. I took the pieces of paper to the lavatory, emptied them in and pulled the plug. As soon as I heard the water gushing I felt better.

The door of the kitchen was open and I saw that there was another path leading to the main road.

And there I was, walking along, not thinking of anything, my eyes fixed on the ground. I walked a long way like that, not looking up, though I passed several people. At last I came to a signpost. I was on the Cirencester road. Something about the word 'miles' written made me feel very tired.

A little farther on the wall on one side of road was low. It was the same wall on which Marston and I had sat that morning, and he had said, 'Do you think we could rest here or will the very stones rise up against us?' I looked round and there was nobody in sight, so I stepped over it and sat down in the shade. It was pretty country, but bare. The white glaring look was still in the sky.

Close by there was a dove cooing. 'Coo away, dove,' I thought. 'It's no use, no use, still coo away, coo away.'

After a while the dazed feeling, as if somebody had hit me on the head, began to go. I thought 'Cirencester – and then a train to London. It's as easy as that.'

Then I realized that I had left my handbag and money, as well as everything else, in the bedroom at the cottage, but imagining walking back there made me feel so tired that I could hardly put one foot in front of the other.

I got over the wall. A car that was coming along slowed down and stopped and the man driving it said, 'Want a lift?'

I went up to the car.

'Where to you want to go?'

'I want to go to London.'

'To London? Well, I can't take you as far as that, but I can get you into Cirencester to catch a train if you like.'

I said anxiously, 'Yes – but I must go back first to the place where I've been staying. It's not far.'

'Haven't time for that. I've got an appointment. I'm late

already and I mustn't miss it. Tell you what — come along with me. If you'll wait till I've done I can take you to fetch your things.'

I got into the car. As soon as I touched him I felt comforted. Some men are like that.

'Well, you look as if you'd lost a shilling and found sixpence.'

Again I had to laugh.

'That's better. Never does any good to be down in the mouth.'

'We're nearly in Cirencester now,' he said after a while. 'I've got to see a lot of people. This is market day and I'm a farmer. I'll take you to a nice quiet place where you can have a cup of tea while you're waiting.'

He drove to a pub in a narrow street. 'This way in.' I followed him into the bar. 'Good afternoon, Mrs Strickland. Lovely day, isn't it? Will you give my friend a cup of tea while I'm away, and make her comfortable? She's very tired.'

'I will, certainly,' Mrs Strickland said, with a swift glance up and down. 'I expect the young lady would like a nice wash too, wouldn't she?' She was dark and nicely got up, but her voice had a tinny sound.

'Oh, I would.'

I looked down at my crumpled white dress. I touched my face for I knew there must be a red mark where I had lain with it pressed against the ground.

'See you later,' the farmer said.

There were brightly polished taps in the ladies' room and a very clean red and black tiled floor. I washed my hands, tried to smooth my dress, and powdered my face — *Poudre Nildé basané* — but I did it without looking in the glass.

Tea and cakes were laid in a small, dark, stuffy room. There were three pictures of Lady Hamilton, Johnny Walker advertisements, china bulldogs wearing sailor caps and two calenders. One said 9 January, but the other was right — 28 July 1914. 'Well, here I am!' He sat heavily down beside me. 'Did Mrs Strickland look after you all right?'

'Very well.'

'Oh, she's a good sort, she's a nice woman. She's known me a long time. Of course, you haven't, have you? But everything's got to have a start.'

Then he said he hadn't done so badly that afternoon and

stretched out his legs, looking pleased, looking happy as the day is long.

'What were you thinking about when I came in? You nearly jumped out of your skin.'

'I was thinking about the time.'

'About the time? Oh, don't worry about that. There's plenty of time.'

He produced a large silver case, took out a cigar and lighted it, long and slow. 'Plenty of time,' he said. 'Dark in here, isn't it? So you live in London, do you.'

'Yes.'

'I've often thought I'd like to know a nice girl up in London.'

His eyes were fixed on Lady Hamilton and I knew he was imagining a really lovely girl – all curves, curls, heart and hidden claws. He swallowed, then put his hand over mine.

'I'd like to feel that when I go up to Town there's a friend I could see and have a good time. You know. And I could give a her a good time too. By God, I could. I know what women like.'

'You do?'

'Yes, I do. They like a bit of loving, that's what they like, isn't it? A bit of loving. All women like that. They like it dressed up sometimes – and sometimes not, it all depends. You have to know, and I know. I just know.'

'You've nothing more to learn, have you?'

'Not in that way I haven't. And they like pretty dresses and bottles of scent, and bracelets with blue stones in them. I know. Well, what about it?' he said, but as if he were joking.

I looked away from him at the calendar and did not answer, making my face blank.

'What about it?' he repeated.

'It's nice of you to say you want to see me again – very polite.'

He laughed. 'You think I'm being polite, do you?' Well, perhaps – perhaps not. No harm in asking, was there? No offence meant – or taken, I hope. It's all right. I'll take you to get your things and catch your train – and we'll have a bottle of something good before we start off. It won't hurt you. It's bad stuff hurts you, not good stuff. You haven't found that out yet, but you will. Mrs Strickland has some good stuff, I can tell you – good enough for me, and I want the best.'

So we had a bottle of Clicquot in the bar.

He said, 'It puts some life into you, doesn't it?'

It did too. I wasn't feeling tired when we left the pub, nor even sad.

'Well,' he said as we got into the car, 'you've got to tell me where to drive to. And you don't happen to know a little song, do you?'

'That was very pretty,' he said when I stopped. 'You've got a very pretty voice indeed. Give us some more.'

But we were getting near the cottage and I didn't finish the next song because I was nervous and worried that I wouldn't be able to tell him the right turning.

At the foot of the path I thought, 'The champagne worked all right.'

He got out of the car and came with me. When we reached the gate leading into the garden he stood by my side without speaking.

They were on the veranda. We could hear their voices clearly.

'Listen, fool.' Julian was saying, 'listen, half-wit. What I said yesterday has nothing to do with what I say today or what I shall say tomorrow. Why should it?'

'That's what you think.' Frankie said obstinately. 'I don't agree with you. It might have something to do with it whether you like it or not.'

'Oh stop arguing, you two.' Marston said. 'It's all very well for you, Julian, but I'm worried about that girl. I'm responsible. She looked so damned miserable. Supposing she's gone and made away with herself. I shall feel awful. Besides, probably I shall be held up to every kind of score and obloquy – as usual. And though it's all your fault you'll escape scot-free – also as usual.'

'Are those your friends?' the farmer asked.

'Well, they're my friends in a way ... I have to go in to get my things. It won't take long.'

Julian said, 'I think, I rather think, Marston, that I hear a female pipe down there. You can lay your fears away. She's not the sort to kill herself. I told you that.'

'Who's that?' the farmer said.

'That's Mr Oakes, one of my hosts.'

'Oh, is it? I don't like the sound of him. I don't like the sound of any of them. Shall I come with you?'

'No, don't. I won't be long.'

I went round by the kitchen into my room, walking very softly. I changed into my dark dress and then began to throw my things into the suitcase. I did all this as quickly as I could, but before I had finished Marston came in, still wearing his black pyjamas crawling with dragons.

'Who were you talking to outside?'

'Oh, that's a man I met. He's going to drive me to Cirencester to catch the London train.'

'You're not offended, are you?'

'Not a bit. Why should I be?'

'Of course, the great Julian can be so difficult,' he murmured. 'But don't think I didn't stick up for you, because I did. I said to him. "It's all very well for you to be rude to a girl I bring down, but what about your loathly Frankie, whom you inflict upon me day after day and week after week and I never say a word? I'm never even sharp to her —" What are you smiling at?'

'The idea of your being sharp to Frankie.'

'The horrid little creature!' Marston said excitedly, 'the unspeakable bitch! But the day will come when Julian will find her out and he'll run to me for sympathy. I'll not give it him. Not after this. . . . Cheer up,' he said. 'The world is big. There's hope.'

'Of course.' But suddenly I saw the women's long, scowling faces over their lupins and their poppies, and my room in Torrington Square and the iron bars of my bedstead, and I thought, 'Not for me.'

'It may all be necessary,' he said, as if he were talking to himself. 'One has to get an entirely different set of values to be any good.'

I said, 'Do you think I could go out through the window? I don't want to meet them.'

'I'll come to the car with you. What's this man like?'

'Well, he's a bit like the man this morning, and he says he doesn't care for the sound of you.'

'Then I think I won't come. Go through the window and I'll hand your suitcase to you.'

He leaned out and said, 'See you in September, Petronella. I'll be back in September.'

I looked up at him. 'All right. Same address.'

The farmer said, 'I was coming in after you. You're well rid of that lot – never did like that sort. Too many of them about.'

'They're all right.'

'Well, tune up,' he said, and I sang 'Mr Brown, Mr Brown, Had a violin, Went around, went around, With his violin.' I sang all the way to Cirencester.

At the station he gave me my ticket and a box of chocolates.

'I bought these for you this afternoon, but I forgot them. Better hurry – there's not much time.

'Fare you well,' he said. 'That's what they say in Norfolk, where I come from.'

'Good-bye.'

'No, say fare you well.'

'Fare you well.'

The train started.

'This is very nice,' I thought, 'My first-class carriage,' and had a long look at myself in the glass for the first time since it had happened. 'Never mind,' I said, and remembered Marston saying 'Never mind, never mind.'

'Don't look so down in the mouth, my girl,' I said to myself. '*Look gay.*'

'Cheer up,' I said, and kissed myself in the cool glass. I stood with my forehead against it and watched my face clouding gradually, then turned because I felt as if someone was staring at me, but it was only the girl on the cover of the chocolate-box. She had slanting green eyes, but they were too close together, and she had a white, square, smug face that didn't go with the slanting eyes. 'I bet you could be a rotten, respectable, sneering bitch too, with a face like that, if you had a chance,' I told her.

The train got into Paddington just before ten. As soon as I was on the platform I remembered the chocolates, but I didn't go back for them. 'Somebody will find you, somebody will look after you, you rotten, sneering, stupid, tight-mouthed bitch,' I thought.

London always smells the same. 'Frowsty,' you think, 'but I'm glad to be back.' And just for a while it bears you up. 'Anything's round the corner,' you think. But long before you get round the corner it lets you drop.

I decided that I'd walk for a bit with the suitcase and get tired and then perhaps I'd sleep. But at the corner of Marylebone Road and Edgware Road my arm was stiff and I put down the suitcase and waved at a taxi standing by the kerb.

'Sorry, miss,' the driver said, 'This gentleman was first.'

The young man smiled. 'It's all right. You have it.'

'*You have it,*' he said. *The other one said,* '*Want a lift?*'

'I can get the next one. I'm not in any hurry.'

'Nor am I.'

The taxi-driver moved impatiently.

'Well, don't let's hesitate any longer,' the young man said, 'or we'll lose our taximeter-cab. Get in — I can easily drop you wherever you're going.'

'Go along Edgware Road,' he said to the driver. 'I'll tell you where in a minute.'

The taxi started.

'Where to?'

'Torrington Square.'

The house would be waiting for me. 'When I pass Estelle's door,' I thought, 'there'll be no smell of scent now.' Then I was back in my small room on the top floor, listening to the church clock chiming every quarter-hour. 'There's a good time coming for the ladies. There's a good time coming for the girls. ...'

I said, 'Wait a minute. I don't want to go to Torrington Square.'

'Oh, you don't want to go to Torrington Square?' He seemed amused and wary, but more wary than amused.

'It's such a lovely night, so warm. I don't want to go home just yet. I think I'll go and sit in Hyde Park.'

'Not Torrington Square,' he shouted through the window.

The taxi drew up.

'Damn his eyes, what's he done that for.'

The driver got down and opened the door.

'Here, where am I going to? This is the third time you've changed your mind since you 'ailed me.'

'You'll go where you're damn well told.'

'Well where am I damn well told?'

'Go to Marble Arch.'

''Yde Park,' the driver said, looking us up and down and grinning broadly. Then he got back into his seat.

'I can't bear some of these chaps, can you?' the young man said.

When the taxi stopped at the end of Park Lane we both got out without a word. The driver looked us up and down again scornfully before he started away.

'What do you want to do in Hyde Park? Look at the trees?'
He took my suitcase and walked along by my side.

'Yes, I want to look at the trees and not go back to the place where I live. Never go back.'

'I've never lived in a place I like,' I thought, 'never.'

'That does sound desperate. Well, let's see if we can find a secluded spot.'

'That chair over there will do,' I said. It was away from people under a tree. Not that people mattered much, for now it was night and they are never so frightening then.

I shut my eyes so that I could hear and smell the trees better. I imagined I could smell water too. The Serpentine – I didn't know we had walked so far.

He said, 'I can't leave you so disconsolate on this lovely night – this night of love and night of stars.' He gave a loud hiccup, and then another. 'That always happens when I've eaten quails.'

'It happens to me when I'm tight.'

'Does it?' He pulled another chair forward and sat down by my side. 'I can't leave you now until I know where you're going with that large suitcase and that desperate expression.'

I told him that I had just come back after a stay in the country, and he told me that he did not live in London, that his name was Melville and that he was at a loose end that evening.

'Did somebody let you down?'

'Oh, that's not important – not half so important as the desperate expression. I noticed that as soon as I saw you.'

'That's not despair, it's hunger.' I said, dropping into the backchat. 'Don't you know hunger when you see it?'

'Well, let's go and have something to eat then, But where?' He looked at me uncertainly. 'Where?'

'We could go to the Apple Tree. Of course, it's a bit early, but we might be able to get kippers or eggs and bacon or sausages and mash.'

'The Apple Tree? I've heard of it. Could we go there?' he said, still eyeing me.

'We could indeed. You could come as my guest. I'm a member. I was one of the first members,' I boasted.

I had touched the right spring – even the feeling of his hand on my arm changed. *Always the same spring to touch before the sneering expression will go out of their eyes and the sneering sound out of their voices. Think about it – it's very important.*

'Lots of pretty girls at the Apple Tree, aren't there?' he said.

'I can't promise anything. It's a bad time of year for the Apple Tree, the singing and the gold.'

'Now what are you talking about?'

'Somebody I know calls it that.'

'But you'll be there.' He pulled his chair closer and looked round cautiously before he kissed me. 'And you're an awfully pretty girl, aren't you? ... The Apple Tree, the singing and the gold. I like that.'

'Better than "Night of love and night of stars"?'

'Oh, they're not in the same street.'

I thought, 'How do you know what's in what street? How do they know who's fifth-rate, who's fifth-rate and where the devouring spider lives?'

'You don't really mind where we go, do you?' he said.

'I don't mind at all.'

He took his arm away. 'It was odd our meeting like that, wasn't it?'

'I don't think so. I don't think it was odd at all.'

After a silence. 'I haven't been very swift in the uptake, have I?' he said.

'No, you haven't. Now, let's be off to the Apple Tree, the singing and the gold.'

'Oh, damn the Apple Tree. I know a better place than that.'

'I've been persuaded to taste it before,' Marston said. *'It tasted exactly as I thought it would.'*

And everything was exactly as I had expected. The knowing waiters, the touch of the ice-cold wine glass, the red plush chairs, the food you don't notice, the gold-framed mirror, the bed in the room beyond that always looks as if its ostentatious whiteness hides dinginess.

But Marston should have said, 'It tastes of nothing, my dear, it tastes of nothing. ...'

When we got out into Leicester Square again I had forgotten Marston and only thought about how, when we had nothing better to do, Estelle and I would go to the Corner House or to some cheap restaurant in Soho and have dinner. She was so earnest when it came to food. 'You must have one good meal a day,' she would say, 'it is *necessary*.' *Escalope de veau* and fried potatoes and brussels sprouts, we usually had, and then *crème caramel* or *compôte de fruits*. And she seemed to be walking along by my side, wearing her blue suit and her white blouse, her high heels tapping. But as we turned the corner by the Hippodrome she vanished. I thought 'I shall never see her again – I know it.'

In the taxi he said, 'I don't forget addresses, do I?'

'No, you don't.'

To keep myself awake I began to sing 'Mr Brown, Mr Brown, Had a violin. ...'

'Are you on the stage?'

'I was. I started my brilliant and successful career like so many others, in the chorus. But I wasn't a success.'

'What a shame! Why?'

'Because I couldn't say "epigrammatic".'

He laughed – really laughed that time.

'The stage manager had the dotty idea of pulling me out of my obscurity and giving me a line to say. The line was "Oh, Lottie, Lottie, don't be epigrammatic". I rehearsed it and rehearsed it, but when it came to the night it was just a blank.'

At the top of Charing Cross Road the taxi was held up. We were both laughing so much that people turned round and stared at us.

'It was one of the most dreadful moments of my life, and I shan't ever forget it. There was the stage manager, mouthing at me from the wings – he was the prompter too and he also played a small part, the family lawyer – and there he was all dressed up in grey-striped trousers and a black tail-coat and top hat and silver side-whiskers, and there I was, in a yellow dress and a large straw hat and a green sunshade and a lovely background of an English castle and garden – half ruined and half not, you know – and a chorus of footmen and maids, and my mind a complete blank.'

The taxi started again. 'Well, what happened?'

'Nothing. After one second the other actors went smoothly on. I remember the next line. It was "Going to Ascot? Well, if you don't get into the Royal Enclosure when you *are* there I'm no judge of character".'

'But what about the audience?'

'Oh, the audience weren't surprised because, you see, they had never expected me to speak at all. Well, here we are.'

I gave him my latchkey and he opened the door.

'A formidable key! It's like the key of a prison,' he said.

Everyone had gone to bed and there wasn't even a ghost of Estelle's scent in the hall.

'We must see each other again,' he said. 'Please. Couldn't you write to met at –' He stopped. 'No, I'll write to you. If you're ever – I'll write to you anyway.'

I said, 'Do you know what I want? I want a gold bracelet with blue stones in it. Not too blue – the darker blue I prefer.'

'Oh, well.' He was wary again. 'I'll do my best, but I'm not one of these plutocrats, you know.'

'Don't you dare to come back without it. But I'm going away for a few weeks. I'll be here again in September.'

'All right, I'll see you in September, Petronella,' he said chirpily, anxious to be off. 'And you've been so sweet to me.'

'The pleasure was all mine.'

He shook his head. 'Now, Lottie, Lottie, don't be epigrammatic.'

I thought, 'I daresay he would be nice if one got to know him. I daresay, perhaps ...' listening to him tapping good-bye on the other side of the door. I tapped back twice and then started up the stairs. Past the door of Estelle's room, not feeling a thing as I passed it, because she had gone and I knew she would not ever come back.

In my room I stood looking out of the window, remembering my yellow dress, the blurred mass of the audience and the face of one man in the front row seen quite clearly, and how I thought, as quick as lightning. 'Help me, tell me what I have forgotten.' But though he had looked, as it seemed, straight into my eyes, and though I was sure he knew exactly what I was thinking, he had not helped me. He had only smiled. He had left me in that moment that seemed like years standing there until through the dreadful blankness of my mind I had heard a high, shrill, cockney voice saying, 'Going to Ascot?' and seen the stage manager frown and shake his head at me.

'My God, I must have looked a fool,' I thought, laughing and feeling the tears running down my face.

'What a waste of good tears !' the other girls had told me when I cried in the dressing-room that night. 'Oh, the waste, the waste, the waste !'

But that did not last long.

'What's the time ?' I thought, and because I wasn't sleepy any longer I sat down in the chair by the window, waiting for the clock outside to strike.

Mysterious Kôr

Full moonlight drenched the city and searched it; there was not a niche left to stand in. The effect was remorseless: London looked like the moon's capital – shallow, cratered, extinct. It was late, but not yet midnight; now the buses had stopped the polished roads and streets in this region sent for minutes together a ghostly unbroken reflection up. The soaring new flats and the crouching old shops and houses looked equally brittle under the moon, which blazed in windows that looked its way. The futility of the black-out became laughable: from the sky, presumably, you could see every slate in the roofs, every whited kerb, every contour of the naked winter flowerbeds in the park; and the lake, with its shining twists and tree-darkened islands would be a landmark for miles, yes, miles, overhead.

However, the sky, in whose glassiness floated no clouds but only opaque balloons, remained glassy-silent. The Germans no longer came by the full moon. Something more immaterial seemed to threaten, and to be keeping people at home. This day between days, this extra tax, was perhaps more than senses and nerves could bear. People stayed indoors with a fervour that could be felt: the buildings strained with battened-down human life, but not a beam, not a voice, not a note from a radio escaped. Now and then under streets and buildings the earth rumbled: the Underground sounded loudest at this time.

Outside the now gateless gates of the park, the road coming downhill from the north-west turned south and became a street, down whose perspective the traffic lights went through their unmeaning performance of changing colour. From the promontory of pavement outside the gates you saw at once up the road and down the street: from behind where you stood, between the gateposts, appeared the lesser strangements of grass and water

216

and trees. At this point, at this moment, three French soldiers, directed to a hostel they could not find, stopped singing to listen derisively to the waterbirds wakened up by the moon. Next, two wardens coming off duty emerged from their post and crossed the road diagonally, each with an elbow cupped inside a slung-on tin hat. The wardens turned their faces, mauve in the moonlight, towards the Frenchmen with no expression at all. The two sets of steps died in opposite directions, and, the birds subsiding, nothing was heard or seen until, a little way down the street, a trickle of people came out of the Underground, around the anti-panic brick wall. These all disappeared quickly, in an abashed way, or as though dissolved in the street by some white acid, but for a girl and a soldier who, by their way of walking, seemed to have no destination but each other and to be not quite certain even of that. Blotted into one shadow, he tall, she little, these two proceeded towards the park. They looked in, but did not go in; they stood there debating without speaking. Then as though a command from the street behind them had been received by their synchronised bodies, they faced round to look back the way they had come.

His look up the height of a building made his head drop back, and she saw his eyeballs glitter. She slid her hand from his sleeve, stepped to the edge of the pavement and said: 'Mysterious Kôr.'

'What is?' he said, not quite collecting himself.

'This is—

'*Mysterious Kôr thy walls forsaken stand,*
Thy lonely towers beneath a lonely moon—'

—this is Kôr.'

'Why,' he said, 'it's years since I've thought of that.' She said: 'I think of it all the time—

'*Not in the waste beyond the swamps and sand,*
The fever-haunted forest and lagoon,
Mysterious Kôr thy walls—'

—a completely forsaken city, as high as cliffs and as white as bones, with no history—'

'But something must once have happened: why had it been forsaken?'

'How could anyone tell you when there's nobody there?'

'Nobody there since how long?'

'Thousands of years.'

'In that case, it would have fallen down.'

'No, not Kôr,' she said with immediate authority. 'Kôr's altogether different; it's very strong; there is not a crack in it anywhere for a weed to grow in; the corners of stones and the monuments might have been cut yesterday, and the stairs and arches are built to support themselves.'

'You know all about it,' he said, looking at her.

'I know, I know all about it.'

'What, since you read that book?'

'Oh, I didn't get much from that; I just got the name. I knew that must be the right name; it's like a cry.'

'Most like the cry of a crow to me.' He reflected, then said: 'But the poem begins with "Not" – "*Not in the waste beyond the swamps and sand—*" And it goes on, as I remember, to prove Kôr's not really anywhere. When a poem says there's no such place—'

'What it tries to say doesn't matter: I see what it makes me see. Anyhow, that was written some time ago, at that time when they thought they had got everything taped, because the whole world had been explored, even the middle of Africa. Every thing and place had been found and marked on some map; so what wasn't marked on any map couldn't be there at all. So *they* thought: that was why he wrote the poem. "*The world is disenchanted*," it goes on. That was what set me off hating civilisation.'

'Well, cheer up,' he said; 'there isn't much of it left.'

'Oh, yes, I cheered up some time ago. This war shows we've by no means come to the end. If you can blow whole places out of existence, you can blow whole places into it. I don't see why not. They say we can't say what's come out since the bombing started. By the time we've come to the end, Kôr may be the one city left: the abiding city. I should laugh.'

'No, you wouldn't,' he said sharply. '*You* wouldn't – at least, I hope not. I hope you don't know what you're saying – does the moon make you funny?'

'Don't be cross about Kôr; please don't, Arthur,' she said.

'I thought girls thought about people.'

'What, these days?' she said. 'Think about people? How can

anyone think about people if they've got any heart? I don't know how other girls manage: I always think about Kôr.'

'Not about me?' he said. When she did not at once answer, he turned her hand over, in anguish, inside his grasp. 'Because I'm not there when you want me – is that my fault?'

'But to think about Kôr *is* to think about you and me.'

'In that dead place?'

'No, ours – we'd be alone there.'

Tightening his thumb on her palm while he thought this over, he looked behind them, around them, above them – even up at the sky. He said finally: 'But we're alone here.'

'That was why I said "Mysterious Kôr."'

'What, you mean we're there now, that here's there, that now's then? ... *I* don't mind,' he added, letting out as a laugh the sigh he had been holding in for some time. 'You ought to know the place, and for all I could tell you we might be anywhere: I often do have it, this funny feeling, the first minute or two when I've come up out of the Underground. Well, well: join the Army and see the world.' He nodded towards the perspective of traffic lights and said, a shade craftily: 'What are those, then?'

Having caught the quickest possible breath, she replied: 'Inexhaustible gases; they bored through to them and lit them as they came up; by changing colour they show the changing of minutes; in Kôr there is no sort of other time.'

'You've got the moon, though: that can't help making months.'

'Oh, and the sun of course; but those two could do what they liked; we should not have to calculate when they'd come or go.'

'We might not have to,' he said, 'but I bet I should.'

'I should not mind what you did, so long as you never said, "What next?"'

'I don't know about "next," but I do know what we'd do first.'

'What, Arthur?'

'Populate Kôr.'

She said: 'I suppose it would be all right if our children were to marry each other?'

But her voice faded out; she had been reminded that they were homeless on this his first night of leave. They were, that was to

say, in London without any hope of any place of their own.
Pepita shared a two-roomed flatlet with a girl friend, in a bye-
street off the Regent's Park Road, and towards this they must
make their half-hearted way. Arthur was to have the sitting-
room divan, usually occupied by Pepita, while she herself had
half of her girl friend's bed. There was really no room for a third,
and least of all for a man, in those small rooms packed with
furniture and the two girls' belongings: Pepita tried to be
grateful for her friend Callie's forbearance – but how could she
be, when it had not occurred to Callie that she would do better
to be away to-night? She was more slow-witted than narrow-
minded – but Pepita felt she owed a kind of ruin to her. Callie,
not yet known to be home later than ten, would be now waiting
up, in her house-coat, to welcome Arthur. That would mean
three-sided chat, drinking cocoa, then turning in: that would be
that, and that would be all. That was London, this war – they
were lucky to have a roof – London, full enough before the
Americans came. Not a place: they would even grudge you
sharing a grave – that was what even married couples
complained. Whereas in Kôr ...

In Kôr ... Like glass, the illusion shattered: a car hummed like
a hornet towards them, veered, showed its scarlet tail-light,
streaked away up the road. A woman edged round a front door
and along the area railings timidly called her cat; meanwhile a
clock near, then another set further back in the dazzling
distance, set about striking midnight. Pepita, feeling Arthur
release her arm with an abruptness that was the inverse of
passion, shivered; whereat he asked brusquely: 'Cold? Well,
which way? – we'd better be getting on.'

Callie was no longer waiting up. Hours ago she had set out the
three cups and saucers, the tins of cocoa and household milk
and, on the gas-ring, brought the kettle to just short of the boil.
She had turned open Arthur's bed, the living-room divan, in the
neat inviting way she had learnt at home – then, with a modest
impulse, replaced the cover. She had, as Pepita foresaw, been
wearing her cretonne house-coat, the nearest thing to a hostess
gown that she had; she had already brushed her hair for the
night, rebraided it, bound the braids in a coronet round her
head. Both lights and the wireless had been on, to make the

room both look and sound gay : all alone, she had come to that peak moment at which company should arrive – but so seldom does. From then on she felt welcome beginning to wither in her, a flower of the heart that had bloomed too early. There she had sat like an image, facing the three cold cups, on the edge of the bed to be occupied by an unknown man.

Callie's innocence and her still unsought-out state had brought her to take a proprietory pride in Arthur ; this was all the stronger, perhaps, because they had not yet met. Sharing the flat with Pepita, this last year, she had been content with reflecting heat of love. It was not, surprisingly, that Pepita seemed, very happy – there were times when she was palpably on the rack, and this was not what Callie could understand. 'Surely you owe it to Arthur,' she would then say, 'to keep cheerful ? So long as you love each other—' Callie's calm brow glowed – one might say that it glowed in place of her friend's ; she became the guardian of that ideality which for Pepita was constantly lost to view. It was true, with the sudden prospect of Arthur's leave, things had come nearer to earth : he became a proposition, and she would have been as glad if he could have slept somewhere else. Physically shy, a brotherless virgin, Callie shrank from sharing this flat with a young man. In this flat you could hear everything : what was once a three-windowed Victorian drawing-room had been partitioned, by very thin walls, into kitchenette, living-room, Callie's bedroom. The living-room was in the centre ; the two others open off it. What was once the conservatory, half a flight down, was now converted into a draughty bathroom, shared with somebody else on the girls' floor. The flat, for these days, was cheap – even so, it was Callie, earning more than Pepita, who paid the greater part of the rent : it thus became up to her, more or less, to express goodwill as to Arthur's making a third. 'Why, it will be lovely to have him here,' Callie said. Pepita accepted the good will without much grace – but then, had she ever much grace to spare ? – she was as restlessly secretive, as self-centred, as a little half-grown black cat. Next came a puzzling moment : Pepita seemed to be hinting that Callie should fix herself up somewhere else. 'But where would I go ?' Callie marvelled when this was at last born in on her. 'You know what London's like now. And, anyway' – here she laughed, but hers was a forehead that coloured as easily as it glowed – 'it wouldn't be proper, would it, me going off and leaving just you and Arthur; I don't know what your mother would say to me. No, we may be a little squashed, but we'll make things ever so homey. I shall not mind playing gooseberry, really, dear.'

But the hominess by now was evaporating, as Pepita and Arthur still and still did not come. At half-past ten, in obedience to the rule of the house, Callie was obliged to turn off the wireless, whereupon silence out of the stepless street began seeping into the slighted room. Callie recollected the fuel target and turned off her dear little table lamp, gaily painted with spots to make it look like a toadstool, thereby leaving only the hanging light. She laid her hand on the kettle, to find it gone cold again and sigh for the wasted gas if not for her wasted thought. Where are they? Cold crept up her out of the kettle; she went to bed.

Callie's bed lay along the wall under the window: she did not like sleeping so close up under glass, but the clearance that must be left for the opening door and cupboards made this the only possible place. Now she got in and lay rigidly on the bed's inner side, under the hanging hems of the window curtains, training her limbs not to stray to what would be Pepita's half. This sharing of her bed with another body would not be the least of her sacrifice to the lovers' love; tonight would be the first night – or at least, since she was an infant – that Callie had slept with anyone. Child of a sheltered middle-class household, she had kept physical distances all her life. Already repugnance and shyness ran through her limbs; she was preyed upon by some more obscure trouble than the expectation that she might not sleep. As to *that*, Pepita was restless; her tossings on the divan, her broken-off exclamations and blurred pleas had been to be heard, most nights, through the dividing wall.

Callie knew, as though from a vision, that Arthur would sleep soundly, with assurance and majesty. Did they not all say, too, that a soldier sleeps like a log? With awe she pictured, asleep, the face that she had not yet, awake, seen – Arthur's man's eyelids, cheek-bones and set mouth turned up to the darkened ceiling. Wanting to savour darkness herself, Callie reached out and put off her bedside lamp.

At once she knew that something was happening – out-doors, in the street, the whole of London, the world. An advance, an extraordinary movement was silently taking place; blue-white beams overflowed from it, silting, dropping round the edges of the muffling black-out curtains. When, starting up, she knocked a fold of the curtain, a beam like a mouse ran across her bed. A searchlight, the most powerful of all time, might have been turned full and steady upon her defended window; finding flaws in the black-out stuff, it made veins and stars. Once gained by this idea of pressure she could not lie down again; she sat tautly, drawn-up knees touching her breasts, and asked herself if there were anything she should do. She parted the curtains, opened them slowly wider, looked out – and was face to face with the moon.

Below the moon, the houses opposite her window blazed black in transparent shadow; and something – was it a coin or a ring? – glittered half-way across the chalk-white street. Light marched in past her face, and she turned to see where it went: out stood the curves and garlands of the great white marble Victorian mantelpiece of that lost drawing-room; out stood, in the photographs turned her way, the thoughts with which her parents had faced the camera, and the humble puzzlement of her two dogs at home. Of silver brocade, just faintly purpled with roses, became her house-coat hanging over the chair. And the moon did more: it exonerated and beautified the lateness of the lovers' return. No wonder, she said to herself, no wonder – if this was the world they walked in, if this was whom they were with. Having drunk in the white explanation, Callie lay down again. Her half of the bed was in shadow, but she allowed one hand to lie, blanched, in what would be Pepita's place. She lay and looked at the hand until it was no longer her own.

Callie woke to the sound of Pepita's key in the latch. But no voices? What had happened? Then she heared Arthur's step. She heard his unslung equipment dropped with a weary, dull sound, and the plonk of his tin hat on a wooden chair. 'Sssh-sssh!' Pepita exclaimed, 'she *might* be asleep!'

Then at last Arthur's voice: 'But I thought you said——'

'I'm not asleep; I'm just coming!' Callie called out with rapture, leaping out from her form in shadow into the moonlight, zipping on her enchanted house-coat over her nightdress, kicking her shoes on, and pinning in place, with a trembling firmness, her plaits in their coronet round her head.

Between these movements of hers she heard not another sound. Had she only dreamed they were there? Her heart beat: she stepped through the living-room, shutting her door behind her.

Pepita and Arthur stood the other side of the table; they gave the impression of being lined up. Their faces, at different levels – for Pepita's rough, dark head came only an inch above Arthur's khaki shoulder – were alike in abstention from any kind of expression; as though, spiritually, they both still refused to be here. Their features looked faint, weathered – was this the work of the moon? Pepita said at once: 'I suppose we are very late?'

'I don't wonder,' Callie said, 'on this lovely night.'

Arthur had not raised his eyes; he was looking at the three cups. Pepita now suddenly jogged his elbow, saying, 'Arthur, wake up; say something; this is Callie – well, Callie, this is Arthur, of course.'

'Why, yes, of course this is Arthur,' returned Callie, whose candid eyes since she entered had not left Arthur's face. Perceiving that Arthur did not know what to do, she advanced round the table to shake hands with him. He looked up, she looked down, for the first time: she rather beheld than felt his red-brown grip on what still seemed her glove of moonlight. 'Welcome, Arthur,' she said. 'I'm so glad to meet you at last. I hope you will be comfortable in the flat.'

'It's been kind of you,' he said after consideration.

'Please do not feel that,' said Callie. 'This is Pepita's home, too, and we both hope – don't we Pepita? – that you'll regard it as yours. Please feel free to do just as you like. I am sorry it is so small.'

'Oh, I don't know,' Arthur said, as though hypnotised; 'it seems a nice little place.'

Pepita, meanwhile, glowered and turned away.

Arthur continued to wonder, though he had once been told, how these two unalike girls had come to set up together – Pepita so small, except for her too-big head, compact of childish brusqueness and of unchildish passion, and Callie, so sedate, waxy and tall – an unlit candle. Yes, she was like one of those candles on sale outside a church; there could be something votive even in her demeanour. She was unconscious that her good manners, those of an old-fashioned country doctor's daughter, were putting the other two at a disadvantage. He found himself touched by the grave good faith with which Callie was wearing that tartish house-coat, above which her face kept the glaze of sleep; and, as she knelt to re-light the gas ring under the kettle, he marked the strong, delicate arch of one bare foot, disappearing into the arty green shoe. Pepita was now too near him ever again to be seen as he now saw Callie – in a sense, he never *had* seen Pepita for the first time: she had not been, and still sometimes was not, his type. No, he had not thought of her twice; he had not remembered her until he began to remember her with passion. You might say he had not seen Pepita coming: their love had been a collision in the dark.

Callie, determined to get this over, knelt back and said: 'Would Arthur like to wash his hands?' When they had heard him stumble down the half-flight of stairs, she said to Pepita: 'Yes, I was so glad you had the moon.'

'Why?' said Pepita. She added: 'There was too much of it.'

'You're tired. Arthur looks tired, too.'

'How would you know? He's used to marching about. But it's all this having no place to go.'

'But, Pepita, you—'

But at this point Arthur came back: from the door he noticed the wireless, and went direct to it. 'Nothing much on now, I suppose?' he doubtfully said.

'No; you see it's past midnight; we're off the air. And, anyway, in this house they don't like the wireless late. By the same token,' went on Callie, friendly smiling, 'I'm afraid I must ask you, Arthur, to take your boots off, unless, of course, you mean to stay sitting down. The people below us—'

Pepita flung off, saying something under her breath, but Arthur, remarking, 'No, I don't mind,' both sat down and began to take off his boots. Pausing, glancing to left and right at the divan's fresh cotton spread, he said: 'It's all right is it, for me to sit on this?'

'That's my bed,' said Pepita. 'You are to sleep in it.'

Callie then made the cocoa, after which they turned in. Preliminary trips to the bathroom having been worked out, Callie was the first to retire, shutting the door behind her so that Pepita and Arthur might kiss each other good night. When Pepita joined her, it was without knocking: Pepita stood still in the moon and began to tug off her clothes. Glancing with hate at the bed, she asked: 'Which side?'

'I expected you'd like the outside.'

'What are you standing about for?'

'I don't really know: as I'm inside I'd better get in first.'

'Then why not get in?'

When they had settled rigidly, side by side, Callie asked: 'Do you think Arthur's got all he wants?'

Pepita jerked her head up. 'We can't sleep in all this moon.'

'Why, you don't believe the moon does things, actually?'

'Well, it couldn't hope to make some of us *much* more screwy.'

Callie closed the curtains, then said: 'What do you mean? And – didn't you hear? – I asked if Arthur's got all he wants.'

'That's what I meant – have you got a screw loose, really?'

'Pepita, I won't stay here if you're going to be like this.'

'In that case, you had better go in with Arthur.'

'What about me?' Arthur loudly said through the wall. 'I can hear practically all you girls are saying.'

They were both startled – rather that than abashed. Arthur, alone in there, had thrown off the ligatures of his social manner: his voice held the whole authority of his sex – he was impatient, sleepy, and he belonged to no one.

'Sorry,' the girls said in unison. Then Pepita laughed soundlessly, making their bed shake, till to stop herself she bit the back of her hand, and this movement made her elbow strike Callie's cheek. 'Sorry,' she had to whisper. No answer: Pepita fingered her elbow and found it, yes, it was quite true, it was wet. 'Look, shut up crying, Callie: what have I done?'

Callie rolled right round, in order to press her forehead closely under the window, into the curtains, against the wall. Her weeping continued to be soundless: now and then, unable to reach her handkerchief, she staunched her eyes with a curtain, disturbing slivers of moon. Pepita gave up marvelling, and soon slept: at least there is something in being dog-tired.

A clock struck four as Callie woke again – but something else had made her open her swollen eyelids. Arthur, stumbling about on his padded feet, could be heard next door attempting to make no noise. Inevitably, he bumped the edge of the table. Callie sat up: by her side Pepita lay like a mummy rolled half over, in forbidding, tenacious sleep. Arthur groaned. Callie caught a breath, climbed lightly over Pepita, felt for her torch on the mantlepiece, stopped to listen again. Arthur groaned again: Callie, with movements soundless as they were certain, opened the door and slipped through to the living-room. 'What's the matter?' she whispered. 'Are you ill?'

'No; I just got a cigarette. Did I wake you up?'

'But you groaned.'

'I'm sorry; I'd no idea.'

'But do you often?'

'I've no idea, really, I tell you,' Arthur repeated. The air of the room was dense with his presence, overhung by tobacco. He must be sitting on the edge of his bed, wrapped up in his overcoat – she could smell the coat, and each time he pulled on the cigarette his features appeared down there, in the fleeting, dull reddish glow. 'Where are you?' he said. 'Show a light.'

Her nervous touch on her torch, like a reflex to what he said, made it flicker up for a second. 'I am just by the door; Pepita's asleep; I'd better go back to bed.'

'Listen. Do you two get on each other's nerves?'

'Not till to-night,' said Callie, watching the uncertain swoops of the cigarette as he reached across to the ash-tray on the edge of the table. Shifting her bare feet patiently, she added: 'You don't see us as we usually are.'

'She's a girl who shows things in funny ways – I expect she feels bad at our putting you out like this – I know I do. But then we'd got no choice, had we?'

'It is really I who am putting you out,' said Callie.

'Well, that can't be helped either, can it? You had the right to stay in your own place. If there'd been more time, we might have gone to the country, though I still don't see where we'd have gone there. It's one harder when you're not married, unless you've got the money. Smoke?'

'No, thank you. Well, if you're all right, I'll go back to bed.'

'I'm glad she's asleep – funny the way she sleeps, isn't it? You can't help wondering where she is. You haven't got a boy, have you, just at present?'

'No, I've never had one.'

'I'm not sure in one way that you're not better off. I can see there's not so much in it for a girl these days. It makes me feel cruel the way I unsettle her: I don't know how much it's me myself or how much it's something the matter that I can't help. How are any of us to know how things could have been? They forget war's not just only war; it's years out of people's lives that they've never had before and won't have again. Do you think she's fanciful?'

'Who, Pepita?'

'It's enough to make her — to-night was the pay-off. We couldn't get near any movie or any place for sitting; you had to fight into the bars, and she hates the staring in bars, and with all that milling about, every street we went, they kept on knocking her even off my arm. So then we took the tube to that park down there, but the place was as bad as daylight, let alone it was cold. We hadn't the nerve — well, that's nothing to do with you.'

'I don't mind.'

'Or else you don't understand. So we began to play — we were off in Kôr.'

'Core of what?'

'Mysterious Kôr — ghost city.'

'Where?'

'You may ask. But I could have sworn she saw it, and from the way she saw it I saw it, too. A game's a game, but what's a hallucination? You begin by laughing, then it gets in you and you can't laugh it off. I tell you, I woke up just now not knowing where I'd been; and I had to get up and feel round this table before I even knew where I was. It wasn't till then that I thought of a cigarette. Now I see why she sleeps like that, if that's where she goes.'

'But she is just as often restless; I often hear her.'

'Then she doesn't always make it. Perhaps it takes me, in some way — Well, I can't see any harm: when two people have got no place, why not want Kôr, as a start? There are no restrictions on wanting, at any rate.'

'But, oh, Arthur, can't wanting want what's human?'

He yawned. 'To be human's to be at a dead loss.' Stopping yawning, he ground out his cigarette: the china tray skidded at the edge of the table. 'Bring that light here a moment — that is, will you? I think I've messed ash all over these sheets of hers.'

Callie advanced with the torch alight, but at arm's length: now and then her thumb made the beam wobble. She watched the lit-up inside of Arthur's hand as he brushed the sheet ; and once he looked up to see her white-nightgowned figure curving above and away from him behind the arc of light.

'What's that swinging ?'

'One of my plaits of hair. Shall I open the window wider ?'

'What, to let the smoke out ? Go on. And how's your moon ?'

'Mine ?' Marvelling over this, as the first sign that Arthur remembered that she was Callie, she uncovered the window, pushed up the sash, then after a minute said : 'Not so strong.'

Indeed, the moon's power over London and the imagination had now declined. The siege of light had relaxed ; the search was over ; the street had a look of survival and no more. Whatever had glittered there, coin or ring, was now invisible or had gone. To Callie it seemed likely that there would never be such a moon again ; and on the whole she felt this was for the best. Feeling air reach in like a tired arm round her body, she dropped the curtains against it and returned to her own room.

Back by her bed, she listened : Pepita's breathing still had the regular sound of sleep. At the other side of the wall the divan creaked as Arthur stretched himself out again. Having felt ahead of her lightly, to make sure her half was empty, Callie climbed over Pepita and got in. A certain amount of warmth had travelled between the sheets from Pepita's flank, and in this Callie extended her sword-cold body : she tried to compose her limbs ; even they quivered after Arthur's words in the dark, words *to* the dark. The loss of her own mysterious expectation, of her love for love, was a small thing beside the war's total of unlived lives. Suddenly Pepita flung out one hand : its back knocked Callie lightly across the face.

Pepita had now turned over and lay with her face up. The hand that had struck Callie must have lain over the other, which grasped the pyjama collar. Her eyes, in the dark, might have been either shut or open, but nothing made her frown more or less steadily : it became certain, after another moment, that Pepita's act of justice had been unconscious. She still lay, as she had lain, in an avid dream, of which Arthur had been the source, of which Arthur was not the end. With him she looked this way, that way, down the wide void pure streets, between statues, pillars and shadows, through arch-ways and colonnades. With him she went up stairs down which nothing but moon came ;

with him trod the ermine dust of the endless halls, stood on terraces, mounted the extreme tower, looked down on the statued squares, the wide, void, pure streets. He was the password, but not the answer: it was to Kôr's finality that she turned.

Sean O'Faolain

An Enduring Friendship

When Georgie Canty saw Louis Golden at the customs counter of the airport he muttered 'Bastard!' under his breath: which was what he hoped most people in Ireland thought of Mr Louis Bloody Well Golden, editor of the *Daily Crucifix*, 'Ireland's One and Only Catholic Daily' – and one too many at that!

Georgie's eyes closed, his mouth zipped tight. His duodenum walked slowly all round his waist with spiked boots. It stuck a redhot sword in through his navel. It pulled his liver out through his ribs. His eyes closed in agony. . . .

He lifted his lids and his eyes swivelled down the counter length at Golden – at his long neck like a heron, his little rabbit's puss with the two white teeth like a nutria, the hunched shoulders of a constipated stork, and the same soapy grin for the customs officer that he probably switched on whenever he'd be talking to a bishop. As he looked at him Georgie wondered if there ever had been a plane crash in which everybody was saved, except one man.

That night at the United Bankers! With himself and Golden, two of a platform of four, debating the motion *That the Irish Are the Most Tolerant Race in the World*. Three sentences. Three not too lengthy sentences about how silly it is for Irishmen to be chasing Freemasons as if they had four horns and two tails; and there he was, the next morning, crucified in the *Crucifix* under a three-column headline – BANKERS DEFEND MASONS – and, on page four, a leading article entitled, 'So This Is Holy Ireland?' signed *Louis Paul Golden*. Naturally he was barely inside the door of the bank before he was called into the parlour.

'I understand, Mr Canty,' old Plummer smiled at him across the carpet with teeth that would clip a hedge, 'I understand that you saw fit to defend Freemasonry in public last night? Is that correct?'

Now, of course every man in the bank knows perfectly well that there isn't a month that old Plumtree Gum doesn't toddle off to the Masonic Hall with his little apron and all the rest of his regalia; and, for all anybody knows, he might be the great Mah Jong of Molesworth Street, he might be the Prince Mason of the Western World. So, what could Georgie do but rub his palms, smile a man-of-the-world smile, and utter these famous last words:

'Irishmen are in many ways absurd ...'

They heard Plummer's roar outside in the Foreign Exchange Department. After that it was ding-dong bell for five minutes. ... Who – would somebody please, *please*, tell him – who ever asked anybody to defend anybody in private or in public? And if, by any possible chance, however remote, anybody ever did happen to require the kind of services of anybody why should anybody think that *his* brilliant services were what was specifically demanded by the occasion? And, furthermore, there were people in this city who were very well equipped to defend themselves. And, furthermore, he himself had lived in this city for fifty-odd years and he had never made any secret of the fact that he was a member of the Worshipful Grand Order, and if he was ever required to defend himself he could do it very well indeed thank you without anybody's assistance! And, further-more, and especially, he would be greatly obliged if people would have the goodness to remember that their job, first, foremost, and before all, was to consider the interests of the institution that paid them and made them, which would be a jolly sight better thing for all concerned than to be going out and opening their bloody gobs to make roaring asses of themselves in the bloody press, and he would be infinitely obliged to Mr Canty if he would remember *that*. And furthermore ...

Not a peep out of Georgie. He sat dumb as a goldfish until he heard the voice of God Almighty bidding him good morning in a voice like a hangman's chaplain, followed by the words: 'I will consider later, Mr Canty, what disciplinary action may be most appropriate to the occasion.' As Georgie walked back over the two and a half miles of marble floor to his cubbyhole not a sound was heard, not a funeral note, except for some scut softly whistling 'Will Ye No' Come Back Again?' He had not done much work in his cubbyhole that day, waiting to be packed off to some back-of-beyond like Killorglin or Cahirciveen. After six weeks without one good night's sleep, he had applied for a week's leave of absence, on a doctor's certificate.

The loud-speaker retailed a female voice in Irish, of which he understood only the word *Gurrabbulluballoo*, which means, 'Thanks.' He opened his eyes to see the queue trailing out. He was the last man on the plane. He took the last seat. He found himself sitting beside the last man in the world he had wanted to see again. Their safety belts got entangled. Golden looked up and at once shot out his paw.

'Georgie Canty, for all the world! Well, isn't this the real McCoy! This is great luck.'

Georgie shook his hand warmly.

'Louis Golden. Well, I'm delighted, simply delighted to see you. Travelling far?'

'Let me help you with that belt,' said Golden, and he tucked Canty in like a baby in its pram. Then he patted his thigh. 'How's tricks? I heard you weren't too well.'

'Not bad, not bad. And yourself? And the missus? All the care doing well?'

As they roared down the runway for the take-off Golden blessed himself piously. Canty thought it just as well to do a fiddle, also, around his third vest button.

'I suppose,' he said presently, trying to suggest (but only suggest) a faint sneer, 'you're off to some ecclesiastical conference?'

Golden leaned over with a confidential, crooked grin and nudged Canty.

'Mattherofact, d'ye know what I was doing the last time I was in Paris? I was touring an Australian Jesuit around the night clubs. He was very agreeably surprised.'

'In which sense?' asked Georgie, modulating between innocence and insinuation. Golden only laughed and waved a tolerant claw.

'Harmless. A bit of leg. Nothing more. The usual routine. We did about five or six of them. Folies Bergère. Bal Tabarin. Chin-Chin. Eve. The Blue Angel. Nothing at all to it.'

Georgie squinted sideways at him, thinking of the moths in the

Bal Tabarin coming out in the altogether.

'Did *you* approve?' he inquired.

'It's not a question of approving.' When he said 'question' his two white teeth went bare. 'It's all a matter of atmosphere. When in Rome, and so on.'

He grabbed the hostess by the hip and ordered two double brandies. This, mind you, at nine-thirty in the morning!

'Morals,' he explained to Georgie, 'morals in the sense of *mores* are always affected by time and place. For example, would you walk down O'Connell Street in the middle of the noonday with nothing on but a Lastex slip?'

'The Guards'd have me in the Bridewell in two ticks.'

'There was a fella walked down the Rue Royale last year with nothin' at all on. He was only fined five francs. Betty Grable could walk down the beach at Biarritz in a G-string and a smile and nobody would look twice at her.'

The brandy was going to Georgie's head. He leaned over and laughed.

'I believe Lady Godiva rode down Broadway wan time in her skin and everybody ran out in wild excitement to see the white horse. But if that be so what's this I hear about the bishops not wanting to see girls wearing cycling shorts?'

'Who would?' cackled Golden, and they went hard at it.

They were still arguing the toss over the Channel, and whether it was the six double brandies, or the elevating sensation of being up in the air, Georgie began, in spite of himself, to find the little runt almost bearable. It was not until the Eiffel Tower appeared out of the smoke that he brought down the question of Freemasons.

'You knew blooming well that night I wasn't defending Freemasonry. But in spite of that, you bastard, you came out in your rotten rag and tore the guts out of me.'

'Editorial policy.' Blandly.

'Do you realize that you nearly cost me my job?' And he told him all about it.

'Ah! No!' cried Louis, genuinely distressed. 'For God's sake! Is that true? Well, now, doesn't that show ye what Freemasons are!'

All the same he stuck to his guns. Georgie had to grant him that he stuck to his guns.

They were still at it as they whirled around the Undying Flame in the bus; and as Georgie had not booked a hotel he went off with Louis; and by the time they were finishing lunch, and two bottles of Nuits Saint Georges, they had arrived at the Arian heresy – about which they both knew sweet damn-all – and were still at Homoiousian and Homoousian at half past four in front of two Otards and the Café de Paris in the blazing sun.

'Now, look, Louis, you flaming scoundrel,' Georgie was saying, 'your trouble is you're a moralist. All you want is an autocratic, oligarchic church laying down the law about everything from cremation to contraceptives. You're a Puritan! That's what you are!'

Louis leaned a gentle hand on Georgie's arm and breathed on him like a father confessor.

'Georgie! I'll tell you something. Here in Paris. As bloke to bloke. I have exactly the same pashuns as you have. But I *know* me pashuns! I *know* them – and they're dynamite! And what's more, the pashuns of every Irishman are dynamite! And double dynamite! And triple dynamite! And if the priests of Ireland are hard on their own people, it's because they know that if they once took the lid off the pashuns of Irish men and Irish women, aye and of Irish children, the country would *blow up*! Look at Saint Paul!'

Georgie looked and saw a smashing blonde. Louis dragged him ashore, and the pair of them took Saint Paul down to the Rue Donau where Golden knew a little bar called, of all things, *Le Crucifix*; and then they took Saint Augustine, who was a bloke Georgie said he never liked – and he didn't care *who* knew it! – across to a bar on the Quatre Septembre where they had four flat Guinnesses for ould Ireland's sake; and then they took the Manichees, and the Jansenists, and Pascal, up to the bar at the Gare du Nord; and then they went up to Sacré Coeur to say a prayer, and lean on the balustrade, and Louis explained all about Modernism to Georgie, and Georgie said it was his cup of tea, and to hell with the Council of Trent anyway for jiggering up everything; and then they had dinner near the old Pigalle, with two more bottles of Nuits Saint Georges; and then nothing would do Louis but to prove he wasn't a Puritan by going off to the Bal Tabarin, where they had two bottles of *champagne obligatoire* at three thousand francs a nose.

All Georgie could remember after that was seeing twelve girls coming out on the platform, with about as much on them, if it was all sewn together, as would make a fair-sized loincloth for one Zulu, and telling Louis, with his arm out to the twelve girls :

'There y'are Jashenist'd shay thatsh shinful ! And you – and you're a fellow I never liked, and I don't care what you think ! – *you* agree with them !'

'No ! Exhplain to ye ! Nothing that God made is shinful. Couldn't be. Shin is in us. Those girls aren't even an occashun of shin. And why ? 'Cos they don't bother us.'

'Bother me,' said Georgie. 'Bother me a helluva lot. That little wan with the green hair would bother Saint Augustine !'

'God's truth ?' asked Louis.

'Struth,' said Georgie.

'Come on out,' said Louis, getting up.

'Sit down,' shouted Georgie, dragging him back.

'C'mout,' said Louis, getting up again.

'Down !' shouts Georgie, hauling him down again.

'Out !' shouts Louis.

'Be quiet !' shouts everybody, and your two men began to shout at everybody else, and to fight one another, and a table gets knocked over, and champagne gets spilled on a girl's dress, and the twelve girls pay no attention at all, only kicking away up in the air like galvanized geese, and the two of them get hauled out and slung out on their backs on the pavement. Like one man they rush back. Like one man they get slung out again. At that they get up and they look into one another's faces, their noses one inch apart.

'You dirty little Freemason !' says Golden, baring his two teeth, and his lips glistening in the moonlight.

'You rotten little Puritan !' says Georgie with the hate of hell in his voice.

At that the two of them stopped dead as if they were a pair of waxworks out of the Musée Grevin, horrified by the sight of the hate in one another's faces. They were so horrified that they burst into a wild fit of laughing. They rocked there in one another's arms, falling over one another with the bitterness of the laughing and the hatred and the shame.

A taxi drew up beside them. They tumbled into it. And the next place they were was in the square in front of Nôtre Dame because Georgie said he wanted to see if the moon could laugh at them as much as it laughed at the gargoyles. The square was empty – it was after one in the morning. The two of them linked arms and began to stroll along the river singing the saddest Irish dirges they knew. Georgie used to say afterwards that he often thought of the poor women in the Hôtel Dieu enduring the pangs of childbirth while the two of them were bawling away about their Wild Irish Rose, and wouldn't she come home again, Kathl-e-e-en !

For the rest of the week they were inseparable.

When Georgie and Louis meet nowadays in the street, they always greet one another warmly. They ask after one another's health. They send their regards to one another's wives. If a companion asks either of them, 'Who was that ?' he will say the name, add, 'Not a bad sort of chap,' and feel the shame of that night burning in him all over again. For, of course, the truth of the whole matter is that once you go on a drunk with a fellow you're stuck with him for life ; and in Ireland every bitter word we say has to be paid for sooner or later in shame, in pity, in kindness, and perhaps even in some queer sort of perverted love.

V. S. PRITCHETT

The Evils of Spain

We took our seats at the table. There were seven of us. It was at one of those taverns in Madrid. The moment we sat down Juliano, the little, hen-headed, red-lipped consumptive who was paying for the dinner and who laughed not with his mouth but by crinkling the skin round his eyes into scores of scratchy lines and showing his bony teeth – Juliano got up and said : 'We are all badly placed.' Fernando and Felix said : 'No, we are not badly placed.' And this started another argument shouting between the lot of us. We had been arguing all the way to the restaurant. The proprietor then offered a new table in a different way. Unanimously we said : 'No,' to settle the row ; and when he brought the table and put it into place and laid a red and white check tablecloth on it, we sat down, stretched our legs, and said : 'Yes. This table is much better.'

Before this we had called for Angel at his hotel. We shook his hand or slapped him on the back or embraced him and two hung on his arm as we walked down the street. 'Ah, Angel, the rogue !' we said, giving him a squeeze. Our smooth Mediterranean Angel ! 'The uncle !' we said. 'The old scoundrel.' Angel smiled, lowering his black lashes in appreciation. Juliano gave him a prod in the ribs and asked him if he remembered, after all these years, that summer at Biarritz. When we had all been together ? The only time we had all been together before ? Juliano laughed by making his eyes wicked and expectant, like one Andalusian reminding another of the great joke they had had the day poor So and So fell down the stairs and broke his neck.

'The day you were nearly drowned,' Juliano said.

Angel's complexion was the colour of white coffee ; his hair, crinkled like a black fern, was parted in the middle, he was rich, soft-palmed, and patient. He was the only well-dressed man

238

among us, the suavest shouter. Now he sat next door but one to
Juliano. Fernando was between them, Juan next to me, and at
the end Felix. They had put Caesar at the head of the table,
because he was the oldest and the largest. Indeed, at his age he
found his weight tiring to the feet.

Caesar did not speak much. He gave his silent weight to the
dinner, letting his head drop like someone falling asleep, and
listening. To the noise we made, his silence was a balance and he
nodded all the time slowly, making everything true. Sometimes
someone told some story about him and he listened to that,
nodding and not disputing it.

But we were talking chiefly of that summer, the one when
Angel (the old uncle!) had nearly been drowned. Then Juan, the
stout, swarthy one, banged the table with his hairy hands and
put on his horn-rimmed glasses. He was the smallest and most
vehement of us, the one with the thickest neck and the deepest
voice, his words like barrels rumbling in a cellar.

'Come on! Come on! Let's make up our minds! What are we
going to eat? Eat! Eat!' he roared.

'Yes,' we cried. 'Drink! What are we going to drink?'

The proprietor, who was in his shirt-sleeves and braces, said it
was for us to decide. We could have anything we wanted. This
started another argument. He stepped back a pace and put
himself in an attitude of self-defence.

'Soup! Soup? Make up your minds about soup! Who wants
soup?' bawled Juan.

'Red wine,' some of us answered. And others: 'Not red,
white.'

'Soup I said,' shouted Juan. 'Yes,' we all shouted. 'Soup.'

'Ah,' said Juan, shaking his head, in his slow miserable
disappointed voice. 'Nobody have any soup. I want some soup.
Nobody soup,' he said sadly to the proprietor.

Juliano was bouncing in his chair and saying, God, he would
never forget that summer when Angel was nearly drowned!
When we had all been together. But Juan said Felix had not been
there and we had to straighten that matter out.

Juliano said: 'They carried him on to the beach, our little
Angel on to the beach. And the beach superintendent came
through the crowd and said: "What's happening?" "Nothing,"
we said. "A man knocked out." "Knocked out?" said the beach

superintendent. "Nothing," we said. "Drowned!" A lot of people left the crowd and ran about over the beach saying: "A man has been drowned." "Drowned," said the beach superintendent. Angel was lying in the middle of them all, unconscious, with water pouring out of his mouth.'

'No! No!' shouted Fernando. 'No. It wasn't like that.'

'How do you mean, it wasn't like that?' cried Juliano. 'I was there.' He appealed to us: 'I was there.'

'Yes, you were there,' we said.

'I *was* there. I was there bringing him in. You say it wasn't like that, but it was like that. We were all there.' Juliano jumped protesting to his feet, flung back his coat from his defying chest. His waistcoat was very loose over his stomach, draughty.

'What happened was better than that,' Fernando said.

'Ah,' said Juliano, suddenly sitting down and grinning with his eyes at everyone, very pleased at his show.

'It was better,' he said.

'How better?' said Juliano.

Fernando was a man who waited for silence and his hour. Once getting possession of the conversation he never let it go, but held it in the long, soothing ecstasy of a pliable embrace. All day long he lay in bed in his room in Fuencarral with the shutters closed, recovering from the bout of the day before. He was preparing himself to appear in the evening, spruce, grey-haired, and meaty under the deep black crescents of his eyebrows, his cheeks ripening like plums as the evening advanced, his blue eyes, which got bloodshot early, becoming mistier. He was a man who ripened and moistened. He talked his way through dinner into the night, his voice loosening, his eyes misting, his walk becoming slower and stealthier, acting every sentence, as if he were swaying through the exalted phase of inebriation. But it was an inebriation purely verbal; an exaltation of dramatic moments, refinements upon situations; and hour after hour passed until the dawn found him sodden in his own anecdotes, like a fruit in rum.

'What happened was,' Fernando said, 'that I was in the sea. And after a while I discovered Angel was in the sea. As you know, there is nothing more perilous than the sea, but with Angel in it the peril is tripled; and when I saw him I was preparing to get as far away as possible. But he was making faces in the water and soon he made such a face, so inhuman, so unnatural, I saw he was drowning. This did not surprise me, for Angel is one of those men who, when he is in the sea, he drowns. There is some psychological antipathy. Now, when I see a man drowning my instinct is to get away quickly. A man drowning is not a man. He is a lunatic. But a lunatic like Angel! But unfortunately he got me before I could get away. There he was,' Fernando stood up and raised his arm, confronting the proprietor of the restaurant, but staring right through that defensive man, 'beating the water, diving, spluttering, choking, spitting, and, seeing he was drowning, for the man *was* drowning, caught hold of me, and we both went under. Angel was like a beast. He clung to me like seaweed. I, seeing this, awarded him a knock-out – zum – but as the tenacity of man increases with unconsciousness, Angel stuck to me like a limpet, and in saving myself there was no escape from saving him.'

'That's true,' said Angel, admiring his fingernails. And Caesar nodded his head up and down twice, which made it true.

Juan then swung round and called out: 'Eat! Food! Let us order. Let us eat. We haven't ordered. We do nothing but talk, not eat. I want to eat.'

'Yes, come on,' said Felix. 'Eat. What's the fish?'

'The fish,' said the proprietor, 'is bacalao.'

'Yes,' everyone cried. 'Bacalao, a good bacalao, a very good one. No, it must be good. No. I can't eat it unless it's good, very good *and* very good.'

'No,' we said. 'Not fish. We don't want it.'

'Seven bacalaos, then?' said the proprietor.

But Fernando was still on his feet.

'And the beach inspector said: "What's his name and address and has he any identity papers?" "Man," I said, "he's in his bathing dress. Where could he keep his papers?" And Juan said: "Get a doctor. Don't stand there asking questions. Get a doctor."'

'That's true,' said Juan gloomily. 'He wasn't dead.'

'Get a doctor, that was it,' Angel said.

'And they got a doctor and brought him round and got half the Bay of Biscay out of him, gallons of it. It astonished me that so much water could come out of a man.'

'And then in the evening' – Juliano leaped up and clipped the story out of Fernando's mouth. 'Angel says to the proprietor of the hotel—'

Juan's head had sunk to his chest. His hands were over his ears.

'Eat,' he bawled in a voice of despair so final that we all stopped talking and gazed at him with astonishment for a few moments. Then in sadness he turned to me, appealing. 'Can't we eat? I am empty.'

'. . . said to the proprietor of the hotel,' Fernando grabbed the tale back from Juliano, 'who was rushing down the corridor with a face like a fish. "I am the man who was drowned this morning." And the proprietor who looked at Angel like a prawn, the proprietor said: "M'sieu, whether you were drowned or not drowned this morning, you are about to be roast. The hotel is on fire."'

'That's right,' we said. 'The hotel was on fire.'

'I remember,' said Felix. 'It began in the kitchen.'

'How in the kitchen?'

'The first time ever I heard it was in the kitchen.'

'But no,' said Angel, softly rising to claim his life story for himself. Juliano clapped his hands and bounced with joy. 'It was not like that.'

'But we were all there, Angel,' Fernando said; but Angel, who spoke very rapidly, said:

'No and no! And the proof of it is. What was I wearing?' He challenged all of us. We paused.

'Tripe,' said Juan to me, hopelessly wagging his head. 'You like tripe? They do it well. Here! Phist!' he called the proprietor through the din. 'Have you tripe, a good Basque tripe? No? What a pity! Can you get me some? Here! Listen,' he shouted to the rest of the table. 'Tripe,' he shouted, but they were engrossed in Angel.

'Pyjamas,' Fernando said. 'When you are in bed you wear your pyjamas.'

'Exactly, and they were not my pyjamas.'

'You say the fire was not in the kitchen,' shouted Fernando, 'because the pyjamas you were wearing were not yours!' And we shouted back at Angel.

'They belonged to the Italian Ambassador,' said Angel, 'the one who was with that beautiful Mexican girl.'

Then Caesar, who, as I have said, was the oldest of us and sat at the head of the table, Caesar leaned his old big pale face forward and said in a hushed voice, putting out his hands like a blind man remembering:

'My God — but what a very beautiful woman she was,' he said. 'I remember her. I have never in my life,' he said speaking all his words slowly and with grave concern, 'seen such a beautiful woman.'

Fernando and Angel, who had been standing, sat down. We all looked in awe at the huge, old-shouldered Caesar with his big pale face and the pockets under his little grey eyes, who was speaking of the most beautiful woman he had ever seen.

'She was there all that summer,' Caesar said. 'She was no longer young.' He leaned forward with his hands on the table. 'What must she have been when she was young?'

A beach, the green sea dancing down white upon it, that Mexican woman walking over the floor of a restaurant, the warm white houses, the night glossy black like the toe of a patent shoe, her hair black. We tried to think how many years ago this was. Brought by his voice to silence us, she was already fading.

The proprietor took his opportunity in our silence. 'The bacalao is done in the Basque fashions with peppers and potatoes. Bring a bacalao,' he snapped to a youth in the kitchen.

Suddenly Juan brought his fists on the table, pushed back his chair, and beat his chest with one fist and then the other. He swore in his enormous voice by his private parts.

'It's eleven o'clock. Eat! For God's sake. Fernando stands there talking and talking and no one listens to anybody. It is one of the evils of Spain. Someone stop him. Eat.'

We all woke up and glared with the defiance of the bewildered, rejecting everything he said. Then what he said to us penetrated. A wave roared over us and we were with him. We agreed with what he said. We all stood up and, by our private parts, swore that he was right. It was one of the evils of Spain.

The soup arrived. White wine arrived.

'I didn't order soup,' some shouted.

'I said "Red wine,"' others said.

'It is a mistake,' the proprietor said. 'I'll take it away.' An argument started about this.

'No,' we said. 'Leave it. We want it.' And then we said the

soup was bad, and the wine was bad and everything he brought was bad, but the proprietor said the soup was good and the wine was good and we said in the end it was good. We told the proprietor the restaurant was good, but he said not very good – indeed, bad. And then we asked Angel to explain about the pyjamas.

H. E. BATES

The Kimono

I

It was the second Saturday of August, 1911, when I came to London for the interview with Kersch and Co. I was just twenty-five. The summer had been almost tropical.

There used to be a train in those days that got into St Pancras, from the North, about ten in the morning. I came by it from Nottingham, left my bag in the cloakroom and went straight down to the City by bus. The heat of London was terrific, a white dust heat, thick with the smell of horse dung. I had to put on my best suit, a blue serge, and it was like a suit of gauze. The heat seemed to stab at me through it.

Kersch and Co. were very nice. They were electrical engineers. I had applied for a vacancy advertised by them. That morning I was on the short list and Mr Alexander Kersch, the son, was very nice to me. We talked a good deal about Nottingham and I asked him if he knew the Brownsons, who were prominent Congregationalists there, but he said no. Everyone in Nottingham, almost, knew the Brownsons, but I suppose it did not occur to me in my excitement that Kersch was a Jew. After a time he offered me a whisky and soda, but I refused. I had been brought up rather strictly, and in any case the Brownsons would not have like it. Finally, Mr Kersch asked me if I could be in London over the week-end. I said yes, and he asked me at once to come in on Monday morning. I knew then that the job was as good as settled and I was trembling with excitement as I shook hands and said good-bye.

I came out of Kersch and Co. just before twelve o'clock. Their offices were somewhere off Cheapside. I forget the name of the street. I only remember, now, how very hot it was. There was something un-English about it. It was a terrific heat, fierce and white. And I made up my mind to go straight back to St Pancras and get my bag and take it to the hotel the Brownsons had recommended to me. It was so hot that I didn't want to eat. I felt that if I could get my room and wash and rest it would be enough. I could eat later. I would go up West and do myself rather well.

Pa Brownson had outlined the position of the hotel so well, both in conversation and on paper, that when I came out of St Pancras with my bag I felt I knew the way to the street as well as if it had been in Nottingham. I turned east and then north and went on turning left and then right, until finally I came to the place where the street with the hotel ought to have been. It wasn't there. I couldn't believe it. I walked about a bit, always coming back to the same place again in case I should get lost. Then I asked a baker's boy where Midhope Street was and he didn't know. I asked one or two more people, and they didn't know either. 'Wade's Hotel,' I would say, to make it clearer, but it was no good. Then a man said he thought I should go back towards St Pancras a bit, and ask again, and I did.

It must have been about two o'clock when I knew that I was pretty well lost. The heat was shattering. I saw one or two other hotels but they looked a bit low class and I was tired and desperate.

Finally I set my bag down in the shade and wiped my face. The sweat on my face was filthy. I was wretched. The Brownsons had been so definite about the hotel and I knew that when I got back they would ask me if I liked it and all about it. Hilda would want to know about it too. Later on, if I got the Kersch job, we should be coming up to it for our honeymoon.

At last I picked up my bag again. Across the street was a little sweet shop and café showing ices. I went across to it. I felt I had to have something.

In the shop a big woman with black hair was tinkering with the ice-cream mixer. Something had gone wrong. I saw that at once. It was just my luck.

'I suppose it's not use asking for an ice?' I said.

'Well, if you wouldn't mind *waiting*.'

'How long?'

'As soon as ever I get this nut fixed on and the freezer going again. We've had a breakdown.'

'All right. You don't mind if I sit down ?' I said.

She said no, and I sat down and leaned one elbow on the tea-table, the only one there was. The woman went on tinkering with the freezer. She was a heavy woman, about fifty, a little swarthy, and rather masterful to look at. The shop was stifling and filled with a sort of yellowish-pink shade cast by the sun pouring through the shop blind.

'I supposed it's no use asking you where Midhope Street is ?' I said.

'Midhope Street,' she said. She put her tongue in her cheek, in thought. 'Midhope Street, I ought to know that.'

'Or Wade's Hotel.'

'Wade's Hotel,' she said. She wriggled her tongue between her teeth. They were handsome teeth, very white. 'Wade's Hotel. No. That beats me.' And then : 'Perhaps my daughter will know. I'll call her.'

She straightened up to call into the back of the shop. But a second before she opened her mouth the girl herself came in. She looked surprised to see me there.

'Oh, here you are, Blanche ! This gentleman here is looking for Wade's Hotel.'

'I'm afraid I'm lost,' I said.

'Wade's Hotel,' the girl said. She too stood in thought, running her tongue over her teeth, and her teeth too were very white, like her mother's. 'Wade's Hotel. I've seen that some-where. Surely ?'

'Midhope Street,' I said.

'Midhope Street.'

No, she couldn't remember. She had on a sort of kimono, loose, with big orange flowers all over it. I remember thinking it was rather fast. For those days it was. It wouldn't be now. And somehow, because it was so loose and brilliant, I couldn't take my eyes off it. It made me uneasy, but it was an uneasiness in which there was pleasure as well, almost excitement. I remember thinking she was really half undressed. The kimono had no neck and no sleeves. It was simply a piece of material that wrapped over her, and when suddenly she bent down and tried to fit the last screw on to the freezer the whole kimono fell loose and I could see her body.

At the same time something else happened. Her hair fell over her shoulder. It was the time of very long hair, the days when girls would pride themselves that they could sit on their pig tails, but here was the longest hair I had ever seen. It was like thick jet-black cotton-rope. And when she bent down over the freezer the pig-tail of it was so long that the tip touched the ice.

'I'm so sorry,' the girl said. 'My hair's always getting me into trouble.'

'It's all right. It just seems to be my unlucky day, that's all.'

'I'm so sorry.'

'Will you have a cup of tea?' the woman said. 'Instead of the ice? Instead of waiting?'

'That's it, Mother. Get him some tea. You *would* like tea, wouldn't you?'

'Very much.'

So the woman went through the counter-flap into the back of the shop to get the tea. The girl and I, in the shop alone, stood and looked at the freezer. I felt queer in some way, uneasy. The girl had not troubled to tighten up her kimono. She let it hang loose, anyhow, so that all the time I could see part of her shoulder and now and then her breasts. Her skin was very white, and once when she leaned forward rather farther than usual I could have sworn that she had nothing on at all underneath.

'You keep looking at my kimono,' she said. 'Do you like it?'

'It's very nice,' I said. 'It's very nice stuff.'

'Lovely stuff. Feel of it. Go on. Just feel of it.'

I felt the stuff. For some reasons, perhaps it was because I had had no food, I felt weak. And she knew it. She must have known it. 'It's lovely stuff. Feel it. I made it myself.' She spoke sweetly and softly, in invitation. There was something electric about her. I listened quite mechanically. From the minute she asked me to feel the stuff of her kimono I was quite helpless. She had me, as it were, completely done up in the tangled maze of the orange and green of its flowers and leaves.

'Are you in London for long? Only to-day?'

'Until Monday.'

'I suppose you booked your room at the hotel?'

'No. I didn't book it. But I was strongly recommended there.'

'I see.'

That was all, only 'I see.' But in it there was something quite maddening. It was a kind of passionate veiled hint, a secret invitation.

'Things were going well,' I said, 'until I lost my way.'

'Oh ?'

'I came up for an interview and I got the job. At least I think I got the job.'

'A bit of luck. I hope it's a good one ?'

'Yes,' I said. 'It is. Kersch and Co. In the City.'

'Kersch and Co ?' she said. 'Not really ? Kersch and Co. ?'

'Yes,' I said. 'Why do you know them ?'

'Know them ? Of course I know them. Everybody knows them. That *is* a bit of luck for you.'

And really I was flattered. She knew Kersch and Co.! She knew that it was a good thing. I think I was more pleased because of the attitude of the Brownsons. Kersch and Co. didn't mean anything to the Brownsons. It was just a name. They had been rather cold about it. I think they would have liked me to get the job, but they wouldn't have broken their hearts if I hadn't. Certainly they hadn't shown any excitement.

'Kersch and Co.,' the girl said again. 'That really *is* a bit of luck.'

Then the woman came in with the tea. 'Would you like anything to eat ?'

'Well, I've had no dinner.'

'Oh! No wonder you look tired. I'll get you a sandwich. Is that all right ?'

'Thank you.'

So the woman went out to get the sandwich, and the girl and I stayed in the shop again, alone.

'It's a pity you booked your room at the hotel,' she said.

'I haven't booked it,' I said.

'Oh! I thought you said you'd *booked* it. Oh! My fault. You *haven't* booked it ?'

'No. Why ?'

'We take people in here,' she said. 'Over the café. It's not central of course. But then we don't charge so much.'

I thought of the Brownsons. 'Perhaps I ought to go to the hotel,' I said.

'We charge three and six,' she said. 'That isn't much, is it ?'

'Oh, no !'

'Why don't you just come up and see the room?' she said. 'Just come up.'

'Well —'

'Come up and see it. It won't eat you.'

She opened the rear door of the shop and in a moment I was going upstairs behind her. She was not wearing any stockings. Her bare legs were beautifully strong and white. The room was over the café. It was a very good room for three and six. The new wall-paper was silver-leaved and the bed was white and looked cool.

And suddenly it seemed silly to go out into the heat again and wander about looking for Wade's Hotel when I could stay where I was.

'Well, what do you think of it?' she said.

'I like it.' She sat down on the bed. The kimono was drawn up over her legs and where it parted at her knees I could see her thighs, strong and white and softly disappearing into the shadow of the kimono. It was the day of long rather prim skirts and I had never seen a woman's leg like that. There was nothing between Hilda and me beyond kissing. All we had done was to talk of things, but there was nothing in it. Hilda always used to say that she would keep herself for me.

The girl hugged her knees. I could have sworn she had nothing on under the kimono.

'I don't want to press you,' she said, 'but I do wish you'd stay. You'd be our first let.'

Suddenly a great wave of heat came up from the street outside, the fierce, horse-smelling, dust-white heat of the earlier day, and I said:

'All right, I'll stay.'

'Oh, you angel!'

The way she said that was so warm and frank that I did not know what to do. I simply smiled. I felt curiously weak with pleasure. Standing there, I could smell suddenly not only the heat but the warmth of her own body. It was sweetish and pungent, the soft odour of sweat and purfume. My heart was racing.

Then suddenly she got up and smoothed the kimono over her knees and thighs.

'My father has just died, you see,' she said. 'We are trying this for a living. You'll give us a start.'

Somehow it seemed too good to be true.

II

I know now that it was. But I will say more of that later, when the time comes.

That evening I came down into the shop again about six o'clock. I had had my tea and unpacked my things and rested. It was not much cooler, but I felt better. I was glad I had stayed.

The girl, Blanche, was sitting behind the counter, fanning herself with the broken lid of a sweet-box. She had taken off her kimono and was wearing a white gauzy dress with a black sash. I was disappointed. I think she must have seen that, because she pouted a bit when I looked at her. In turn I was glad she pouted. It made her lips look full-blooded and rich and shining. There was something lovely about her when she was sulky.

'Going out ?' she said.

'Yes,' I said. 'I thought of going up West and celebrating over Kersch and Co.'

'Celebrating ? By yourself ?'

'Well,' I said. 'I'm alone. There's no one else.'

'Lucky you.'

I knew what she meant in a moment. 'Well,' I said, almost in a joke, 'why don't you come ?'

'Me ?' she said, eyes wide open. 'You don't mean it. Me ?'

'I do,' I said. 'I do mean it.'

She got up. 'How long can you wait ? I'll just change my dress and tell mother.'

'No hurry at all,' I said, and she ran upstairs.

I have said nothing about how old she was. In the kimono she looked about twenty, and in the white dress about the same age, perhaps a little younger. When she came down again that evening she looked nearer twenty-six or twenty-seven. She looked big and mature. She had changed from the white dress into a startling yellow affair with a sort of black coatee cut away at the hips. It was so flashy that I felt uneasy. It was very tight too : the skirt so tight that I could see every line of her body, the bodice filled tight in turn with her big breasts. I forget what her hat was like. I rather fancy I thought it was rather silly. But later she took it off.

'Well, where shall we go?' she said.

'I thought of going up West and eating and perhaps dropping in to hear some music.'

'Music. Isn't that rather dull?'

'Well, a play then.'

'I say,' she said, 'don't let's go up West. Let's go down to the East End instead. We can have some fun. It'll do you good to see how the Jews live. If you're going to work for a firm of Jews you ought to know something about them. We might have some Jewish food. I know a nice place.'

So we took a bus and went. In the Mile End Road we had a meal. I didn't like it. The food didn't smell very nice. It was spiced and strong and rather strange to eat. But Blanche liked it. Finally she said she was thirsty. 'Let's go out of here and have a drink somewhere else,' she said. 'I know a place where you can get beautiful wine, cheap.' So we went from that restaurant to another. We had some cheese and a bottle of wine – asti, I think it was. The place was Italian. The evening was stifling and everywhere people were drinking heavily and fanning themselves limply against the heat. After the wine I began to feel rather strange. I wasn't used to it and I hardly knew what I was doing. The cheese was rather salty and made me thirsty. I kept drinking almost unconsciously and my lips began to form syllables roundly and loosely. I kept staring at Blanche and thinking of her in the kimono. She in turn would stare back and we played a kind of game, carrying on a kind of conversation with glances, burning each other up, until at last she said:

'What's your name? You haven't told me yet.'

'Arthur,' I said. 'Arthur Lawson.'

'Arthur.'

The way she said it set my heart on fire. I just couldn't say anything: I simply sat looking at her. There was an intimacy then, at that moment, in the mere silences and glances between us, that went far beyond anything I had known with Hilda.

Then she saw something on the back of the menu that made her give a little cry.

'Oh, there's a circus! Oh, let's go! Oh, Arthur, you must take me.'

So we went there too. I forget the name of the theatre and really, except for some little men and women with wizened bird faces and beards, there is nothing I remember except one thing. In the middle of the show was a trapeze act. A girl was swinging backwards and forwards across the stage in readiness to somersault and the drum was rolling to rouse the audience to excitement. Suddenly the girl shouted 'I can't do it!' and let loose. She crashed down into the stalls and in a minute half the audience were standing up in a pandemonium of terror.

'Oh! Arthur, take me out.'

We went out directly. In those days women fainted more often and more easily than they do now, and I thought Blanche would faint too. As we came out into the street she leaned against me heavily and clutched my arm.

'I'll get a cab and take you home,' I said.

'Something to drink first.'

I was a bit upset myself. We had a glass of port in a public house. It must have been about ten o'clock. Before long, after the rest and the port, Blanche's eyes were quite bright again.

Soon after that we took the cab and drove home. 'Let me lean against you,' she said. I took her and held her. 'That's it,' she said. 'Hold me. Hold me tight.' It was so hot in the cab that I could hardly breathe and I could feel her face hot and moist too. 'You're so hot,' I said. She said it was her dress. The velvet coatee was too warm. 'I'll change it as soon as I get home,' she said. 'Then we'll have a drink. Some ice-cream in lemonade. That'll be nice.'

In the cab I looked down at her hair. It was amazingly black. I smiled at it softly. It was full of odours that were warm and voluptuous. But it was the blackness of it that was so wonderful and so lovely.

'Why do they call you Blanche?' I said. 'When you're so black. Blanche means white.'

'How do you know I'm not white underneath?' she said.

I could not speak. No conversation I had ever had with a woman had ever gone within miles of that single sentence. I sat dazed, my heart racing. I did not know what to do. 'Hold me tight,' she said. I held her and kissed her.

I got out of the cab mechanically. In the shop she went straight upstairs. I kept thinking of what she had said. I was wild with a new and for me a delicious excitement. Downstairs the shop was in darkness and finally I could not wait for her to come down again. I went quickly upstairs to meet her.

She was coming across the landing as I reached the head of the stairs. She was in the kimono, in her bare feet.

'Where are you?' she said softly. 'I can't see you.' She came a second later and touched me.

'Just let me see if mother has turned your bed back,' she whispered.

She went into my bedroom. I followed her. She was leaning over the bed. My heart was racing with a sensation of great longing for her. She smoothed the bed with her hands and, as she did so, the kimono, held no longer, fell right apart.

And as she turned again I could see, even in the darkness, that she had nothing on underneath it at all.

III

On the following Monday morning I saw Kersch and Co. again and in the afternoon I went back to Nottingham. I had been given the job.

But curiously, for a reason I could not explain, I was no longer excited. I kept thinking of Blanche. I suppose, what with my engagement to Hilda Brownson and so on, I ought to have been uneasy and a little conscience-stricken. I was uneasy, but it was a mad uneasiness and there was no conscience at all in it. I felt reckless and feverish, almost desperate. Blanche was the first woman I had known at all on terms of intimacy, and it shattered me. All my complacent values of love and women were smashed. I had slept with Blanche on Saturday night and again on Sunday and the effect on me was one of almost catastrophic ecstasy.

That was something I had never known at all with Hilda: I had never come near it. I am not telling this, emphasising the physical side of it and singling out the more passionate implications of it, merely for the sake of telling it. I want to make clear that I had undergone a revolution: a revolution brought about, too, simply by a kimono and a girl's bare body underneath it. And since it was a revolution that changed my whole life it seems to me that I ought to make the colossal effect of it quite clear, now and for always.

I know, now, that I ought to have broken it off with Hilda at once. But I didn't. She was so pleased at my getting the Kersch job that to have told her would have been as cruel as taking away a doll from a child. I couldn't tell her.

A month later we were married. My heart was simply not in it. I wasn't there. All the time I was thinking of and, in imagination, making love to Blanche. We spent our honeymoon at Bournemouth in September. Kersch and Co. had been very nice and the result was that I was not to take up the new appointment until the twenty-fifth of the month.

I say appointment. It was the word the Brownsons always used. From the very first they were not very much in love with my going to work in London at all and taking Hilda with me. I myself had no parents, but Hilda was their only child. That put what seemed to me a snobbish premium on her. They set her on a pedestal. My job was nothing beside Hilda. They began to dictate what we should do and how and where we ought to live, and finally Mrs Brownson suggested that we all go to London and choose the flat in which we were to live. I objected. Then Hilda cried and there was an unpleasant scene in which Pa Brownson said that he thought I was unreasonable and that all Mrs Brownson was trying to do was to ensure that I could give Hilda as good a home as she had always had. He said something else about God guiding us as He had always guided them. We must put our trust in God. But God or no God, I was determined that if we were going to live in a flat in London the Brownsons shouldn't choose it. I would choose it myself. Because even then I knew where, if it was humanly possible, I wanted it to be.

In the end I went to London by myself. I talked round Hilda, and Hilda talked round her mother, and her mother, I suppose, talked round her father. At any rate I went. We decided on a flat at twenty-five shillings a week if we could get it. It was then about the twentieth of September.

I went straight from St Pancras to Blanche. It was a lovely day, blue and soft. It was a pain for me merely to be alive. I got to the shop just as Blanche was going out. We almost bumped into each other.

'Arthur!'

The way she said it made me almost sick with joy. She had on a tight fawn costume and a little fussy brown hat. 'Arthur! I was just going out. You just caught me. But mother can go instead.

Oh! Arthur.' Her mother came out of the back room and in a minute Blanche had taken off her hat and costume and her mother had gone out instead of her, leaving us alone in the shop.

We went straight upstairs. There was no decision, no asking, no consent in it at all. We went straight up out of a tremendous equal passion for each other. We were completely in unison, in desire and act and consummation and everything. Someone came in the shop and rang the bell loudly while we were upstairs, but it made no difference. We simply existed for each other. There was no outside world. She seemed to me then amazingly rich and mature and yet sweet. She was like a pear, soft and full-juiced and overflowing with passion. Beside her Hilda seemed like an empty eggshell.

I stayed with the Hartmans that night and the next. There were still three days to go before the Kersch job began. Then I stayed another night. I telegraphed Hilda, 'Delayed. Returning certain to-morrow.'

I never went. I was bound, heart and soul, to Blanche Hartman. There was never any getting away from it. I was so far gone that it was not until the second day of that second visit that I noticed the name Hartman at all.

'I'm going to stay here,' I said to Blanche. 'Lodge here and live with you. Do you want me?'

'Arthur, Arthur.'

'My God,' I said. 'Don't.' I simply couldn't bear the repetition of my name. It awoke every sort of fierce passion in me.

Then after a time I said: 'There's something I've got to tell you.'

'I know,' she said. 'About another girl. It doesn't matter. I don't want to hear. I could tell you about other men.'

'No, but listen,' I said. 'I'm married.' I told her all about Hilda.

'It doesn't matter,' she said. 'It makes no difference. You could be a Mormon and it wouldn't matter.'

And after that, because it mattered nothing to her, it mattered nothing to me. There is no conscience in passion. When I did think of Hilda and the Brownsons it was like the squirt of a syphon on to a blazing furnace. I really had no conscience at all. I walked out of one life into another as easily as from one room into another.

The only difficulty was Kersch and Co. It was there that Hilda would inquire for me as soon as I failed to turn up.

Actually I got out of the Kersch difficulty as easily as I got out of the rest. I didn't go back there either.

IV

I went on living with Blanche until the war broke out. I got another job. Electrical engineers were scarcer in those days. Then, as soon as the war broke out, I joined up.

In a way it was almost a relief. Passion can go too far and one can have too much of it. I was tired out by a life that was too full of sublimity. It was not that I was tired of Blanche. She remained as irresistible to me as when I had first seen her in the green and orange kimono. It was only that I was tired of the constant act of passion itself. My spirit, as it were, had gone stale and I needed a rest.

The war gave it to me. As soon as I came home for my first leave I knew it was the best thing that could have happened to me. Blanche and I went straight back to the almost unearthly plane of former intimacy. It was the old almost catastrophic ecstasy.

I say almost catastrophic. Now, when I think of it, I see that it was really catastrophic. One cannot expect a woman to feed off the food of the gods and then suddenly, because one man among a million is not there, to go back on a diet of nothing at all. I am trying to be reasonable about this. I am not blaming Blanche. It is the ecstasy between us that I am blaming. It could not have been otherwise than catastrophic.

I always think it odd that I did not see the catastrophe coming before it did. But perhaps if I had seen it coming it would have ceased to be a catastrophe. I don't know. I only know that I came home in 1917, unexpectedly, and found that Blanche was carrying on with another man.

I always remembered that Mrs Hartman looked extraordinarily scared as I walked into the shop that day. She was an assured, masterful woman and it was not at all like her to be scared. After a minute or so I went upstairs and in my bedroom a man was just buttoning up his waistcoat. Blanche was not there, but I understood.

I was furious, but the fury did not last. Blanche shattered it. She was a woman to whom passion was as essential as bread. She reminded me of that. But she reminded me also of something else. She reminded me that I was not married to her.

'But the moral obligation!' I raged.

'It's no good,' she said. 'I can't help it. It's no more than kissing to me. Don't be angry, honey. If you can't take me as I am you're not bound to take me at all.'

And in the end she melted my fury. 'What's between us is different from all the rest,' she said. I believed her and she demonstrated it to me too. And I clung to that until the end of the war.

But when I came home finally it had gone farther than that. There was more than one man. They came to the shop, travellers in the street-trade, demobilised young officers with cars. They called while I was at my job.

I found out about it. This time I didn't say anything. I did something instead. I gave up what the Brownsons would have called my appointment.

'But what have you done that for?' Blanche said.

'I can't stand being tied to a job any more,' I said. 'I'll work here. We'll develop the shop. There's money in it.'

'Who's going to pay for it?'

'I will.'

Just before I married Hilda I had nearly a hundred and fifty pounds in the bank. I had had it transferred to a London branch and it was almost all of it still there. I drew it out and in the summer of 1919 I spent nearly £80 of it on renovating the Hartman's shop. Blanche was delighted. She supervised the decorations and the final colour scheme of the combined shop and café was orange and green.

'Like your kimono,' I said. 'You remember it? That old one?'

'Oh! Arthur. I've got it.'

'Put it on,' I said.

She went upstairs and put it on. In about a minute I followed her. It was like old times. It brought us together again.

'Tell me something,' I said. 'That first day, when I came in. You hadn't anything on underneath, had you?'

'No,' she said. 'I'd just had a bath and it was all I had time to slip on.'

'By God, kiss me.'

She kissed me and I held her very tight. Her body was thicker and heavier now, but she was still lovely. It was all I asked. I was quite happy.

Then something else happened. I got used to seeing men in the shop. Most of them shot off now when they saw me, but one day when I came back from the bank there was a man in the living-room.

He was an oldish chap, with pepper and salt hair cut rather short.

'Hello,' I said, 'what's eating you?' I got to be rather short with any man I saw hanging about the place.

'Nothing's eating me,' he said. 'It's me who wants something to eat.'

'Oh! Who are you?'

'My name's Hartman,' he said.

I looked straight at his hair. It was Blanche's father. And in a minute I knew that he was out of prison.

I don't know why, but it was more of a shock to me than Blanche's affairs with other men. Blanche and I could fight out the question of unfaithfulness between ourselves, but the question of a criminal in the house was different.

'He isn't a criminal,' Blanche said. 'He's easily led and he was led away by others. Be kind to him, honey.'

Perhaps I was soft. Perhaps I had no right to do anything. It was not my house, it was not my father. Blanche was not even my wife. What could I possibly do but let him stay?

That summer we did quite well with the new café. We made a profit of nine and very often ten or eleven pounds a week. Hartman came home in May. In July things began to get worse. Actually, with the summer at its height, they ought to have been better. But the takings dropped to six and even five pounds. Blanche and her mother kept saying that they couldn't understand it.

But I could. Or at least I could after a long time. It was Hartman. He was not only sponging on me, but robbing the till too. All the hard-earned savings of the shop were being boozed away by Hartman.

I wanted to throw him out. But Blanche and her mother wouldn't hear of it. 'He's nothing but a damned scoundrel,'

I shouted.

'He's my father,' Blanche said.

That was the beginning of it. I date the antogonism between us and also the estrangement between us from that moment. It was never the same afterwards. I could stand Blanche being nothing more or less than a whore, but it was the thought of the old man and the thought of my own stupidity and folly that enraged me and finally broke me up.

Perhaps I shouldn't have written the word whore, and I wouldn't have done if it wasn't for the fact that, as I sit here, my heart is really almost broken.

V

I am sitting in what used to be my bedroom. We have changed it into a sitting-room now. We ought to have it done up. We haven't had new paper on it for seven or eight years.

I am just fifty. I think Blanche is just about fifty, too. She is out somewhere. It's no use thinking where. Passion is still as essential to her as bread. It means no more to her and I have long since given up asking where she goes. And somehow – and this is a damnable part of it all – I am still fond of her, but gently and rather foolishly now. What I feel for her most is regret. Not anger and not passion. I couldn't keep up with her pace. She long since outdistanced me in the matter of emotions.

Mrs Hartman is dead. I am sorry. She was likeable and though sometimes I didn't trust her I think she liked me. Hartman still hangs on. I keep the till-money locked up, but somehow he picks the locks, and there it is. He's too clever for me and I can't prove it. I feel as if, now, I am in a prison far more completely than any Hartman was ever in. It is a bondage directly inherited from that first catastrophic passion for Blanche. It's that, really, that I can't escape. It binds me irrevocably. I know that I shall never escape.

Last night, for instance, I had a chance to escape. I know of course that I'm a free man and that I am not married to Blanche and that I could walk out now and never come back. But this was different.

Hilda asked for me. I was in the shop, alone, just about six o'clock. I was looking at the paper. We don't get many people in the café now, but I always have the evening paper, in case. This district has gone down a lot and the café of course has gone down with it. We don't get the people in that we did. And as I was reading the paper the wireless was on. At six o'clock, the dance band ended and in another moment or two someone was saying my name.

'Will Arthur Lawson, last heard of in London twenty-five years ago, go at once to the Nottingham Infirmary, where his wife, Hilda Lawson, is dangerously ill.'

That was all. No one but me, in the house I mean, heard it. Afterwards no one mentioned it. Round here they think my name is Hartman. It was as though it had never happened.

But it was for me all right. When I heard it I stood stunned, as though something had struck me. I almost died where I stood, at the foot of the stairs.

Then after a bit I got over it enough to walk upstairs to the sitting-room. I did not know quite what I was doing. I felt faint and I sat down. I thought it over. After a minute I could see that there was no question of going. If it had been Blanche – yes. But not Hilda. I couldn't face it. And I just sat there and thought not of what I should do but what I might have done.

I thought of that hot day in 1911, and the Kersch job and how glad I was to get it. I thought about Hilda. I wondered what she looked like now and what she had done with herself for twenty-five years and what she had suffered. Finally I thought of that catastrophic ecstasy with Blanche, and then of the kimono. And I wondered how things might have gone if the Hartmans' ice-cream freezer had never broken and if Blanche had been dressed as any other girl would have been dressed that day.

And thinking and wondering, I sat there and cried like a child.

Angus Wilson

Et Dona Ferentes

'I'll have a cigarette too, Mother' said Monica to Mrs. Rackham, 'it'll help to keep the midges off. That's why I always hate woods so. Oh don't worry, Elizabeth' she added as she saw her own daughter's look of alarm. 'That's why I *hate* woods, but there are hundreds and hundreds of more important reasons why I *love* them – especially pine woods. To begin with there's the scent, and *you* can say what you like, Edwin' she smiled up at her husband, who was frowning as he cut inexpertly at a block of wood with a pocket knife 'about its being a hackneyed smell. But apart from the scent, there's the effect of light and shade. The only time that you can really see the sunlight out of doors is when it shines through dark trees like these. When you're in it, you're always too hot or too dazzled to notice anything. So you see, darling' she turned again to her daughter 'I *do* love pinewoods.' For a moment she lay back, but the smoke from her cigarette got into her eyes and soon she was stubbing it out on the bed of pine-needles beneath. 'How I *do* hate cigarettes' she cried 'and how I *do* hate hating them. It puts one at such a social disadvantage. Oh! it's all right for you, Mother, everyone in your generation smoked, and *smoked* determinedly; and it's all right for Elizabeth, when she's eighteen – don't let's talk of it there's only two years – nobody will even think of smoking, it'll be so dowdy; but with women in the forties like me there was always that awful choice – to smoke or not to smoke – and I chose not to, and there I am of course on occasions like parties and things with nothing to do with my hands. Now let's all lie back and relax for a quarter of an hour' she went on and the nervous tension in her voice seemed even greater than before as she said it 'and then we can have a drink before lunch. Don't you think it was clever of me to remember to bring gin? People

262

always forget it on picnics and yet it's so lovely to be able to have a drink without needing to be jolly. I hope nobody is going to be jolly, by the way. I forbid anyone to be jolly,' she said with mock sternness and then turning to her son who was watching a squirrel in a nearby tree 'Richard, darling, take that knife away from your father before he does himself an injury'.

'It wouldn't be a very serious injury, Mother, and then Elizabeth could show her prowess as a First Aider or whatever they're called in the Guides' said Richard, but nevertheless he moved slowly towards his father. Before he could offer assistance, however, a tall fair haired youth had sprung forward.

'Allow me, please, Mr. Newman' he said, the stiffness of his foreign English relieved by the charm and intimacy of his smile 'I am very able to cut wood with these kind of knives'.

'That's very kind of you, Sven' said Monica 'there you are, darling, you see, Sven has manners. I'm surprised you weren't able to learn a few, Richard, when you were staying with him in Sweden. I'm afraid we lost all our manners here while we were busy fighting the war'.

Two sharp points of red glowed suddenly on the Swedish boy's high cheekbones and his already slanting eyes narrowed and blinked.

Edwin Newman glared angrily at his wife, his prominent Adam's apple jerking convulsively above his open-necked shirt. He placed a hand of Sven's shoulder.

'You have given us so many useful lessons since you arrived, Sven, if you use the same charm to re-educate us in everyday courtesy, we shall be fortunate' he said.

'You are too kind to say these many good things to me, Mr. Newman' replied the boy 'I hope I shall not quite fail to deserve them'.

'You two ought to be talking in Latin' said Richard 'You sound like Dr. Johnson, Dad, when he met famous foreign scholars. By the way, Grannie, have you been getting at Sven about his reading ? I can't persuade him to read anything decent like De Quincey or Dickens or Coleridge. He seems to think for some reason or other that he's got to wade through "Rasselas" in order to "appreciate literature" as he calls it. I must say I shouldn't have thought even you would have inflicted that torture upon anyone'.

Mrs. Rackham's heavy square-jawed face lost its look of grimness for a moment as she spoke to her beloved grandson.

'I am delighted to hear of a blow being struck at this neo-romantic nonsense. Like Miss Deborah I think that nothing but good can arise from reading the works of the great Lexicographer. Continue to read Rasselas,' she said to Sven 'and you may yet know what the English language should really sound like. Take no notice of Richard's attempts to lure you into reading Dickens. He only wants you to fall under a railway train like a famous English retired officer, Captain Brown, whose unhealthy interest in Boz led him to that horrid end.'

'That just shows how little you understand about it, Grannie. Captain Brown was reading Pickwick and Pickwick's nothing to do with the real Dickens. Anyhow it was Pickwick in weekly parts which couldn't happen now.'

'Isn't it time you two stopped all this Who's Who in Literature' said Edwin, 'In any case, if Sven's going to waste his time on novels surely he might read modern authors like Huxley or even Lawrence.'

'Dear Edwin' replied Mrs. Rackham 'Even I know that Huxley or even Lawrence' and she imitated her son-in-law's hesitant tones 'daring though they may be are not *modern* authors'.

'In any case I am reading Rasselas because it is demanded for the higher examination. I am not really so greatly interested to read books'. Sven lay back and stretched his arms out to a spot where the sunlight had broken through 'I think I prefer more to follow outdoor games when the sun shines, like Elizabeth does' and he smiled lazily towards the clearing where Elizabeth was staking little wooden sticks around a clump of late bluebells.

Seen upside down it's more like a cat's than a satyr's thought Edwin.

Elizabeth only scowled 'This isn't an outdoor game' she said 'I'm just messing around. Come down to the stream with me, Mummie' she called.

'May I come too?' said Mrs. Rackham. Elizabeth gave no answer, but Monica looked pleased and held out her hand to assist her mother from the ground. The family likeness showed clearly as they walked away – three generations – hand in hand.

'It's the most lovely stream, Mummie' said Elizabeth, squeezing Monica's arm. 'I wish we had it all for our own'.

'Yes' said Monica 'I would plant Japanese irises here – the dark purple kind with the spear-like leaves to contrast with the yellow flags. It's funny how profuse Nature is with yellow, now if I had made the Universe I should have had much more contrast of colour and more subtlety too with wild flowers. I wonder if fritillary would grow here, the place could do with something a bit more strange'.

'But Mummie, it would be awful to change it when it's so beautiful'.

'I don't think so, darling' said Monica 'I don't know, of course, but I've always thought that was a false sort of romanticism. I don't believe you really become aware of the beauty of a scene until you see how it could be made more beautiful. What do you think, Mother?'

Mrs. Rackham smiled. 'I think I just see the stream and the meadows behind' she said 'and then I feel a great sense of peace and solitude'.

'Oh yes, that of course' cried her daughter 'but there's something else too. You have to look at it properly surely to see the patterns of shape and colour and that's when you see what's needed to complete them'. She thought for a moment, then added 'Yes, I'm sure you have to do that, otherwise it's all a blur and you don't really see anything'.

'Look, Mummie, those holes' cried Elizabeth 'I think there must be badgers. If you were here at night you would see them come down to drink'.

'I should like that' said Monica 'When there was no moon – at dusk or dawn – with black water and those nightmare deformed willow-trees and then lumbering grey shapes coming down to drink. But not by moonlight, that would be too expected'.

'We've been imagining the badgers drinking in the stream' said Elizabeth to her father when they returned.

'Is that one of Brock's nightly prowls?' asked Edwin.

'No, darling', replied Monica '*not* Brock and *not* nightly prowls. Just badgers drinking. There were rabbits, too, but they weren't wearing sky blue shorts, they were just brown rabbits with white tails'. Then seeing her husband's hurt expression, she put her hand on his arm 'Never mind, darling', she said 'You like imagining in that whimsical way, I don't; but I think it's only because I don't know how to'.

Edwin smiled. 'How about that gin you were talking about?' he asked.

'It's in the shaker, darling, with some French. You do the shaking, you're so professional'.

Indeed with his boyish face and long black hair, dressed in a saxeblue Aertex shirt and navy blue Daks Edwin looked very much like some barman from a smart bar in Cannes or like some cabaret turn. He seemed almost to be guying the part as he waved the shaker to and fro, dancing up and down, and singing grotesquely 'Hold that Tiger'.

'Idiot' cried Monica, and, relenting further, she turned to Sven 'Do respectable fathers of families ever behave so absurdly in Sweden?'

'I do not imagine Mr. Newman a father of a family, I imagine him to have continual youth'.

Monica turned away sharply 'At eighteen, of course, one can imagine so many ridiculous things' she said.

But Edwin ended his dance with a mock bow.

'The spirit of youth is infectious' he declared. Sven lay back and laughed with delight, showing his regular, white teeth.

It was while they were eating their lunch that Edwin got on to his hobby horse.

'There's supposed to be a Saxon camp across on that hill over there' he said, pointing to the East. 'If my theory is right it may well be an example of a Saxon settlement existing alongside a British one'.

He was so used to a completely silent audience that he was quite startled when Sven said 'Can that really be?'

'I believe so, but it's a view which is only gradually gaining ground' said Edwin and he looked across at Sven who sat clasping his legs, with his knees up to his chin, staring seriously before him. It's like talking to Pan, he thought, and he went on hurriedly 'Of course the whole of this Thames Valley area is very important from the point of view of Saxon migrations. It's almost certain that a great part of the inhabitants of Wessex came from the East and crossed the river near here at Dorchester'.

'But that is most interesting' said Sven. 'Do you really think so?' asked Elizabeth and then turning away contemptuously she added 'I don't believe you know anything about it'.

'That is true' said the boy 'but your father makes the story so alive'.

'If you're really interested we might go to the edge of the wood and see the hill from a closer vantage point', suggested Edwin.

Sven was on his feet immediately 'I should like that so much' he exclaimed.

'Are you coming, Richard?' asked his father, but Richard was deep in a first reading of *The Possessed* and merely shook his head.

Mr. Newman bounded lightly across the treetrunks that lay in the path, his sandals thumping against his heels.

'Of course when I say that Saxons and British dwelt side by side, I don't deny that there *were* cases of horrible violence' they could hear him saying, and Sven's answering voice replying 'But violence, I think, is often so beautiful'.

'How happy Edwin seems' said Mrs. Rackham to her daughter 'That boy's quite right, he *has* got the spirit of "continual youth" as he called it'.

Monica made no answer 'I'm going down to the stream again' she said.

'I've never seen him look so young and gay' went on Mrs. Rackham.

'How funny' said her daughter, as she walked away 'I was just thinking how absurd he looked, like a scout-master or something.'

If I was one of those Virginia Woolf mothers, thought Mrs. Rackham, I should have been told what all this means long ago. It's much better as it is, however, she decided. Fond as I am of Monica, I wouldn't be able to help, whatever may be wrong. She has no power of resignation, no ability to seek refuge, she insists on fighting, on living even when life is unpleasant. Edwin, too, has that same total absorption in the affair of the moment. They want to wring every drop out of life. She smiled as she thought how they must despise her for living so much in books. A secondhand life they would probably call it. I prefer to have my people pre-digested, she decided, it's easier, yes and wiser. To-day's undercurrents, for instance, how wearying! ... and life was so short. She turned to her book, then laughed out loud as it came to her how little even she profited from her reading. Let me remember Miss Woodhouse's folly in interfering in the affairs of others she said, and began her twenty-third reading of *Emma*.

Monica took the lime green coat she was carrying over her arm and placed it on a large white stone by the edge of the stream. Then she sat down and rippled her fingers through the water. Every now and again she dabbed her forehead or smoothed her eyelids with her wet fingers. The afternoon had become intensely hot, there seemed to be no breath of air anywhere. Overhead, mosquitoes and midges hummed so that she was forced to pluck some wild mint from the stream to attempt to drive them away. The mint grew so shallowly that the whole plant came away suddenly as she touched it, and mud from the roots splashed over her white dress. Eveything seemed discordant to her – the yellow green of her coat against the emerald grass, the crimson ribbons of the large straw hat which lay at her side against a clump of pink campion. Suddenly she saw a creature slithering up the trunk of an old tree, a creature brown-grey like the tree itself – it was a tree-creeper, but for a moment the little bird seemed to her like a rat. The rusty bullocks further up the stream stamped and swished their tails as they tried to drive the horseflies from their dung-caked flanks. There were always creatures like that who lived upon dirt, who nosed it out and unearthed it, however deeply it was hidden, however long, yes, even though all trace of it seemed vanished for twenty years, she thought. A shallow, vain, egocentric creature like that, with those untrustworthy, mocking cat's eyes. Twenty years ago, when they were first married and Edwin had told her, she had been so anxious to help. There had been incidents, it was true, but they had been so unimportant and they had become closer through fighting them together. But now after twenty years she felt she could do nothing; her pride was too hurt. All this fortnight, since the holiday began, she had been telling herself it could not be true and yet she knew she was not mistaken, to-day especially she felt sure of it. What could have altered things to make it possible? she reflected. It was true that she had been a bit uncertain in her feelings herself this year, but Edwin had understood so well that it was change of life that was coming to her early. Change of life had such strange results, that must be it – she seized on the idea eagerly – it was all fancy. How horrible that anything purely physical could make one believe such things and how cruel to Edwin that she had indulged them. How cruelly she had behaved, even if it were true, and somehow she felt again that it was. She had withdrawn her sympathy at the very moment Edwin needed it most: it was easy enough to realize that with one's mind, she thought, but the emotional revulsion was so great after twenty years' forgetfulness that she might only overcome it when events had moved beyond her reach. Whatever happens, she thought, I shall be so much to blame; and to Elizabeth who came running towards her along the bank of the stream she said aloud.

'If anything should go wrong, darling, in our lives, always remember I am to blame. I hadn't the courage to do as I should.'

The moment she had said it she could have bitten her tongue out. The child was already too inclined to histrionics in this new phase of schoolgirl religious enthusiasm through which she was passing. Monica's fears were quite justified, Elizabeth rose at once to the situation, though she had no idea of the meaning of her mother's words.

'Brave Mummie' she said, putting her hand on Monica's arm.

Monica spoke almost harshly 'No, darling, *not* brave Mummie. Self-dramatizing Mummie, if you like, Mummie who's got the heroine's part quite pat at rehearsals and in the wings, but who always fluffs her words when it comes to the night. Anything you like, my dear, but not *brave* Mummie'.

Mummie's so strange and sarcastic sometimes, thought Elizabeth, anyone but me might think she was bitter, but I know her better. I know how brave and true and kind she is. I understand Daddy too, how much he needs my love. Richard never thinks about anything but his old books, so I have to help both of them. It's a kind of secret I have with myself – and God, she thought quickly. God loves and knows them all, even Grannie though she laughs at him. It's true what Miss Anstruther says – life's ever so exciting for anyone who's found Him; always something new and worthwhile to do, not just silly messing around with boys like Penelope Black and all those drips. That's what Sven wants, a lot of silly girls swooning about over him, like soppy Sinatra. That's what he would like from me, for all he keeps on saying I'm only a kid, but there's no time for waste of time Miss Anstruther says. I wish Sven hadn't come here, it's all been beastly since he did. It's ever since he came that Mummy's been snappy and Daddy keeps on showing off, not that it's for Sven, he wouldn't want to show off for a little pipsqueak like him. I oughtn't to talk like that about him, I must learn to love him. Love everyone, pray for them and set a good example that's all we can do. I can help all of them even Sven if I show how Christ wants us to live. People don't say so, but they're watching us Christians all the time, Miss Anstruther says. Ye are the salt of the Earth. A City that is set on a hill cannot be hid.

Monica's voice suddenly broke into her daughter's thoughts.

'Look, darling! On that larch tree there. See? A jay'. There, indeed very close at hand sat a jay preening its rose feathers, its pastel shades harmonizing delicately with the soft green catepillars of the larch. Suddenly it rose, with a flash of blue-green wing feathers, and flew off, screaming harshly. Immediately all the birds in the wood seemed to break into chattering. A cold wind blew across the stream. Monica shivered and drew her coat round her shoulders. 'I think there's a storm coming up, darling' she said 'Let's go back to Grannie'.

'I think there's a storm coming up, but I'm glad we came all the same' said Edwin, as, somewhat out of breath, he reached the crest of the hills. 'We've gone much further than I ever intended, but the time's passed so quickly in talking. I'm afraid the others may get rather anxious, but still I think one has a right to enjoy oneself in one's own way sometimes, don't you?' Then not waiting for answer the continued. 'The Saxon settlement must have run right across the chain to the left here. Down below, you see, is Milkford, the outskirts run right up to the foot of the hills. It's quite an important town still, a sort of watering place, but it was even more important in medieval times. Of course there's nothing earlier, really, than thirteenth century' he said apologetically 'but the castle's quite interesting – fifteenth century, you know, when the fortress is turning into the country house. We might run down and look at it later, would you like that?' he asked.

'That would be most nice' said Sven 'but for some minutes I should like to rest here, please. The heat renders me most tired' and indeed beads of sweat were trickling down his brown chest where the line of his shirt lay open almost to his stomach.

Edwin turned away 'Yes, you lie there a bit while I explore round the place' but he did not move far off. Suddenly Sven broke the silence.

'That is so lovely, your signet-ring. I should much like one of the same kind' he said.

'Would you?' said Edwin. 'We must see what we can do about it'.

Sven did not answer. It was nice to lie here in the sun and to feel that one was being watched, admired. It was boring staying with these Newmans. Richard, with his books had been bad enough at home, but there it did not matter, if he did not choose to come out swimming or skiing with the girls, he could be left behind. But here there were no girls, no sports, only books and talking and talking. He had hoped to watch the English girls bathing and to go dancing with them; they were said to be prudish, but all the same he was usually very irresistible. They would have run their hands through his hair like Karen, who looked so pretty when her own hair blew across her face and she smiled with those white teeth through the salt spray; or they would have stroked his fine brown legs as Sigrid when she buried them in the sand and he brought his face close to her firm white breasts showing through her costume; or perhaps even an English girl more bold than the others would lie naked and soft under him on the sand like little Lili who had licked the salt sweat from his chest when he had done his part with her – different girls, but all of them, all of them wanting him as he had a right to be wanted, so handsome he felt that sometimes he also wanted himself. But here there were no girls only books and talking. He had hoped much of Richard's sister, but she was only a child of sixteen and even so she was taken up with some rubbish about religion. With Mrs. Newman, too, he had thought he might have so much fun, after all she was not as old as Mrs. Thomas, the American woman, who had taken him out to cabarets and dances and given him presents last year when he was only seventeen. It had been most pleasant and he had learned from her so much that was useful. But this bitch treated him as though he was a child, it made him so glad that now he could hurt her. Even if Richard had made him his hero like Ekki Blomquist who followed him around with admiring eyes, little Ekki whom he liked to protect and pet and tease – but Richard thought only of his books. No, it was only Mr. Newman who had been kind to him and who admired him. He looked so gay and fine for forty-seven, he would be very pleased if he could look so at that age. But all the same it was very disturbing, it would not be pleasant if so kind a man should behave stupidly, it would be necessary to be very polite and very firm. For a little while still it would be nice to continue to be admired, also he would like to have the present of the ring, also he would like to make that bitch unhappy. Not that he liked to be naughty but it was not pleasant when one was not admired. What strange little white shells there were on the ground, like little Lili's ears, or his own curls when they fell from the nape of his neck at the barber's shop.

The same little crustacea lay all around Edwin, pressed into the soft ground by the tightly winding mesh of mossgrass. Little balls of rabbit droppings were scattered here and there. The hillside was carpet smooth but for an occasional red and yellow vetch that rose above the even level. Edwin peered closely at the turf, but he noticed nothing for his thoughts were far away.

If only I could collect my ideas, thought Edwin, but the blood pounds so at my temples. If only I could piece together how it had all led up to this. I think I have been feeling shut in by them all for a long time now, at any rate all this year. Richard with his books and Elizabeth with this priggish religious talk, and lately even Monica has seemed to be so sure of her values, so determinedly living in a world of beauty. All the best that's written, only the actions God approves, only the most beautiful in nature and art – it almost sickens me at times. It all seems to come out in their lack of charity to Sven. I wanted so to be kind to him, to show him that he was wanted, to make up for their priggish lack of courtesy. I understood what they meant when they said he was materialistic, animal, superficial, vain – but in some degree I felt that I was too and I wanted them to realize that. The children will always be afraid of physical pleasure in sex, afraid of their own bodies' lusts, afraid of the lusts of others for them. It's worse, somehow, when Mrs. Rackham's here because I can see the stunted shy, self-satisfied life they're heading for. But Monica is different, all the years she has understood my feelings about it, and at times has shared in them gloriously, but recently she's changed, 'trying to put sex in its perspective' she would call it, but that's only another name for avoiding it because it's distasteful. It's true she's given me this physical reason but she said it so eagerly that it seemed like an excuse for doing what she's wanted to do for years. And now this has happened. What I thought to be kindness and sympathy for a rebel has re-awakened the old feeling of twenty years ago, the old sensual pattern of Gilbert and Heinrich and Bernard and the others, only more violently as it seems, and the blood is pulsing in my head as it used to then, only more loudly.

Suddenly he heard himself saying in a clear, artificial voice 'I'm so glad that we should have become such good friends, Sven, and I hope you are too. I don't expect you realize what a very lonely man I am in some ways. Oh ! I know how lucky I am in my family, but they're terribly narrow. I felt perhaps that you were feeling that too. Richard, for example' by now Edwin was talking at break neck speed 'he lives in books, takes no pleasure in the life around him. Now you must find that very strange, being so strong and lithe and well-made. Yes I'm afraid the truth of the matter is that my family are all what we call in England kill-joys, that is they get no real fun out of life. That's what I've so admired about you, you obviously get so *much* fun out of life. I think it's probably because I've allowed my wife to dominate the family so. You'll think it funny of me to say so, but I'm not really very much of a woman's man. I think woman are inclined rather to be kill-joys. Do *you* think so ?'

'Do I ?' said Sven 'do I think that women kill joy ? No, oh no. Certainly not that' and he began to shake with laughter, but seeing Edwin's face twisted with combined excitement and alarm he controlled his amusement and added 'but I think I so well understand what you may mean, you must tell me about this. But not here, I think, for it is now getting so dark and a rain spot has fallen on my face so that I think there will be a storm. Shall you not tell me in the town down there ?'

'Of course !' said Edwin eagerly and he began to clamber down the hill. 'We'll go into Milkford and I'll ring up from there to say we've been caught by the storm. If we can't get a car we may have to stay the night there. You won't mind that, will you? It'll give us a real chance to get to know each other, and they say the Bull's really a very decent old pub'.

At first there had only been a few heavy drops of rain falling through the trees in the wood. Richard, who had reached the death of Stefan Trofimovich, positively refused to move, and even Mrs. Rackham who was being once more horrified and entranced by the vulgarity of Mrs. Elton preferred to take no notice. Then quite suddenly the storm had burst over their heads – the picnic things all shook under the blast of the thunder-clap and the whole wood was lit up by a great fork of lightning which seemed to strike obliquely at the nearby stream. Before a second and more deafening thunder clap had sounded, Mrs. Rackham had jumped to her feet.

'Come on, Richard, pack up the picnic basket. We mustn't stay under these trees with this lightning about. Make for the car and the clearing. Help me with the rugs, Elizabeth. Monica,' she called 'don't stand there, my dear, we'll all get drenched soon if we don't move, apart from the danger of the lightning'.

But Monica stood a little away from them, her face chalk-white and her eyes round with terror. As the next fork of lightning zigzagged viciously in front of them she began to scream.

'Edwin, Edwin! My God! where are you? Oh pray God nothing happens. We must find him, we must find him' and she turned and ran down the little path. She had hardly gone a few paces when she tripped on a tree root and fell on her face, bruising her cheek and cutting the side of her chin.

Richard made as though to move towards her and then blushing scarlet, turned in the direction of the car. But already Elizabeth had run to her mother and, throwing herself on her she sobbed.

'Mummie, darling, Mummie darling, let's go away from this place.'

'For heaven's sake, Monica', said Mrs. Rackham 'pull yourself together. You're scaring the child out of her wits.' She took her daughter's arm and started to pull her to her feet, but Monica pulled her arm away roughly 'We must find him' she said and began to weep bitterly.

'Stop this at once' said Mrs. Rackham sternly 'Edwin's perfectly capable of looking after himself' and she led her sobbing daughter to the car. By now the rain was pouring down. Monica's fashionable hair style was washed across on to her face and strands of hair got stuck to the cut on her chin, meanwhile the blood ran down on to the white dress beneath. As they came to the clearing there was a blinding flash of lightning, followed by a crash. In a few moments smoke was ascending from the other side of the stream – one of the larches had been struck.

'*You* must drive, Richard' said Mrs. Rackham 'Your mother's not at all well' and she helped her daughter into the back, as she did so she heard her mumbling 'Oh God! don't let it happen! Oh God! don't let it happen!' That any daughter of mine should be superstitious over a storm, she thought.

'It's lucky, there's only the four of us this time' said Richard, as he started the car.

Elizabeth kicked his leg 'You silly, thoughtless idiot, don't let Mummie hear you' she said.

I've failed again, thought Richard. When I was reading about Stefan Trofimovich's death, I wanted to be there so that I could make him happy, to tell him that for all his faults I knew he was a good man. But when my own mother is in trouble I can't say anything. It all sounds alright in books, but when I see people's faces – all that redness, wetness and ugliness and the noises they make – I feel ashamed for them and then I'm speechless and that makes me angry and I say cruel things. It was just like that when Sven was unhappy over that girl, I wanted to be his friend as Alyosha was to Kolya, to tell him that I knew he was often bad, but that I didn't mind but it was no good because I couldn't show any sympathy. I shall always live like this, cut off, although I think I understand more clearly than others. But how can I speak to Mother of her fears about Sven and that they are absurd? No I must always be shut in like this.

Nevertheless when they arrived home, he took his mother's arm 'Don't worry, darling, nothing could happen I'm sure' he whispered. But Monica did not hear him, she was listening to the maid.

'Mr. Newman phoned, ma'am, to say that he and Mr. Sodeblom are stranded at Milkford and will be staying the night'.

Monica walked straight into the drawing-room and sat, with set face, upon the sofa. 'I am very tired, my dears, I'll have my dinner in my room. Mother would you be very kind and see Agnes in the kitchen, I don't want to be worried.'

Richard and Elizabeth began to speak at once, as Mrs. Rackham went from the room.

'Can I get you some books, Mother?'

'Shall I help you to undress, Mummie?'

But such offers were premature, for at that moment a car sounded in the drive outside and a few minutes later Edwin rushed breathlessly into the room.

'Oh! you're here before us' he exclaimed 'So you got my message. As the storm cleared, I thought it wasn't necessary to stay the night'.

Sven had come into the room very quietly behind Edwin and now his voice sounded, speaking very slowly.

'Mr. Newman was so kind, he was so anxious that I should stay and see Milkford. But I thought you would be alarmed at our absence, Mrs. Newman. See, however, he has bought me this lovely ring, the stone has so strange a name – garnet. But he has not forgotten you, Mrs. Newman' and as Edwin motioned him to be silent, he went on 'But, no, Mr. Newman, you must show your wife the gift or she will be upset that you gave me so lovely a ring and nothing for her. Look, it is a beautiful sapphire pendant, is it not a lovely stone? I chose it for you myself, I have a great taste for jewels.'

Monica got to her feet 'It is a pity' she said 'that you speak such ghastly English. You say unfortunate things that a boy of your age cannot understand' and she walked from the room.

A few moments later Mrs. Rackham returned. 'Look' said Sven 'at the lovely pendant the kind Mr. Newman has bought for Mrs. Newman.'

'Oh! but Edwin how sweet of you! It's charming looking' said his mother-in-law.

'But Mrs. Newman does not at all seem to like it' said Sven.

'Oh! she will to-morrow' said Mrs. Rackham 'she's very overtired to-night, the storm upset her a lot'.

The rainfall ceased after dinner and there was a calming silence as Monica sat before her dressing table, talking to her mother. Suddenly Edwin came into the room. He began to talk quickly as thought he feared interruption.

'I've been talking to the children' he said 'and Sven thinks he ought to return home by the next boat – that is in three days – I think he's probably right. He's got his exams coming on and I don't know that it's been quite his sort of holiday or' and he laughed 'that we're exactly his sort of family'.

Monica said nothing, but Mrs. Rackham declared approvingly 'I'm sure it's a very wise decision'.

'I'm glad you think so' he said 'because I was wondering if you'd mind looking after the three of them until he goes. I've suddenly remembered *Don Giovanni* comes off next week and it may not be done again for some time'. He put his hand on his wife's shoulder. 'Would you like to go up to the flat for two nights on our own?' he asked.

Monica nodded her head 'Yes, darling' she said 'I would'.

'You'll have to wear that new pendant to celebrate' said Mrs. Rackham.

'No' said Monica 'I shan't do that. I don't think I shall ever wear that pendant. And now' she said, gathering her dressing-gown around her 'I must go and see that all Sven's clothes are properly mended. I can't have Mrs. Sodeblom thinking we didn't look after the child, she was so good to Richard' and she swept from the room.

Safe, thought Edwin, safe, thank God! But the room seemed without air, almost stifling. He threw open one of the windows and let in a refreshing breeze that blew across from the hills.

DYLAN THOMAS

The Vest

He rang the bell. There was no answer. She was out. He turned the key.

The hall in the late afternoon light was full of shadows. They made one almost solid shape. He took off his hat and coat, looking sideways, so that he might not see the shape, at the light through the sitting-room door.

'Is anybody in?'

The shadows bewildered him. She would have swept them up as she swept the invading dust.

In the drawing-room the fire was low. He crossed over to it and sat down. His hands were cold. He needed the flames of the fire to light up the corners of the room. On the way home he had seen a dog run over by a motorcar. The sight of the blood had confused him. He had wanted to go down on his knees and finger the blood that made a round pool in the middle of road. Someone had plucked at his sleeve, asking him if he was ill. He remembered that the sound and strength of his voice had drowned the first desire. He had walked away from the blood, with the stained wheels of the car and the soaking blackness under the bonnet going round and round before his eyes. He needed the warmth. The wind outside had cut between his fingers and thumbs.

She had left her sewing on the carpet near the coal-scuttle. She had been making a petticoat. He picked it up and touched it, feeling where her breasts would sit under the yellow cotton. That morning he had seen her with her head enveloped in a frock. He saw her, thin in her nakedness, as a bag of skin and henna drifting out of the light. He let the petticoat drop on to the floor again.

Why, he wondered, was there this image of the red and broken dog? It was the first time he had seen the brains of a living

278

creature burst out of the skull. He had been sick at the last yelp and the sudden caving of the dog's chest. He could have killed and shouted, like a child cracking a blackbeetle between its fingers.

A thousand nights ago, she had lain by his side. In her arms, he thought of the bones of her arms. He lay quietly by her skeleton. But she rose next morning in the corrupted flesh.

When he hurt her, it was to hide his pain. When he struck her cheek until the skin blushed, it was to break the agony of his own head. She told him of her mother's death. Her mother had worn a mask to hide the illness at her face. He felt the locust of that illness on his own face, in the mouth and the fluttering eyelid.

The room was darkening. He was too tired to shovel the fire into life, and saw the last flame die. A new coldness blew in with the early night. He tasted the sickness of the death of the flame as it rose to the tip of his tongue, and swallowed it down. It ran around the pulse of the heart, and beat until it was the only sound. And all the pain of the damned. The pain of a man with a bottle breaking across his face, the pain of a cow with a calf dancing out of her, the pain of the dog, moved through him from his aching hair to the flogged soles of his feet.

His strength returned. He and the dripping calf, the man with the torn face, and the dog on giddy legs, rose up as one, in one red brain and body, challenging the beast in the air. He heard the challenge in his snapping thumb and finger, as she came in.

He saw that she was wearing her yellow hat and frock.

'Why are you sitting in the dark?' she said.

She went into the kitchen to light the stove. He stood up from his chair. Holding his hands out in front of him as though they were blind, he followed her. She had a box of matches in her hand. As she took out a dead match and rubbed it on the box, he closed the door behind him. 'Take off your frock,' he said.

She did not hear him, and smiled.

'Take off your frock,' he said.

She stopped smiling, took out a live match and lit it.

'Take off your frock,' he said.

He stepped towards her, his hands still blind. She bent over the stove. He blew the match out.

'What is it?' she said.

His lips moved, but he did not speak.

'Why?' she said.

He slapped her cheek quite lightly with his open hand.

'Take off your frock,' he said.

He heard her frock rustle over her head, and her frightened sob as he touched her. Methodically his blind hands made her naked.

He walked out of the kitchen, and closed the door.

In the hall, the one married shadow had broken up. He could not see his own face in the mirror as he tied his scarf and stroked the brim of his hat. There were too many faces. Each had a section of his features, and each a stiffened lock of his hair. He pulled up the collar of his coat. It was a wet winter night. As he walked, he counted the lamps. He pushed a door open and stepped into the warmth. The room was empty. The woman behind the bar smiled as she rubbed two coins together. 'It's a cold night,' she said.

He drank up the whisky and went out.

He walked on through the increasing rain. He counted the lamps again, but they reached no number.

The corner bar was empty. He took his drink into the saloon, but the saloon was empty.

The Rising Sun was empty.

Outside, he heard no traffic. He remembered that he had seen nobody in the streets. He cried aloud in a panic of loneliness:

'Where are you, where are you?'

Then there was traffic, and the windows were blazing. He heard singing from the house on the corner.

The bar was crowded. Women were laughing and shouting. They spilt their drinks over their dresses and lifted their dresses up. Girls were dancing on the sawdust. A woman caught him by the arm, and rubbed his face on her sleeve, and took his hand in hers and put it on her throat. He could hear nothing but the voices of the laughing women and the shouting of the girls as they danced. Then the ungainly women from the seats and the corners rocked towards him. He saw that the room was full of women. Slowly, still laughing, they gathered close to him.

He whispered a word under his breath, and felt the old sickness turn sour in his belly. There was blood before his eyes.

Then he, too, burst into laughter. He stuck his hands deep in the pockets of his coat, and laughed into their faces.

His hand clutched around a softness in his pocket. He drew out his hand, the softness in it.

The laugther died. The room was still. Quiet and still, the women stood watching him.

He raised his hand up level with his eyes. It held a piece of soft cloth.

'Who'll buy a lady's vest,' he said, 'Going, going, ladies, who'll buy a lady's vest.'

The meek and ordinary women in the bar stood still, their glasses in their hands, as he leant with his back to the counter and shouted with laughter and waved the bloody cloth in front of them.

MURIEL SPARK

The First Year of My Life

I was born on the first day of the second month of the last year of
the First World War, a Friday. Testimony abounds that during
the first year of my life I never smiled. Everyone who knew me
then has told me so. They tried very hard, singing and bouncing
me up and down, jumping around, pulling faces. Many times I
was told this later by my family and their friends; but, anyway, I
knew it at the time.

You will shortly be hearing of that new school of psychology,
or maybe you have heard of it already, which after long and far-
adventuring research and experiment has established that all of
the young of the human species are born omniscient. Babies, in
their waking hours, know everything that is going on everywhere in the world; they can tune in to any conversation they
choose, switch on to any scene. We have all experienced this
power. It is only after the first year that it was brainwashed out
of us; for it is demanded of us by our immediate environment
that we grow to be of use to it in a practical way. Gradually, our
know-all brain-cells are blacked out, although traces remain in
some individuals in the form of E.S.P., and in the adults of some
primitive tribes.

It is not a new theory. Poets and philosophers, as usual, have
been there first. But scientific proof is now ready and to hand.
Perhaps the final touches are being put to the new manifesto in
some cell at Harvard University. Any day now it will be given to
the world, and the world will be convinced.

Let me therefore get my word in first, because I feel pretty
sure, now, about the authenticity of my remembrance of things
past. My autobiography, as I very well perceived at the time,
started in the very worst year that the world had ever seen so far.
Apart from being born bedridden and toothless, unable to raise

282

myself on the pillow or utter anything but farmyard squawks or police-siren wails, my bladder and bowels totally out of control, I was further depressed by the curious behaviour of the two-legged mammals around me. There were those black-dressed people, females of the species to which I appeared to belong, saying they had lost their sons. I slept a great deal. Let them go and find their sons. It was like a special pin for my nappies which my mother or some other hoverer dedicated to my care was always losing. These careless women in black lost their husbands and their brothers. Then they came to visit my mother and clucked and crowed over my cradle. I was not amused.

'Babies never really smile till they're three months old,' said my mother. 'They're not *supposed* to smile till they're three months old.'

My brother, aged six, marched up and down with a toy rifle over his shoulder:

> The grand old Duke of York
> He had ten thousand men;
> He marched them up to the top of the hill
> And he marched them down again.
>
> And when they were up, they were up.
> And when they were down, they were down.
> And when they were neither down nor up
> They were neither up nor down.

'Just listen to him!'
'Look at him with his rifle!'

I was about ten days old when Russia stopped fighting. I tuned in to the Czar, a prisoner, with the rest of the family, since evidently the country had put him off his throne and there had been a revolution not long before I was born. Everyone was talking about it. I tuned in to the Czar. 'Nothing would ever induce me to sign the treaty of Brest-Litovsk,' he said to his wife. Anyway, nobody had asked him to.

At this point I was sleeping twenty hours a day to get my strength up. And from what I discerned in the other four hours of the day I knew I was going to need it. The Western Front on my frequency was sheer blood, mud, dismembered bodies, blistered crashes, hectic flashes of light in the night skies, explosions, total terror. Since it was plain I had been born into a bad moment in the history of the world, the future bothered me, unable as I was to raise my head from the pillow and as yet only twenty inches long. 'I truly wish I were a fox or a bird,' D.H.Lawrence was writing to somebody. Dreary old creeping Jesus. I fell asleep.

Red sheets of flame shot across the sky. It was 21st March, the fiftieth day of my life, and the German Spring Offensive had started before my morning feed. Infinite slaughter. I scowled at the scene, and made an effort to kick out. But the attempt was feeble. Furious, and impatient for some strength, I wailed for my feed. After which I stopped wailing but continued to scowl.

> The grand old Duke of York
> He had ten thousand men ...

They rocked the cradle. I never heard a sillier song. Over in Berlin and Vienna the people were starving, freezing, striking, rioting and yelling in the streets. In London everyone was bustling to work and muttering that it was time the whole damn business was over.

The big people around me bared their teeth; that meant a smile, it meant they were pleased or amused. They spoke of ration cards for meat and sugar and butter.

'Where will it all end?'

I went to sleep. I woke and tuned in to Bernard Shaw who was telling someone to shut up. I switched over to Joseph Conrad, who, strangely enough, was saying precisely the same thing. I still didn't think it worth a smile, although it was expected of me any day now. I got on to Turkey. Women draped in black huddled and chattered in their harems; yak-yak-yak. This was boring, so I came back to home base.

In and out came and went the women in British black. My mother's brother, dressed in his uniform, came coughing. He had been poison-gassed in the trenches. '*Tout le monde à la bataille*!' declaimed Marshal Foch the old swine. He was now Commander-in-Chief of the Allied Forces. My uncle coughed from deep within his lungs, never to recover but destined to return to the Front. His brass buttons gleamed in the firelight. I weighed twelve pounds by now; I stretched and kicked for exercise, seeing that I had a lifetime before me, coping with this crowd. I took six feeds a day and kept most of them down by the time the *Vindictive* was sunk in Ostend harbour, on which day I kicked with special vigour in my bath.

In France the conscripted soldiers leapfrogged over the dead on the advance and littered the fields with limbs and hands, or drowned in the mud. The strongest men on all fronts were dead before I was born. Now the sentries used bodies for barricades and the fighting men were unhealthy from the start. I checked my toes and fingers, knowing I was going to need them. *The Playboy of the Western World* was playing at the Court Theatre in London, but occasionally I beamed over to the House of Commons which made me drop off gently to sleep. Generally, I preferred the Western Front where one got the true state of affairs. It was essential to know the worst, blood and explosions and all, for one had to be prepared, as the boy scouts said. Virginia Woolf yawned and reached for her dairy. Really, I preferred the Western Front.

In the fifth month of my life I could raise my head from my pillow and hold it up. I could grasp the objects that were held out to me. Some of these things rattled and sqawked. I gnawed on them to get my teeth started. 'She hasn't smiled yet ?' said the dreary old aunties. My mother, on the defensive, said I was probably one of those late smilers. On my wavelength Pablo Picasso was getting married and early in that month of July the Silver Wedding of King George V and Queen Mary was celebrated in joyous pomp at St. Paul's Cathedral. They drove through the streets of London with their children. Twenty-five years of domestic happiness. A lot of fuss and ceremonial handing over of swords went on at the Guildhall where the King and Queen received a cheque for £53,000 to dispose of for charity as they thought fit. *Tout le monde à la bataille* ! Income tax in England had reached six shillings in the pound. Everyone was talking about the Silver Wedding; yak-yak-yak, and ten days later the Czar and his family, now in Siberia, were invited to descend to a little room in the basement. Crack, crack, went the guns ; screams and blood all over the place, and that was the end of the Romanoffs. I flexed my muscles. 'A fine healthy baby,' said the doctor ; which gave me much satisfaction.

Tout le monde à la bataille ! That included my gassed uncle. My health had improved to the point where I was able to crawl in my playpen. Bertrand Russell was still cheerily in prison for writing something seditious about pacifism. Tuning in as usual to the Front Lines it looked as if the Germans were winning all the battles yet losing the war. And so it was. The upper-income people were upset about the income tax at six shillings to the pound. But all women over thirty got the vote. 'It seems a long time to wait,' said one of my drab old aunts, aged twenty-two. The speeches in the House of Commons always sent me to sleep which was why I missed, at the actual time, a certain oration by Mr Asquith following the armistice on 11 November. Mr Asquith was a greatly esteemed former prime minister later to be an Earl, and had been ousted by Mr Lloyd George. I clearly heard Asquith, in private, refer to Lloyd George as 'that damned Welsh goat'.

The armistice was signed and I was awake for that. I pulled myself on to my feet with the aid of the bars of my cot. My teeth were coming through very nicely in my opinion, and well worth all the trouble I was put to in bringing them forth. I weighed twenty pounds. On all the world's fighting fronts the men killed in action or dead of wounds numbered 8,538,315 and the warriors wounded and maimed were 21,219,452. With these figures in mind I sat up in my high chair and banged my spoon on the table. One of my mother's black-draped friends recited:

I have a rendezvous with Death
At some disputed barricade,
When spring comes back with rustling shade
And apple blossoms fill the air—
I have a rendezvous with Death.

Most of the poets, they said, had been killed. The poetry made them dab their eyes with clean white handkerchiefs.

Next February on my first birthday, there was a birthday-cake with one candle. Lots of children and their elders. The war had been over two months and twenty-one days. 'Why doesn't she smile?' My brother was to blow out the candle. The elders were talking about the war and the political situation. Lloyd George and Asquith, Asquith and Lloyd George. I remembered recently having switched on to Mr Asquith at a private party where he had been drinking a lot. He was playing cards and when he came to cut the cards he tried to cut a large box of matches by mistake. On another occasion I had seen him putting his arm around a lady's shoulder in a Daimler motor car, and generally behaving towards her in a very friendly fashion. Strangely enough she said, 'If you don't stop this nonsense immediately, I'll order the chauffeur to stop and I'll get out.' Mr Asquith replied, 'And pray, what reason will you give?' Well anyway it was my feeding time.

The guests arrived for my birthday. It was so sad, said one of the black widows, so sad about Wilfred Owen who was killed so late in the war, and she quoted from a poem of his:

> *What passing-bells for these who die as cattle?*
> *Only the monstrous anger of the guns.*

The children were squealing and toddling around. One was sick and another wet the floor and stood with his legs apart gaping at the puddle. All was mopped up. I banged my spoon on the table of my high chair.

> But I've a rendezvous with Death
> At midnight in some flaming town;
> When spring trips north again this year,
> And I to my pledged word am true,
> I shall not fail that rendezvous.

More parents and children arrived. One stout man who was warming his behind at the fire, said, 'I always think those words of Asquith's after the armistice were so apt ...'

They brought the cake close to my high chair for me to see, with the candle shining and flickering above the pink icing. 'A pity she never smiles.'

'She'll smile in time,' my mother said, obviously upset.

'What Asquith told the House of Commons just after the war,' said that stout gentleman with his backside to the fire, '—so apt, what Asquith said. He said that the war has cleansed and purged the world, by God! I recall his actual words: "All things have become new. In this great cleansing and purging it has been the privilege of our country to play her part ..."'

That did it. I broke into a decided smile and everyone noticed it, convinced that it was provoked by the fact that my brother had blown out the candle on the cake. 'She smiled' my mother exclaimed. And everyone was clucking away about how I was smiling. For good measure I crowed like a demented raven. 'My baby's smiling!' said my mother.

'It was the candle on her cake,' they said.

The cake be damned. Since that time I have grown to smile quite naturally, like any other healthy and house-trained person, but when I really mean a smile, deeply felt from the core, then to all intents and purposes it comes in response to the words uttered in the House of Commons after the First World War by the distinguished, the immaculately dressed and the late Mr Asquith.

DORIS LESSING

England versus England

'I think I'll be off,' said Charlie. 'My things are packed.' He had made sure of getting his holdall ready so that his mother wouldn't. 'But it's early,' she protested. Yet she was already knocking red hands together to rid them of water while she turned to say goodbye: she knew her son was leaving early to avoid the father. But the back door now opened and Mr Thornton came in. Charlie and his father were alike: tall, overthin, big-boned. The old miner stooped, his hair had gone into grey wisps, and his hollow cheeks were coal-pitted. The young man was still fresh, with jaunty fair hair and alert eyes. But there were scoops of strain under his eyes.

'You're alone,' said Charlie involuntarily, pleased, ready to sit down again. The old man was not alone. Three men came into view behind him in the light that fell into the yard from the door, and Charlie said quickly: 'I'm off, Dad, it's good-bye till Christmas.' They all came crowding into the little kitchen, bringing with them the spirit of facetiousness that seemed to Charlie his personal spiteful enemy, like a poltergeist always standing in wait somewhere behind his right shoulder. 'So you're back to the dreaming spires,' said one man, nodding goodbye. 'Off to t'places of learning,' said another. Both were smiling. There was no hostility in it, or even envy, but it shut Charlie out of his family, away from his people. The third man, adding his tribute to this, the most brilliant son of the village said: 'You'll be coming back to a right Christmas with us, then, or will you be frolicking with t'lords and t'earls you're the equal of now?'

'He'll be home for Christmas,' said the mother sharply. She turned her back on them, and dropped potatoes one by one from a paper bag into a bowl.

'For a day or so, any road,' said Charlie, in obedience to the

289

prompting spirit. 'That's time enough to spend with t'hewers of wood and t'drawers of water.' The third man nodded, as if to say: 'That's right! and put back his head to let out a relieved bellow. The father and the other two men guffawed with him. Young Lennie pushed and shoved Charlie encouragingly and Charlie jostled back, while the mother nodded and smiled because of the saving horseplay. All the same, he had not been home for nearly a year, and when they stopped laughing and stood waiting for him to go, their grave eyes said that they were remembering this fact.

'Sorry I've not had more time with you, son,' said Mr Thornton, 'but you know how 'tis.'

The old miner had been union secretary, was now chairman, and had spent his working life as miners' representative in a dozen capacities. When he walked through the village, men at a back door, or women in an apron, called: 'Just a minute, Bill,' and came after him. Every evening Mr Thornton sat in the kitchen, or in the parlour when the television was claimed by the children, giving advice about pensions, claims, work rules, allowances; filling in forms; listening to tales of trouble. Ever since Charlie could remember, Mr Thornton had been less his father than the father of the village. Now the three miners went into the parlour, and Mr Thornton laid his hand on his son's shoulder, and said: 'It's been good seeing you,' nodded, and followed them. As he shut the door he said to his wife: 'Make us a cup of tea, will you, lass?'

'There's time for a cup, Charlie,' said the mother, meaning there was no need for him to rush off now, when it was unlikely any more neighbours would come in. Charlie did not hear. He was watching her slosh dirty potatoes about under the running tap while with her free hand she reached for the kettle. He went to fetch his raincoat and his holdall listening to the nagging inner voice which he hated, but which he felt as his only protection against the spiteful enemy outside: 'I can't stand it when my father apologizes to me – he was apologizing to me for not seeing more of me. If he wasn't as he is, better than anyone else in the village, and our home the only house with real books in it, I wouldn't be at Oxford. I wouldn't have done well at school, so it cuts both ways.' The words, cut both ways, echoed uncannily in his inner ear, and he felt queasy, as if the earth he stood on was shaking. His eyes cleared on the sight of his mother, standing in front of him, her shrewd, non-judging gaze on his face. 'Eh, lad,' she said, 'you don't look any too good to me.' 'I'm all right,' he said hastily, and kissed her, adding: 'Say my piece to the girls when they come in.' He went out, with Lennie behind him.

The two youths walked in silence past fifty crammed lively brightly lit kitchens whose doors kept opening as the miners came in from the pit for their tea. They walked in silence along the fronts of fifty more houses. The fronts were all dark. The life of the village, even now, was in the kitchens where great fires roared all day on the cheap coal. The village had been built in the thirties by the company, now nationalized. There were two thousand houses, exactly alike, with identical patches of carefully tended front garden, and busy back yards. Nearly every house had a television aerial. From every chimney poured black smoke.

At the bus stop Charlie turned to look back at the village, now a low hollow of black, streaked and spattered with sullen wet lights. He tried to isolate the gleam from his own home, while he thought how he loved his home and how he hated the village. Everything about it offended him, yet as soon as he stepped inside his kitchen he was received into warmth. That morning he had stood on the front step and looked out on lines of grey stucco houses on either side of grey tarmac; on grey ugly lamp-posts and greyish hedges, and beyond to the grey minetip and the neat black diagram of the minehead.

He had looked, listening while the painful inner voice lectured: 'There's nothing in sight, not one object or building anywhere, that is beautiful. Everything is so ugly and mean and graceless that it should be bulldozed into the earth and out of the memory of man.' There was not even a cinema. There was a post office, and attached to it a library that had romances and war stories. There were two miners' clubs for drinking. And there was television. These were the amenities for two thousand families.

When Mr Thornton stood on his front step and looked forth he smiled with pride and called is children to say: 'You're never seen what a miners' town can be like. You couldn't even imagine the conditions. Slums, that's what they used to be. Well, we've put an end to all that ... Yes, off you go to Doncaster, I suppose, dancing and the pictures – that's all you can think about. And you take it all for granted. Now, in our time ...'

And so when Charlie visited his home he was careful that none of his bitter criticisms reached words, for above all, he could not bear to hurt his father.

A group of young miners came along for the bus. They wore smartly shouldered suits, their caps set at angles, and scarves flung back over their shoulders. They greeted Lennie, looked to see who the stranger was, and when Lennie said: 'This is my brother,' they nodded and turned quickly to board the bus. They went upstairs, and Lennie and Charlie went to the front downstairs. Lennie looked like them, with a strong cloth cap and a jaunty scarf. He was short, stocky, strong – 'built for t'pit,' Mr Thornton said. But Lennie was in a foundry in Doncaster. No pit for him, he said. He had heard his father coughing through all the nights of his childhood, and the pit wasn't for him. But he had never said this to his father.

Lennie was twenty. He earned seventeen pounds a week, and wanted to marry a girl he had been courting for three years now. But he could not marry until the big brother was through college. The father was still on the coal face, when by rights of age he should have been on the surface, because he earned four pounds a week more on the face. The sister in the office had wanted to be a schoolteacher, but at the moment of decision all the extra money of the family had been needed for Charlie. It cost them two hundred pounds a year for his extras at Oxford. The only members of the family not making sacrifices for Charlie were the schoolgirl and the mother.

It was half an hour on the bus, and Charlie's muscles were set hard in readiness for what Lennie might say, which must be resisted. Yet he had come home thinking: Well, at least I can talk it out with Lennie, I can be honest with him.

Now Lennie said facetiously, but with an anxious loving inspection of his brother's face: 'And what for do we owe the pleasure of your company, Charlie boy? You could have knocked us all over with a feather when you said you were coming this weekend.'

Charlie said angrily: 'I got fed up with t'earls and t'dukes.'

'Eh,' said Lennie quickly, 'but you didn't need to mind *them*, they didn't mean to rile you.'

'I know they didn't.'

'Mum's right,' said Lennie, with another anxious but carefully brief glance, 'you're not looking too good. What's up?'

'What if I don't pass t'examinations,' said Charlie in a rush.

'Eh, but what is this, then? You were always first in school. You were the best of everyone. Why shouldn't you pass, then?'

'Sometimes I think I won't,' said Charlie lamely, but glad he had let the moment pass.

Lennie examined him again, this time frankly, and gave a movement like a shrug. But it was a hunching of the shoulders against a possible defeat. He sat hunched, his big hands on his knees. On his face was a small critical grin. Not critical of Charlie, not at all, but of life.

His heart beating painfully with guilt, Charlie said: 'It's not as bad as that, I'll pass.' The inner enemy remarked softly: 'I'll pass, then I'll get a nice pansy job in a publisher's office with the other wet-nosed little boys, or I'll be a sort of clerk. Or I'll be a teacher – I've not talent for teaching, but what's the matter? Or I'll be on the management side of industry, pushing people like Lennie around. And the joke is, Lennie's earning more than I shall for years.' The enemy behind his right shoulder began satirically tolling a bell and intoned: 'Charlie Thornton, in his third year at Oxford, was found dead in a gas-filled bed-sittingroom this morning. He had been overworking. Death from natural causes.' The enemy added a loud rude raspberry and fell silent. But he was waiting: Charlie could feel him there waiting.

Lennie said: 'Seen a doctor, Charlie boy?'

'Yes. He said I should take it easy a bit. That's why I came home.'

'No point killing yourself working.'

'No, it's not serious, he just said I must take it easy.'

Lennie's face remained grave. Charlie knew that when he got home he would say to the mother: 'I think Charlie's got summat on his mind.' And his mother would say (while she stood shaking chips of potato into boiling fat): 'I expect sometimes he wonders is the grind worth it. And he sees you earning, when he isn't.' She would say, after a silence during which they exchanged careful looks: 'It must be hard for him, coming here, everything different, then off he goes, everything different again.'

'Shouldn't worry, Mum.'

'I'm not worrying. Charlie's all right.'

The inner voice enquired anxiously : 'If she's on the spot about the rest, I suppose she's right about the last bit too – *I suppose I am all right?*'

But the enemy behind his right shoulder said : 'A man's best friend is his mother, she never lets a thing pass.'

Last year he had brought Jenny down for a weekend, to satisfy the family's friendly curiosity about the posh people he knew these days. Jenny was a poor clergyman's daughter, bookish, a bit of a prig, but a nice girl. She had easily navigated the complicated currents of the weekend, while the family waited for her to put on 'side'. Afterwards Mrs Thornton had said, putting her finger on the sore spot : 'That's a right nice girl. She's a proper mother to you, and that's a fact.' The last was not a criticism of the girl, but of Charlie. Now Charlie looked with envy at Lennie's responsible profile and said to himself : Yes, he's a man. He has been for years, since he left school. Me, I'm a proper baby, and I've got two years over him.

For above everything else, Charlie was made to feel, every time he came home, that these people, his people, were serious ; while he and the people with whom he would now spend his life (if he passed the examinations) were not serious. He did not believe this. The inner didactic voice made short work of any such idea. The outer enemy could, and did, parody it in a hundred ways. His family did not believe it, they were proud of him. Yet Charlie felt it in everything they said and did. They protected him. They sheltered him. And above all, they still paid for him. At his age, his father has been working in the pit for eight years.

Lennie would be married next year. He already talked of a family. He, Charlie (if he passed the examination), would be running around licking people's arses to get a job, Bachelor of Arts, Oxford, and a drug on the market.

They had reached Doncaster. It was raining. Soon they would pass where Doreen, Lennie's girl, worked. 'You'd better get off here,' Charlie said. 'You'll have all that drag back through the wet.' 'No, s'all right, I'll come with you to the station.'

There were another five minutes to go. 'I don't think it's right, the way you get at Mum,' Lennie said, at last coming to the point.

'But I haven't said a bloody word,' said Charlie, switching without having intended it into his other voice, the middle-class voice which he was careful never to use with his family except in joke. Lennie gave him a glance of surprise and reproach and said: 'All the same. She feels it.'

'But it's bloody ridiculous.' Charlie's voice was rising. 'She stands in that kitchen all day, pandering to our every whim, when she's not doing housework or making a hundred trips a day with that blood coal ...' In the Christmas holidays, when Charlie had visited home last, he had fixed up a bucket on the frame of an old pram to ease his mother's work. This morning he had seen the contrivance collapsed and full of rainwater in the back yard. After breakfast Lennie and Charlie had sat at the table in their shirt-sleeves watching their mother. The door was open into the back yard. Mrs Thornton carried a shovel whose blade was nine inches by ten, and was walking back and forth from the coalhole in the yard, through the kitchen, into the parlour. On each inward journey, a small clump of coal balanced on the shovel. Charlie counted that his mother walked from the coalhole to the kitchen fire and the parlour fire thirty-six times. She walked steadily, the shovel in front, held like a spear in both hands, and her face frowned with purpose. Charled had dropped his head on to his arms and laughed soundlessly until he felt Lennie's warning gaze and stopped the heave of his shoulders. After a moment he had sat up, straight-faced. Lennie said: 'Why do you get at Mum, then?' Charlie said: 'But I haven't said owt.' 'No, but she's getting riled. You always show what you think, Charlie boy.' As Charlie did not respond to his appeal – for far more than present charity – Lennie went on: 'You can't teach an old dog new tricks.' 'Old! She's not fifty!'

Now Charlie said, continuing the early conversation: 'She goes on as if she were an old woman. She wears herself out with nothing – she could get through all the work she has in a couple of hours if she organized herself. Or if just for once she told us where to get off.'

'What'd she do with herself then?'

'Do? Well, she could do something for herself. Read. Or see

friends. Or something.'

'She feels it. Last time you went off she cried.'

'She *what*?' Charlie's guilt almost overpowered him, but the inner didactic voice switched on in time and he spoke through it: 'What right have we to treat her like a bloody servant? Betty likes her food this way and that way, and Dad won't eat this and that, and she stands there and humours the lot of us – like a servant.'

'And who was it last night said he wouldn't have fat on his meat and changed it for hers?' said Lennie smiling, but full of reproach.

'Oh, I'm just as bad as the rest of you,' said Charlie, sounding false. 'It makes me wild to see it,' he said, sounding sincere. Didactically he said: 'All the women in the village – they take it for granted. If someone organized them so that they had half a day to themselves sometimes, they'd think they were being insulted – they can't stop working. Just look at Mum, then. She comes into Doncaster to wrap sweets two or three times a week – well, she actually loses money on it, by the time she's paid bus fares. I said to her, "You're actually losing money on it," and she said: "I like to get out and see a bit of life." A bit of life! Wrapping sweets in a bloody factory. Why can't she just come into town of an evening and have a bit of fun without feeling she has to pay for it by wrapping sweets, sweated bloody labour? And she actually loses on it. It doesn't make sense. They're human beings, aren't they? Not just ...'

'Not just what?' asked Lennie angrily. He had listened to Charlie's tirade, his mouth setting harder, his eyes narrowing. 'Here's the station,' he said in relief. They waited for the young miners to clatter down and off before going forward themselves. 'I'll come with you to your stop,' said Charlie; and they crossed the dark, shiny, grimy street to the opposite stop for the bus which would take Lennie back to Doreen.

'It's no good thinking we're going to change, Charlie boy.'

'Who said change?' said Charlie excitedly; but the bus had come, and Lennie was already swinging on to the back. 'If you're in trouble just write and say,' said Lennie, and the bell pinged and his face vanished as the lit bus was absorbed by the light-streaked drizzling darkness.

There was half an hour before the London train. Charlie stood with the rain on his shoulders, his hands in his pockets, wondering whether to go after his brother and explain – what ? He bolted across the street to the pub near the station. It was run by an Irishman who knew him and Lennie. The place was still empty, being just after opening time.

'It's you then,' said Mike, drawing him a pint of bitter without asking. 'Yes, it's me,' said Charlie, swinging himself up on to a stool.

'And what's in the great world of learning ?'

'Oh Jesus, *no* !' said Charlie. The Irishman blinked, and Charlie said quickly : 'What have you gone and tarted this place up for ?'

The pub had been panelled in dark wood. It was ugly and comforting. Now it had half a dozen bright wallpapers and areas of shining paint, and Charlie's stomach moved again, light filled his eyes, and he sat his elbows hard down for support, and put his chin on his two fists.

'The youngsters like it,' said the Irishman. 'But we've left the bar next door as it was for the old ones.'

'You should have a sign up : Age This Way,' said Charlie. 'I'd have known where to go.' He carefully lifted his head off his fists, narrowing his eyes to exclude the battling colours of the wallpapers, the shine of the paint.

'You look bad,' said the Irishman. He was a small, round, alcoholically cheerful man who, like Charlie, had two voices. For the enemy – that is, all the English whom he did not regard as a friend, which meant people who were not regulars – he put on an exaggerated brogue which was bound, if he persisted, to lead to the political arguments he delighted in. For friends like Charlie he didn't trouble himself. He now said : 'All work and no play.'

'That's right,' said Charlie. 'I went to the doctor. He gave me a tonic and said I am fundamentally sound in wind and limb. "You are sound in wind and limb," he said,' said Charlie, parodying an upper-class English voice for the Irishman's pleasure.

Mike winked, acknowledging the jest, while his professionally humorous face remained serious. 'You can't burn the candle at both ends,' he said in earnest warning.

Charlie laughed out. 'That's what the doctor said. You can't burn the candle at both ends, he said.'

This time, when the stool he sat on, and the floor beneath the stool, moved away from him, and the glittering ceiling dipped and swung, his eyes went dark and stayed dark. He shut them and gripped the counter tight. With his eyes still shut he said facetiously : 'It's the clash of cultures, that's what it is. It makes me light-headed.' He opened his eyes and saw from the Irishman's face that he had not said these words aloud.

He said aloud : 'Actually the doctor was all right, he meant well. But Mike, I'm not going to make it, I'm going to fail.'

'Well, it won't be the end of the world.'

'*Jesus*. That's what I like about you, Mike, you take a broad view of life.'

'I'll be back,' said Mike, going to serve a customer.

A week ago Charlie had gone to the doctor with a cyclostyled leaflet in his hand. It was called 'A Report Into the Increased Incidence of Break-down Among Undergraduates'. He had underlined the words :

> Young men from working-class and lower-middle-class families on scholarships are particularly vulnerable. For them, the gaining of a degree is obviously crucial. In addition they are under the continuous strain of adapting themselves to middle-class mores that are foreign to them. They are victims of a clash of standards, a clash of cultures, divided loyalties.

The doctor, a young man of about thirty, provided by the college authorities as a sort of father figure to advise on work problems, personal problems and (as the satirical alter ego took pleasure in pointing out) on clash-of-culture problems, glanced once at the pamphlet and handed it back. He had written it. As, of course, Charlie had known. 'When are your examinations ?' he asked. *Getting to the root of the matter, just like Mum,* remarked the malevolent voice from behind Charlie's shoulder.

'I've got five months, doctor, and I can't work and I can't sleep.'

'For how long ?'

'It's been coming on gradually.' *Every since I was born,* said the enemy.

'I can give you sedatives and sleeping pills, of course, but that's not going to touch what's really wrong.'

Which is, all this unnatural mixing of the classes. Doesn't do, you know. People should know their place and stick to it. 'I'd like some sleep pills, all the same.'

'Have you got a girl?'

'Two.'

The doctor paid out an allowance of man-of-the-world sympathy, then shut off his smile and said: 'Perhaps you'd be better with one?'

Which, my mum figure, or my lovely bit of sex? 'Perhaps I would at that.'

'I could arrange for you to have some talks with a psychiatrist — well, not if you don't want,' he said hastily, for the alter ego had exploded through Charlie's lips in a horselaugh and: 'What can the trick cyclist tell me I don't know?' He roared with laughter, flinging his legs up; and an ashtray went circling around the room on its rim. Charlie laughed, watched the ashtray, and thought: There, I knew all the time it was a poltergeist sitting there behind my shoulder. I swear I never touched that damned ashtray.

The doctor waited until it circled near him, stopped it with his foot, picked it up, laid it back on the desk. 'It's no point your going to him if you feel like that.'

All avenues explored, all roads charted.

'Well now, let's see, have you been to see your family recently?'

'Last Christmas. No, doctor, it's not because I don't want to, it's because I can't work there.' *You try working in an atmosphere of trade union meetings and the telly and the pictures in Doncaster. You try it, doc. And besides all my energies go into not upsetting them. Because I do upset them. My dear doc, when we scholarship boys jump our class, it's not we who suffer, it's our families. We are an expense, doc. And besides — write a thesis, I'd like to read it ... Call it: Long-term effects on working-class or lower-middle-class family of a scholarship child whose existence is a perpetual reminder that they are nothing but ignorant non-cultured clods. How's that for a thesis, doc? Why, I do believe I could write it myself.*

'If I were you, I'd go home for a few days. Don't try to work at all. Go to the pictures. Sleep and eat and let them fuss over you. Get this prescription made up and come and see me when you get back.

'Thanks, doc, I will.' *You mean well*.

The Irishman came back to find Charlie spinning a penny, so intent on this game that he did not see him. First he spun it with his right hand, anticlockwise, then with his left, clockwise. The right hand represented his jeering alter ego. The left hand was the didactic and rational voice. The left hand was able to keep the coin in a glittering spin for much longer than the right.

'You ambidextrous ?

'Yes, always was.'

The Irishman watched the boy's frowning, teeth-clenched concentration for a while, then removed the untouched beer and poured him a double whisky. 'You drink that and get on the train and sleep.'

'Thanks, Mike. Thanks.'

'That was a nice girl you had with you last time.'

'I've quarrelled with her. Or rather, she's given me the boot. And quite right too.'

After a visit to the doctor Charlie had gone straight to Jenny. He had guyed the interview while she sat, gravely listening. Then he had given her his favourite lecture on the crass and unalterable insensibility of anyone anywhere born middle-class. No one but Jenny ever heard this lecture. She said at last : 'You *should* go and see a psychiatrist. No, don't you see, it's not fair.'

'Who to, me ?'

'No, me. What's the use of shouting at me all the time ? You should be saying these things to him.'

'*What* ?'

'Well, surely you can see that. You spend all your time lecturing me. You make use of me, Charles.' (She always called him Charles.)

What she was really saying was : 'You should be making love to me, not lecturing me.' Charlie did not really like making love to Jenny. He forced himself when her increasingly tart and accusing manner reminded him he ought to. He had another girl, whom he disliked, a tall crisp middle-class girl called Sally. She called him, mocking : Charlie Boy. When he had slammed out of Jenny's room, he had gone to Sally and fought his way into her bed. Every act of sex with Sally was a slow, cold subjugation of her by him. That night he had said, when she lay at last, submissive, beneath him: 'Horny-handed son of toil wins by his unquenched virility beautiful daughter of the moneyed classes. And doesn't she love it.'

'Oh yes I do, Charlie boy.'

'I'm nothing but a bloody sex symbol.'

'Well,' she murmured, already self-possessed, freeing herself, 'that's all I am to you.' She added defiantly, showing that she did care, and that it was Charlie's fault: 'And I couldn't care less.'

'Dear Sally, what I like about you is your beautiful honesty.'

'Is that what you like about me? I thought it was the thrill of beating me down.'

Charlie said to the Irishman: 'I've quarrelled with everyone I know in the last weeks.'

'Quarrelled with your family too?'

'*No,*' he said, appalled, while the room again swung around him. 'Good Lord no,' he said in a different tone – grateful. He added savagely: 'How could I? I can never say anything to them I really think.' He looked at Mike to see if he had actually said these words aloud. He had, because now Mike said: 'So you know how I feel. I've lived thirty years in this mucking country, and if you arrogant sods knew what I'm thinking half the time...'

'Liar. You say whatever you think, from Cromwell to the Black and Tans and Casement. You never let up. But it's not hurting yourself to say it.'

'Yourself, is it?'

'Yes. But it's all insane. Do you realize how insane it all is, Mike? There's my father. Pillar of the working class. Labour Party, trade union, the lot. But I've been watching my tongue not to say I spent last term campaigning about – he takes it for granted even *now* that the British should push the wogs around.'

'You're a great nation,' said the Irishman. 'But it's not your personal fault, so drink up and have another.'

Charlie drank his first Scotch, and drew the second glass towards him. 'Don't you see what I mean?' he said, his voice rising excitedly. 'Don't you see that it's all *insane*? There's my mother, her sister is ill and it looks as if she'll die. There are two kids, and my mother'll take them both. They're nippers, three and four, it's like starting a family all over again. She thinks nothing of it. If someone's in trouble, she's the mug, every time.

But there she sits and says: "Those juvenile offenders ought to be flogged until they are senseless." She reads it in the papers and so she says it. She said it to me and I kept my mouth shut. And they're all alike.'

'Yes, but you're not going to change it, Charlie, so drink up.'

A man standing a few feet down the bar had a paper sticking out of his pocket. Mike said to him: 'Mind if I borrow your paper for the winners, sir?'

'Help yourself.'

Mike turned the paper over to the back page. 'I had five quid on today,' he said 'Lost it. Lovely bit of horseflesh, but I lost it.'

'Wait,' said Charlie excitedly, straightening the paper so he could see the front page. WARDROBE MURDERER GETS SECOND CHANCE, it said. 'See that?' said Charlie. 'The Home Secretary says he can have another chance, they can review the case, he says.'

The Irishman read, cold-faced. 'So he does,' he said.

'Well, I mean to say, there's some decency left, then. I mean if the can can be reviewed it shows they do *care* about something at least.'

'I don't see it your way at all. It's England versus England, that's all. Fair play all round, but they'll hang the poor sod on the day appointed as usual.' He turned the newspaper and studied the race news.

Charlie waited for his eyes to clear, held himself steady with one hand flat on the counter, and drank his second double. He pushed over a pound note, remembering it had to last three days, and that now he had quarrelled with Jenny there was no place for him to stay in London.

'No, it's on me,' said Mike 'I asked you. It's been a pleasure seeing you, Charlie. And don't take the sins of the world on your personal shoulders, lad, because that doesn't do anyone any good, does it, now?'

'See you at Christmas, Mike, and thanks.'

He walked carefully out into the rain. There was no solitude to be had on the train that night, so he chose a compartment with one person in it, and settled himself in a corner before looking to see who it was he had with him. It was a girl. He saw then that she was pretty, and then that she was upper-class. Another Sally, he thought, sensing danger, seeing the cool, self-sufficient little face. Hey, there, Charlie, he said to himself, keep yourself in order, or you've had it. He carefully located himself : *he,* Charlie was now a warm, whisky-comforted belly, already a little sick. Close above it, like a silent loudspeaker, was the source of the hectoring voice. Behind his shoulder waited his grinning familiar. *He must keep them all apart.* He tested the didactic voice : It's not her fault, poor bitch, victim of the class system, she can't help she sees everyone under her like dirt ... But the alcohol was working strongly and meanwhile his familiar was calculating : She's had a good look, but can't make me out. My clothes are right, my haircut's on the line, but there's something that makes her wonder. She's waiting for me to speak, then she'll make up her mind. Well, first I'll get her, and then I'll speak.

He caught her eyes and signalled an invitation, but it was an aggressive invitation, to make it as hard for her as he could. After a bit, she smiled at him. Then he roughened his speech to the point of unintelligibility and said : 'Appen you'd like t'window up ? What wi' t'rain and t'wind and all.'

'What ?' she said sharply, her face lengthening into such a comical frankness of shock that he laughed out, and afterwards enquired impeccably : 'Actually it is rather cold, isn't it ? Wouldn't you like to have the window up ?' She picked up a magazine and shut him out, while he watched, grinning, the blood creep up from under her neat collar to her hairline.

The door slid back ; two people came in. They were a man and his wife, both small, crumpled in face and flesh, and dressed in their best for London. There was a fuss and a heaving of suitcases and murmured apologies because of the two superior young people. Then the woman, having settled herself in a corner, looked steadily at Charlie, while he thought : 'Deep calls to deep, *she* knows who I am all right, she's not foxed by the trimmings. He was right, because soon she said familiarly : 'Would you put the window up for me, lad ? It's a rare cold night and no mistake.'

Charlie put up the window, not looking at the girl, who was hiding behind the magazine. Now the woman smiled, and the man smiled too, because of her ease with the youth.

'You comfortable like that, father ?' she asked.

'Fair enough,' said the husband on the stoical note of the

confirmed grumbler.

'Put your feet up beside me, any road,'

'But I'm all right, lass,' he said bravely. Then, making a favour of it, he loosened his laces, eased his feet inside too-new shoes, and set them on the seat beside his wife.

She, for her part, was removing her hat. It was of shapeless grey felt, with a pink rose at the front. Charlie's mother owned just such a badge of respectability, renewed every year or so at the sales. Hers was always bluish felt, with a bit of ribbon or coarse net, and she would rather be seen dead than without it in public.

The woman sat fingering her hair, which was thin and greying. For some reason, the sight of her clean pinkish scalp shining through the grey wisps made Charlie wild with anger. He was taken by surprise, and again summoned himself to himself, making the didactic voice lecture : 'The working woman of these islands enjoys a position in the family superior to that of the middle-class woman, etc., etc., etc.' This was an article he had read recently, and he continued to recite from it, until he realized the voice had become an open sneer, and was saying : 'Not only is she the emotional bulwark of the family, but she is frequently the bread-winner as well, such as wrapping sweets at night, sweated labour for pleasure, anything to get out of the happy home for a few hours.'

The fusion of the two voices, the nagging inside voice, and the jeer from the dangerous force outside, terrified Charlie, and he told himself hastily : 'You're drunk, that's all, now keep your mouth shut, for God's sake.'

The woman was asking him : 'Are you feeling all right ?'

'Yes, I'm all right,' he said carefully.

'Going all the way to London ?'

'Yes, I'm going all the way to London.'

'It's a long drag.'

'Yes, it's a long drag.'

At this echoing dialogue, the girl lowered her magazine to give him a sharp contemptuous look, up and down. Her face was now smoothly pink, and her small pink mouth was judging.

'You have a mouth like a rosebud,' said Charlie, listening horrified to these words emerging from him.

The girl jerked up her magazine. The man looked sharply at

Charlie, to see if he had heard alright, and then at his wife, for guidance. The wife looked doubtfully at Charlie, who offered her a slow desperate wink. She accepted it, and nodded at her husband: boys will be boys. They both glanced warily at the shining face of the magazine.

'We're on our way to London too,' said the woman.

'So you're on your way to London.'

Stop it, he told himself. He felt a foolish slack grin on his face, and his tongue was thickening in his mouth. He shut his eyes, trying to summon Charlie to his aid, but his stomach was rolling, warm and sick. He lit a cigarette for support, watching his hands at work. 'Lily-handed son of learning wants a manicure badly,' commented a soft voice in his ear; and he saw the cigarette poised in a parody of a cad's gesture between displayed nicotined fingers. Charlie, smoking with poise, sat preserving a polite, sarcastic smile.

He was in the grip of terror. He was afraid he might slide off the seat. He could no longer help himself.

'London's a big place, for strangers,' said the woman.

'But it makes a nice change,' said Charlie, trying hard.

The woman, delighted that a real conversation was at last under way, settled her shabby old head against a leather bulge, and said: 'Yes, it does make a nice change.' The shine of the leather confused Charlie's eyes; he glanced over at the magazine, but its glitter, too, seemed to invade his pupils. He looked at the dirty floor, and said: 'It's good for people to get a change now and then.'

'Yes, that's what I tell my husband, don't I, father? It's good for us to get away now and then. We have a married daughter in Streatham.'

'It's a great thing, family ties.'

'Yes, but it's a drag,' said the man. 'Say what you like, but it is. After all, I mean, when all is said and done.' He paused, his head on one side, with a debating look, waiting for Charlie to take it up.

Charlie said: 'There's no denying it, say what you like, I mean, there's no doubt about *that*.' And he looked interestedly at the man for his reply.

The woman said: 'Yes, but the way I look at it, you've got to get *out* of yourself sometimes, look at it that way.'

'It's all very well,' said the husband, on a satisfied but grumbling note, 'but if you're going to do that, well, for a start-off, it's an expense.'

'If you don't throw a good penny after a bad one,' said Charlie judiciously. 'I mean, what's the point?'

'Yes, that's it,' said the woman excitedly, her old face animated. 'That's what I say to father, what's the point if you don't sometimes let yourself go?'

'I mean, life's bad enough as it is,' said Charlie, watching the magazine slowly lower itself. It was laid precisely on the seat. The girl now sat, two small brown-gloved hands in a ginger-tweeded lap, staring him out. Her blue eyes glinted into his, and he looked quickly away.

'Well, I can see that right enough,' said the man. 'but there again, you've got to know where to stop.'

'That's right,' said Charlie, 'you're dead right.'

'I know it's all right for some,' said the man, 'I know that, but if you're going to do that, you've got to consider. That's what I think.'

'But father, you know you enjoy it, once you're there and Joyce has settled you in your own corner with your own chair and your cup to yourself.'

'Ah,' said the man, nodding heavily, 'but it's not as easy as that, now, is it? Well, I mean, that stands to reason.'

'Ah,' said Charlie, shaking his head, feeling it roll heavily in the socket of his neck, 'but if you're going to consider at all, then what's the point? I mean, what I think is, for a start-off, there's no doubt about it.'

The woman hesitated, started to say something, but let her small bright eyes falter away. She was beginning to colour.

Charlie went on compulsively, his head turning like a clockwork man's: 'It's what you're used to, that's what I say, well I mean. *Well,* and there's another thing, when all is said and done, and after all, if you're going to make one thing with another ...'

'Stop it,' said the girl, in a sharp high voice.

'It's a question of principle,' said Charlie, but his head had stopped rolling and his eyes had focussed.

'If you don't stop I'm going to call the guard and have you put in another compartment' said the girl. To the old people she said in a righteous scandalized voice: 'Can't you see he's laughing at you? Can't you see?' She lifted the magazine again.

The old people looked suspiciously at Charlie, dubiously at each other. The woman's face was very pink and her eyes bright and hot.

'I think I am going to get forty winks,' said the man, with general hostility. He settled his feet, put is head back, and closed his eyes.

Charlie said: 'Excuse me,' and scrambled his way to the corridor over the legs of the man, then the legs of the woman, muttering: 'Excuse me, excuse me, I'm sorry.'

He stood in the corridor, his back jolting slightly against the shifting wood of the compartment's sides. His eyes were shut, his tears running. Words, no longer articulate, muttered and jumbled somewhere inside him, a stream of frightened protesting phrases.

Wood slid against wood close to his ear, and he heard the softness of clothed flesh on wood.

'If it's that bloody little bint I'll kill her,' said a voice, small and quiet, from his diaphragm.

He opened his murderous eyes on the woman. She looked concerned.

'I'm sorry,' he said, stiff and sullen, 'I'm sorry, I didn't mean ...'

'It's all right,' she said, and laid her two red hands on his crossed quivering forearms. She took his two wrists, and laid his arms gently down by his sides. 'Don't take on,' she said, 'it's all right, it's all right, son.'

The tense rejection of his flesh caused her to take a step back from him. But there she stood her ground and said: 'Now look, son, there's no point taking on like that, well, is there? I mean to say, you've got to take the rough with the smooth, and there's no other way of looking at it.'

She waited, facing him, troubled but sure of herself.

After a while Charlie said: 'Yes, I suppose you're right.'

She nodded and smiled, and went back into the compartment. After a moment, Charlie followed her.

WILLIAM TREVOR

Angels at the Ritz

The game was played when the party, whichever party it happened to be, had thinned out. Those who stayed on beyond a certain point – beyond, usually, about one o'clock – knew that the game was on the cards and in fact had stayed for that reason. Often, as one o'clock approached, there were marital disagreements about whether or not to go home.

The game of swapping wives and husbands, with chance rather than choice dictating the formations, had been practised in this outer suburb since the mid-1950s. The swinging wives and husbands of that time were now passing into the first years of elderliness, but their party game continued. In the outer suburb it was most popular when the early struggles of marriage were over, after children had been born and were established at school, when there were signs of marital wilting that gin and tonic did not cure.

'I think it's awfully silly,' Polly Dillard pronounced, addressing her husband on the evening of the Ryders' party.

Her husband, whose first name was Gavin, pointed out that they'd known for years that the practice was prevalent on Saturday-night parties in the outer suburb. There'd been, he reminded her, the moment at the Meacocks' when they'd realised they'd stayed too late, when the remaining men threw their car-keys on to the Meacocks' carpet and Sylvia Meacock began to tie scarves over the eyes of the wives.

'I mean, it's silly Sue and Malcolm going in for it. All of a sudden, out of the blue like that.'

'They're just shuffling along with it, I suppose.'

Polly shook her head. Quietly, she said that in the past Sue and Malcolm Ryder hadn't been the kind to shuffle along with things. Sue had sounded like a silly schoolgirl, embarrassed and

308

not looking her in the eye when she told her.

Gavin could see she was upset, but one of the things about Polly since she'd had their two children and had come to live in the outer suburb was that she was able to deal with being upset. She dealt with it now, keeping calm, not raising her voice. She'd have been the same when Sue Ryder averted her eyes and said that she and Malcolm had decided to go in, too, for the outer suburb's most popular party game. Polly would have been astonished and would have said so, and then she'd have attempted to become reconciled to the development. Before this evening came to an end she really would be reconciled, philosophically accepting the development as part of the Ryders' middle age, while denying that it could ever be part of hers.

'I suppose,' Gavin said, 'it's like a schoolgirl deciding to let herself be kissed for the first time. Don't you remember sounding silly then, Polly?'

She said it wasn't at all like that. Imagine, she suggested, finding yourself teamed up with a sweaty creature like Tim Gruffydd. Imagine any schoolgirl in her senses letting Tim Gruffydd within two million miles of her. She still couldn't believe that Sue and Malcolm Ryder were going in for stuff like that. What on earth happened to people? she asked Gavin, and Gavin said he didn't know.

Polly Dillard was thirty-six, her husband two years older. Her short fair hair had streaks of grey in it now. Her thin, rather long face wasn't pretty but did occasionally seem beautiful, the eyes deep blue, the mouth wide, becoming slanted when she smiled. She herself considered that nothing matched properly in her face and that her body was too lanky and her breasts too slight. But after thirty-six years she'd become used to all that, and other women envied her figure and her looks.

On the evening of the Ryders' party she surveyed the features that did not in her opinion match, applying eyeshadow in her bedroom looking-glass and now and again glancing at the reflection of her husband, who was changing from his Saturday clothes into clothes more suitable for Saturday night at the Ryders': a blue corduroy suit, pink shirt and pinkish tie. Of medium height, fattening on lunches and alcohol, he was dark-haired and still handsome, for his chunky features were only just beginning to trail signs of this telltale plumpness. By profession

Gavin Dillard was a director of promotional films for television, mainly in the soap and detergent field.

The hall-door bell rang as Polly rose from the chair in front of her looking-glass.

'I'll go,' he said, adding that it would be Estrella, their babysitter.

'Estrella couldn't come, I had to ring Problem. Some Irish-sounding girl it'll be.'

'Hannah McCarthy,' a round-faced girl at the door said. 'Are you Mr Dillard, sir?'

He smiled at her and said he was. He closed the door and took her coat. He led her through a white, spacious hall into a sitting-room that was spacious also, with pale blue walls and curtains. One child was already in bed, he told her, the other was still in his bath. Two boys, he explained: Paul and David. His wife would introduce her to them.

'Would you like a drink, Hannah?'

'Well, I wouldn't say no to that, Mr Dillard.' She smiled an extensive smile at him. 'A little sherry if you have it, sir.'

'And how's the old country, Hannah?' He spoke lightly, trying to be friendly, handing her a glass of sherry. He turned away and poured himself some gin and tonic, adding a sliver of lemon. 'Cheers, Hannah!'

'Cheers, sir! Ireland, d'you mean, sir? Oh, Ireland doesn't change.'

'You go back, do you?'

'Every holidays. I'm in teacher training, Mr Dillard.'

'I was at the Cork Film Festival once. A right old time we had.'

'I don't know Cork, actually. I'm from Listowel myself. Are you in films yourself, sir? You're not an actor, Mr Dillard?'

'Actually I'm a director.'

Polly entered the room. She said she was Mrs Dillard. She smiled, endeavouring to be as friendly as Gavin had been, in case the girl didn't feel at home. She thanked her for coming at such short notice and presumably so far. She was wearing a skirt that Gavin had helped her to buy in Fenwick's only last week, and a white lace blouse she'd had for years, and her jade beads. The skirt, made of velvet, was the same green as the jade. She took the babysitter away to introduce her to the two children.

Gavin stood with his back to the fire, sipping at his gin and tonic. He didn't find it puzzling that Polly should feel so strongly about the fact that Sue and Malcolm Ryder had reached a certain stage in their marriage. The Ryders were their oldest and closest friends. Polly and Sue had known one another since they'd gone together to the Misses Summers' nursery school in Putney. Perhaps it was this depth in the relationship that caused Polly to feel so disturbed by a new development in her friend's life. In his own view, being offered a free hand with an unselected woman in return for agreeing that some man should maul his wife about wasn't an attractive proposition. It surprised him that the Ryders had decided to go in for this particular party game, and it surprised him even more that Malcolm Ryder had never mentioned it to him. But it didn't upset him.

'All right?' Polly enquired from the doorway, with her coat on. The coat was brown and fur-trimmed and expensive: she looked beautiful in it, Gavin thought, calm and collected. Once, a long time ago, she had thrown a milk-jug across a room at him. At one time she had wept a lot, deploring her lankiness and her flat breasts. All that seemed strangely out of character now.

He finished his drink and put the glass down on the mantelpiece. He put the sherry bottle beside the babysitter's glass in case she should feel like some more, and then changed his mind and returned the bottle to the cabinet, remembering that they didn't know the girl: a drunk babysitter – an experience they'd once endured – was a great deal worse than no babysitter at all.

'She seems very nice,' Polly said in the car. 'She said she'd read to them for an hour.'

'An hour? The poor girl!'

'She loves children.'

It was dark, half-past eight on a night in November. It was raining just enough to make it necessary to use the windscreen-wipers. Automatically, Gavin turned the car radio on: there was something pleasantly cosy about the glow of a car radio at night when it was raining, and the background whirr of the wind-screenwipers and the wave of warmth from the heater.

'Let's not stay long,' he said.

It pleased her that he said that. She wondered if they were dull not to wish to stay, but he said that was nonsense.

He drove through the sprawl of their outer suburb, all of it new, disguised now by the night. Orange street lighting made the façades of the carefully-designed houses seem different, changing the colours, but the feeling of space remained, and the uncluttered effect of the unfenced front gardens. Roomy Volvo estate-cars went nicely with the detached houses. So did Vauxhall Victors, and big bus-like Volkswagens. Families were packed into such vehicles on summer Saturday mornings, for journeys to cottages in the Welsh hills or in Hampshire or Herts. The Dillards' cottage was in the New Forest.

Gavin parked the car in Sandiway Crescent, several doors away from the Ryders' house because other cars were already parked closer to it. He'd have much preferred to be going out to dinner in Tonino's with Malcolm and Sue, lasagne and peperonata and a carafe of Chianti Christina, a lazy kind of evening that would remind all of them of other lazy evenings. Ten years ago they'd all four gone regularly to Tonino's trattoria in Greek Street, and the branch that had opened in their outer suburb was very like the original, even down to the framed colour photographs of A.C. Milan.

'Come on *in*!' Sue cried jollily at Number Four Sandiway Crescent. Her face was flushed with party excitement, her large brown eyes flashed adventurously with party spirit. Her eyes were the only outsize thing about her: she was tiny and black-haired, as pretty as a rose-bud.

'Gin?' Malcolm shouted at them from the depths of the crowded hall. 'Sherry, Polly? Burgundy?'

Gavin kissed the dimpled cheek that Sue Ryder pressed up to him. She was in red, a long red dress that suited her, with a red band in her hair and red shoes.

'Yes, wine please, Malcolm,' Polly said, and when she was close enough she slid her face towards his for the same kind of embrace as her husband had given his wife.

'You're looking edible, my love,' he said, a compliment he'd been paying her for seventeen years.

He was an enormous man, made to seem more so by the smallness of his wife. His features had a mushy look. His head, like a pink sponge, was perched jauntily on shoulders that had once been a force to reckon with in rugby scrums. Although he was exactly the same age as Gavin, his hair had balded away to almost nothing, a rim of fluff not quite encircling the sponge.

'You're looking very smart yourself,' Polly said, a statement that might or might not have been true: she couldn't see him properly because he was so big and she was so close to him, and she hadn't looked when she'd been further away. He was wearing a grey suit of some kind and a blue-striped shirt and the tie of the Harlequins' Rugby Club. Usually he looked smart: he probably did now.

'I'm feeling great,' he said. 'Nice little party we're having, Poll.'

It wasn't really little. Sixty or so people were in the Ryders' house, which was similar to the Dillards' house, well-designed and spacious. Most of the downstairs rooms, and the hall, had coffee-coloured walls, an experiment of Sue's which she believed had been successful. For the party, the bulkier furniture had been taken out of the coffee-coloured sitting-room, and all the rugs had been lifted from the parquet floor. Music came from a tape-recorder, but no one was dancing yet. People stood in small groups, smoking and talking and drinking. No one, so far, appeared to be drunk.

All the usual people were there: the Stubbses, the Burgesses, the Pedlars, the Thompsons, the Stevensons, Sylvia and Jack Meacock, Philip and June Mulally, Oliver and Olive Gramsmith. Tim and Mary-Ann Gruffyd and dozens of others. Not all of them lived in the outer suburb; and some were older, some younger, than the Ryders and the Dillards. But there was otherwise a similarity about the people at the party: they were men who had succeeded or were in the process of succeeding, and women who had kept pace with their husbands' advance. No one looked poor at the Ryders' party.

At ten o'clock there was food, smoked salmon rolled up and speared with cocktail sticks, chicken *vol-au-vent* or beef Strog-anoff with rice, salads of different kinds, stilton and brie and port salut, and meringues. Wine flowed generously, white burgundy and red. Uncorked bottles were distributed on all convenient surfaces.

The dancing began when the first guests had eaten. To 'Love of the Loved', Polly danced with a man whose name she didn't know, who told her he was an estate agent with an office in Jermyn Street. He held her rather close for a man whose name she didn't know. He was older than Polly, about fifty, she reckoned, and smaller. He had a foxy moustache and foxy hair, and a round stomach, like a ball, which kept making itself felt. So did his knees.

In the room where the food was Gavin sat on the floor with Sylvia and Jack Meacock, and a woman in an orange trouser suit, with orange lips.

'Ralphie wouldn't come,' this woman said, balancing food in the hollow of a fork. 'He got cross with me last night.'

Gavin ate from his fingers a *vol-au-vent* full of chicken and mushrooms that had gone a little cold. Jack Meacock said nothing would hold him back from a party given by the Ryders. Or any party, he added, guffawing, given by anyone. Provided there was refreshment, his wife stipulated. Well naturally, Jack Meacock said.

'He wouldn't come,' the orange woman explained, 'because he thought I misbehaved in Olive Gramsmith's kitchen. A fortnight ago, for God's sake!'

Gavin calculated he'd had four glasses of gin and tonic. He corrected himself, remembering the one he'd had with the babysitter. He drank some wine. He wasn't entirely drunk, he said to himself, he hadn't turned a certain corner, but the corner was the next thing there was.

'If you want to kiss someone you kiss them,' the orange woman said. 'I mean, for God's sake, he'd no damn right to walk into Olive Gramsmith's kitchen. I didn't see you,' she said, looking closely at Gavin. 'You weren't there, were you?'

'We couldn't go.'

'You were there,' she said to the Meacocks. 'All over the place.'

'We certainly were!' Jack Meacock guffawed through his beef Stroganoff, scattering rice on to the coffee-coloured carpet.

'Hullo,' their hostess said, and sat down on the carpet beside Gavin, with a plate of cheese.

'You mean you've been married twelve years?' the estate agent said to Polly. 'You don't look it.'

'I'm thirty-six.'

'What's your better half in? Is he here?'

'He directs films. Advertisements for TV. Yes, he's here.'

'That's mine.' He indicated with his head a woman who wasn't dancing, in lime-green. She was going through a bad patch, he said: depressions.

They danced to 'Sunporch Cha-Cha-Cha', Simon and Garfunkel.

'Feeling O.K. ?' the estate agent enquired, and Polly said yes, not understanding what he meant. He propelled her towards the mantelpiece and took from it a glass of white burgundy Polly had left there. He offered it to her and when she'd taken a mouthful he drank some from it himself. They danced again. He clutched her more tightly with his arms and flattened a cheek against one of hers, rasping her with his moustache. With dead eyes, the woman in lime-green watched.

At other outer-suburb parties Polly had been through it all before. She escaped from the estate agent and was caught by Tim Gruffydd, who had already begun to sweat. After that another man whose name she didn't know danced with her, and then Malcolm Ryder did.

'You're edible tonight,' he whispered, the warm mush of his lips damping her ear. 'You're really edible, my love.'

'Share my cheese,' Sue offered in the other room, pressing brie on Gavin.

'I need more wine,' the woman in orange said, and Jack Meacock pushed himself up from the carpet. They all needed more wine, he pointed out. The orange woman predicted that the next day she'd have a hangover and Sylvia Meacock, a masculine-looking woman, said she'd never had a hangover in forty-eight years of steady drinking.

'You going to stay a while ?' Sue said to Gavin. 'You and Polly going to stay ?' She laughed, taking one of his hands because it was near to her. Since they'd known one another for such a long time it was quite in order for her to do that.

'Our babysitter's unknown,' Gavin explained. 'From the bogs of Ireland.'

The orange woman said the Irish were bloody.

'Jack's Irish, actually,' Sylvia Meacock said.

She went on talking about that, about her husband's child-hood in County Down, about an uncle of his who used to drink a bottle and a half of whiskey a day – on top of four glasses of stout, with porridge and bread, for his breakfast. If you drank at all you should drink steadily, she said.

Gavin felt uneasy, because all the time Sylvia Meacock was

talking about the drinking habits of her husband's uncle in County Down Sue clung on to his hand. She held it lightly, moving her fingers in a caress that seemed to stray outside the realm of their long friendship. He was in love with Polly: he thought that deliberately, arraying the sentiment in his mind as a statement, seeing it suspended there. There was no one he'd ever known whom he'd been fonder of than Polly, or whom he respected more, or whom it would upset him more to hurt. Seventeen years ago he'd met her in the kitchens of the Hotel Belvedere, Penzance, where they had both gone to work for the summer. Five years later, having lived with one another in a flat in the cheaper part of Maida Vale, they'd got married because Polly wanted to have children. They'd moved to the outer suburb because the children needed space and fresh air, and because the Ryders, who'd lived on the floor above theirs in Maida Vale, had moved there a year before.

'She'll be all right,' Sue said, returning to the subject of the Irish babysitter. 'She could probably stay the night. She'd probably be delighted.'

'Oh, I don't think so, Sue.'

He imagined without difficulty the hands of men at the party unbuttoning Polly's lace blouse, the hands of Jack Meacock or the sweaty hands of Tim Gruffydd. He imagined Polly's clothes falling on to a bedroom carpet and then her thin, lanky nakedness, her small breasts and the faint mark of her appendix scar. 'Oh, I say!' she said in a way that wasn't like her when the man, whoever he was, took of his own clothes. Without difficulty either, Gavin imagined being in a room himself for the same purpose, with the orange woman or Sylvia Meacock. He'd walk out again if he found himself in a room with Sylvia Meacock and he'd rather be in a room with Sue than the orange woman. Because he wasn't quite sober, he had a flash of panic when he thought of what might be revealed when the orange trouser-suit fell to the floor: for a brief, disturbing moment he felt it was actually happening, that in the bonhomie of drunkenness he'd somehow agreed to the situation.

'Why don't we dance?' Sue suggested, and Gavin agreed.

'I think I'd like a drink,' Polly said to Philip Mulally, an executive with Wolsey Menswear. He was a grey shadow of a man, not at all the kind to permit himself or his wife to be a party to sexual games. He nodded seriously when Polly interrupted their dance to say she'd like a drink. It was time in any case, he revealed, that he and June were making a move homewards.

'I love you in that lace thing,' Malcolm Ryder whispered boringly as soon as Polly stopped dancing with Philip Mulally. He was standing waiting for her.

'I was saying to Philip I'd like a drink.'

'Of course you must have a drink. Come and quaff a brandy with me, Poll.' He took her by the hand and led her away from the dancers. The brandy was in his den, he said.

She shook her head, following him because she had no option. Above the noise of Cilla Black singing 'Anyone Who Had a Heart' she shouted at him that she'd prefer some more white burgundy, that she was actually feeling thirsty. But he didn't hear her, or didn't wish to. 'Ain't misbehaving,' the foxy estate agent mouthed at her as they passed him, standing on his own in the hall. It was an expression that was often used, without much significance attaching to it, at parties in the outer suburb.

'Evening all,' Malcolm said in the room he called his den, closing the door behind Polly. The only light in the room was from a desk-lamp. In the shadows, stretched on a mock-leather sofa, a man and a woman were kissing one another. They parted in some embarrassment at their host's jocular greeting, revealing themselves, predictably, as a husband and another husband's wife.

'Carry on, folks,' Malcolm said.

He poured Polly some brandy even though she had again said that what she wanted was a glass of burgundy. The couple on the sofa got up and went away, giggling. The man told Malcolm he was an old bastard.

'Here you are,' Malcolm said, and then to Polly's distaste he placed his mushy lips on hers and exerted some pressure. The brandy glass was in her right hand, between them: had it not been there, she knew the embrace would have been more intimate. As it was, it was possible for both of them to pretend that what had occurred was purely an expression of Malcolm Ryder's friendship for her, a special little detour to show that for all these years it hadn't been just a case of two wives being friends and the husbands tagging along. Once, in 1965, they'd all gone to the Italian Adriatic together and quite often Malcolm had given her a kiss and a hug while telling her how edible she was. But somehow – perhaps because his lips hadn't been so mushy in the past – it was different now.

'Cheers!' he said, smiling at her in the dimness. For an unpleasant moment she thought he might lock the door. What on earth did you do if an old friend tried to rape you on a sofa in his den?

With every step they made together, the orange woman increased her entwinement of Oliver Gramsmith. The estate agent was dancing with June Mulally, both of them ignoring the gestures of June Mulally's husband, Philip, who was still anxious to move homewards. The Thompsons, the Pedlars, the Stevensons, the Suttons, the Heeresmas and the Fultons were all maritally separated. Tim Gruffydd was clammily tightening his grasp of Olive Gramsmith, Sylvia Meacock's head lolled on the shoulder of a man called Thistlewine.

'Remember the Ritz?' Sue said to Gavin.

He did remember. It was a long time ago, years before they'd all gone together to the Italian Adriatic, when they'd just begun to live in Maida Vale, one flat above the other, none of them married. They'd gone to the Ritz because they couldn't afford it. The excuse had been Polly's birthday.

'March the twenty-fifth,' he said. '1961.' He could feel her breasts, like spikes because of the neat control of her brassière. He'd become too flabby, he thought, since 25 March, 1961.

'What fun it was!' With her dark, petite head on one side, she smiled up at him. 'Remember it all, Gavin?'

'Yes, I remember.'

'I wanted to sing that song and no one would let me. Polly was horrified.'

'Well, it was Polly's birthday.'

'And of course we couldn't have spoiled that.' She was still smiling up at him, her eyes twinkling, the tone of her voice as light as a feather. Yet the words sounded like a criticism, as though she were saying now – fourteen years later – that Polly had been a spoilsport, which at the time hadn't seemed so in the least. Her arms tightened around his waist. Her face disappeared as she sank her head against his chest. All he could see was the red band in her hair and the hair itself. She smelt of some pleasant scent. He liked the sharpness of her breasts. He wanted to stroke her head.

'Sue fancies old Gavin, you know.' Malcolm said in his den.

Polly laughed. He had put a hand on her thigh and the fingers were now slightly massaging the green velvet of her skirt and the flesh beneath it. To have asked him to take his hand away or to have pushed it away herself would have been too positive, too much a reflection of his serious mood rather than her own determinedly casual one. A thickness had crept into his voice. He looked much older than thirty-eight; he'd worn less well than Gavin.

'Let's go back to the party, Malcolm.' She stood up, dislodging his hand as though by accident.

'Let's have another drink.'

He was a solicitor now, with Parker, Hille and Harper. He had been, in fact, a solicitor when they'd all lived in the cheaper part of Maida Vale. He'd still played rugby for the Harlequins then. She and Gavin and Sue used to watch him on Saturday afternoons, in matches against the London clubs, Rosslyn Park and Blackheath, Waterloo, London Welsh, London Irish, and all the others. Malcolm had been a towering wing three-quarter, with a turn of speed that was surprising in so large a man: people repeatedly said, even newspaper commentators, that he should play for England.

Polly was aware that it was a cliché to compare Malcolm as he had been with the blubbery, rather tedious Malcolm beside whom it was unwise to sit on a sofa. Naturally he wasn't the same. It was probably a tedious life being a solicitor with Parker, Hille and Harper day after day. He probably did his best to combat the blubberiness, and no man could help being bald. When he was completely sober, and wasn't at a party, he could still be quite funny and nice, hardly tedious at all.

'I've always fancied you, Poll,' he said. 'You know that.'

'Oh, nonsense, Malcolm!'

She took the brandy glass from him, holding it between them in case he should make another lurch. He began to talk about sex. He asked her if she'd read, a few years ago, about a couple in an aeroplane, total strangers, who had performed the sexual act in full view of the other passengers. He told her a story about

Mick Jagger on an aeroplane, at the time when Mick Jagger was making journeys with Marianne Faithfull. He said the springing system of Green Lane buses had the same kind of effect on him. Sylvia Meacock was lesbian, he said. Olive Gramsmith was a slapparat. Philip Mulally had once been seen hanging about Shepherd Market, looking at the tarts. He hadn't been faithful to Sue, he said, but Sue knew about it and now they were going to approach all that side of things in a different way. Polly knew about it, too, because Sue had told her: a woman in Parker, Hille and Harper had wanted Malcolm to divorce Sue, and there'd been, as well, less serious relationships between Malcolm and other women.

'*Since you went away the days grow long,*' sang Nat King Cole in the coffee-coloured sitting-room, '*and soon I'll hear ole winter's song*'. Some guests, in conversation, raised their voices above the voice of Nat King Cole. Others swayed to his rhythm. In the sitting-room and the hall and the room where the food had been laid out there was fog of cigarette smoke and the warm smell of burgundy. Men sat together on the stairs, talking about the election of Margaret Thatcher as leader of the Conservative party. Women had gathered in the kitchen and seemed quite happy there, with glasses of burgundy in their hands. In a bedroom the couple who had been surprised in Malcolm's den continued their embrace.

'Don't dare move,' she warned Gavin, releasing his hand in order to poke among the records. She found what she wanted and placed in on the turn-table of the gramophone. The music began just before she turned the tape-recorder off. A cracked female voice sang: '*That certain night, the night we met, there was magic abroad in the air ...*'

'Listen to it,' Sue said, taking Gavin's hand again and drawing him on to the dancing area.

'*There were angels dining at the Ritz, and a nightingale sang in Berkeley Square.*'

The other dancers, who'd been taken aback by the abrupt change of tempo, slipped into the new rhythm. The two spiky breasts again depressed Gavin's stomach.

'Angels of a kind we were,' Sue said. 'And fallen angels now, Gavin? D'you think we've fallen?'

Once in New York and once in Liverpool he'd made love since

his marriage, to other girls. Chance encounters they'd been, irrelevant and unimportant at the time and more so now. He had suffered from guilt immediately afterwards, but the guilt had faded, with both girls' names. He could remember their names if he tried : he once had, when suffering from about of indigestion in the night. He had remembered precisely their faces and their naked bodies and what each encounter had been like, but memories that required such effort hadn't seemed quite real. It would, of course, be different with Sue.

'Fancy Sue playing that,' her husband said, pausing outside the den with Polly. 'They've been talking about the Ritz, Poll.'

'Goodness !' With a vividness that was welcome antidote to Malcolm's disclosure about the sex-life of his guests, the occasion at the Ritz returned to her. Malcolm said :

'It was my idea, you know. Old Gavin and I were boozing in the Hoop and he suddenly said, "It's Polly's birthday next week," and I said, "For God's sake ! Let's all go down to the Ritz."'

'You had oysters, I remember,' She smiled at him, feeling better because they were no longer in the den, and stronger because of the brandy. Malcolm would have realised by now how she felt, he wouldn't pursue the matter.

'We weren't much more than kids.' He seized her hand in a way that might have been purely sentimental, as though he was inspired by the memory.

'My twenty-second birthday. What an extraordinary thing it was to do !'

In fact, it had been more than that. Sitting in the restaurant with people she liked, she'd thought it was the nicest thing that had ever happened to her on her birthday. It was absurd because none of them could afford it. It was absurd to go to the Ritz for a birthday treat : martinis in the Rivoli Bar because Malcolm said it was the thing, the gilt chairs and the ferns. But the absurdity hadn't mattered because in those days nothing much did. It was fun, they enjoyed being together, they had a lot to be happy about. Malcolm might yet play rugby for England. Gavin was about to make his break-through into films. Sue was pretty, and Polly that night felt beautiful. They had sat there carelessly laughing, while deferential waiters simulated the gaiety of their mood. They had drunk champagne because Malcolm said they must.

With Malcolm still holding her hand, she crossed the spacious hall of Number Four Sandiway Crescent. People were beginning to leave. Malcolm released his hold of her in order to bid them goodbye.

She stood in the doorway of the sitting-room watching Gavin and Sue dancing. She lifted her brandy glass to her lips and drank from it calmly. Her oldest friend was attempting to seduce her husband, and for the first time in her life she disliked her. Had they still been at the Misses Summers' nursery school she would have run at her and hit her with her fists. Had they still been in Maida Vale or on holiday on the Italian Adriatic she would have shouted and made a fuss. Had they been laughing in the Ritz she'd have got up and walked out.

They saw her standing there, both of them almost in the same moment. Sue smiled at her and called across the coffee-coloured sitting-room, as though nothing untoward were happening. 'D'you think we've fallen, Polly ?' Her voice was full of laughter, just like it had been that night. Her eyes still had their party gleam, which probably had been there too.

'Let's dance, Poll,' Malcolm said, putting his arm around her waist from behind.

It made it worse when he did that because she knew by the way he touched her that she was wrong: he didn't realise. He probably thought she'd enjoyed hearing all that stuff about Philip Mulally hanging about after prostitutes and Olive Gramsmith being a slapparat, whatever a slapparat was.

She finished the brandy in her glass and moved with him on to the parquet. What had happened was that the Ryders had had a conversation about all this. They'd said to one another that this was how they wished – since it was the first time – to make a sexual swap. Polly and Gavin were to be of assistance to their friends because a woman in Parker, Hille and Harper had wanted Malcolm to get a divorce and because there'd been other relationships. Malcolm and Sue were approaching all that side of things in a different way now, following the fashion in the outer suburb since the fasion worked wonders with wilting marriages.

'Estrella babysitting, is she ?' Malcolm asked. 'All right if you're late, is she ? You're not going to buzz off, Poll ?'

'Estrella couldn't come. We had to get a girl from Problem.'

He suggested, as though the arrangement were a natural one and had been practised before, that he should drive her home when she wanted to go. He'd drive the babysitter from Problem home also. 'Old Gavin won't want to go,' he pronounced, trying to make it all sound like part of his duties as host. To Polly it sounded preposterous, but she didn't say so. She just smiled as she danced with him.

They'd make these plans quite soberly presumably, over breakfast or when there was nothing to watch on television, or in bed at night. They'd discussed the game that people played with car-keys or playing cards, or by drawing lots in other ways. They'd agreed that neither of them cared for the idea of taking a chance. 'Different,' Malcolm had probably quite casually said, 'if we got the Dillards.' Sue wouldn't have said anything then. She might have laughed, or got up to make tea if they were watching the television, or turned over and gone to sleep. On some other occasion she might have drifted the conversation towards the subject again and Malcolm would have known that she was interested. They would then have worked out a way of interesting their oldest friends. Dancing with Malcolm, Polly watched Gavin's mouth descended to touch the top of Sue's head. He and Sue were hardly moving on the dance-floor.

'Well, that's fixed up then.' Malcolm said. He didn't want to dance any more. He wanted to know that it was fixed up, that he could return to his party for an hour or so, with something to look forward to. He would drive her home and Gavin would remain. At half-past one or two, when the men threw their car-keys on to the carpet and the blind-folded women each picked one out, Gavin and Sue would simply watch, not taking part. And when everyone went away Gavin and Sue would be alone with all the mess and the empty glasses. And she would be alone with Malcolm.

Polly smiled at him again, hoping he'd take the smile to mean that everything was fixed because she didn't want to go on dancing with him. If one of them had said, that night in the Ritz, that for a couple of hours after dinner they should change partners there'd have been a most unpleasant silence.

Malcolm patted her possessively on the hip. He squeezed her forearm and went away, murmuring that people might be short of drink. A man whom she didn't know, excessively drunk, took her over, informing her that he loved her. As she swayed around the room with him, she wanted to say to Sue and Malcolm and Gavin that yes, they had fallen. Of course Malcolm hadn't done his best to combat his blubberiness, of course he didn't make efforts. Malcolm was awful, and Sue was treacherous. When people asked Gavin if he made films why didn't he ever reply that the films he made were television commercials? She must have fallen herself, for it was clearly in the nature of things, but she couldn't see how.

'It's time we went home, Sue,' Gavin said.

'Of course it isn't, Gavin.'

'Polly – '

'You're nice, Gavin.'

He shook his head. He whispered to her, explaining that Polly wouldn't ever be a party to what was being suggested. He said that perhaps they could meet some time, for a drink or for lunch. He would like to, he said; he wanted to.

She smiled. That night in the Ritz, she murmured, she hadn't wanted to be a blooming angel. 'I wanted you,' she murmured.

'That isn't true.' He said it harshly. He pushed her away from him, wrenching himself free of her arms. It shocked him that she had gone so far, spoiling the past when there wasn't any need to. 'You shouldn't have said that, Sue.'

'You're sentimental.'

He looked around for Polly and saw her dancing with a man who could hardly stand up. Some of the lights in the room had been switched off and the volume of the tape-recorder had been turned down. Simon and Garfunkel were whispering about Mrs Robinson. A woman laughed shrilly, kicking her shoes across the parquet.

Sue wasn't smiling any more. The face that looked up at him through the gloom was hard and accusing. Lines that weren't laughter-lines had developed round the eyes: lines of tension and probably fury, Gavin reckoned. He could see her thinking: he had led her on, he had kissed the top of her head. Now he was suggesting lunch some time, dealing out the future to her when the present was what mattered. He felt he'd been rude.

'I'm sorry, Sue.'

They were standing in the other dancers' way. He wanted to dance again himself, to feel the warmth of her small body, to feel

her hands, and to smell her hair, and to bend down and touch it
again with his lips. He turned away and extricated Polly from
the grasp of the drunk who had claimed to love her. 'It's time to
go home,' he said angrily.

'You're never going, old Gavin,' Malcolm protested in the
hall. 'I'll run Poll home, you know.'

'I'll run her home myself.'

In the car Polly asked what had happened, but he didn't tell
her the truth. He said he'd been rude to Sue because Sue had said
something appalling about one of her guests and that for some
silly reason he'd taken exception to it.

Polly did not believe him. He was making an excuse, but it
didn't matter. He had rejected the game the Ryders had wanted
to play and he had rejected it for her sake. He had stood by her
and shown his respect for her, even though he had wanted to
play the game himself. In the car she laid her head against the
side of his shoulder. She thanked him, without specifying what
she was grateful for.

'I feel terrible about being rude to Sue,' he said.

He stopped the car outside the house. The light was burning in
the sitting-room window. The babysitter would be half asleep.
Everything was as it should be.

'I'd no right to be rude,' Gavin said, still in the car.

'Sue'll understand.'

'I don't know that she will.'

She let the silence gather, hoping he'd break it by sighing or
saying he'd telephone and apologise tomorrow, or simply saying
he'd wait in the car for the babysitter. But he didn't sigh and he
didn't speak.

'You could go back,' she said calmly, in the end, 'and say
you're sorry. When you've driven the babysitter home.'

He didn't reply. He sat gloomily staring at the steering-wheel.
She thought he began to shake his head, but she wasn't sure.
Then he said:

'Yes, perhaps I should.'

They left the car and walked together on the short paved path
that led to their hall-door. She said that what she felt like was a
cup of tea, and then thought how dull that sounded.

'Am I dull, Gavin?' she asked, whispering in case the words
somehow carried in to the babysitter. Her calmness deserted her

for a moment. 'Am I?' she repeated, not whispering any more, not caring about the babysitter.

'Of course you're not dull. Darling, of course you aren't.'

'Not to want to stay? Not to want to go darting into beds with people?'

'Oh, don't be silly. Polly. They're all dull except you, darling. Every single one of them.'

He put his arms around her and kissed her, and she knew that he believed what he was saying. He believed she hadn't fallen as he and the Ryders had, that middle age had dealt no awful blows. In a way that seemed true to Polly, for it had often occurred to her that she, more than the other three, had survived the outer suburb. She was aware of the pretences but could not pretend herself. She knew every time they walked into the local Tonino's that the local Tonino's was just an Italian joke, a sham compared with the reality of the original in Greek Street. She knew that the party they'd just been to was a squalid little mess. She knew that when Gavin enthused about a fifteen-second commercial for soap his enthusiasm was no cause for celebration. She knew the suburb for what it was, its Volvos and Vauxhalls, its paved paths in unfenced front gardens, it crescents and avenues and immature trees, and the games its people played.

'All right, Polly?' he said, his arms still about her, with tenderness in his voice.

'Yes, of course.' She wanted to thank him again, and to explain that she was thanking him because he had respected her feelings and stood by her. She wanted to ask him not to go back and apologise, but she couldn't bring herself to do that because the request seemed fussy. 'Yes, of course I'm all right,' she said.

In the sitting-room the babysitter woke up and reported that the children had been as good as gold. 'Not a blink out of either of them, Mrs Dillard.'

'I'll run you home,' Gavin said.

'Oh, it's miles and miles.'

'It's our fault for living in such a godforsaken suburb.'

'Well, it's terribly nice of you, sir.'

Polly paid her and asked her again what her name was because she'd forgotten. The girl repeated that it was Hannah McCarthy. She gave Polly her telephone number in case Estrella shouldn't be available on another occasion. She didn't at all mind coming out so far, she said.

When they'd gone Polly made tea in the kitchen. She placed the tea-pot and a cup and saucer on a tray and carried the tray upstairs to their bedroom. She was still the same as she'd always been, they would say to one another, lying there, her husband and her friend. They'd admire her for that, they'd share their guilt and their remorse. But they'd be wrong to say she was the same.

She took her clothes off and got into bed. The outer suburb was what it was, so was the shell of middle age: she didn't complain because it would be silly to complain when you were fed and clothed and comfortable, when your children were cared for and warm, when you were loved and respected. You couldn't forever weep with anger, or loudly deplore yourself and other people. You couldn't hit out with your fists as though you were back at the Misses Summers' nursery school in Putney. You couldn't forever laugh among the waiters at the Ritz just because it was fun to be there.

In bed she poured herself a cup of tea, telling herself that what had happened tonight – and what was probably happening now – was reasonable and even fair. She had rejected what was distasteful to her, he had stood by her and had respected her feelings: his unfaithfulness seemed his due. In her middle-age calmness that was how she felt. She couldn't help it.

It was how she had fallen, she said to herself, but all that sounded silly now.

J. G. BALLARD

The Intensive Care Unit

Within a few minutes the next attack will begin. Now that I am surrounded for the first time by all the members of my family it seems only fitting that a complete record should be made of this unique event. As I lie here – barely able to breathe, my mouth filled with blood and every tremor of my hands reflected in the attentive eye of the camera six feet away – I realize that there are many who will think my choice of subject a curious one. In all senses, this film will be the ultimate home-movie, and I only hope that whoever watches it will gain some idea of the immense affection I feel for my wife, and for my son and daughter, and of the affection that they, in their unique way, feel for me.

It is now half an hour since the explosion, and everything in this once elegant sitting-room is silent. I am lying on the floor by the settee, looking at the camera mounted safely out of reach on the ceiling above my head. In this uneasy stillness, broken only by my wife's faint breathing and the irregular movement of my son across the carpet, I can see that almost everything I have assembled so lovingly during the past years has been destroyed. My Sèvres lies in a thousand fragments in the fireplace, the Hokusai scrolls are punctured in a dozen places. Yet despite the extensive damage this is still recognizably the scene of a family reunion, though of a rather special kind.

My son David crouches at his mother's feet, chin resting on the torn Persian carpet, his slow movement marked by a series of smeared hand-prints. Now and then, when he raises his head, I can see that he is still alive. His eyes are watching me, calculating the distance between us and the time it will take him to reach me. His sister Karen is little more than an arm's length away, lying beside the fallen standard lamp between the settee and the fireplace, but he ignores her. Despite my fear, I feel a powerful

328

sense of pride that he should have left his mother and set out on this immense journey towards me. For his own sake I would rather he lay still and conserved what little strength and time are left to him, but he presses on with all the determination his seven-year-old body can muster.

My wife Margaret, who is sitting in the armchair facing me, raises her hand in some kind of confused warning, and then lets it fall limply on to the stained damask arm-rest. Distorted by her smudged lipstick, the brief smile she gives me might seem to the casual spectator of this film to be ironic or even threatening, but I am merely struck once again by her remarkable beauty. Watching her, and relieved that she will probably never rise from her armchair again, I think of our first meeting ten years ago, then as now within the benevolent gaze of the television camera.

The unusual, not to say illicit, notion of actually meeting my wife and children in the flesh had occurred to me some three months earlier, during one of our extended family breakfasts. Since the earliest days of our marriage Sunday mornings had always been especially enjoyable. There were the pleasures of breakfast in bed, of talking over the papers and whatever else had taken place during the week. Switching to our private channel, Margaret and I would make love, celebrating the deep peace of our marriage beds. Later, we would call in the children and watch them playing in their nurseries, and perhaps surprise them with the promise of a visit to the park or circus.

All these activities, of course, like our family life itself, were made possible by television. At that time neither I nor anyone else had ever dreamed that we might actually meet in person. In fact, age-old though rarely invoked ordinances still existed to prevent this – to meet another human being was an indictable offence (especially, for reasons I then failed to understand, a member of one's own family, presumably part of some ancient system of incest taboos). My own upbringing, my education and medical practice, my courtship of Margaret and our happy marriage, all occurred within the generous rectangle of the television screen. Margaret's insemination was of course by AID, and like all children David's and Karen's only contact with their mother was during their brief uterine life.

In every sense, needless to say, this brought about an immense increase in the richness of human experience. As a child I had been brought up in the hospital créche, and thus spared all the psychological dangers of a physically intimate family life (not to mention the hazards, aesthetic and otherwise, of a shared domestic hygiene). But far from being isolated I was surrounded by companions. On television I was never alone. In my nursery I played hours of happy games with my parents, who watched me from the comfort of their homes, feeding on to my screen a host of video-games, animated cartoons, wild-life and family serials which together opened the world to me.

My five years as a medical student passed without my ever needing to see a patient in the flesh. My skills in anatomy and physiology were learned at the computer display terminal. Advanced techniques of diagnosis and surgery eliminated any need for direct contact with an organic illness. The probing camera, with its infra-red and X-ray scanners, its computerized diagnostic aids, revealed far more than any unaided human eye.

Perhaps I was especially adept at handling these complex keyboards and retrieval systems – a finger-tip sensitivity that was the modern equivalent of the classical surgeon's operative skills – but by the age of thirty I had already established a thriving general practice. Freed from the need to visit my surgery in person, my patients would merely dial themselves on to my television screen. The selection of these incoming calls – how tactfully to fade out a menopausal housewife and cut to a dysenteric child, while remembering to cue in separately the anxious parents – required a considerable degree of skill, particularly as the patients themselves shared these talents. The more neurotic patients usually far exceeded them, presenting themselves with the disjointed cutting, aggressive zooms and split-screen techniques that went far beyond the worst excesses of experimental cinema.

My first meeting with Margaret took place when she called me during a busy morning surgery. As I glanced into what was still known nostalgically as 'the waiting room' – the visual display projecting brief filmic profiles of the day's patients – I would customarily have postponed to the next day any patient calling without an appointment. But I was immediately struck, first by her age – she seemed to be in her late twenties – and then by the remarkable pallor of this young woman. Below close-cropped blonde hair her underlit eyes and slim mouth were set in a face that was almost ashen. I realized that, unlike myself and everyone else, she was wearing no make-up for the cameras. This accounted both for her arctic skin-tones and for her youthless appearance – on television, thanks to make-up, everyone of whatever age was 22, the cruel divisions of chronology banished for good.

It must have been this absence of make-up that first seeded the idea, to flower with such devastating consequences ten years later, of actually meeting Margaret in person. Intrigued by her unclassifiable appearance, I shelved my other patients and began our interview. She told me that she was a masseuse, and after a polite preamble came to the point. For some months she had been concerned that a small lump in her left breast might be cancerous.

I made some reassuring reply, and told her that I would examine her. At this point, without warning, she leaned forward, unbuttoned her shirt and exposed her breast.

Startled, I stared at this huge organ, some two feet in diameter, which filled my television screen. An almost Victorian code of visual ethics governed the doctor/patient relationship, as it did all social intercourse. No physician ever saw his patients undressed, and the location of any intimate ailments was always indicated by the patient by means of diagram slides. Even among married couples the partial exposure of their bodies was a comparative rarity, and the sexual organs usually remained veiled behind the most misty filters, or were coyly alluded to by the exchange of cartoon drawings. Of course, a clandestine pornographic channel operated, and prostitutes of both sexes plied their wares, but even the most expensive of these would never appear live, instead substituting a pre-recorded film-strip of themselves at the moment of climax.

These admirable conventions eliminated all the dangers of personal involvement, and this liberating affectlessness allowed those who so wished to explore the fullest range of sexual possibility and paved the way for the day when a truly guilt-free sexual perversity and, even, psychopathology might be enjoyed by all.

Staring at the vast breast and nipple, with their uncompromising geometries, I decided that my best way of dealing with this eccentrically frank young woman was to ignore any lapse from convention. After the infra-red examination confirmed that the suspected cancer nodule was in fact a benign cyst she buttoned her shirt and said:

'That's a relief. Do call me, doctor, if you ever need a course of massage. I'll be delighted to repay you.'

Though still intrigued by her, I was about to roll the credits at the conclusion of this bizarre consultation when her casual offer lodged in my mind. Curious to see her again, I arranged an appointment for the following week.

Without realizing it, I had already begun my courtship of this unusual young woman. On the evening of my appointment, I half-suspected that she was some kind of novice prostitute. However, as I lay discreetly robed on the recreation couch in my sauna, manipulating my body in response to Margaret's instructions, there was not the slightest hint of salaciousness. During the evenings that followed I never once detected a glimmer of sexual awareness, though at times, as we moved through our exercises together, we revealed far more of our bodies to each other than many married couples. Margaret, I realized, was a sport, one of those rare people with no sense of self-consciousness, and little awareness of the prurient emotions she might arouse in others.

Our courtship entered a more formal phase. We began to go out together – that is, we shared the same films on television, visited the same theatres and concert halls, watched the same meals prepared in restaurants, all within the comfort of our respective homes. In fact, at this time I had no idea where Margaret lived, whether she was five miles away from me or five hundred. Shyly at first, we exchanged old footage of ourselves, of our childhoods and schooldays, our favourite foreign resorts.

Six months later we were married, at a lavish ceremony in the most exclusive of the studio chapels. Over two hundred guests attended, joining a huge hook-up of television screens, and the service was conducted by a priest renowned for his mastery of the split-screen technique. Pre-recorded films of Margaret and myself taken separately in our own sitting-rooms were projected against a cathedral interior and showed us walking together down an immense aisle.

For our honeymoon we went to Venice. Happily we shared the panoramic views of the crowds in St Mark's Square, and gazed at the Tintorettos in the Academy School. Our wedding night was a triumph of the director's art. As we lay in our respective beds (Margaret was in fact some thirty miles to the south of me, somewhere in a complex of vast high-rises), I courted Margaret with a series of increasingly bold zooms, which she countered in a sweetly teasing way with her shy fades and wipes. As we undressed and exposed ourselves to each other the screens merged into a last oblivious close-up . . .

From the start we made a handsome couple, sharing all our interests, spending more time on the screen together than any couple we knew. In due course, through AID, Karen was conceived and born, and soon after after her second birthday in the residential crèche she was joined by David.

Seven further years followed of domestic bliss. During this period I had made an impressive reputation for myself as a paediatrician of advanced views by my championship of family life – this fundamental unit, as I described it, of intensive care. I repeatedly urged the installation of more cameras throughout the homes of family members, and provoked vigorous controversy when I suggested that families should bathe together, move naked but without embarrassment around their respective bedrooms, and even that fathers should attend (though not in close-up) the births of their children.

It was during a pleasant family breakfast together that there occurred to me the extraordinary idea that was so dramatically to change our lives. I was looking at the image of Margaret on the screen, enjoying the beauty of the cosmetic mask she now wore – even thicker and more elaborate as the years passed, it made her grow younger all the time. I relished the elegantly stylized way in which we now presented ourselves to each other – fortunately we had moved from the earnestness of Bergman and the more facile mannerisms of Fellini and Hitchcock to the classical serenity and wit of René Clair and Max Ophuls, though the children, with their love of the hand-held camera, still resembled so many budding Godards.

Recalling the abrupt way in which Margaret had first revealed herself to me, I realized that the logical extension of Margaret's frankness – on which, effectively, I had built my career – was that we should all meet together in person. Throughout my entire life, I reflected, I had never once seen, let alone touched, another human being. Whom better to begin with than my own wife and children?

Tentatively I raised the suggestion with Margaret, and I was delighted when she agreed.

'What an odd but marvellous idea! Why on earth has no one suggested it before?'

We decided instantly that the archaic interdiction against meeting another human being deserved simply to be ignored.

Unhappily, for reasons I failed to understand at the time, our first meeting was not a success. To avoid confusing the children, we deliberately restricted the first encounter to ourselves. I remember the days of anticipation as we made preparations for Margaret's journey – an elaborate under-taking, for people rarely travelled, except at the speed of the television signal.

An hour before she arrived I disconnected the complex security precautions that sealed my house from the world outside, the electronic alarm signals, steel grilles and gas-tight doors.

At last the bell rang. Standing by the internal portcullis at the end of the entrance hall, I released the magnetic catches on the front door. A few seconds later the figure of a small, narrow-shouldered woman stepped into the hall. Although she was over twenty feet from me I could see her clearly, but I almost failed to realize that this was the wife to whom I had been married for ten years.

Neither of us was wearing make-up. Without its cosmetic mask Margaret's face seemed pasty and unhealthy, and the movements of her white hands were nervous and unsettled. I was struck by her advanced age and, above all, by her small size. For years I had known Margaret as a huge close-up on one or other of the large television screens in the house. Even in long-shot she was usually larger than this hunched and diminutive woman hovering at the end of the hall. It was difficult to believe that I had ever been excited by her empty breasts and narrow thighs.

Embarrassed by each other, we stood without speaking at opposite ends of the hall. I knew from her expression that Margaret was as surprised by my appearance as I was by her own. In addition, there was a curiously searching look in her eye, an element almost of hostility that I had never seen before.

Without thinking, I moved my hand to the latch of the portcullis. Already Margaret had stepped back into the doorway, as if nervous that I might seal her into the hall forever. Before I could speak, she had turned and fled.

When she had gone I carefully checked the locks on the front door. Around the entrance hung a faint and not altogether unpleasant odour.

After this first abortive meeting Margaret and I returned to the happy peace of our married life. So relieved was I to see her on the screen that I could hardly believe our meeting had ever taken place. Neither of us referred to the disaster, and to the unpleasant emotions which our brief encounter had prompted.

During the next few days I reflected painfully on the experience. Far from bringing us together, the meeting had separated us. True closeness, I now knew, was television closeness – the intimacy of the zoom lens, the throat microphone, the close-up itself. On the television screen there were no body odours or strained breathing, no pupil contractions and facial reflexes, no mutual sizing up of emotions and advantage, no distrust and insecurity. Affection and compassion demanded distance. Only at a distance could one find that true closeness to another human being which, with grace, might transform itself into love.

Nevertheless, we inevitably arranged a second meeting. Why we did so I have still not understood, but both of us seemed to be impelled by those very motives of curiosity and distrust that I assumed we most feared. Calmly discussing everything with Margaret, I learned that she had felt the same distaste for me that I in turn had felt for her, the same obscure hostility.

We decided that we would bring the children to our next meeting, and that we would all wear make-up, modelling our behaviour as closely as possible on our screen life together. Accordingly, three months later, Margaret and myself, David and Karen, that unit of intensive care, came together for the first time in my sitting-room.

Karen is stirring. She has rolled across the shaft of the broken standard lamp and her body faces me across the blood-stained carpet, as naked as when she stripped in front of me. This provocative act, presumably intended to jolt some incestuous fantasy buried in her father's mind, first set off the explosion of violence which has left us bloody and exhausted in the ruins of my sitting-room. For all the wounds on her body, the bruises that disfigure her small breasts, she reminds me of Manet's *Olympia*, perhaps painted a few hours after the visit of some psychotic client.

Margaret, too, is watching her daughter. She sits forward, eyeing Karen with a gaze that is both possessive and menacing. Apart from a brief lunge at my testicles, she has ignored me. For some reason the two women have selected each other as their chief targets, just as David has vented almost all his hostility on me. I had not expected the scissors to be in his hand when I first slapped him. He is only a few feet from me now, ready to mount his last assault. For some reason he seemed particularly outraged by the display of teddy bears I had mounted so carefully for him, and shreds of these dismembered animals lie everywhere on the floor.

Fortunately I can breathe a little more freely now. I move my head to take in the ceiling camera and my fellow combatants. Together we present a grotesque aspect. The heavy television make-up we all decided to wear has dissolved into a set of bizarre halloween masks.

All the same, we are at last together, and my affection for them overrides these small problems of mutual adjustment. As soon as they arrived, the bruise on my son's head and my wife's bleeding ears betrayed the evidence of some potentially lethal scuffle. I knew that it would be a testing time. But at least we are making a start, in our small way establishing the possibility of a new kind of family life.

Everyone is breathing more strongly, and the attack will

clearly begin within a minute. I can see the bloody scissors in my son's hand, and remember the pain as he stabbed me. I brace myself against the settee, ready to kick his face. With my right arm I am probably strong enough to take on whoever survives the last confrontation between my wife and daughter. Smiling at them affectionately, rage thickening the blood in my throat, I am only aware of my feelings of unbounded love.

Ian McEwan

Solid Geometry

In Melton Mowbray in 1875 at an auction of articles of 'curiosity and worth', my great-grandfather, in the company of M his friend, bid for the penis of Captain Nicholls who died in Horsemonger jail in 1873. It was bottled in a glass twelve inches long, and, noted my great-grandfather in his diary that night, 'in a beautiful state of preservation'. Also for auction was 'the unnamed portion of the late Lady Barrymore. It went to Sam Israels for fifty guineas.' My great-grandfather was keen on the idea of having the two items as a pair, and M dissuaded him. This illustrates perfectly their friendship. My great-grandfather the excitable theorist, M the man of action who knew when to bid at auctions. My great-grandfather lived for sixty-nine years. For forty-five of them, at the end of every day, he sat down before going to bed and wrote his thoughts in a diary. These diaries are on my table now, forty-five volumes bound in calf leather, and to the left sits Capt. Nicholls in the glass jar. My great-grandfather lived on the income derived from the patent of an invention of his father, a handy fastener used by corset-makers right up till the outbreak of the First World War. My great-grandfather liked gossip, numbers and theories. He also liked tobacco, good port, jugged hare and, very occasionally, opium. He liked to think of himself as a mathematician, though he never had a job, and never published a book. Nor did he ever travel or get his name in *The Times*, even when he died. In 1869 he married Alice, only daughter of the Rev. Toby Shadwell, co-author of a not highly regarded book on English wild flowers. I believe my great-grandfather to have been a very fine diarist, and when I have finished editing the diaries and they are published I am certain he will receive the recognition due to him. When my work is over I will take a long holiday, travel somewhere cold and clean and treeless, Iceland or the Russian Steppes. I used to think that at the end of it all I would try, if it was possible, to divorce my wife Maisie, but now there is no need at all.

Often Maisie would shout in her sleep and I would have to wake her.

'Put your arm around me,' she would say. 'It was a horrible dream. I had it once before. I was in a plane flying over a desert. But it wasn't really a desert. I took the plane lower and I could see there were thousands of babies heaped up, stretching away into the horizon, all of them naked and climbing over each other. I was running out of fuel and I had to land the plane. I tried to find a space, I flew on and on looking for a space ...'

'Go to sleep now,' I said through a yawn. 'It was only a dream.'

'No,' she cried. 'I mustn't go to sleep, not just yet.'

'Well, *I* have to sleep now,' I told her. 'I have to be up early in the morning.'

She shook my shoulder. 'Please don't go to sleep yet, don't leave me here.'

'I'm in the same bed,' I said. 'I won't leave you.'

'It makes no difference, don't leave me awake ...' But my eyes were already closing.

Lately I have taken up my great-grandfather's habit. Before going to bed I sit down for half and hour and think over the day. I have no mathematical whimsies or sexual theories to note down. Mostly I write out what Maisie has said to me and what I have said to Maisie. Sometimes, for complete privacy, I lock myself in the bathroom, sit on the toilet seat and balance the writing-pad on my knee. Apart from me there is occasionally a spider or two in the bathroom. They climb up the waste pipe and crouch perfectly still on the glaring white enamel. They must wonder where they have come to. After hours of crouching they turn back, puzzled, or perhaps disappointed they could not learn more. As far as I can tell, my great-grandfather made only one reference to spiders. On 8 May 1906, he wrote, 'Bismarck is a spider.'

In the afternoons Maisie used to bring me tea and tell me her nightmares. Usually I was going through old newspapers, compiling indexes, cataloguing items, putting down this volume, picking up another. Maisie said she was in a bad way. Recently she had been sitting around the house all day glancing at books on psychology and the occult, and almost every night she had bad dreams. Since the time we exchanged physical blows, lying in wait to hit each other with the same shoe outside the bathroom, I had had little sympathy for her. Part of her problem was jealousy. She was very jealous ... of my great-grandfather's forty-five-volume diary, and of my purpose and energy in editing it. She was doing nothing. I was putting down one volume and picking up another when Maisie came in with the tea.

'Can I tell you my dream?' she asked. 'I was flying this plane over a kind of desert ...'

'Tell me later, Maisie,' I said. 'I'm in the middle of something here.' After she had gone I stared at the wall in front of my desk and thought about M, who came to talk and dine with my great-grandfather regularly over a period of fifteen years up until his sudden and unexplained departure one evening in 1898. M, whoever he might have been, was something of an academic, as well as a man of action. For example, on the evening of 9 August 1870, the two of them are talking about positions for love-making and M tells my great-grandfather that copulation *a posteriori* is the most natural way owing to the position of the clitoris and because other anthropoids favour this method. My great-grandfather, who copulated about half-a-dozen times in his entire life, and that with Alice during the first year of their marriage, wondered out loud what the Church's view was and straight away M is able to tell him that the seventh-century theologian Theodore considered copulation *a posteriori* a sin ranking with masturbation and therefore worthy of forty penances. Later in the same evening my great-grandfather produced mathematical evidence that the maximum number of positions cannot exceed the prime number seventeen. M scoffed at this and told him he had seen a collection of drawings by Romano, a pupil at Raphael's, in which twenty-four positions where shown. And, he said, he had heard of a Mr F.K. Forberg who had accounted for ninety. By the time I remembered the tea Maisie had left by my elbow it was cold.

An important stage in the deterioration of our marriage was reached as follows. I was sitting in the bathroom one evening writing out a conversation Maisie and I had had about the Tarot pack when suddenly she was outside, rapping on the door and rattling the door-handle.

'Open the door,' she called out. 'I want to come in.'

I said to her, 'You'll have to wait a few minutes more. I've almost finished.'

'Let me in now,' she shouted. 'You're not using the toilet.'

'Wait,' I replied, and wrote another line or two. Now Maisie was kicking the door.

'My period has started and I need to get something.' I ignored her yells and finished my piece, which I considered to be particularly important. If I left it till later certain details would be lost. There was no sound from Maisie now and I assumed she was in the bedroom. But when I opened the door she was standing right in my way with a shoe in her hand. She brought the heel of it sharply down on my head, and I only had time to move slightly to one side. The heel caught the top of my ear and cut it badly.

'There,' said Maisie, stepping round me to get to the bathroom, 'now we are both bleeding,' and she banged the door shut. I picked up the shoe and stood quietly and patiently outside the bathroom holding a handkerchief to my bleeding ear. Maisie was in the bathroom about ten minutes and as she came out I caught her neatly and squarely on the top of her head. I did not give her time to move. She stood perfectly still for a moment looking straight into my eyes.

'You worm,' she breathed, and went down to the kitchen to nurse her head out of my sight.

During supper yesterday Maisie claimed that a man locked in a cell with only the Tarot cards would have access to all knowledge. She had been doing a reading that afternoon and the cards were still spread about the floor.

'Could he work out the street plan of Valparaiso from the cards?' I asked.

'You're being stupid,' she replied.

'Could it tell him the best way to start a laundry business, the best way to make an omelette or a kidney machine?'

'Your mind is so narrow,' she complained. 'You're so narrow, so predictable.'

'Could he,' I insisted, 'tell me who M is, or why ...'

'Those things don't matter,' she cried. 'They're not necessary.'

'They are still knowledge. Could he find them out?'

She hesitated. 'Yes, he could.'

I smiled, and said nothing.

'What's so funny?' she said. I shrugged, and she began to get angry. She wanted to be disproved. 'Why did you ask all those pointless questions?'

I shrugged again. 'I just wanted to know if you really meant *everything*.'

Maisie banged the table and screamed, 'Damn you! Why are you always trying me out? Why don't you say something real?' And with that we both recognized we had reached the point where all our discussions led and we became bitterly silent.

Work on the diaries cannot proceed until I have cleared up the mystery surrounding M. After coming to dinner on and off for fifteen years and supplying my great-grandfather with a mass of material for his theories, M simply disappears from the pages of the diary. On Tuesday 6 December, my great-grandfather invited M to dine on the following Saturday, and although M came, my great-grandfather in the entry for that day simply writes, 'M to dinner.' On any other day the conversation at these meals is recorded at great length. M had been to dinner on Monday 5 December, and the conversation had been about geometry, and the entries for the rest of that week are entirely given over to the same subject. There is absolutely no hint of antagonism. Besides, my great-grandfather *needed* M. M provided his material, M knew what was going on, he was familiar with London and he had been on the Continent a number of times. He knew all about socialism and Darwin, he had an acquaintance in the free love movement, a friend of James Hinton. M was *in* the world in a way which my great-grandfather, who left Melton Mowbray only once in his lifetime, to visit Nottingham, was not. Even as a young man my great-grandfather preferred to theorize by the fireside; all he needed was the materials M supplied. For example, one evening in June 1884 M, who was just back from London, gave my great-grandfather an account of how the streets of the town were fouled and clogged by horse dung. Now in that same week my great-grandfather had been reading the essay by Malthus called 'On the Principle of Population'. That night he made an excited entry in the diary about a pamphlet he wanted to write and have published. It was to be called 'De Stercore Equorum'. The pamphlet was never published and probably never written, but there are detailed notes in the diary entries for the two weeks folllowing that evening. In 'De Stercore Equorum' ('Concerning Horseshit') he assumed geometric growth in the horse population, and working from detailed street plans he predicted that the metropolis would be impassable by 1935. By impassable he took to mean an average thickness of one foot (compressed) in every major street. He described involved experiments outside his own stables to determine the compressibility of horse dung, which he managed to express mathematically. It was all pure theory, of course. His result rested on the assumption that no dung would be shovelled aside in the fifty years to come. Very likely it was M who talked my great-grandfather out of the project.

One morning, after a long dark night of Maisie's nightmares, we were lying side by side in bed and I said,

'What is it you really want? Why don't you go back to your job? These long walks, all this analysis, sitting around the house, lying in bed all morning, the Tarot pack, the nightmares ... what is it you want?'

And she said, 'I want to get my head straight,' which she had said many times before.

I said, 'Your head, your mind, it's not like a hotel kitchen, you know, you can't throw stuff out like old tin cans. It's more like a river than a place, moving and changing all the time. You can't make rivers flow straight.'

'Don't go through all that again,' she said. 'I'm not trying to make rivers flow straight, I'm trying to get my head straight.'

'You've got to *do* something,' I told her. 'You can't do nothing. Why not go back to your job? You didn't have nightmares when you were working. You were never so unhappy when you were working.'

'I've got to stand back from all that,' she said. 'I'm not sure what any of it means.'

'Fashion,' I said, 'it's all fashion. Fashionable metaphors, fashionable reading, fashionable malaise. What do you care about Jung, for example? You've read twelve pages in a month.'

'Don't go on,' she pleaded, 'you know it leads nowhere.'

But I went on.

'You've never been anywhere,' I told her, 'you've never done anything. You're a nice girl without even the blessing of an unhappy childhood. Your sentimental Buddhism, this junk-shop mysticism, joss-stick therapy, magazine astrology ... none of it is yours, you've worked none of it out for yourself. You fell into it, you fell into a swamp of respectable intuitions. You haven't the originality or passion to intuit anything yourself beyond your own unhappiness. Why are you filling your mind with other people's mystic banalities and giving yourself nightmares?' I got out of bed, opened the curtains and began to get dressed.

'You talk like this was a fiction seminar,' Maisie said. 'Why are you trying to make things worse for me?' Self-pity began to well up from inside her, but she fought it down. 'When you are talking,' she went on, 'I can feel myself, you know, being screwed up like a piece of paper.'

'Perhaps we *are* in a fiction seminar,' I said grimly. Maisie sat up in bed staring at her lap. Suddenly her tone changed. She patted the pillow beside her and said softly,

'Come over here. Come and sit here. I want to touch you, I want you to touch me ...' But I was sighing, and already on my way to the kitchen.

In the kitchen I made myself some coffee and took it through to my study. It had occurred to me in my night of broken sleep that a possible clue to the disappearance of M might be found in the pages of geometry. I had always skipped through them before because mathematics does not interest me. On the Monday, December 5th, 1898, M and my great-grandfather discussed the *vescia piscis*, which apparently is the subject of Euclid's first proposition and a profound influence on the ground plans of many ancient religious buildings. I read through the account of the conversation carefully, trying to understand as best I could the geometry of it. Then, turning the page, I found a lengthy anecdote which M told my great-grandfather that same evening when the coffee had been brought in and the cigars were lit. Just as I was beginning to read Maisie came in.

'And what about you,' she said, as if there had not been an hour break in our exchange, 'all you have is books. Crawling over the past like a fly on a turd.'

I was angry, of course, but I smiled and said cheerfully, 'Crawling? Well, at least I'm moving.'

'You don't speak to me any more,' she said, 'you play me like a pinball machine, for points.'

'Good morning, Hamlet,' I replied, and sat in my chair waiting patiently for what she had to say next. But she did not speak, she left, closing the study door softly behind her.

'In September 1870,' M began to tell my great-grandfather,

I came into the possession of certain documents which not only invalidate everything fundamental to our science of solid geometry but also undermine the whole canon of our physical laws and force one to redefine one's place in Nature's scheme. These papers outweigh in importance the combined work of Marx and Darwin. They were entrusted to me by a young American mathematician, and they are the work of David Hunter, a mathematician too and a Scotsman. The American's name was Goodman. I had corresponded with his father over a number of years in connection with his work on the cyclical theory of menstruation which, incredible enough, is still widely discredited in this country. I met the young Goodman in Vienna where, along with Hunter and mathematicians from a dozen countries, he had been attending an international conference on mathematics. Goodman was pale and greatly disturbed when I met him, and planned to return to America the following day even though the conference was not yet half complete. He gave the papers into my care with instructions that I was to deliver them to David Hunter if I was ever to learn of his whereabouts. And then, only after much persuasion and insistence on my part, he told me what he had witnessed on the third day of the conference. The conference met every morning at nine thirty when a paper was read and a general discussion ensued. At eleven o'clock refreshments were brought in and many of the mathematicians would get up from the long, highly polished table round which they were all gathered and stroll about the large, elegant room and engage in informal discussions with their colleagues. Now, the conference lasted two weeks, and by a long-standing arrangement the most eminent of the mathematicians read their papers first, followed by the slightly less eminent, and so on, in a descending hierarchy throughout the two weeks, which caused, as it is wont to do among highly intelligent men, occasional but intense jealousies. Hunter, though a brilliant mathematician, was young and virtually unknown outside his university, which was Edinburgh. He had applied to deliver what he described as a very important paper on solid geometry, and since he was of little account in this pantheon he was assigned to read to the conference on the last day but one, by which time many of the most important figures would have returned to their respective countries. And so on the third morning, as the servants were bringing in the refreshments, Hunter stood up suddenly and addressed his colleagues just as they were rising from their seats. He was a large, shaggy man and, though young, he had about him a certain presence which reduced the hum of conversation to a complete silence.

'Gentlemen,' said Hunter, 'I must ask you to forgive this improper form of address, but I have something to tell you of the utmost importance. I have discovered the plane without a surface.' Amid derisive smiles and gentle bemused laughter, Hunter picked up from the table a large white sheet of paper. With a pocket-knife he made an incision along its surface about three inches long and slightly to one side of its centre. Then he made some rapid, complicated folds and, holding the paper aloft so all could see, he appeared to draw one corner of it through the incision, and as he did so it disappeared.

'Behold, gentlemen,' said Hunter, holding out his empty hands towards the company, 'the plane without a surface.'

Maisie came into my room, washed now and smelling faintly of perfumed soap. She came and stood behind my chair and placed her hands on my shoulders.

'What are you reading?' she said.

'Just bits of the diary which I haven't looked at before.' She began to massage me gently at the base of my neck. I would have found it soothing if it had still been the first year of our marriage. But it was the sixth year and it generated a kind of tension which communicated itself the length of my spine. Maisie wanted something. To restrain her I placed my right hand on her left, and, mistaking this for affection, she leaned forward and kissed under my ear. Her breath smelled of toothpaste and toast. She tugged at my shoulder.

'Let's go in the bedroom,' she whispered. 'We haven't made love for nearly two weeks now.'

'I know,' I replied, 'you know how it is ... with my work.' I felt no desire for Maisie or any other woman. All I wanted to do was turn the next page of my great-grandfather's diary. Maisie took her hands off my shoulders and stood by my side. There was such a sudden ferocity in her silence that I found myself tensing like a sprinter on the starting line. She stretched forward and picked up the sealed jar containing Capt. Nicholls. As she lifted it his penis drifted dreamily from one end of the glass to the other.

'You're so COMPLACENT,' Maisie shrieked, just before she hurled the glass bottle at the wall in front of my table. Instinctively I covered my face with my hands to shield off the shattering glass. As I opened my eyes I heard myself saying,

'Why did you do that? That belonged to my great-grand-father.' Amid the broken glass and rising stench of formaldehyde lay Capt. Nicholls, slouched across the leather covers of a volume of the diary, grey, limp and menacing, transformed from a treasured curiosity into a horrible obscenity.

'That was a terrible thing to do. Why did you do that?' I said again.

'I'm going for a walk,' Maisie replied, and slammed the door this time as she left the room.

I did not move from my chair for a long time. Maisie had destroyed an object of great value to me. It had stood in his study while he lived, and then it had stood in mine, linking my life with his. I picked a few splinters of glass from my lap and stared at the 160-year-old piece of another human on my table. I looked at it and thought of all the homunculi which had swarmed down its length. I thought of all the places it had been, Cape Town, Boston, Jerusalem, travelling in the dark, fetid inside of Capt. Nicholl's leather breeches, emerging occasionally into the dazzling sunlight to discharge urine in some jostling public place. I thought also of all the things it had touched, all the molecules, of Capt. Nicholl's exploring hands on lonely unrequited nights at sea, the sweating walls of cunts of young girls and old whores, their molecules must still exist today, a fine dust blowing from Cheapside to Leicestershire. Who knows how long it might have lasted in its glass jar. I began to clear up the mess. I brought the rubbish bucket in from the kitchen. I swept and picked up all the glass I could find and swabbed up the formaldehyde. Then, holding him by just one end, I tried to ease Capt. Nicholls on to a sheet of newspaper. My stomach heaved as the foreskin began to come away in my fingers. Finally, with my eyes closed, I succeeded, and wrapping him carefully in the newspaper, I carried him into the garden and buried him under the geraniums. All this time I tried to prevent my resentment towards Maisie filling my mind. I wanted to continue with M's story. Back in my chair I dabbed at a few spots of formaldehyde which had blotted the ink, and read on.

For as long as a minute the room was frozen, and with each successive second it appeared to freeze harder. The first to speak was Dr Stanley Rose of Cambridge University, who had much to lose by Hunter's plane without a surface. His reputation, which was very considerable indeed, rested upon his 'Principles of Solid Geometry'.

'How dare you, sir. How dare you insult the dignity of this assembly with a worthless conjuror's trick.' And bolstered by the rising murmur of concurrence behind him, he added, 'You should be ashamed, young man, thoroughly ashamed.' With that, the room erupted like a volcano. With the exception of young Goodman, and of the servants who still stood by with the refreshments, the whole room turned on Hunter and directed at him a senseless babble of denunciation, invective and threat. Some thumped on the table in their fury, others waved their clenched fists. One very frail German gentleman fell to the floor in an apoplexy and had to be helped to a chair. And there stood Hunter, firm and outwardly unmoved, his head inclined slightly to one side, his fingers resting lightly on the surface of the long polished table. That such an uproar should follow a worthless conjuror's trick clearly demonstrated the extent of the underlying unease, and Hunter surely appreciated this. Raising his hand, and the company falling suddenly silent once more, he said,

'Gentlemen, your concern is understandable and I will effect another proof, the ultimate proof.' This said, he sat down and removed his shoes, stood up and removed his jacket, and then called for a volunteer to assist him, at which Goodman came forward. Hunter strode through the crowd to a couch which stood along one of the walls, and while he settled himself upon it he told the mystified Goodman that when he returned to England he should take with him

Hunter's papers and keep them there until he came to collect them. When the mathematicians had gathered round Hunter rolled on to his stomach and clasped his hands behind his back in a strange posture to fashion a hoop with his arms. He asked Goodman to hold his arms in that position for him, and rolled on his side where he began a number of strenuous jerking movements which enabled him to pass one of his feet through the hoop. He asked his assistant to turn him on his other side, where he performed the same movements again and succeeded in passing his other foot between his arms, and at the same time bent his trunk in such a way that his head was able to pass through the hoop in the opposite direction to his feet. With the help of his assistant he began to pass his legs and head past each other through the hoop made by his arms. It was then that the distinguished assembly vented, as one man, a single yelp of utter incredulity. Hunter was beginning to disappear, and now, as his legs and head passed through his arms with greater facility, seemed even to be drawn through by some invisible power, he was almost gone. And now ... he was gone, quite gone, and nothing remained.

M's story put my great-grandfather in a frenzy of excitement. In his diary that night he recorded how he tried 'to prevail upon my guest to send for the papers upon the instant' even though it was by now two o'clock in the morning. M, however, was more sceptical about the whole thing. 'Americans,' he told my great-grandfather, 'often indulge in fantastic tales.' But he agreed to bring along the papers the following day. As it turned out M did not dine with my great-grandfather that night because of another engagement, but he called round in the late afternoon with the papers. Before he left he told my great-grandfather he had been through them a number of times and 'there was no sense to be had out of them.' He did not realize then how much he was underestimating my great-grandfather as an amateur mathematician. Over a glass of sherry in front of the drawing-room fire the two men arranged to dine together again at the end of the week, on Saturday. For the next three days my great-grandfather hardly paused from his reading of Hunter's theorems to eat or sleep. The diary is full of nothing else. The pages are covered with scribbles, diagrams and symbols. It seems that Hunter had to devise a new set of symbols, virtually a whole new language, to express his ideas. By the end of the second day my great-grandfather had made his first breakthrough. At the bottom of a page of mathematical scribble he wrote, 'Dimensionality is a function of consciousness.' Turning to the entry for the next day I read the words, 'It disappeared in my hands'. He had re-established the plane without a surface. And there, spread out in front of me, were step by step instructions on how to fold the piece of paper. Turning the next page I suddenly understood the mystery of M's disappearance. Undoubtedly encouraged by my great-grandfather, he had taken part that evening in a scientific experiment, probably in a spirit of great scepticism. For here my great-grandfather had drawn a series of small sketches illustrating what at first glance looked like yoga positions. Clearly they were the secret of Hunter's disappearing act.

My hands were trembling as I cleared a space on my desk. I selected a clean sheet of typing paper and laid it in front of me. I fetched a razor blade from the bathroom. I rummaged in a drawer and found an old pair of compasses, sharpened a pencil and fitted it in. I searched through the house till I found an accurate steel ruler I had once used for fitting window panes, and then I was ready. First I had to cut the paper to size. The piece that Hunter had so casually picked up from the table had obviously been carefully prepared beforehand. The length of the sides had to express a specific ratio. Using the compasses I found the centre of the paper and through this point I drew a line parallel to one of the sides and continued it right to the edge. Then I had to construct a rectangle whose measurements bore a particular relation to those of the sides of the paper. The centre of this rectangle occurred on the line in such a way as to dissect it by the Golden Mean. From the top of this rectangle I drew intersecting arcs, again of specified proportionate radii. This operation was repeated at the lower end of the rectangle, and when the two points of intersection were joined I had the line of incision. Then I started work on the folding lines. Each line seemed to express, in its length, angle of incline and point of intersection with other lines, some mysterious inner harmony of numbers. As I intersected arcs, drew lines and made folds, I felt I was blindly operating a system of the highest, most terrifying form of knowledge, the mathematics of the Absolute. By the time I had made the final fold the piece of paper was the shape of a geometric flower with three concentric rings arranged round the incision at the centre. There was something so tranquil and perfect about this design, something so remote and compelling, that as I stared into it I felt myself going into a light trance and my mind becoming clear and inactive. I shook my head and glanced away. It was time now to turn the flower in on itself and pull it through the incision. This was a delicate operation and now my hands were trembling again. Only by staring into the centre of the design could I calm myself. With my thumbs I began to push the sides of the paper flower towards the centre, and as I did so I felt a numbness settle over the back of my skull. I pushed a little further, the paper glowed whiter for an instant and then it *seemed* to disappear. I say 'seemed' because at first I could not be sure whether I could feel it still in my hands and not see it, or see it but not feel it, or whether I could sense it had disappeared while its external properties remained. The numbness had spread right across my head and shoulders. My senses seemed inadequate to grasp what was happening. 'Dimensionality is a function of consciousness,' I thought. I brought my hands together and there was nothing between them, but even when I opened them again and saw nothing I could not be sure the paper flower had completely gone. An impression remained, an after-image not on the retina but on the mind itself. Just then the door opened behind me, and Maisie said,

'What are you doing?'

I returned as if from a dream to the room and to the faint smell of formaldehyde. It was a long, long time ago now, the destruction of Capt. Nicholls, but the smell revived my resentment, which spread through me like the numbness. Maisie slouched in the doorway, muffled in a thick coat and woollen scarf. She seemed a long way off, and as I looked at her my resentment merged into a familiar weariness of our marriage. I thought, why did she break the glass? Because she wanted to make love? Because she wanted a penis? Because she was jealous of my work, and wanted to smash the connection it had with my great-grandfather's life?

'Why did you do it?' I said out loud, involuntarily. Maisie snorted. She had opened the door and found me hunched over my table staring at my hands.

'Have you been sitting there all afternoon,' she asked,

'thinking about *that* ?' She giggled. 'What happened to it, anyway ? Did you suck it off ?'

'I buried it,' I said, 'under the geraniums.'

She came into the room a little way and said in a serious tone, 'I'm sorry about that, I really am. I just did it before I knew what was happening. Do you forgive me ?' I hesitated, and then, because my weariness had blossomed into a sudden resolution, I said,

'Yes, of course I forgive you. It was only a prick in pickle,' and we both laughed. Maisie came over to me and kissed me, and I returned the kiss, prising open her lips with my tongue.

'Are you hungry ?' she said, when we were done with kissing. 'Shall I make some supper ?'

'Yes,' I said. 'I would love that.' Maisie kissed me on the top of my head and left the room, while I turned back to my studies, resolving to be as kind as I possibly could to Maisie that evening.

Later we sat in the kitchen eating the meal Maisie had cooked and getting mildly drunk on a bottle of wine. We smoked a joint, the first one we had had together in a very long time. Maisie told me how she was going to get a job with the Forestry Commission planting trees in Scotland next summer. And I told Maisie about the conversation M and my great-grandfather had had about *a posteriori,* and about my great-grandfather's theory that there could not be more than the prime number of seventeen positions for making love. We both laughed, and Maisie squeezed my hand, and lovemaking hung in the air between us, in the warm fug of the kitchen. Then we put our coats on and went for a walk. It was almost a full moon. We walked along the main road which runs outside our house and then turned down a narrow street of tightly packed houses with immaculate and minute front gardens. We did not talk much, but our arms were linked and Maisie told me how very stoned and happy she was. We came to a small park which was locked and we stood outside the gates looking up at the moon through the almost leafless branches. When we came home Maisie took a leisurely hot bath while I browsed in my study, checking on a few details. Our bedroom is a warm, comfortable room, luxurious in its way. The bed is seven foot by eight, and I made it myself in the first year of our marriage. Maisie made the sheets, dyed them a deep, rich blue and embroidered the pillow cases. The only light in the room shone through a rough old goatskin lampshade. Maisie bought from a man who came to the door. It was a long time since I had taken an interest in the bedroom. We lay side by side in the tangle of sheets and rugs, Maisie voluptuous and drowsy after her bath and stretched full out, and I propped up on my elbow. Maisie said sleepily,

'I was walking along the river this afternoon. The trees are beautiful now, the oaks, the elms ... there are two copper beeches about a mile past the footbridge, you should see them now ... ahh, that feels good.' I had eased her on to her belly and was caressing her back as she spoke. 'There are blackberries, the biggest ones I've ever seen, growing all along the path, the elderberries, too. I'm going to make some wine this autumn ...' I leaned over her and kissed the nape of her neck and brought her arms behind her back. She liked to be manipulated in this way and she submitted warmly. 'And the river is really still,' she was saying. 'You know, reflecting the trees, and the leaves are dropping into the river. Before the winter comes we should go there together, by the river, in the leaves. I found this little place. No one goes there ...' Holding Maisie's arms in position with one hand, I worked her legs towards the 'hoop' with the other. '... I sat in this place for half an hour without moving, like a tree. I saw a water-rat running along the opposite bank, and different kinds of ducks landing on the river and taking off. I heard these plopping noises in the river but I didn't know what they were and I saw two orange butterflies, they almost came on my hand.' When I had her legs in place Maisie said, 'Position number eighteen,' and we both laughed softly. 'Let's go there tomorrow, to the river,' said Maisie as I carefully eased her head towards her arms. 'Careful, careful, that hurts,' she suddenly shouted, and tried to struggle. But it was too late now, her head and legs were in place in the hoop of her arms, and I was beginning to push them through, past each other. 'What's happening?' cried Maisie. Now the positioning of her limbs expressed the breathtaking beauty, the nobility of the human form, and, as in the paper flower, there was a fascinating power in its symmetry. I felt the trance coming on again and the numbness settling over the back of my hand. As I drew her arms and legs through, Maisie appeared to turn in on herself like a sock. 'Oh God,' she sighed, 'what's happening?' and her voice sounded very far away. Then she was gone ... and not gone. Her voice was quite tiny, 'What's happening?' and all that remained was the echo of her question above the deep-blue sheets.

The following biographical and bibliographical notes are, inevitably, highly selective. Where an author has had a *collected stories* published I have indicated this as well as listing his or her more important individual collections together with an indication of other writing and the basic facts of the life. No attempt has been made to provide critical assessments.

James Graham Ballard (1930–   ) was born of English parents in Shanghai and lived there until he was fifteen. During the Second World War he was interned for two and a half years by the Japanese in a civilian prison camp. This experience provided some of the background for his best-known novel, *Empire of the Sun* (1984). He was repatriated in 1946 and, after leaving school, read medicine at King's College, Cambridge. He then became a copy writer, a Covent Garden porter and an RAF pilot. He is a widower, with three children. He has contributed to all the leading science fiction magazines, has published ten novels, including *The Drowned World* (1962) and *High Rise* (1975), and a dozen collections of stories including *The Terminal Beach* (1964), *The Disaster Area* (1967), *The Atrocity Exhibition* (1970), *Vermilion Sands* (1973) and *Myths of the Near Future* (1982) (from which 'The Intensive Care Unit' is taken).

Herbert Ernest Bates (1905–1974) was born in Rushden, Northamptonshire and educated at Kettering Grammar School. He went to live in Kent after his marriage in 1931 and resided there until his death. He had four children. His chief recreations were fishing, cricket and gardening but he confessed not really to be happy except when writing. His first novel, *The Two Sisters* (1926) launched him on a prolific career, his twenty-five or so novels including *Fair Stood the Wind for France*, *The Purple Plain*, *Oh! To Be In England* and *The Darling Buds of May*. He published hundreds of short stories collected in over twenty volumes including *Thirty Tales*, *My Uncle Silas* and *Seven by Five: 35 stories by H.E.Bates 1926–1961* with a preface by Henry Miller. He also wrote two volumes of stories about his experiences with the RAF during World War Two, brought together in 1952 as *The Stories of Flying Officer 'X'*. In addition he published three volumes of autobiography, and a study of *The Modern Short Story*. Many of his novels and stories were filmed and televised.

ARNOLD BENNETT (1867–1931) was the eldest son of a solicitor. Born in Hanley, Staffordshire, he was educated at Middle School, Newcastle under Lyme. In 1891, while employed as a clerk to a London firm of solicitors, the family with whom he lodged in Chelsea encouraged him to write and enter for a literary competition in the magazine *Tit Bits*, which he won. This success led him into journalism, and 'A Letter Home' was published in the *Yellow Book* (1895). His first novel, *A Man from the North*, followed in 1898, and from 1896–1900 he edited *Woman* magazine. In 1902 he published the first of his serious novels about life in the Potteries, *Anna of the Five Towns*, and lived in Paris. His other novels included *The Old Wives' Tale* (1908), *Clayhanger* (1910), *The Card* (1911) and *Riceyman Steps* (1923). In the last years of his life he contributed a weekly book column to the *Evening Standard* which made him the most powerful literary journalist in Britain. His collections of short stories included *Tales of the Five Towns* (1905) – from which 'The Idiot' is taken – *The Matador of the Five Towns* (1912), *The Grim Smile of the Five Towns* (1907), *Elsie and the Child* (1924) and *The Woman Who Stole Everything* (1927). He was married to a French wife, from whom he separated; and died from typhoid.

ELIZABETH BOWEN (1899–1973) was born of a landed Anglo-Irish family in Dublin. She spent much of her childhood at the family home in County Cork which she inherited in 1930. She married Alan Cameron, an ex-Army officer, and they lived in London for ten years. Her best work memorialised the life and world of Anglo-Irish gentry, and London during the Second World War. She published ten novels, including *The Death of the Heart* (1938) and *The Heat of the Day* (1949), a history of her family, and several other non-fiction books as well as seven volumes of short stories including *Encounters* (1923), *The Cat Jumps* (1934), *The Demon Lover* (1945) and *A Day in the Dark* (1965). Her *Collected Stories*, introduced by Angus Wilson, were published in 1980 (Cape).

GILBERT KEITH CHESTERTON (1874–1936) was born on Camden Hill, London and educated at St Paul's School. He later studied art at the Slade School and literature at University College, London. By the time he was twenty-one he was well-launched in journalism and as a reviewer. He achieved fame in 1905 with the publication of *Heretics*.

Essays, literary and art criticism, poetry, history and novels (including *The Napoleon of Notting Hill* (1904) and *The Man Who Was Thursday* (1908)) followed in the next thirty years. Much associated with Hilaire Belloc, Chesterton became a Roman Catholic in 1922. He is perhaps best remembered for his five collections of short stories about the unassuming East Anglican Roman Catholic priest, Father Brown, who first appeared in *The Innocence of Father Brown* (1911) – from which 'The Honour of Israel Gow' is taken – followed by *The Wisdom of Father Brown, The Incredulity of Father Brown, The Secret of Father Brown* and *The Scandal of Father Brown*.

JOSEPH CONRAD (1857–1924), christened Jósef Teodor Konrad Naleçz Korzeniowski, was born in Berdiczew, Poland. He became a sailor when aged seventeen, serving in the French marines from 1874–8. He first reached England in 1878, becoming a naturalised British subject in 1886, the year he obtained his Master Mariner's certificate, retiring from the sea in 1893. He married in 1896, and had two sons. He died at Bishopsbourne, Kent, and is buried in Canterbury. He wrote many novels, novellas and stories. His first novel *Almayer's Folly* was published in 1895. Others included *An Outcast of the Islands* (1896), *The Nigger of the 'Narcissus'* (1897), *Lord Jim* (1900) and *Nostromo* (1904). His stories, too, dealt much with the sea, volumes including *Tales of Unrest* (1898), *Youth* (1902), *Typhoon* (1903), *A Set of Six* (1908), *'Twixt Land and Sea* (1912), *Within the Tides* (1915) and *Tales of Hearsay* (1925) (one of the four stories in it being 'The Tale').

WALTER DE LA MARE (1873–1956) was born in Kent of well-off parents and educated at St Paul's Choir School. Aged sixteen, he began to work for an oil company, where he remained for twenty years. In his mid-twenties he started to contribute stories and poems to magazines, and published many collections of poetry for adults and children, including *Peacock Pie* (1913). Several collections were amalgamated in *Collected Rhymes and Verses* (1970) and *Collected Poems* (1979). He wrote novels and children's stories, including *Memoirs of a Midget* (1921). His numerous volumes of short stories, for adults and children, included *Broomsticks* (1925), *The Lord Fish* (1933) and *The Scarecrow* (1945). In 1950 *The Collected Tales* (from which 'Bad Company' is taken) was published. He was awarded the Companion of Honour in 1948, the Order of Merit in 1953, and is buried in St Paul's Cathedral.

MONTAGUE RHODES JAMES (1862–1936) was educated at Eton and at King's College, Cambridge, where, from 1905 to 1918, he was Provost. He published a number of books on bibliographical, historical and artistic subjects and had a special interest in archaeology, taking part in excavations in Cyprus. From 1904 to 1908 he was director of the Fitzwilliam Museum, Cambridge, and Vice-Chancellor of the University, 1913–15. He was awarded the Order of Merit in 1930. His two volumes of stories, *Ghost Stories of an Antiquity* (from which 'Oh, Whistle, and I'll Come to You, My Lad' is taken) and *More Ghost Stories*, were published respectively in 1904 and 1911.

JAMES JOYCE (1882–1941) was born in Dublin, one of, according to his father, sixteen or seventeen children. He was educated by the Jesuits at Clongowes Wood College, then Belvedere College, Dublin. In 1898 he attended the Dublin College of the Royal University where he studied philosophy and languages. In October 1902 he went to Paris but returned the following year as his mother was dying. He taught at a school in Dalkey until he married Nora Barnacle in 1904. He and his wife went to live in Zurich and later Trieste where he taught languages at the Berlitz school. He returned to Dublin in 1912, when he was unsuccessful in having *Dubliners* privately published. He spent World War One in Zurich in great poverty with his wife and two children. From 1920 he lived in Paris. *Dubliners*, published in 1914, was Joyce's only collection of stories. ('A Painful Case' is taken from it.) *Ulysses* was published in 1922, *Finnegans Wake* in 1939.

RUDYARD KIPLING (1865–1936) was born in Bombay, a cousin of Stanley Baldwin. From his schooldays at United Service College, Westward Ho!, emanated *Stalky & Co* (1899). In 1882 he joined the staff of Lahore *Civil and Military Gazette*, and wrote especially about the imperial race doing justice and upholding law. He became known through stories and verse including *Departmental Ditties* (1886), *Plain Tales from the Hills, Soldiers Three* and *Wee Willie Winkie* (1888). The next year he settled in London, eventually moving to Burwash. His books included *The Light That Failed* (1891), the two *Jungle Books* (1894–5), *Captains Courageous* (1897), *Just So Stories* (1902), *Kim* (1901), *Puck of Pook's Hill* (1906) and *A School History of England* (1911). ('Dayspring Mishandled' is taken from *Limits and Renewals* (1932).) He was awarded the Nobel Prize for Literature but refused the poet laureateship and the Order of Merit thrice. The best selection of his stories is contained in *A Choice of Kipling's Prose*, edited by Craig Raine (Faber and Faber, 1987).

DAVID HERBERT LAWRENCE (1885–1930) was born at Eastwood, Nottinghamshire, one of five children of a miner and an ex-school-teacher. He was frequently ill as a child and later developed tuberculosis as well as growing up in poverty. With the assistance of a scholarship he attended Nottingham High School for three years but aged fifteen he was obliged to take a job as a clerk in a surgical goods factory and then became a pupil teacher. In 1906, having saved the £20 fee, he took up a scholarship at Nottingham University College to study for a teacher's certificate. He taught for two years at an elementary school in Croydon but, after the death of his mother, he became seriously ill and had to give up teaching. In 1912 he met Frieda Weekley, wife of his old professor at Nottingham. She was six years older than Lawrence and had three children; they fell in love and eloped to Germany. Their life was frequently violent but they remained together till his death. His novels included *The White Peacock* (1911), *Sons and Lovers* (1913), *The Rainbow* (1915), *Women in Love* (1916) and *Lady Chatterley's Lover* (1928). He was a prolific poet and travel writer, too, and published various volumes of short stories including *The Prussian Officer* (1914), *England, My England* (1922) and *The Woman Who Rode Away* (1928). *The Collected Stories* were published by Heinemann in three volumes in 1955.

DORIS LESSING (1919–) was born in Persia of British parents who moved when she was five to a farm in Southern Rhodesia. She left school at fifteen and worked as a nursemaid, then as a shorthand typist and telephone operator in Salisbury. After the breakup of her first marriage she became involved in radical politics. In 1945 she remarried, but in 1949 left for England, where she has lived since, with her youngest child and the manuscript of her first novel, *The Grass is Singing* (1950). The year 1956 saw her last visit to the country where she grew up, the authorities declaring her a prohibited immigrant after her return to England. She has published over a dozen novels including the quintet *Children of Violence*, *The Golden Notebook* (1962), *Briefing for a Descent into Hell* (1971) and *Memoirs of a Survivor* (1975). Her stories have been variously collected, as *Collected African Stories* in two volumes (Michael Joseph, 1973) and, also in two volumes, as *Collected Stories* (Cape, 1978). ('England versus England' was included in *A Man and Two Women* (1963) and appeared in *Collected Stories, Volume 1 : To Room Nineteen*.)

IAN MCEWAN (1948–) was born in London. He is married, with one child. In 1976 he won the Somerset Maugham Award for his first book, *First Love, Last Rites* (from which 'Solid Geometry' is taken). A second volume of stories, *In Between the Sheets*, followed in 1978. He has also written three novels, *The Cement Garden* (1978), *The Comfort of Strangers* (1981) and *The Child in Time* (1987), as well as a couple of television plays.

KATHERINE MANSFIELD (1888–1923) was born in Wellington, New Zealand, educated at Queen's College, London (1903–6), returned to New Zealand for two years to study music, then came back to London in 1908. In 1909 she married but left her husband after a few days. She became pregnant by another man: the child was stillborn. In 1911 she met John Middleton Murry, whom she married in 1918. She suffered from tuberculosis and, in 1922, entered the institute run by Gurdjieff near Fontainebleau, hoping to regain spiritual and physical health, but died. Three of her five collections of stories – *In a German Pension* (1911), *Bliss* (1920) (from which 'Je Ne Parle Pas Français' is taken) and *The Garden Party* (1922) – were published during her lifetime, *The Doves' Nest* (1923) and *Something Childish* (1924) posthumously. *The Stories of Katherine Mansfield*, edited by Antony Alpers, was published in 1984 (Oxford University Press).

WILLIAM SOMERSET MAUGHAM (1874–1965) was born in Paris, the fourth surviving son of a lawyer attached to the British embassy. His mother died when he was eight, his father of cancer in 1884, and William was sent to Whitstable to live with a childless aunt and clergyman uncle. Educated at King's School, Canterbury and at Heidelberg University, he then trained as a doctor at St Thomas's Hospital, London. *Liza of Lambeth* (1897) was the first of innumerable novels including *The Moon and Sixpence* (1919) and *Cakes and Ale* (1930). By 1908 he was a highly successful playwright but abandoned the stage in 1933 to travel and concentrate on short stories, novels and travel books. *A Writer's Notebook* (1949) comprised extracts from the notebooks he had kept since he was eighteen. *The Summing Up* (1938) was his autobiography. He married the interior decorator Syrie Maugham in 1917 but they spent most of their time apart. For most of his life he lived with Gerald Haxton. From 1926 he lived at Cap Ferrat on the French Riviera. He was created a Companion of Honour in 1954. *The Complete Short Stories* (Heinemann) were published in three volumes in 1951.

SEAN O'FAOLAIN (1900–   ) was born in Cork, the son of a policeman. He studied at University College, Cork. In his early 20s he joined the Irish Republican Army where he eventually became 'director of publicity'. In 1926 he went to Harvard University and stayed in America for three years before returning to Europe, to London, to teach, by which time he was married and a father. One of his three children is the writer Julia O'Faolain. When his first book, a collection of stories, *Midsummer Night's Madness*, was published in 1932 it was banned in Ireland but this did not deter him from returning to live there. He has remained ever since (currently living in Dunlaoire), making his living mostly as a journalist and publishing more than twenty books including novels, biography, travel, his autobiography, *Vive moi!*, a critical account of *The Short Story*, and various volumes of stories including *Teresa* (1947), *I Remember, I Remember* (1962), *The Heat of the Day* (1966) and *Foreign Affairs* (1976). His *Collected Stories* have been published in three volumes (Constable: 1980, 1981, 1987).

SIR VICTOR SAWDON PRITCHETT (1900–   ) was born in Ipswich, the son of a travelling salesman, and spent a peripatetic childhood in the provinces and various London suburbs before attending Alleyn's School, Dulwich, which he left at fifteen to work in the leather trade. He went to Paris aged twenty-one, then became a journalist in Ireland and Spain before settling to a literary life in London. Primarily a writer of stories, he has also written novels, biography, travel books, two volumes of autobiography (*A Cab at the Door* and *Midnight Oil*) and much literary criticism. His collections of stories include *The Spanish Virgin* (1930), *You Make Your Own Life* (1938) (from which 'The Evils of Spain' is taken), *When My Girl Comes Home* (1961) and *The Camberwell Beauty* (1974). His *Collected Stories* were published in 1982, and *More Collected Stories* in 1983 (both Chatto & Windus).

JEAN RHYS (1894–1979) was born in Dominica, West Indies. She came to England aged sixteen, and spent one term at the Royal Academy of Dramatic Art, having to leave when her father died. She drifted into a series of hopeless jobs – chorus girl, mannequin, artist's model – and began to write when the first of her three marriages broke up. At the time she was living in Paris, and was taken up by Ford Madox Ford, who wrote an enthusiastic introduction to her first book and collection of stories, *The Left Bank* (1927). Other books were *Postures* (1928, reprinted in 1969 as *Quartet*), *After Leaving Mr Mackenzie* (1930), *Voyage in the Dark* (1934) and *Good Morning, Midnight* (1939). With the outbreak of the Second World War, her work went out of print and she dropped from sight. Nearly twenty years later she was rediscovered. In 1966 her fifth and final novel, *Wild Sargasso Sea*, won the W.H.Smith Award. Her other collections of stories were *Tigers Are Better-Looking* (1968) – from which 'Till September Petronella' is taken – and *Sleep It Off Lady* (1976). *The Collected Short Stories*, edited by Diana Athill, were published in 1987 (Deutsch).

'SAKI' (HECTOR HUGH MUNRO) (1870–1916) was born in Burma but came to England less than two years later to be brought up by two formidable aunts in a village near Barnstaple, North Devon: Aunt Augusta and Aunt Tom were the basis for the monstrous women of his short stories. In 1893 he joined the Burmese military police but was invalided home. In 1900 he wrote political satire for the *Westminster Gazette*, and from 1902 to 1908 was correspondent for the *Morning Post* in Poland, Russia and Paris. He wrote two novels, *The Unbearable Bassington* (1912) and *When William Came* (1913). His collections of stories were *Reginald* (1904), *Reginald in Russia* (1910), *The Chronicles of Clovis* (1911), *Beasts and Super-Beasts* (1914), *The Toys of Peace* (1919) and *The Square Egg* (1924). In 1914 he enlisted as a trooper and was killed in France, shot through the head while resting in a crater.

MURIEL SPARK (1918–   ), of Scottish-Jewish descent, was born in Edinburgh, and educated at James Gillespie's School for Girls there. She then spent some years in Central Africa but returned to Britain during the Second World War. She worked in the Political Intelligence Department of the Foreign Office. Subsequently she edited two poetry magazines and published poetry, criticism and biography. In 1951 she won an *Observer* short story competition, following which she won many awards including the James Tait Black and an Italia Prize. She became a Roman Catholic in 1954. Divorced, with one child, she lives in Italy. She has published nearly twenty novels including *The Comforters* (1957), *Memento Mori* (1959), *The Ballard of Peckham Rye* (1960), *The Prime of Miss Jean Brodie* (1961), which was successfully filmed, *The Abbess of Crewe* (1974) and *The Takeover* (1976). Her two collections of stories, *The Go-Away Bird* (1958) and *Voices at Play* (1961) were brought together in *Collected Stories I* (1967) and, with additional and later stories, in *The Stories of Muriel Spark* (Bodley Head, 1987).

DYLAN THOMAS (1914–1953) was born in Swansea, son of the English master at Swansea Grammar School, where he himself was educated. He began writing poetry while still at school, and worked in Swansea as a journalist before moving to London in 1934, his first volume of verse, *18 Poems*, appearing in that year. In 1937 he married Caitlin Macnamara. They settled for a time in Laugharne, Wales, returning there permanently in 1949. In 1950 he undertook the first of his lecture tours to the United States of America, dying there on his fourth. As well as his poetry, and the radio play *Under Milk Wood*, he wrote a considerable amount of prose including *The Map of Love* (1939), *Portrait of the Artist as a Young Dog* (1955), *Adventures in the Skin Trade* (1955) and *A Prospect of the Sea* (1955). 'The Vest' was not collected until it was included in *Early Prose Writings* (1971) and appears also in *The Collected Stories* (Dent, 1983).

WILLIAM TREVOR (1922–   ) was born in County Cork in 1928 and spent his childhood in provincial Ireland, being educated at St Columba's College and at Trinity College, Dublin. For a while he worked as a sculptor, then won the Hawthornden Prize with his second novel, *The Old Boys*, since when he has won many honours for his work: the Royal Society of Literature Award, the Allied Irish Banks Prize for Literature and the Whitbread Prize for Fiction. He is married, with two sons. He has published eleven novels including *Mrs Eckdorf in O'Neill's Hotel* (1969), *Elizabeth Alone* (1973) and *The Children of Dynmouth* (1976). His collections of stories include *The Day We Got Drunk on Cake* (1967), *The Ballroom of Romance* (1972), *Angels at the Ritz* (1975), *Lovers of their Time* (1978) and *The News from Ireland* (1986). Many of his stories have been televised.

HERBERT GEORGE WELLS (1866–1946) was the son of an unsuccessful tradesman. His penurious childhood profoundly influenced his voluminous writing. He was educated at a commercial school and by wide reading, and apprenticed successively to pharmacy and drapery. In 1883–4 he became student assistant at Midhurst grammar school, eventually teaching at Holt Academy, Wrexham and Henley House School, Kilburn, before becoming, in 1891, tutor at University Tutorial College. In the 1890s he found a ready market for short stories, and began to publish his fantastic and imaginative romances, usually based on scientific fact, ranging from *The Time Machine* (1895) and *The Invisible Man* (1897) to *The Shape of Things to Come* (1933). Novels drawing on his own experience included *Kipps* (1905), *Tono-Bungay* (1909) and *The History of Mr Polly* (1910). Later influential books were *The Outline of History* (1920), *The Science of Life* (1931) and *The Fate of Homo Sapiens* (1939). His *Experiment in Autobiography* (1934) was a substantial contribution to social history. ('The Truth about Pyecraft' was published in *Twelve Stories and a Dream* (1903) and is included in *The Complete Short Stories of H. G. Wells* (1927).

SIR ANGUS WILSON (1913–   ) was born in Bexhill, Sussex. A South African childhood was followed by education at Westminster School, then three years at Merton College, Oxford. He worked for some years in the Foreign Office, then as Deputy Superintendent of the Reading Room of the British Museum. His first book, *The Wrong Set* (from which 'Et Dona Ferentes' is taken) was published when he was thirty-five in 1949. *Such Darling Dodos* followed in 1950 and a third volume of stories, *A Bit Off the Map*, in 1957. In 1955 he resigned from the Museum, and lived in Suffolk until a few years ago when he moved to the South of France. When in Suffolk, he was a professor of English Literature at the University of East Anglia. He has published books about Zola, Dickens and Kipling, much criticism and a play as well as eight novels including *Hemlock and After* (1952), *Anglo-Saxon Attitudes* (1956), *The Middle Age of Mrs Eliot* (1958), *The Old Men at the Zoo* (1961), *Late Call* (1964) and *Setting the World on Fire* (1980). His *Collected Stories* were published in 1987 (Secker & Warburg).

SIR PELHAM GRENVILLE WODEHOUSE (1881–1975) was born in Guildford, the son of a civil servant who became a judge in Hong Kong. He was brought up in England by various aunts, and educated at Dulwich College. He soon abandoned a banking career in Hong Kong for literature, his stories being published extensively in magazines. His first novel was published in 1902, and thereafter there were over 120 books. *The Man with Two Left Feet* (1917) was the collection of stories which introduced Bertie Wooster and Jeeves. Unnumerable volumes followed, including *My Man Jeeves* (1919), *The Inimitable Jeeves* (1923) and *Carry On, Jeeves* (1925) – from which 'Jeeves and the Hard-boiled Egg' is taken. He was also highly successful in musical comedy, the theatre and Hollywood. He was captured by the Germans at Le Touquet in 1940, interned and then released but not allowed to leave Germany. He accepted an invitation to broadcast to America, which caused a scandal in the UK and resulted in his returning to America after the war and, in 1955, taking American citizenship. He was, though, eventually knighted.

VIRGINIA WOOLF (1882–1941) was the daughter of Leslie Stephen and Julia Duckworth. She was born at Hyde Park Gate, London where she lived with her sister (later Vanessa Bell) and her brothers until her father's death in 1904. The Stephen children then moved to Blooms-bury. In 1912 she married the publisher Leonard Woolf, and was already working on her first novel, *The Voyage Out*, published in 1915. In 1917 she and her husband founded The Hogarth Press. For much of her life she was mentally ill, and this eventually led to her drowning herself in the River Ouse near her home at Rodmell, Sussex. Her novels included *Mrs Dalloway* (1925), *To the Lighthouse* (1927), *The Waves* (1931), *Orlando* (1928) and *Between the Acts* (1941). ('Lappin and Lapinova' is taken from her only collection of stories, *A Haunted House*, published posthumously in 1944.)

ACKNOWLEGEMENT AND COPYRIGHTS

Acknowledgements are due to the following for permission to include in this book stories in copyright:

The author and Margaret Hanbury for 'The Intensive Care Unit' from *Myths of the Near Future* (Jonathan Cape) by J.G.Ballard; copyright © J.G.Ballard 1977;

The estate of H.E.Bates and Laurence Pollinger Ltd for 'The Kimono' from *Seven by Seven* (Michael Joseph) by H.E.Bates; copyright © H.E.Bates 1937;

The estate of Elizabeth Bowen and Curtis Brown Ltd for 'Mysterious Kôr' from *The Demon Lover* (Jonathan Cape) by Elizabeth Bowen; copyright © Elizabeth Bowen 1945;

The executors of the author's estate and The Society of Authors for 'A Painful Case' from *Dubliners* (Jonathan Cape) by James Joyce; copyright © James Joyce 1914;

The author and Jonathan Clowes Ltd for 'England versus England' from *A Man and Two Women* (MacGibbon & Kee) by Doris Lessing; copyright © Doris Lessing 1963;

The author and Rogers, Coleridge & White for 'Solid Geometry' from *First Love, Last Rites* (Jonathan Cape) by Ian McEwan; copyright © Ian McEwan 1975;

The literary trustees and The Society of Authors for 'Bad Company' from *A Beginning and other stories* (Faber and Faber) by Walter de la Mare; copyright © Walter de la Mare 1950;

William Heinemann Ltd and A.P.Watt Ltd for 'The Four Dutchmen' from *The Complete Short Stories* by W.Somerset Maugham; copyright © W.Somerset Maugham 1951;

The author and A.P.Watt Ltd for 'Enduring Friendship' from *The*